Drawing on a wealth of personal experience, Mark Moody-Stuart's book reminds us of the urgent need for responsible corporate leadership, particularly in the extractives industries, which have suffered a poor track record in the past. Responsible leadership is necessary to develop trust between governments and business, to create the conditions to lift millions out of poverty, and to promote inclusive growth and protect the environment.
Kofi Annan, former UN Secretary-General

There is much to be learned from this fascinating book, which draws on many practical examples and explains the way they were addressed by a man who is both deeply thoughtful and possessed of a powerful moral conscience. The lessons are relevant not only to current generations of business managers, but to all who want to understand the interface of industry and the geo-political world.
Sir Robert Wilson KCMG, former Executive Chairman of Rio Tinto plc; former Chairman of BG Group plc

This is an insightful book from a business leader who is willing to discuss openly the dilemmas and shortcomings of business in the area of human rights. Mark Moody-Stuart draws on his experience representing oil companies in developing countries and in later years chairing the board of the UN Global Compact. His reasons for championing what can be achieved by coalitions involving business, governments and civil society are highly relevant to the twin challenges of a post-2015 sustainable development agenda and a robust climate agreement.
Mary Robinson, former President of Ireland and UN High Commissioner for Human Rights; President of the Mary Robinson Foundation – Climate Justice

Mark Moody-Stuart brings a unique perspective as a corporate leader deeply engaged with civil society and NGOs. He provides insightful assessment of what works and doesn't work when seeking to loosen the grip of oppressive governments and reduce violence. He forthrightly takes us into the challenges of decision-making within international companies. He demonstrates how complex it is to find the right balance between the responsibilities of governments, companies and civil society – and how important it is to try.
Daniel Yergin, author of *The Quest: Energy, Security, and the Remaking of the Modern World* and *The Prize*

Whether he came by it innately or learned it in the school of hard knocks, Sir Mark Moody-Stuart, former chief executive of Shell, is a member of a rare species: a business statesman, one who understands the corporation as a social institution not merely an undertaking for private gain. In *Responsible Leadership*, Moody-Stuart draws on his vast range of professional experiences to illuminate the complex issues and dilemmas of corporate social responsibility, and he explains why getting it right requires an 'all hands on deck' approach. Everyone, from new students of the subject to seasoned professionals, will find gems of insight and valuable examples in this book.

John G. Ruggie, Harvard University, former UN Special Representative for Business & Human Rights

[Mark's] compassion and profound sense of service has found a larger stage than his own generous personal philanthropy. Through changing how business behaves, he is helping to rewrite the terms of modern society. An unlikely perhaps, but very effective, revolutionary.

Mark Malloch-Brown, former UN Deputy Secretary-General

In the Nineties, engaging Shell was seen by some as akin to dining with the Devil. But Sir Mark Moody-Stuart tops my list of mainstream business pioneers in the linked areas of ethics and sustainability. Read his account of dining with real devils: those responsible for human rights abuses. His book makes uncomfortable reading because it challenges our preconceptions. Highly recommended.

John Elkington, co-founder, Environmental Data Services (ENDS), SustainAbility and Volans

A wonderful anatomy of what it takes to be a sustainable and ethical business, from one of the earliest and most distinguished proponents of responsible leadership. Wide-ranging in its scope and perceptive in its analysis, this is an important contribution for any modern manager keen to understand what it takes to operate responsibly in today's highly complex and interdependent world.

Paul Polman, Chief Executive, Unilever

Mark Moody-Stuart's experience in the development of some of the first efforts at sustainable business and the creation of the United Nations Global Compact make essential reading for anyone interested in the evolution of international business sustainability since the cold war. His account of life in international business is a timely reminder that the fight against corruption depends on a unified response from companies, governments and civil society.
Huguette Labelle, Chair, Transparency International

This book is a true treasure chest of wisdom and practical guidance on many of the issues which business and policy leaders should know more about. A testimony of responsible leadership, it should be a must-read for the next generation of business leaders in all regions of the world.
Georg Kell, Executive Director, UN Global Compact Office

Sir Mark Moody-Stuart's brilliance and insight into the complexities and challenges facing international businesses today is a must-read for all in business. The breadth and depth of his unparalleled experiences, shaped by his lifetime of living and working overseas, place him in a category of unique experts who truly understand what it means to lead responsibly in a global world.
Cynthia Carroll, former Chief Executive, Anglo American plc

Globalisation has transformed the world. Globalisation is not an abstract process. The profit-seeking firm lies at its core. Unfortunately, few scholars and journalists understand fully the role of the global corporation and few business leaders write about the role their firms have played in this process. Mark Moody-Stuart's book fills a critically important gap in the literature. Based on his own wide experience with Shell, as well as with Anglo American and the UN's Global Compact, his book sheds invaluable light on almost every key issue in globalisation, including politics, international relations, corporate governance, corruption, energy and the environment, poverty reduction, inequality and social justice. Based on deep real-world knowledge, his book provides a realistic but optimistic view of the challenges involved in intelligently regulating the global corporation in the interests of the whole of mankind. It should be compulsory reading for anyone interested in the real world of globalisation.
Peter Nolan, Chong Hua Professor of Chinese Development; Director, Centre of Development Studies, University of Cambridge

A fascinating, thoughtful and wise book. Perceptive analysis of the range of critical global issues facing big business today is leavened with revealing anecdotes from a life of interacting with everyone from presidents and prime ministers to oil drillers and community activists. Sir Mark Moody-Stuart has thought deeply about the multiple dilemmas and challenges that spring up at the interface of business and society, and writes candidly and engagingly about them. This is a highly recommended read.

Daniel Litvin, author of *Empires of Profit: Commerce, Conquest and Corporate Responsibility*; founder and director of Critical Resource

Responsible Leadership

RESPONSIBLE LEADERSHIP

Lessons from the Front Line of Sustainability and Ethics

Mark Moody-Stuart

Greenleaf
PUBLISHING

© 2014 Greenleaf Publishing Limited

Published by Greenleaf Publishing Limited
Aizlewood's Mill
Nursery Street
Sheffield S3 8GG
UK
www.greenleaf-publishing.com

Cover by LaliAbril.com

Printed in the UK on environmentally friendly, acid-free paper
from managed forests by CPI Group (UK) Ltd, Croydon

British Library Cataloguing in Publication Data:
   A catalogue record for this book is available from the British Library.

   ISBN-13: 978-1-906093-96-9 [hardback]
   ISBN-13: 978-1-78353-077-9 [PDF ebook]
   ISBN-13: 978-1-78353-078-6 [ePub ebook]

Contents

Acknowledgements vii

Foreword by Sir Robert Wilson ix

Foreword by Mark Malloch-Brown xiii

Preface xvii

Introduction 1

1 Differing development outcomes and their causes 5

2 Coalitions, governments and doing the right thing 36

3 The United Nations Global Compact 53

4 Some alternatives in countries with military rule or
  human rights abuses: Sanctions or withdrawal 77

5 Dining with the devil: Engaging with those guilty of
  human rights abuses 109

6 Markets are essential, but they cannot do everything 127

7 Oil, gas and climate change 138

8 Corruption: The biggest market failure of all 170

9 Enterprise solutions to poverty and development 200

10 Lessons from China on poverty eradication 226

11 1995: Shell's *annus horribilis* and its consequences 242

12 Embedding values and principles 263

13 Changes in structure and governance: Do they matter? 284

14 Differences in remuneration and wealth in companies
    and societies 308

15 The business of not-for-profit enterprises 324

    Afterword 336
    Index 350

Figures and boxes

Figures

4.1 Letter to Colin Powell, US Secretary of State, 2003 90

4.2 Reply to letter to Colin Powell, US Secretary of State, 2003 93

Boxes

2.1 The Voluntary Principles on Security and Human Rights 40

3.1 Global Compact: initial nine principles 54

3.2 Protect, Respect and Remedy Framework 71

11.1 Article requested for *Greenpeace Business* 247

11.2 Shell's revised General Business Principles, 1997 258

Acknowledgements

I owe a great deal to all colleagues for whom and with whom I have worked over the last decades in different parts of the world in situations from boardrooms to rig floors and mines. Apart from those whose contribution is acknowledged at relevant points in the text, I would like to name three exploration geologists for whom I worked and who guided and inspired my early Shell career: Jake Schweighauser, Myles Bowen and Ruedi Wegmann. Alas, all have now died. To them I would add Cambridge geologist Peter Friend under whose guidance I worked in the Arctic for several years. Adegoke Ademiluyi and Godwin Omene and their families helped me and my family understand and appreciate Nigeria and Nigerians. Gönül Çapan and Puan Noraini, academics both, did more than just teach me Turkish and Malay but also clarified for me the subtleties of their societies. Any manager knows how much we owe to our personal assistants: Patricia, Stephen, Bingül, Nazan, Pek Tin, Suyin, Valentine, Barbara and Erica have helped me in six different countries and were all invaluable supporters, daily companions and advisers. Robin Aram in Shell and Edward Bickham in Anglo American, each with strong links to civil society and the outside world, are people with whom I frequently discussed the companies' position in society and the rights, wrongs and possible outcomes of various policies and actions; I believe every chief executive needs a kind of corporate conscience with whom such matters can be explored. Robin White at Shell guided me around the pitfalls of television journalism, often travelling with me and interpreting what I said or did with healthy journalistic scepticism; people at the top of organisations need someone to bring such a realistic perspective and I remain grateful for his. Wendy Pritchard likewise supplied this internally within Shell. Georg Kell of the UN Global Compact is someone with whom I have interacted with great pleasure on an almost weekly basis over the last decade; his contribution to the Global Compact has been seminal. I am grateful to my publisher John Stuart of Greenleaf Publishing for advice on this book and to Monica Allen for her editing. Pam Simmonds ran her sharp eye over the manuscript and fixed text and subjunctives alike. I should also like to thank those with whom I have interacted at various points who kindly took time to read the text and make thoughtful comments. Lastly I would like to thank my family of many generations older and younger; they have provided and still provide a framework for my life and establish a connection to many walks of everyday life, demonstrating an unwritten system of accepted values against which actions are readily though unconsciously screened.

Foreword

Sir Robert Wilson KCMG, former Executive Chairman of Rio Tinto plc;
former Chairman of BG Group plc

Mark Moody-Stuart's book is not a conventional business book. Nor is it what we usually think of as an autobiography. Happily, it fits somewhere in between, because these are the reflections on a lifetime of international experience from a man whose career culminated in leadership of one of the biggest companies in the world: Shell. And for dessert, so to speak, after his executive career in Shell he went on to lead one of the world's largest mining companies, Anglo American, as non-executive Chairman.

It is a fact of life that the extractive industries, both oil and gas and mining, face a wide range of ethical and practical challenges: environmental; relationships with national governments, regional governments and local communities; the economic and social consequences of major resource projects; bribery and corruption in many different forms; human rights. The list goes on.

The extractive industries are sometimes caricatured as archetypal capitalists: red in tooth and claw. Doubtless there have been some instances, mainly in the distant past, which give substance to this image, but it is a long way from the reality of today's leading companies. The subtitle to Mark's book, 'Lessons from the Front Line of Sustainability and Ethics', is therefore singularly apt. There is much to be learned from this fascinating book, which draws on many practical examples and explains the way they were addressed by a man who is both deeply thoughtful and possessed of a powerful moral conscience. The lessons are relevant not only to current generations of business managers, but to all who want to understand the interface of industry and the geo-political world. It would help if more of our political leaders (not just in Britain), took time to understand the essence of responsible capitalism, and that it is something much more complex than the superficial inanities which sometimes seem to characterise their thoughts. The failure of some companies to live up to the rhetoric of their public relations is an obvious cause of cynicism. Perhaps, though, there is a more fundamental problem. The time-horizon for a politician in the democratic world is generally fixed somewhere between tomorrow morning's headlines and the next general election. The time-horizon of a responsible leader in the capital-intensive extractive industries is (or should be) measured in decades.

Bribery and corruption is one aspect of responsible capitalism where there is no ambiguity about what is right. Companies should have no part of it. It will soon become clear to the reader, though, that there are often no simple black-and-white answers to some of the dilemmas that Mark addresses. For example, should companies be held accountable, by virtue of their economic influence, for the actions of their host governments, when the latter are guilty of human rights abuses or gross corruption? Some will say yes, because it is the companies that are providing the financial means of the government remaining in power as well as the wealth that some of them would steal. Others will say no: foreign companies have no mandate to involve themselves in issues that are for sovereign governments to resolve and, indeed, any use by companies of their economic power would be the antithesis of good governance. If outside influence is to be brought to bear on host governments, it should be by other sovereign governments or the multilateral agencies, not by corporations.

There are many occasions when there are grey areas, where the 'right' or ethical course of action is a matter of judgement rather than a self-evident certainty. I include in this category the fraught area of trade-offs.

For example, there may be an environmental cost (perhaps permanent, perhaps temporary) associated with a project that yields economic and welfare benefits. Such trade-off decisions should be made by government, but sometimes governments lack the experience and knowledge needed. And sometimes the costs may be borne by one part of the community (e.g. those living close to a project), but the benefits might largely accrue to others (e.g. the urban elite). How and by whom should these issues be addressed? The industry participant may have relevant experience and insight, but, of course, it also has a vested interest and will rarely be seen as an impartial adviser. Those familiar with the debate about airport capacity around London will know that there are no simple solutions when trade-offs are involved, even in a relatively sophisticated society. No wonder, then, that resources companies, which frequently face comparable problems in countries with relatively untested government institutional infrastructure, have sometimes been party to poor decisions.

I hope that this book will reach a wide readership, including not only aspirant leaders in the extractive industries, but also politicians, investors, multilateral agencies and NGOs. Major companies cannot be built and sustained by the simple pursuit of profit this year and next. Long-term success, perhaps especially in the extractive industries, which have such long time-horizons, requires enlightened self-interest. The so-called 'soft' issues relating to the environment, health and safety, and employment practices, contributing meaningfully to the long-term welfare of host societies and everything else that constitutes good corporate citizenship, should now be seen as central parts of the business process. There are instances, too, when the scale of a resources project is so large relative to the host economy that the project company may find it necessary to assume many of the characteristics of a development agency. Sometimes this has been done rather well, but the company must focus on helping to build institutional capability so that the host government can take on its responsibilities as soon as possible.

Many of the challenges and dilemmas that Mark has experienced and described are not, of course, unique to Shell or to Anglo American. Whatever our sphere, we are all likely to do better if we learn from one another's experiences as well as our own. As Mark observes, industry is at its most effective when it can act collectively, or at least in coalitions. This is surely the path to a better future. The Global Compact, with which Mark has been closely associated, is one such example but this is very high-level, and the principles, while very important, are necessarily broad. It should be complementary to more focused industry-level cooperation.

This book includes an interesting retrospective view on the Brent Spar saga in 1995. Mark comments that 'Shell learned that not all problems can be solved simply by technical analysis . . . we need to listen . . . and address concerns.' How true! In my view this has probably been the biggest single source of error in the extractive industries: a belief that, if we have made the right technical assessment, it will speak for itself and there is no need for serious engagement with the concerns expressed by civil society, especially if they are scientifically unsound.

Sir Robert Wilson
January 2014

Foreword

Mark Malloch-Brown, former UN Deputy Secretary-General

The ground has shifted under the resource extraction industries. Mark Moody-Stuart was one of the first to notice and certainly one of the very first to do something about it. The old operating assumptions about what it took to get oil and gas or minerals out of the ground were overtaken by a whole new set of 'above ground' requirements that can be summarised in the phrase 'permission to operate'.

As a chief of Shell, he had seen for himself how a crass environmental mistake, such as Shell's attempt to bury an oil platform deep in the ocean, could cut into public trust and risk turning a familiar and respected consumer brand into a pariah and target of threatened consumer boycotts. A sensitive and committed manager, I am sure he also saw what this did to his people. What had been a source of pride, working for a company that adventurously scoured the world to bring home the oil and gas that fired the modern economy, had suddenly become a cause for embarrassment at the school gate or neighbourhood drinks party.

He emerged as the thoughtful spokesman for an industry that recognised that it had to recover the trust, not just of its consumers and shareholders, but of the communities where it worked. By their nature, oil and gas, and then minerals when he became Chairman of Anglo American, are often extracted from the world's difficult neighbourhoods, where governance is weak and inequalities of income and access to education and health are high. In the Niger Delta, for example, following what many Nigerians saw as its complicity in the then military regime's execution of Ken Saro Wiwa, Mark saw how Shell has struggled to overcome a legacy of political distrust and environmental damage.

All of this for Mark has proved a crucible in which his experiences, sometimes no doubt painful, hardened into a deep commitment to a new way of doing business. This has put a premium on industry sectors, well beyond his own, establishing voluntary standards of conduct and being open and forthcoming about reporting compliance. It is not just about sustaining the trust of cautious institutional investors, but about restoring a much broader social trust for business and its place in the modern political economy. This book is the personal journey of reflection and discovery that has carried him to a leading role as a businessman in the UN's Global Compact, as well as to a broader role in international standard setting for business conduct.

It has made Mark an unlikely revolutionary. His compassion and profound sense of service has found a larger stage than his own generous personal philanthropy. Through changing how business behaves, he is helping to rewrite the terms of modern society. Whether it is adopting standards of disclosure around environmental and social policies, anti-corruption compliance, or encouraging much more ambitious development provision in deprived communities where companies are operating collectively; it amounts to a small revolution in corporate behaviour.

And as the state and company struggle in very different national contexts to find some kind of accommodation, Mark's wise quiet words should be a source of wisdom to many. He has now been at this long enough to have seen both the post-1989, pre-2008 world when business seemed to rule supreme, and the world since then where big government has returned. In the first, markets were king and governments seemed to have been pushed to the sidelines. Then, the appeal of people like Mark to international business was essentially not to exploit their dominance, and to resist the ability to up sticks and move from Hungary to Mexico or Thailand to Sri Lanka depending on changing labour costs and convenience. Companies seemed in an age of fluid global capital flows to be masters of their own fate, and countries were the supplicants who fought for their attention and investment. In that context the main message was couched in terms of social responsibility, and not over-reaching and abusing this corporate power in an era of globalisation.

Now, good corporate behaviour has a much more immediate interest. Since the financial crisis, the state is back in the economy. From the state capitalism of China, to the busy regulatory activism of the EU or Washington, business has no longer got the world to itself! It needs to win friends. Just as 1989 and the fall of the Berlin Wall seemed to have discredited government's role in markets, so the global financial crisis similarly upended business's brief supremacy, and re-established respect for both state-led capitalism as in China and a much more highly government-regulated business environment in the West. Like so many pendulums, it has no doubt now swung too far in this new direction.

Nevertheless, for business it has become critical to win the confidence of regulators and legislators alike. Companies must demonstrate they are acting in a broader interest, and understand that in addition to being run for profit and innovation there is also a social bottom line that must be respected. Further, this is not just a case to be made in global forums like the UN or before national governments and parliaments, but also in those communities at the bottom of the pyramid where the oil rig, mine or factory is located.

This is Mark's story: how a quietly spoken, supremely well-mannered English gentleman has brought this urgent message of corporate good neighbourliness and global social responsibility to the boardrooms and conference rooms of both business and the UN. An unlikely perhaps, but very effective, revolutionary.

Mark Malloch-Brown
January 2014

Preface

This is not an autobiography, at least in the conventional sense. Rather, I have tried to address the myriad of issues and dilemmas that have confronted me in a career working in the extractive sector and living in ten different countries. The emphasis is on these issues and dilemmas and not on the sequence of events.

However, no matter how balanced and impartial we may try to be, we are all products of our backgrounds, training and life experiences. In interpreting what a person says about events, it is useful to have an idea of this background and the likely biases. For this reason, I have given in an Afterword at the end of this book a more chronological account of my upbringing and the events that have shaped my life. This covers the period from my early years up to 1990 and the ten countries in which I have lived and worked. My time at the very top of Shell and as Chairman of Shell and Anglo American from 1990 to 2009 and on many commercial and not-for-profit boards up to the present is directly reflected in the views and experiences in the main text. The reader can choose whether to read this Afterword or not, and whether to do so before or after reading the rest of the book.

For those not involved in business, I hope that this book may give them some insight into the kinds of issues and problems that a business faces and perhaps suggest some ways to interact. For those in business, I hope that the book will be of some interest in shedding light through one person's view of approaches to what will be reasonably familiar problems. I will be very satisfied if this book can go some way in encouraging people from the different segments of society to work together to address objectives that are common to all parts of society. If the book leads any young person to understand that business is so much more than just a matter of making money, that would be a bonus.

Introduction

One of the great privileges of having lived and worked in many different countries with my wife Judy and our family is not just getting to know countries and their people—and in some cases their languages—at a level that is denied to the short-term visitor, but of following their subsequent evolution and development. For the rest of your life you prick up your ears when there is an item on the news about a particular country and you imagine how your friends and colleagues are coping with some, perhaps momentous, event. You also hear directly from friends whom you meet again later how things are going and what the outcome was of particular political or social movements. And there is always the fascination of 'what happened to so-and-so?' This relates not just to the ten countries where I have lived and worked. I have visited oil and mining operations in some 40 other countries, often making a point of not just visiting operations to which I had a connection, but also engaging in what I call 'industrial tourism'. That involves observing standards of living and examining the drivers of the economy outside the main cities. Through that you begin to learn what the people of the country themselves regard as important.

Experiencing and observing the evolution of societies and economies in various countries over several decades one faces the unavoidable question of why in some countries the process of development has been a relatively happy and successful one, while in others it has repeatedly sunk into quagmires of failure. Where the economy was heavily dependent on natural resource revenues, was this a fundamental cause of difficulties? To what extent were the actions of extractive companies, or indeed the individual managers in those companies, responsible for such failures? Or is success or failure more dependent on the behaviour and motivation of individual governments and national leaders? If governments, and indeed systems of governance, play a major role, what is the responsibility of companies and individuals to attempt to influence outcomes? History shows that there are clearly significant dangers in this. The historical precedents are the Honourable East India Company in India, in whose army my great-great-great-grandfather served from 1764 to 1804, or, a century later, the British South Africa Company founded by Cecil John Rhodes.[1] These companies effectively took over all the responsibilities of the state in their areas of influence. A more modern example is the United Fruit Company in Central America influencing or controlling governments, which gave us the phrase 'banana republic'. The company's efforts may even have been initially intended simply to bring order and system to a country to allow businesses to operate, but this slides easily into behaviour that preferentially benefits the company. On the other hand, in the absence of some reforming efforts a government may continue to pursue courses of action and behaviour that lead to disaster. For example, as elsewhere in the world, Shell in Nigeria pursued a policy of strict non-interference in local politics. Some argue that Shell could and should have used its undoubted economic power in some way to force changes of behaviour on successive Nigerian governments. I believe that it is inappropriate and improper for individual companies to go beyond offering advice, but readers will form their own opinion.

The history of the last 20 years or so has, however, shown that coalitions of companies and civil society organisations can exert a positive influence on outcomes, particularly when addressing specific challenges such as ensuring that timber is sourced only from sustainably managed

1 For an excellent review of the activities of these and other companies see D. Litvin, *Empires of Profit: Commerce, Conquest and Corporate Responsibility* (New York/London: Texere, 2003).

forests or working to prevent the use of diamonds to fund conflicts.[2] This approach provides much more legitimacy than a single company acting alone could have. How are such coalitions best formed? What is the role of international sanctions and what are the alternatives to sanctions? What is the role of markets as opposed to regulations? What happens when markets fail, as could be argued in the case of climate change, or are severely distorted by endemic corruption? What are the particular challenges for companies and individuals of operating in countries where governments are guilty of human rights abuses? Or should companies simply withdraw?

How can we stimulate the development of enterprises and economies so that they can escape from the spirals of poverty, debt and ongoing development aid? What can we learn from the remarkable changes that have taken place in China where hundreds of millions of people have been lifted out of poverty through economic development, albeit with significant collateral environmental damage and at the cost of individual freedom?

When it comes to how individual global companies work, what can companies learn from the failures of development that occur with somewhat depressing frequency? How can the well-intentioned values and principles expressed by almost all responsible companies actually be embedded practically and acted on credibly by the thousands of people working for the company around the world? Do all employees really believe in or support the values that the corporation is espousing?

These are difficult questions and no one could provide answers to all of them in a single book. What this book does attempt to do is to give personal examples and observations on how some of these questions have been or are being addressed in specific cases. My hope is that this will be useful to all those who are studying or struggling on the ground with some of these issues in companies, business schools and civil society organisations around the world.

---

2 For example, by the Forest Stewardship Council, a coalition of civil society organisations and businesses, or through the Kimberley Process, which involves governments as well as civil society and business.

A few words of warning. I have not kept a diary and I am well aware that human memory is not only fallible but also selective. Furthermore, in describing the evolution of certain economies and societies I have radically simplified what are very complex developments about which many learned treatises could, and have been, written. My objective is to highlight trends and methods that appear to have been successful in the hope that they can be replicated, or at least experimented with further. There are no panaceas or magic bullets, as no two countries or companies are alike. In a scientific experiment, if one recreates the conditions exactly the result will be the same. Because we humans learn and anticipate, the same is not true of our organisations. We do not necessarily respond to the same stimulus in the way that we did on the previous occasion. This is why economics is not a science; it is also why life and learning is both a challenge and a pleasure.

Chapter 1

Differing development outcomes and their causes

For the past 45 years I have been involved with the extraction of natural resources, first oil and gas and later metals and minerals. The industry in which I was involved was often a very major contributor to the host economy. In some cases the outcome has been positive, in others much less so. I do not subscribe to the inevitability of the 'resource curse' theory propounded by Jeffrey Sachs and others, which seeks to demonstrate that countries blessed with natural resource income have poorer economic and social development.[1] I have certainly often observed many of the ills ascribed to resource development—corruption, negative impacts on other sectors of the economy and unwise dependency on ongoing resource income. The picture is more complex and mixed than often portrayed. Here are three examples that I have followed over the last 45 years: Oman, Malaysia and Nigeria.

---

1 J.D. Sachs and A.M. Warner, *Natural Resource Abundance and Economic Growth* (NBER Working Paper 5398; Cambridge, MA: National Bureau of Economic Research, 1995; ideas.repec.org/p/nbr/nberwo/5398.html); R.M. Auty, *Sustaining Development in Mineral Economies: The Resource Curse Thesis* (London: Routledge, 1993); P. Collier, *Natural Resources, Development and Conflict: Channels of Causation and Policy Interventions* (Washington, DC: World Bank, 2004).

Oman

When I first worked as a field geologist in the Sultanate of Oman in 1967 and 1968, the country was in what could be described as a mediaeval state. There were only a couple of doctors for a population of over a million, and diseases such as the eye infection trachoma were endemic in the Bedu people of the desert and mountains. Education was basic, consisting often of only studying the Koran. Female genital mutilation was still practised. Prison could mean a ball chained to an ankle. I recall visiting the Wali, or governor, of Nizwa, a town to the north-west of the capital city of Muscat but on the other side of the Oman (Hajar) Mountains, which run along the eastern side of the country and rise to around 10,000 feet (3,000 metres) forming some of the most spectacular scenery in the Middle East. In the courtyard of Nizwa fort, the residence and office of the Wali, there was a man sweeping the dusty floor, picking up his chain and shifting his ball every few steps. One of our workers, Hamid Nasser, returned to his village for a break after having been earlier involved in a dispute over water with a neighbour and sentenced to two weeks in prison for breaching the peace. At that time there had apparently been no vacant leg irons available, but on his return to the village from our camp he was caught and put in irons. This consisted of a ball and chain with a heavy soft iron ring beaten around the ankle. When Hamid did not return after his break, a party went in search. When he was located—somewhat embarrassed by his predicament—his release was negotiated. The irons were struck off in an alarming process involving an anvil and a sledgehammer.

Along the Batinah coast on the Indian Ocean fishermen lived in *barasti* huts made of palm fronds. As in mediaeval Britain, revenue was still collected at internal toll gates through which caravans to the coastal souks or markets had to pass.

The then Sultan, Said bin Taimur, was what I regard as a pioneer of anti-globalisation. He believed that development of the country should come slowly and in line with Omani customs and values. He felt that the country could benefit from Western investment and technology to produce oil, but that the process, proceeds and impacts should be carefully managed. Western experts and their families should be kept separate so that Western influences did not have an adverse effect on society. In principle this idea is not a bad one, and in fact it is not unlike the ideas of those who believe that the 'resource curse' could be kept at bay by ensuring that resource income should only be accessed when the structures of society are sufficiently developed to handle the income. However, there are many practical difficulties to this approach. We field geologists lived in a tented camp and moved around the country by helicopter, accompanied at all times by a representative of the sultan. To ensure that our impact on society was limited, we were forbidden among other things to bring medical cases back to the medical facilities on the coast that were available to us in the oil industry. I remember a young boy of about 12 in the mountains who was suffering from a gunshot wound in his shoulder. The wound had been treated with a traditional and unhygienic poultice and was plainly infected. The boy was feverish. Knowing that we could not take him back to the coast in Oman, we offered to fly him to the neighbouring emirate of Sharjah where we knew British military medical facilities would be available. The family were not prepared to let the boy go alone, so we offered to take as many as wanted to go by truck on what was perhaps a five- or six-hour journey. After much discussion, the family decided to let the infection and fever run its course; God would decide on the outcome. I have often thought since of the boy dying from septicaemia, as he almost certainly did. The power of a helicopter and our relative wealth was of little relevance in that situation. The family were perhaps of the same mind as Sultan Said bin Taimur, although much of the rest of the population were not.

I developed an enormous respect for the Omani people. They were, and are, modest and yet very confident of their own position and values. Wherever we went, even in remote areas, people would gather round us and invite us for a traditional coffee. I could manage the long traditional to-and-fro Arabic greeting, but when that ran its course after a couple of minutes and we got on to the serious business of 'the news' I was stuck. Those who spoke Arabic told of their enquiries after progress in the war in Vietnam and the price of gold and silver—we still paid many local crews in silver Maria Theresa thalers, dated 1780 as are they all.[2] The Bedu people in the desert with few possessions would willingly share their last cup of coffee with you, prepared with ritual hospitality over a small fire of twigs. To ensure that we could get our work done before the inevitable hospitality, we would circle the helicopter to make sure no one was in sight before we landed and commenced our geological work, but no matter where this was, most likely within 20 minutes there would be a boy or girl beside the helicopter and the rest of the group followed soon after. The most popular gifts we could give in return were the heavy linen sample bags in which we collected rock specimens. These are invaluable for nomadic people who often leave possessions hanging in trees or bushes.

As ordained by Sultan Said bin Taimur, we had an Omani representative with us wherever we went. The Wali of whatever district we were in would nominate the representative from one of the tribesmen standing around his fort. At a moment's notice the nominee would gather his gun and his few belongings and, leaving a message for his family, join us in the helicopter. Although he had probably hardly been in a Land Rover, let alone a helicopter, he would follow us in doing his seat belt up as if it was a perfectly normal event. The only change on his dignified face would be a tiny smile at the corners of his mouth as the helicopter lifted off. Omanis have stiffer upper lips than your average modern Brit!

The writ of Sultan Said bin Taimur did not run unchallenged over the whole of the Sultanate. There was still a rebellion in Dhofar in the south. We were challenged in the wild and beautiful Musandam peninsula in the north, where tribesmen still carried their trademark stone or metal axes. We were also shot at by tribesmen near the Wahiba sands in

2 Although there was printed currency available both in Oman and in what were then the Trucial States, later to become the United Arab Emirates, the most trusted currency was in the form of Maria Theresa thalers dated 1780 and showing the head of Hapsburg Empress Maria Theresa. The silver content of these was known and trusted. When the supply ran short, additional coins were struck in London with exactly the same images, silver content and 1780 date. I believe that the practice was challenged in an international court by the Austrian government, but the practice was upheld as the currency was not being adulterated albeit the money supply increased.

the centre of the country. Fortunately, this was at the extreme range of the most common tribal weapon, the Martini Henry rifle, which fired a large handmade lead ball. The damage was limited to scratches from fragmenting balls and a dent in the helicopter as we beat a hasty and undignified retreat.

While some resented the presence of strangers from outside their tribal group, others sought the changes taking place elsewhere in the region. The then almost ubiquitous little transistor radio was bringing not just news of Vietnam to the Sultanate, but news of developments elsewhere in the Middle East, of Gamal Abdel Nasser in Egypt, of the Organization of the Petroleum Exporting Countries (OPEC), of other Gulf kingdoms and emirates and of education and healthcare in hospitals. A slow development from the status quo was untenable and in 1970 Sultan Said bin Taimur was replaced in a bloodless coup by his son Qaboos bin Said. The father left in waiting RAF transport for London, where he was accommodated in comfort by his son.

The steady development of Oman then began and the results of the subsequent 40 years of wise and enlightened leadership by Sultan Qaboos bin Said are remarkable. The Sultanate is held up as an example of good development by the United Nations Development Programme. Healthcare is universal and statistics such as those on child mortality a source of pride. I have not seen a case of trachoma for years. Housing is good, and there are no longer *barasti* huts to be seen along the coast, just neat small villages. There is a bi-cameral parliament, with the lower house, the Majlis Al-shura, being elected from a list that has evolved from one nominated by the Sultan to open nomination. Women stand and are elected, although there are more women in the upper house, which is appointed by the Sultan, who has pointed out to me in conversation that he is less conservative than the electorate. The education system is excellent with a university that attracts students from other countries. There are televised discussions with ministers in which they can be challenged. The Sultan still goes on an annual tour of part of the Sultanate, living with his ministers, often in tented camps, and being accessible to all members of the local population.

As in any country there are challenges. The largest is employment for the growing population of young educated Omanis. There is also the inescapably finite nature of oil and gas reserves on which the economy has grown. This is addressed both by having investment in a reserve fund, and also in planning production so that at any one time the hydrocarbon reserves are there to allow production at the same level for at least a further ten years. The development of a sustainable tourism industry based on spectacular Indian Ocean beaches, desert and mountains is helped by Oman's traditional yet tolerant and liberal culture. There is heavy investment in port and rail facilities and ancillary industry, which take advantage of Oman's location at the mouth of the Gulf and Indian Ocean coastline. There is a well-functioning stock exchange.

Because of its relatively modest oil and gas production and much larger population than most of its Gulf neighbours, Oman has never been excessively wealthy. Perhaps because of this, the excessive consumerist culture and mass tourism of some of the other Gulf countries has been avoided. Through wise and inclusive government the country has escaped the problems of civil and sometimes religious strife that have affected its southern neighbour Yemen. Formed by the uneasy combination of the former North and South Yemen, the one traditional and tribal and the other secular and socialistic, Yemen has thus struggled to develop using its admittedly more modest resources. I believe that many of these differences are not down to chance, but due to the quality of leadership and wise use of economic resources by the government. Resources have been largely a blessing for Oman.

Malaysia

When we first travelled to Malaysia in the late 1960s it was a country with an economy largely dependent on primary industries—rubber, tin, timber, palm oil, and oil and gas. While wealthier than Oman, the population was ethnically divided. Certainly in Peninsular Malaysia, although less so in the East Malaysian states of Sabah and Sarawak, one could guess the occupation of an individual by their ethnic origins.

Malays dominated the civil service, the police and the army, and rural subsistence agriculture and fishing. Commerce was largely the domain of the Chinese, while Indians worked in the rubber and palm oil plantations or drove the taxis in the towns. One of the great achievements of the last 40 years is that this is no longer true. That is not to say that divisions and stresses no longer exist, but the picture has radically changed. The economy has also broadened so that it is no longer dependent on primary industries, and now includes thriving manufacturing and financial service sectors.

The change probably had its origins in the riots in Malaysia on 13 May 1969 when in the aftermath of an election many hundreds of Chinese were killed in communal riots and thousands of people rendered homeless when their houses were burned. As in Singapore, which suffered racial riots five years earlier, all of Malaysia's ethnic groups stared into the abyss of the deadly racial violence that has effectively destroyed many countries since. Citizens of different groups realised that compromises were necessary if strife and bloodshed were to be avoided. Singapore and Malaysia, with different racial balances and different economic histories, have taken somewhat different routes to addressing what is essentially the same issue. I do not think it is for outsiders to judge which method is more appropriate. Although attention is often focused on Singapore's indubitably faster economic growth, a true comparison is difficult given the large geographic and historical differences and the need to take into account non-economic factors. We can just be very grateful that through the chosen method of resolution major bloodshed has been avoided and the two societies have found harmonious ways to develop economically in ways of which any nation could be proud.

In Singapore the approach was one of legal equality between different ethnic groups, combined with a bilingual approach, firmly guided by what is essentially a single dominant party. In Malaysia politics has always been more pluralistic, with different parties, predominantly ethnically based, coming together into an alliance, but with a single national language. Historically, when a new or different group challenges the alliance in one or other state and wins, the result has often been simply their subsequent co-option into the alliance, which has therefore sometimes come to resemble a form of winners club. The reward is generally a degree of government patrimony of a type certainly not unknown in Western democracies.

A key element, and one of the drivers for the social changes, was positive discrimination by means of the controversial New Economic Policy (NEP), which mandated an element of ownership for *bumiputra* shareholders—essentially Malay and other indigenous groups.[3] This was not imposed overnight, but if a business wanted to restructure, raise capital or expand by building new facilities, then the requirements had to be fulfilled before permission would be granted. There were undoubtedly abuses—fronting or so-called Ali Baba organisations, advantageous deals by the politically connected or indeed effectively by political parties. However, considerable amounts of the investments were made through what were essentially investment trusts such as Permodalan Nasional Berhad (PNB) or the pilgrims' fund, Tabung Haji. These organisations provided savings vehicles for *bumiputras*, deploying the funds in advantaged shareholdings often acquired from firms seeking to meet the requirements of the NEP. In the 1980s in Shell we also worked with Tabung Haji to find a solid remunerative outlet for their savings funds. An outlet for some of these was created by putting in place financing for a refinery expansion through one of the first Islamic bonds (what would now be known as a 'sukuk').[4] This form of collective *bumiputra* investment meant that while an individual could

---

3 The term *bumiputra*, literally meaning a 'son of the soil', differentiates the indigenous population of Malays and some others from the Chinese and Indian populations, which are largely the result of British colonial labour practices and migration in colonial times. There is a also a small and centuries-old Chinese population on the west coast of the Malay peninsula, some indeed Muslim, which resulted from trade and which has its own long-established customs incorporating many Malay practices.

4 This was certainly the first such Islamic bond or sukuk in Malaysia and I have been assured by the former head of the Malaysian Stock Exchange, Zarinah Anwar, that she considered it one of the first in the world. Since Zarinah is a former Shell employee and finance director in Malaysia, she may not be entirely impartial in her judgement, but it was certainly a pioneering move.

realise his or her investment to deploy in, for example, the purchase of a house or car, the *bumiputra* element was maintained.

This contrasts with the South African process of Black Economic Empowerment (BEE), where shares have more often been acquired by individuals or black-owned companies, often supported by loans from the company seeking to meet empowerment criteria. When the individual or organisation wishes to release capital, sales are often made on the open market, so that the shareholding reverts essentially to that of the market as a whole, with no specific black component. In discussions with South African ministers on the process and aims of BEE, I was never able to engage their interest in the Malaysian model. Attention often focused on the political and historical differences between the two countries and on one or two failures. There are of course many differences, but there were, nonetheless, some two decades of Malaysian experience to draw on, both successes and failures, before the South African process was embarked on.

In Malaysia, the main oil-producing concessions are offshore and initially were held largely by Exxon in Peninsular Malaysia and by Shell in the East Malaysian states of Sabah and Sarawak. In the 1970s, Malaysia decided to form a national oil company, Petronas, and to convert all concessions to production-sharing contracts. As the oil and gas had so far been developed without a national oil company, the international oil companies were less than enthusiastic. There were arguments that this would simply lead to another layer of overhead and unnecessary expenditure; the performance of national oil companies elsewhere had not always been good, not least because they had often been starved of development capital by their short-sighted or financially pressed governments.

At the time, for reasons of efficiency, Shell's operations in East Malaysia were largely run from a long-established operational base in Brunei, an independent sultanate that lay sandwiched between the Malaysian states of Sabah and Sarawak. This was plainly untenable, and discussions began with Petronas to recreate operations bases in Malaysia. Shell's operations were essentially in East Malaysia, while the fields off Peninsular Malaysia were operated by Esso Malaysia, later a part of Exxon. The

Malaysian approach was essentially pragmatic, but none the less firm. While content to have foreign operations, there was a strong desire to establish a national oil company and Petronas, or Petroleum Nasional, was formed. After initial skirmishes, we in Shell approached the project with a determination to make the inevitable work. Petronas needed operational experience but acknowledged that they did not yet have the staff or all the skills necessary. Long-established traditional concession agreements were converted into production-sharing contracts, in which the ownership of the oil remains clearly with the state but there is a contract that allows an operator to recover capital and operating costs from a share of production. An area off the Baram Delta in Sarawak with a number of Shell-operated oilfields was identified and turned into a joint venture. This was staffed jointly and run as an independent joint venture between Shell and Petronas, but operated by the nascent Petronas operating arm Petronas Carigali. In this way there was no loss of efficiency and Petronas gained vital operating experience. Likewise, under Malaysian employment laws Shell had to demonstrate that it was developing and promoting Malaysian staff in line with the ethnic balance of the population. The plans had to be approved by Petronas, but as a result of the joint operating experience and their own operations, Petronas had a realistic view of what experience and performance were needed from staff of whatever background. So, although there was healthy pressure to accelerate the process of achieving balance, there were no ill-judged short cuts and no undue protection of any underperformers. Petronas has grown to be one of the relatively few highly respected national oil companies. Although Shell was certainly not initially supportive of the formation of a national oil company, the subsequent cooperation can be a source of some pride on both sides.

It is by no means just in the oil and gas industry that there were changes. Malaysia transformed itself from an economy in which licences were needed for any industrial activity to a much more open economy. Light manufacturing, in particular electronics, was encouraged and grew rapidly and effectively, providing liberating employment for many young Malay women. The Malaysian Industrial Development Authority (MIDA) transformed itself from a government licensing agency to an effective single point of investment promotion with the declared mission of 'Positioning Malaysia for Global Competitiveness'. I had the honour in the 1980s to sit on the MIDA board as the sole Non-Malaysian, so I was able to see this transformation in action at first hand. I recall a discussion on whether a licence should be given to a toy manufacturer. Were not things such as Barbie dolls essentially frivolous and should we not encourage more serious industries? I argued that the critical thing was the standard of operation—working conditions, employment creation, environmental impact, and health and safety—rather than the nature of the product, providing of course the product was not damaging. Our children were never Barbie enthusiasts, but choices of toys should be made by parents (or aunts and uncles), not by government departments. The interesting question is not whether 'frivolous' toys such as Barbie dolls should or should not be made in a country such as Malaysia, but why they are almost never made in the countries of Africa, where the development of light manufacturing has been limited.[5]

No one contributed more to the leadership of the Malaysian development process than Mahathir bin Mohamad, Prime Minister of Malaysia from 1981 to 2003. Dr Mahathir is no stranger to controversy—his early book *The Malay Dilemma* (written in 1970) provides much of the rationale for the New Economic Policy and has been denounced by some as racist. Whether or not you agree with all his policies, Dr Mahathir achieved something over his 22 years in power that anyone who has led a major global company would salute. Almost as if Malaysia was a corporation, through leadership, he created a spirit of alignment between citizens of every background, focused on the belief that '*Malaysia boleh*'[6]—that Malaysia could achieve whatever any other country could achieve and do so at a world-leading level.

---

5 Part of the explanation, certainly in countries without significant natural resource dependency, is the poor communication infrastructure, particularly in landlocked countries. High internal tariff barriers and unattractive conditions for foreign direct investment has in many cases also played a part. It is good to see that in the fast-growing African economies, manufacturing activity is beginning to be established.

6 'Malaysia can!'

I first became aware of this process in the 1980s when it was announced that Malaysia would build the tallest flagpole in the world, presumably with the world's largest national flag flying from it. This would be on the Padang[7] in Kuala Lumpur, the green sports field cum parade ground in the colonial centre of the city, down one side of which ran the long-verandaed mock-Tudor building of the Royal Selangor Club, a watering hole of the colonial and local elites since 1884. Cynics greeted this announcement with some mirth, tinged with irritation if they were cricketers as well as cynics, as the project would reportedly shave a piece off the boundary of the cricket pitch. They did not laugh for long.

Next came the twin Petronas Towers, shining, modernistic shafts of offices, malls and restaurants, which were for a while the tallest buildings in the world. Apart from their intrinsic architectural attraction, the towers became familiar to cinema audiences as a result of a Sean Connery/Catherine Zeta-Jones scene in the film *Entrapment*. It is interesting that, for approximately the same building cost, Malaysia got a global icon, a valuable commercial property, a tourist attraction and a source of pride for all Malaysians, while Britain got the Millennium Dome, a 'temporary' tented dome structure with original contents of questionable taste.

Another of Dr Mahathir's brain children is Putrajaya, a purpose-built city housing the administrative centres of Malaysia. The many buildings and bridges are impressive, with mixtures of architectural styles—Mughal and Islamic, but sometimes with columns capped by capitals that are almost pharaonic. The impression is grand and spacious, and the setting is around an artificial lake. Once when visiting Dr Mahathir in his vast office in the Perdana Putra, looking out to the lake and the magnificent national mosque Masjid Putra, the Prime Minister pointed out that the lake was bigger than the one in Canberra—the administrative centre of Australia. Therein lies the key. This is a project of national pride, a symbol of unity. The very grand Lutyens buildings in New Delhi[8] and the 'new' cities of Brasilia, Canberra, and indeed Abuja in Nigeria

---

7 Renamed Merdeka Square in 1990.
8 The Chairman of Shell India, Vikram Mehta, remarked to me on my first visit, 'You can see from these buildings, Mark, that you Brits never planned to leave.'

all had the same aim. But when one sees a rural Malay family standing with pride on one of the great bridges in Putrajaya, one knows that for Malaysia it really works, however over the top it might seem to some.

The list of projects is long—infrastructure, car manufacturing, petro-chemical and steel plants, tourism venues, a Formula One track, and a modern stock exchange. Not all of these have been successful. However, Malaysia has enough confidence not to agonise over failures, but to move on to the next thing. The question as to what extent the sound legacy of Dr Mahathir and his own predecessors will survive remains an open one. Dr Mahathir himself has been very critical, perhaps some-times unfairly, of his successors. At least they have the advantage of an economy and society that has transformed itself by the intelligent and pragmatic use of its resources. As in Oman, I believe that much of this transformation is down to leadership.

Nigeria

In the late 1960s, in contrast to Oman and Malaysia, Nigeria was split by a bloody civil war. While there was still a Dhofari separatist move-ment in Oman at the time and there were the racial riots of 1969 in Malaysia, none of these could compare with the all-out land and aerial warfare of the Nigerian Civil War in which well over a million peo-ple died (estimates go up to 3 million deaths in all). The war, which lasted from 6 July 1967 to 15 January 1970, had complex roots. Looked at from today's perspective it appears to be a war of secession on the part of the oil-rich Eastern Region, proclaimed the Republic of Biafra, but while the rights to oil revenue were clearly a major factor, there were other deeper and more complex causes. At the time of independ-ence Nigeria, whose external boundaries were essentially a product of the process of colonisation, was made up of three regions. Very sim-ply put, in the Hausa/Fulani north there was a hierarchy of traditional Islamic emirs and an essentially authoritarian system, while in the east, the dominant Igbo tradition was one of communities with strong con-sultative processes. The east was also strongly influenced by Catholic missionaries and standards of education and literacy were high. The system in the largely Yoruba west also had a hierarchy of chiefs and traditional rulers, but was much less rigid than the north. There was more economic development and a mixture of Christianity and Islam and indeed, as in the east, a strong animist tradition.

It was perhaps almost inevitable that these three major regions with different social, educational and religious traditions should struggle to develop a common modus operandi. Furthermore, in a country that embraces a quarter of the population of Africa, it is impossible to give a feel of the rich complexity of groupings in a few sentences. One constantly gains new insights and is surprised by both some aspect of history or some new development in this great country. The first of many military coups in Nigeria took place in 1966, partly as a result of one of Nigeria's many disputed elections. During the coup, the prime minister and the premiers of the Northern and Western Regions were killed. The coup failed, but General Ironsi, the head of the army, took charge and was installed as president. Ironsi was in fact an Igbo from the Eastern Region, and in the coup aftermath, with the inevitable executions, suspicions exploded. The predominance of prominent northerners and westerners killed in the coup raised anti-Igbo feelings and there were massacres of Igbo Christians living in the north. General Ironsi was in turn replaced by a coup led by Colonel Murtala Muhammed, whose name is familiar to any traveller through the eponymous international airport in Lagos. General Ironsi was captured and killed by some of the coup members. These were the first violent manifestations of the lasting stresses between the major regions of Nigeria.

Colonel Yakubu Gowon, a Sandhurst-trained Christian northerner from a minority tribe who had been Ironsi's Chief of Staff in the army, was installed as Head of the Federal Military Government, a post which he held for the next nine years.

The migration of tens of thousands of Igbos fleeing from the north in the aftermath of the coup placed strains on the federal structure and the military governor of the Eastern Region, Colonel Ojukwu, declared that if a federal government could not protect its citizens, the Igbo had a right to establish a state that could.[9] In May 1967 Ojukwu declared the Republic of Biafra. The federal government invaded the east to prevent secession and the civil war began.

There is no doubt that underlying the communal and political stresses and strains was concern over control of revenues from the very large oil reserves that had been found largely lying in the east. The issue of the division of revenue between the oil-producing regions and the rest of the country has been an underlying factor in Nigerian politics ever since, and indeed is one of the most sensitive issues in almost every resource-rich country.

The civil war dragged on for two and a half years. Apart from the military losses civilian casualties were high, with starvation brought about by the blockade of the south. Pictures of starving Biafran children aroused much public sympathy in the Western world, but Britain and the Soviet Union supported the federal government militarily, while France supported Biafra. External political considerations were probably influenced by a desire to establish or maintain friendly relations with whoever controlled the oil. Shell was the major concession holder along with BP as partners. Although the main oil production lay in the east there was much potential in the western part of the Delta that was developed rapidly as the civil war progressed. French companies had little or no presence at that time. The war ended in January 1970 with the surrender of Biafran forces. Colonel Ojukwu fled to Côte d'Ivoire.

---

9 This was the first time that I heard the expression of a state's 'duty to protect', which is expanded on in the 'Guiding Principles on Business and Human Rights: Implementing the United Nations "Protect, Respect and Remedy" Framework' developed by John Ruggie, former UN Special Representative on Business and Human Rights, and approved unanimously by the UN Human Rights Council. These principles emphasise the duty of a state to protect the human rights of its people, the responsibility of businesses to respect such rights and the need for there to be access to remedy when rights are infringed. In an excellent book Ruggie describes the processes that he used to achieve unanimous support from business and civil society groups previously at loggerheads on the difficult subject of the extent of responsibility of businesses for human rights in the countries in which they operate. See J.G. Ruggie, *Just Business: Multinational Corporations and Human Rights* (New York: Norton, 2013).

In 1975 Murtala Muhammed, the leader of the coup that had appointed Gowon, took control of the country while Gowon was abroad at a meeting of the Organisation of African Unity. Murtala Muhammed was himself assassinated in 1976 in an abortive coup and was replaced as Head of the Federal Military Government by his colleague Olesegun Obasanjo.

I arrived in Nigeria in mid-1979 with our family, just nine years after the end of the civil war, to become divisional manager of the Western Division of Shell–BP Petroleum Development, the operator of the unincorporated joint venture in which the Nigerian National Petroleum Corporation (NNPC) held 60% and Shell and BP 20% each. Although the company was headquartered in Lagos, the Eastern and Western Divisions, which produced the oil, were based in Port Harcourt and Warri respectively. My opposite number in the east was Babs Kumolu, later to be succeeded by Emeka Achebe. I learnt much from these two Nigerians, as I did from Godwin Omene and Adegoke Ademiluyi, respectively operations and administration managers in the Western Division.

On the plane to Lagos from London, I happened to sit next to a British businessman who lived in Lagos and was well connected commercially with the military government. Among many stories of life in Lagos he told me that within ten days Shell would no longer have a foreign partner. Arriving in Lagos I dutifully reported this somewhat Delphic statement to Peter Holmes, the chief executive of Shell in Nigeria. Peter, who later became chairman of the Shell Group as a whole, was an inveterate traveller in Nigeria and the author of an outstanding book of photographs of Nigeria (and later of Turkey). He was a historian, with a great interest in the country and an affection for its people. He did not, however, believe the information that I passed on. With hindsight I should have made a bet with him—Peter frequently made bets with people, and normally won them—for the prediction proved to be correct. For reasons that were never explicit, but related somehow to Britain's approach to Rhodesia (the Lancaster House conference that resulted in the formation of Zimbabwe was later that same year) or due to Britain's (and the then partly state-owned BP's) approach to oil sanctions on South Africa, the Nigerian government nationalised the Nigerian holdings of

BP. The actual mechanism was important. Although the NNPC share in the unincorporated joint venture rose to 80% as Nigeria took over BP's share, the BP shares in the joint venture operator Shell–BP Petroleum Development were 'extinguished' so that the company that ran the operations became 100% Shell-owned and thus just Shell Petroleum Development Company of Nigeria (SPDC).

In a classic oil industry unincorporated joint venture (JV) one party to the JV is appointed 'operator'. The operator prepares budgets for approval by all partners. The operating and capital budgets are then funded by means of 'cash calls' on the JV partners. The partners in turn each receive their share of the products of the JV, oil and gas, which they can dispose of as they wish, paying tax in line with the relevant legislation and of course funding further development.

To the great relief of the staff, this meant that the operator was a Shell company that adopted Shell standards and the Shell ethos. Employment conditions and financial controls were Shell's. During my time in Nigeria we had a system of anniversary awards for all levels of staff celebrating 10, 15, 20 or 25 years with the company. The occasion was marked by a bonus of up to a month's salary for the bigger anniversaries and involved an individual discussion with the divisional manager. These were fascinating discussions on subjects ranging from experiences in the civil war to ritual murder or the death of kings and cannibalism in ethnic or community disputes. I would often ask staff why they had remained working for Shell for so long, for if they worked for the government not only would they not have to work so hard, but they could probably run a business on the side as well. Or if they worked for a contractor, they might well be paid more. The invariable answer, which puzzled me at first, was that it was the 'administration' in Shell that was the attraction. I soon came to realise that this 'administration' did not just mean that you got paid your salary regularly and on time, but that the working environment was well ordered, smooth running and basically fair and incorrupt. The power and water supply was not interrupted. If you were an engineer and designed something you had the satisfaction of seeing it actually built and functioning. The result was a self-reinforcing mechanism; if you were that sort of person you were attracted to that sort of environment, in spite of the smaller opportunities for personal enrichment. I am not suggesting that Shell in Nigeria was a global model of efficiency, but people normally overlook the achievement of running an organisation producing the equivalent of about a third of UK North Sea peak production in an environment where much of the government infrastructure around it was under severe strain if not actually collapsing.

The JV was naturally subject to the controls of the regulatory wing of NNPC. It was also critically dependent on NNPC as JV partner not only approving the budgets but also providing its share of the funds necessary for investment when it came to the 'cash call'. Over the years this has proved to be a major constraint. When NNPC is under pressure from the government to pass on the maximum of oil revenue to the government for whatever reason, the funding of the actual operations inevitably bears the brunt of the shortfall. The JV budget could be a billion dollars short and as with any funding cuts difficult decisions on priorities had to be taken.

Shortly after our arrival in Nigeria the country returned to civilian government. To the great credit of Olesegun Obasanjo, after 13 years of military rule and four military coups or attempted coups, he stuck to his promise of returning the country to civilian rule under a constitution similar to that of the United States, with a President, Senate and House of Representatives.[10] While at the time of independence there were three major regions in the Federation, the number of states had been increased by Gowon to 12 just before the civil war; when we arrived in 1979 there were 19 states; today there are 36. Each ethnic group or community wanted its own state, which brought with it requirements for a state capital, a governor, a state assembly and appropriate state commission-

---

10 President Obasanjo deserves great credit for this. He was the first African military leader to leave office and return power to a civilian government and it was many years before others followed. Nineteen years later Obasanjo was himself democratically elected President of Nigeria and served with distinction. In the interim he was involved in Transparency International, the global anti-corruption NGO. He was also imprisoned and sentenced to death for treason by a military successor, Sani Abacha, a sentence fortunately commuted.

ers for different departments. All required appropriate buildings and of course personal transport. The opportunities for 'leakage' of oil revenue flowing from the federal government back to the states multiplied.

The 1979 election was won by the National Party of Nigeria led by Shehu Shagari, a northerner who had been private secretary to the assassinated prime minister and a minister in the Gowon administration.

The new administration embarked on major spending on road and housing infrastructure together with an agricultural reform programme intended to encourage the formation of large agro-industries. The result was not very successful. Corruption in the major projects was significant. Two major steel projects were embarked on, one in Warri with Western technology and one with Russian technology in Ajaokuta. The former was completed but has never produced more than a fraction of its installed capacity and has closed completely several times. The latter was commissioned in the early 1980s and produced at about half of its capacity. Production dwindled and the plant closed in 1996. It was privatised in 2005. There have been continuous problems with supplies, financing and infrastructure.[11]

With the arrival of the civilian government, Shell ran in each of its operating divisions three-day seminars for elected politicians. In the Western Division this meant engaging groups of state assembly members every month. We had technical presentations on how the oil was produced, measured and handled. We explained the finances of the industry, pointing out to an initially incredulous audience that the marginal tax rate was such that of every million dollars of incremental revenue generated most went to the federal government and less than five thousand dollars remained with Shell. We also explained that an oil price rise above a ceiling of around 26 dollars a barrel had no influence on oil company profits. We demonstrated how the bulk of staff and key positions were held by Nigerians—I would often be the only non-Nigerian presenting to them.

11 The failure of some Nigerian projects is not solely due to actions or inactions on the part of the Nigerian side, but unfortunately also sometimes due to the peddling by Western companies of inappropriate technologies or flawed economic models.

One of the most popular presentations was that given by Chief Ohunyon, who ran the agricultural element of our community relations programmes. The Chief was the best community relations person that I encountered in my Shell career and an extremely practical person. Chief Ohunyon would describe how in the 1960s and early 1970s a bacterial blight had decimated the cassava crop in Nigeria, with catastrophic consequences given that cassava was the staple food in the Delta. With oil production spreading and increasing at that time, Chief Ohunyon would explain his fears of a link being made between oil and the bacterial blight. He would explain how in the 1950s an exotic weed had spread rapidly across Nigeria. Depending on its time of arrival in a region it was variously known as 'Elizabeth Weed' after the visit of the Queen of England in 1956 or as 'Awolowo' weed. The latter reference was to a well-known Yoruba politician Obafemi Awolowo, who travelled extensively in Nigeria and, being a politician, popped up everywhere like the weed. So a major programme was embarked on with the help of the International Institute for Tropical Agriculture in Ibadan to multiply blight-resistant forms of cassava selected by the Institute and get them adopted by local growers. The Chief would hold meetings of farmers, asking them to identify the best and the worst farmer in a village. Both would be given the new disease-resistant cuttings to grow in half of their plots. At harvest time there would be a party and it could be demonstrated that whether you were a good or bad farmer your yield increased spectacularly. Bundles of cuttings were sold—the price was low but the Chief would point out that if the cutting were not given a value they might well end up as firewood. The programme was a major success, but was little known. A similar programme was started to introduce fish farming in the mangrove swamps of the Delta.

The seminars always included a field trip by helicopter to oil production stations and to the major oil export terminal at Forcados. Assembly members could ask to vary the programme to visit particular villages or areas from which they had heard complaints. The trip was always monitored by Operations Manager Godwin Omene via the radio and the oilfield microwave communications system. What often impressed the assembly members most was that in the Delta, however much they deviated from the programme, Godwin would rearrange the transport and the helicopters would get them back to Warri on time. At that time there was probably no other area of Nigerian life where this was possible.

Nigeria in the 1960s had been the world's major producer of palm oil. In fact I recalled an older colleague telling me that when the volume of mineral oil production had passed oil palm production in the late 1950s, there had been a celebration. Today Malaysia and Indonesia each produce some ten times as much palm oil as Nigeria. In spite of the Shagari government efforts, there was no major agricultural revival. While part of this is due to land tenure issues and organisation there is no doubt that the dependence on oil income played its part. Not only was the industry a magnet for employment and business, but the resulting over-valued exchange rate resulted in cheap agricultural imports undercutting domestic production.

Corruption in Nigeria has never been a particularly secretive thing. I recall the headlines announcing that a senator had been found to have been corruptly involved in the issuance of permits for the import of rice. I somewhat naïvely assumed that this would be the end of his political career. My Nigerian colleagues assured me that he would merely keep his head down for a little while and then return to politics and indeed this proved to be the case. This approach is of course not so unusual in Western democracies.

In late 1983 the civilian Shagari administration was brought to an end by a coup that installed Major General Muhammadu Buhari as head of state. The coup was not unwelcome as many saw advantages in a military hierarchy with only one control structure to satisfy as opposed to a multi-state civilian structure with many more mouths suckling at the national revenues. But then the Nigerian people had not yet experienced the extraordinary excesses of the Abacha regime. Buhari had been Minister of Petroleum and Mineral Resources and later the head of NNPC in the 1970s. The reasons for the coup were flawed elections and the rampant corruption during the Shagari administration. Buhari did indeed institute a drive against corruption and it may well have been his insistence on pushing ahead with investigations into corruption in defence contracts that led some of those possibly involved to mount a coup, which placed General Ibrahim Babangida at the head of government in 1985.

General Babangida declared that there would be a return to civilian rule in 1990, but in the event there were a series of delays. In the process two new competing parties were set up by the military government. Elections took place, but the results were annulled. In 1993 General Babangida handed over the presidency to a transitional civilian president, Ernest Shonekan. Shonekan was a respected civilian businessman with a distinguished business career culminating in his being chief executive of the United Africa Company, a subsidiary of Unilever, which from the 1970s onwards had an increasing Nigerian public shareholding in compliance with Nigerian regulations. Shonekan was also a non-executive director of Shell in Nigeria.

Ernest Shonekan's presidency was short-lived as within three months he was deposed by General Sani Abacha and Nigeria entered a particularly dark period that only ended in 1998 with Abacha's death aged 54. Abacha's rule was marked by severe human rights abuses, including the execution in 1995 of Ken Saro-Wiwa and eight other Ogoni activists who had campaigned both for Ogoni autonomy and against Shell (see Chapter 11). Former President Obasanjo, who was vocal in his opposition to corruption and involved with the international anti-corruption organisation Transparency International, had earlier been arrested for treason and condemned to death, later commuted to life imprisonment. There is also no doubt that during the Abacha regime several billion dollars was sent to accounts abroad in the name of Abacha family members, much of which has not been recovered. Abacha reportedly died of a heart attack but there is much speculation that he was in fact murdered, with stories involving prostitutes and poison disguised as Viagra pills. The truth will probably never be known but it seems to me highly likely that he was in fact murdered.

Abacha's death marked a turning point for Nigeria. A Provisional Ruling Council headed by General Abdulsalemi Abubakar quickly paved the way for elections. Political prisoners, including former President Obasanjo, were released and campaigning began. General Abubakar thus followed General Obasanjo as the second Nigerian military ruler to oversee a transition to democracy. In 1999 Olesegun Obasanjo was elected President as head of the People's Democratic Party (PDP). Ironically he gained strong support in the north and in the east but less in his own Yoruba homeland in the west, partly because of an alternative Yoruba candidate.

Thus began independent Nigeria's longest period of democratic rule, which has continued to the present day. President Obasanjo was re-elected in 2003 and was then succeeded in 2007 by the election of Umaru Yar'Adua, also of the PDP. On Yar'Adua's death after a long illness Vice President Goodluck Jonathan was sworn in as President.

The democratic governments face enormous challenges. Corruption is still endemic. There is large-scale criminal theft of crude oil coupled with artisanal refining in the Delta. There has also been at times armed strife close to civil war in the Delta. There are religious and ethnic tensions elsewhere in the country. Much of the infrastructure is in a very poor state. Although the Nigerian Liquefied Natural Gas scheme has successfully exported Nigerian gas for more than a decade, much gas produced in association with oil is still wastefully flared though the lack of infrastructure.

Environmental damage and pollution in the Niger Delta is generally blamed on the oil industry and on Shell in particular, as the major operator in the onshore area. Oil production is of course the ultimate origin of the oil pollution but the causes are multiple and complex.

The earliest major pollution incident was in the Civil War when the major Trans Niger pipeline was cut and the oil set on fire by retreating troops. The result was a large area of baked and tar soaked soil, difficult to remediate and remediation efforts have often been impeded by the local population.

There is no doubt that in the rush to increase production after the civil war, maintenance schedules were not always followed, exacerbated by the inability or unwillingness of the Nigerian National Petroleum Corporation to contribute to its share of the joint venture funding. Leaks due to corrosion are well documented, and in such cases compensation for damage is paid and the local community employed in clean-up operations. However, corrosion leaks are by no means the only source of pollution (and Shell would claim that they have always been a relatively minor one). In ascending order of damage the other causes are as follows:

1. In the 1970s and 1980s it was quite common for villagers to steal the flowlines for use in house construction or possibly as scrap. During my time in Nigeria, a kilometre or more of line could be stolen in a night and the cut up lines were visible in local building construction

2. More serious were cases where lines were deliberately cut to cause pollution. Motives ranged from compensation for damages to a desire for local employment in the clean-up operation. If such sabotage was documented by a joint team of government officials and Shell staff, clean-up would be carried out, but no compensation was paid

3. In the 1990s, a much more damaging and large-scale form of activity developed: tapping the normally buried lines at river crossings to allow theft of the oil, which is loaded into barges and taken offshore to tankers. There is often significant pollution of the river through leaks either during or after the operation. Shell has at various times estimated of the amount of oil stolen have been from 150,000 to 250,000 barrels a day, while I have seen estimates of up to 400,000 barrels a day from the Nigerian Ministry of Finance. This illegal activity is referred to in Nigeria as 'bunkering'. Shell helicopters would photograph these operations and report them with geographical coordinates to the authorities. Assuming only 100,000 barrels a day and a conservative price per barrel of $50, the annual revenue would be $1.8 billion, leaving ample funds to discourage interference

4. The last and perhaps most damaging form of environmental pollution is that caused by artisanal refining of crude oil. During the civil war the Biafran side developed a technique of refining light crude oil in drums over pits with open fires of burning crude oil. This technique has been resurrected on a significant

scale, and crude from the burning pits leaks into the environment, with damage being further increased as the heavy and not easily used residues are simply tipped into the rivers. In 2011 the United Nations Environmental Programme (UNEP) reported that remote sensing revealed that in Bodo West, in Bonny Local Government Area, an increase in artisanal refining between 2007 and 2011 has been accompanied by a 10% loss of healthy mangrove cover.[12]

The root cause of these activities was deprivation and a lack of development in the oil-producing areas. The Shell efforts in community development programmes and in generating employment in its supply chain while at the same time urging the federal government to increase the percentage of oil revenue applied to projects in the oil-producing areas have had an impact, but an insufficient one. No solution to the problems of pollution and clean-up will be found unless all the parties cooperate. This will require each party to be quite open about its failings and its part in arriving at the present situation. The oil companies and Shell in particular will have to play a major role, but that on its own will never be sufficient. Cooperation of many different parties is needed to achieve results.

Nigeria has now had successive civilian presidents hailing ethnically from each of the three original major regions. They have struggled with some success against the endemic problems and have in many cases been served by very able ministers of integrity. Nigeria is a dynamic country with many citizens of world-class ability. It will take time, but if all the actors, including those in the oil industry can stay the course, Nigeria may yet achieve its potential.

I have not covered the particular role of Shell in Nigeria and the traumatic events connected with the execution in 1995 of Ken Saro-Wiwa as this is the subject of Chapter 11. The object of this brief and simplified description of Nigeria's political development in the last 40 years is to contrast it with that of Oman and Malaysia. It is indubitable that

---

12 UNEP, *Environmental Assessment of Ogoniland* (Nairobi: UNEP, 2011; postconflict.unep.ch/publications/OEA/UNEP_OEA.pdf).

competition for and suspicion over the likely use of oil revenues played a part. Likewise the revenue generated by oil has meant that there have been the funds available to government for excesses of all kinds. Yet one can see that many of the historical issues were not related to oil and oil income. If we want to avoid a repetition of the Nigerian experience the arguments are more complex than just oil. Natural resource revenues can certainly be part of the problem, but as we have seen elsewhere, they can also contribute to the solution. The major question is whether there is a government that provides a framework for development and use of the funds in the interest of the population at large.

The importance of government— and what is the role of business when government fails?

The revenues from the production of oil and gas had a significant impact on the economies of Oman, Malaysia and Nigeria. I derive some satisfaction and a little pride in the contribution of oil and gas to the developmental success of Oman and Malaysia. If you feel some pride in success, you have to accept a share of the blame when the outcome has been less happy, as in Nigeria.

How much of the difference is in fact due to the actions of oil companies and how much to those of others, most notably the government? In each of the cases cited, Shell was the dominant company. The principles behind the Shell approach were also the same: there was a strong commitment to not interfering in local politics, not making political contributions and not indulging in bribery. The people in Shell involved in the operations were the same or at least brought up in the same ethos. My own personal beliefs and behaviours did not change rapidly with a shift from country to country; neither did those of Shell people generally, although there has indeed rightly been a shift as we learned lessons over the years. There were Omanis working in Nigeria, Malaysians working in Oman and Nigerians working in both Malaysia and Oman. Although the operating environment was different, the approach and principles were the same. I have often joked that if you run up the steps of a Shell-built operational office in Miri in Sarawak and Warri in Nigeria, you sense exactly the same slightly unusual tread depth and spacing, which cause you to stumble. The staircases were designed by Shell engineers from the same manual and design specifications. The polemical film *The Corporation*[13] was right in postulating that one can in a sense ascribe individual personal traits to a corporate body. However, although corporations can indeed be seen as having inherited personal characteristics from their founders, their history and through the natural replication of recruitment, they are as varied as any group of individuals. *The Corporation* was quite wrong in selecting traits from individual corporations and then combining them to build a stereotypical picture of the entire band of corporations. The makers of the film deduce from that stereotype that corporations collectively show the characteristic of a psychopath. Such stereotyping is as inadmissible for the race of corporations or business people as it is for the Irish, Poles, Arabs or Jews, or indeed lawyers or bankers, although generalisations in the latter cases appear to be admissible.

So if the company involved is not the determinant of outcome, is it perhaps some characteristic of the people that leads to the difference? Each of the countries discussed above has a different history, two of them including periods of British colonisation. Colonial experiences probably did have an impact, particularly in the case of Nigerian internal and external borders. Each has strong civil society and strong social customs. As the public education system came to a point of near collapse, many well-educated Nigerians were frustrated by the feeling that their children would not benefit from as good an education in Nigeria as they had. As a result, groups of parents got together and organised private schools. Family values are strong in all three countries, perhaps particularly so in Nigeria where the family and the wider family in the community are of great importance. There is much that Nigeria could teach Britain in this area. Religion too is important in all three societies,

---

13 *The Corporation* (2003) is a Canadian documentary film written by J. Bakan and directed by J. Abbott and M. Achbar. It includes a scene in which my wife Judy is seen serving tea to demonstrators on the lawn of our house in Sussex.

whether Islam or Christianity. So I do not think you can ascribe the differences in outcome to some kind of disaggregation of society.

The obvious big difference is in national leadership. In the last 40 years both Oman and Malaysia have been blessed by having single strong leaders for either all of the time or a substantial part of it. More importantly, these leaders had a clear vision for their country and worked towards it, making plain what they regarded as important for the country. You may not agree with everything that they have done, but there is no doubt in my mind that this provided a framework for coherent economic and social development. In contrast to Oman and Malaysia, Nigeria has had six military coups and almost 30 years of military government during the same period. The rule was certainly strong and sometimes brutal during periods of military government. For example, in an effort to stem the wave of armed robberies in the 1970s and 1980s, there was a mandatory death sentence for armed robbery, with executions taking place in public by firing squad with the robbers tied to posts on Bar Beach in Lagos. Although two of the military rulers, generals Olesegun Obasanjo and Abdulsalemi Abubakar, to their great credit, oversaw elections and a transfer to democratic government, many of the seven military rulers were mainly guided by the interests, financial and otherwise, of themselves, their families and their particular clique.

All of this was well known at the time, so the question arises as to what are the responsibilities of a company in such situations and what can or should a company do to influence the outcome.

When I joined Shell in the 1960s from university it was a period when there was global concern over multinational companies influencing or exerting control over national governments.[14] As mentioned, the activities of the United Fruit Company in Central America influencing and controlling governments was the origin of the term 'banana republic'. Later the Nigerian singer Fela Kuti was to sing of 'ITT, International T'ief T'ief'. Two strong elements of Shell corporate culture were that we

14 The activities of multinationals from the East India Company through United Fruit to Nike and Shell are well described in D. Litvin, *Empires of Profit: Commerce, Conquest and Corporate Responsibility* (New York/London: Texere, 2003).

did not get involved in local politics or make political payments and we did not bribe people.

Thirty years or so ago, certainly while we were living in Nigeria, I and many of my colleagues believed that as a company it was our responsibility to run an effective operation to international standards with appropriate environmental controls, to pay our taxes honestly in the country in which the income was earned, not to bribe people or make political payments, to run a sound staff development system based on merit where nationals had training and opportunity to develop within the organisation and in Shell operations around the world, and to build relations with communities around our operations based on fair dealings, local contracting and community projects. If the government took the revenue from the operation and spent it on foolish grandiose projects, or in the worst case corruptly applied it or transferred it to personal Swiss bank accounts, that was regrettable, but not in the end the responsibility of a corporation that was a guest in the country. In other words, our responsibility stopped with our operations or in our close neighbourhood. We could express an opinion and offer advice on what we saw as the best way forward, we could do what we could to ameliorate the negative consequences of government action, but in the end such matters were very much in the realm of national sovereignty with which we absolutely should not tamper.

The extent of a corporation's responsibility in countries of weak government or effectively no government is one of the most difficult dilemmas faced by corporations. Over the years my views have inevitably changed. Simply saying that in the absence of properly enforced standards a company should abide by generally accepted international standards does not come near to addressing the issue. That is what in any case we endeavoured to do, although as can be seen from Chapter 11 on events in Nigeria local constraints sometimes make this difficult. The issue is what to do when a government, be it elected or military, acts persistently in a way that is dishonest or detrimental to the interests of the country. When such behaviour persists, even in the wider sphere beyond the company's own activities, it is clearly in the interests of a company, let alone society, to take action to prevent it. Persistent misallocation of resources, corruption and theft destroy the development of a country. People inevitably turn to a company that over the years has had a major role in the economy of the country and enquire as to the benefits to the nation. In the absence of visible national development benefits, the operations of the company become untenable. At that point the argument that the company paid billions of dollars honestly in tax revenue is of little use, however accurate it might be and however much the failures are actually the result of an incapable or corrupt government misapplying the revenue.

Having said that, I still do not believe that a company should try and act in isolation. Suggesting that a foreign company should actively work against a government is not something that most people would see as desirable. Citizens do not welcome a foreign company taking unilateral decisions on what is right, even if the actions of a government are seen not to be in the best interests of the country. Besides, who determines what those interests or best interests are? It should certainly not be the executives of a single company. Many international non-governmental organisations (NGOs) believe that they can determine such interests and are not shy in telling corporations what they should do. While some of this is thoughtful input, I do not believe that this is the answer either.

So what about a collective industry position? This suffers from the same challenge as that of a company acting alone. Business is not trusted (and I would argue should not be trusted) with such decisions. Human nature being what it is, a bias in favour of business will almost certainly creep in over time.

Each of the actors—companies, NGOs, labour organisations where they exist, local and national governments—bears responsibility. They need to express their views. I believe that this is most effectively done by forming coalitions across society. The different participants help to keep each other honest and to rein in the self-interest should it rear its head in one or other sector of society.

Such coalitions are not pie in the sky. Their formation in various areas is one of the most hopeful developments of the last ten to twenty years. They come in many forms. While such coalitions are a constructive development, they take time to form and their progress is often halting and imperfect. They do lend hope in what is often an almost hopeless situation. The alternatives are not attractive. On the one hand, companies can carry on to the best of their ability within their own sphere of operations and claim that any further action goes beyond their responsibilities and capabilities.[15] On the other hand, they can simply withdraw, either leaving the field open to others with fewer scruples or leaving the country largely without the economic means of development. In my opinion it is far better to stay and try to play a part in a collective approach to improvement, while running your own operation in line with your own standards.

15 The work of the UN Secretary-General's Special Representative on Business and Human Rights developed the invaluable UN Guiding Principles for Business and Human Rights, which does much to clarify the differing responsibilities of business and governments.

Chapter 2

Coalitions, governments and doing the right thing

Cooperative efforts are most effective when they are focused on a clear but limited objective. Their formation often follows a common path. First someone identifies an issue—some problem for society. This could be a question of labour conditions, an environmental or human rights issue or a question of equity. Although issues are sometimes raised initially within a corporation, the most common initial source is a civil society organisation or sometimes a labour union. This may be accompanied by some form of public campaign, but most often initially it is not, although nowadays social media is bringing greater immediacy and awareness to such campaigns. When an issue is first raised with a company or a group of companies in an industry, the reaction is fairly predictable. It will be argued that the factors affecting the issue are not within the control of companies—it is a matter for government. Or it will be claimed that the issue is not as widespread as suggested and that things are not really so bad. Or that it would require industry-wide effort to have any impact. Companies, like NGOs, are human organisations and they suffer from the natural conservatism of all human organisations—they like to carry on doing what they have been doing successfully for years and tend to resist any change to a smoothly running system.

Of course, the counter to all of these arguments is the same. It is only through some form of collective action involving the cooperation of other elements of society that many issues can be addressed. In spite of initial scepticism, more thoughtful companies will agree to sit down with some policy NGOs to see what could be done to address the issue, even if they are initially sceptical of the possibility of progress or of finding a practical solution. While this is going on there is sometimes simultaneously a public campaign, often driven by NGOs whose speciality is campaigning, even against some of the very companies engaged in the discussions.

I recall sitting on a panel in Bali in one of the ministerial pre-meetings in the run-up to the World Summit on Sustainable Development in 2002—these pre-meetings for grand UN Summits take place in different parts of the world and often in attractive places. The government officials and others taking part often know each other quite well as the caravan moves from region to region. In this case the panel was organised by Greenpeace to discuss action needed to address climate change. As well as their campaigning and direct action wing, Greenpeace have an excellent and well-informed climate strategy group. Also on the panel was Margaret Beckett, then UK Secretary of State for Environment, Food and Rural Affairs, as well as someone from The Body Shop in Indonesia. The panel was interesting and the discussion very constructive. On the way out, someone from Greenpeace was handing out invitations to a side event at which they would name the top ten global corporate criminals. When I asked my Greenpeace fellow panel member whether Shell was in their top ten he replied that he did not know—that was handled by a different department in Greenpeace. His answer gave me a pretty clear indication and Shell was indeed one of the top ten. Some business people regard this as quite unacceptable and therefore find it difficult to work with or trust some NGOs. I am personally quite relaxed about it. Campaigning NGOs need to campaign, if nothing else because their funding supporters expect it of them. One cannot expect an across-the-board truce. No civil society organisation can afford to become so close to a corporation that it ceases to criticise them where it feels it is necessary. All one can ask for is that the criticism is honest and based on facts.

Around the year 2000 there seems to have been a particular surge in the formation of coalitions addressing specific issues, at least in the extractive industries, although initiatives such as the Forest Stewardship Council[1] and the WWF/Unilever Marine Stewardship Council[2] project for sustainable fisheries started earlier.[3] The question is to what extent such coalitions merely influence the behaviour of international corporations and to what extent they begin to support and help an individual government in its fundamental role in building a governance framework within which business and other parts of society can carry out their roles.

Initiatives such as the Marine Stewardship Council and the Forest Stewardship Council have had a major impact on their respective sectors. They harness the power of consumer choice in relatively high-income markets. Consumers look for the logo when making their choice of fish or wood and paper-based products. The coalitions include companies active in these sectors and set challenging but achievable standards. Fisheries and forests have benefited on a significant scale. So have the companies. Through its foresight in being a leader Unilever has benefited, not only in its fish business, but across other lines as well. Anglo American's former paper subsidiary Mondi has certified more than a million hectares of productive forest in Russia under the Forest Stewardship Council scheme, undoubtedly protecting areas which under the

1 The Forest Stewardship Council (FSC) originated in California in 1990 when a group of timber users, traders and representatives of environmental and human rights organisations met to address the need for a system that could credibly identify well-managed forests as the sources of responsibly produced wood products https://ic.fsc.org/about-us.1.htm). The FSC certifies products as being from sustainable forests.

2 The Marine Stewardship Council (MSC) was first established by Unilever, the world's largest buyer of seafood, and WWF, the international conservation organisation, in 1997 to agree standards for sustainable fisheries. See www.msc. org.

3 For a full review of the history of coalitions see D. Grayson and J. Nelson *Corporate Responsibility Coalitions: The Past, Present, and Future of Alliances for Sustainable Capitalism* (Sheffield, UK: Greenleaf Publishing; Stanford, CA: Stanford University Press, 2013).

Soviet system were in grave danger of degradation, in spite of the clear Soviet regulations that should have prevented it. Although these initiatives, along with other similar approaches, have undoubtedly made serious contributions to sustainable development, the impact on government frameworks is more peripheral. Such initiatives demonstrate to governments that such steps towards sustainability are not impractical and do not damage business. Whether or not a government seeks to apply such approaches more widely is a matter of choice.

The Voluntary Principles on Security and Human Rights

In 2000, as a result of incidents in Colombia and Nigeria,[4] the Voluntary Principles on Security and Human Rights were developed between leading extractive industry companies including BP and Shell, human rights NGOs such as Human Rights Watch and Amnesty International and the US State Department and the UK Foreign and Commonwealth Office. All participants accepted that in countries with a high level of violence, armed security forces might be necessary to protect both company personnel and operations. In both Nigeria and Colombia, and indeed also in Sudan, companies had turned to governments to assist in the provision of that security. In all three cases there had been incidents in which such security forces, whether directly or indirectly linked to companies,

---

4 In Colombia, there were repeated attacks on oil transportation pipelines and other facilities by armed insurgent groups such as the Revolutionary Armed Forces of Colombia (FARC). Security was provided by government forces as well as by private security. There were controversial incidents involving security forces associated with BP operations. In Nigeria, armed government security forces acting broadly in support of Shell operations in the Niger Delta, attacked a village and killed several villagers in response to the murder by the community of at least one security force member. While both companies would point out that such actions were carried out by government forces not subject to corporate control, both companies acknowledged that there were major problems and dangers associated with the involvement of government security forces and welcomed proposals by human rights groups to address the issue.

had been involved in human rights abuses. Yet the alternative of having private armed security was often neither desirable nor possible.

The Voluntary Principles provide a well-thought-out series of steps through which a company should go in relation to security in such cases (see Box 2.1).

Box 2.1 **The Voluntary Principles on Security and Human Rights**

The Voluntary Principles propose a sequence of steps that a company should undertake when considering the use of security, armed or otherwise. This includes ensuring proper training for government security forces if these are used:

- Conduct a comprehensive assessment of human rights risks associated with security, with a particular focus on complicity

- Engage appropriately with public and private security in conflict-prone areas

- Institute proactive human rights screenings of and trainings for public and private security forces

- Ensure that the use of force is proportional and lawful

- Develop systems for reporting and investigating allegations of human rights abuses[5]

The first step is an analysis of whether armed security is indeed needed. Does it really add security or does it simply increase risk? If it is necessary, are the rules of engagement clear?[6] Are security staff properly

---

5 Full details can be found at www.voluntaryprinciples.org/what-are-the-voluntary-principles.

6 A quarrying operation in the Philippines operated by the Swiss company Holcim was attacked by armed insurgents. Although no one was injured, all the arms of the security guards were seized. Analysing the incident, Holcim concluded that it was possible that the main objective of the attack was in fact to obtain arms. The company changed to a policy of having no armed security. This took some time to achieve as it was necessary to reassure employees that this would not increase the risks to them and also to convince the local

trained in the use of arms and under what conditions their use might be acceptable? If government security forces are being used, the same questions apply. In Colombia companies, including Anglo American, have arranged for the training of many hundreds of members of government security forces in human rights awareness in relation to their duties and the use of arms. The need for the keeping of proper records and the use of video filming of operations is emphasised. If a security operation is filmed it improves the behaviour of all parties, both the security forces and those whom they are endeavouring to control. Furthermore, if there are subsequent complaints about behaviour there is useful evidence. It is not foolproof; many regard the use of films as intimidating and fear that such records may be used to highlight and target activists later.

Through such activities, the behaviour of the national security forces in general begins to improve. The governance fabric of the country is strengthened in a way that does not impinge on national sovereignty. Indeed governments in some cases request the help of companies in contributing to the training of police and security forces.

Shell and Turkey: working with military rule

A policy of not employing armed security is not always easy to implement. At the time of return to civilian rule in Turkey after the military coup in September 1980, the government was anxious to ensure that key facilities were protected. The 1980 coup had ended a period of extreme and violent division in Turkish society. Political murders had been running at some 25 a day. Universities, schools and shopkeepers such as butchers and bakers were labelled as either right or left wing.

---

population that the security guards were indeed unarmed and did not simply have weapons concealed. The policy has been successful and there have been no repeats of the initial incident (UN Global Compact and Principles for Responsible Investment with KPMG, *Responsible Business Advancing Peace: Examples from Companies, Investors and Global Compact Local Networks*, [New York: UNGC, 2013; www.unglobalcompact.org/docs/issues_doc/Peace_and_Business/ B4P_Resource_Package_company.pdf]: 25-28).

Even moustaches, very common in Turkey, were political, being right or left wing depending on whether they turned down below the corner of the mouth. The military intervention stopped the bloodshed. Over a million small arms, and sometimes not so small arms, were handed over in a fairly draconian amnesty. There were undoubtedly excesses. Many were arrested and a number of executions were carried out. However, the number of death sentences was only the equivalent of two to three days worth of political murders before the coup. Whatever the rights or wrongs of individual cases, a pragmatist would argue that in human terms the price was worth paying. Certainly very many more innocent people died in the anarchy preceding the coup.

When we arrived in Turkey in 1982, peace had returned and the return to elected civilian government was about to take place. Shell staff would tell us over dinner what a relief it was to have their children return safely every day from school or university and not be worried about them being caught in some mayhem. The leader of the military intervention, General Kenan Evren, became President as a guarantor of the constitution on which there was a referendum during the transition. General Evren had famously despatched the pre-coup party leaders of left and right, Demirel and Ecevit, to a form of house arrest in a rather nice hotel in Çannakale on the eastern side of the Dardanelles. He admonished them to look across the strait to the Gallipoli Peninsula and to ponder the sacrifices made by their countrymen in defending Turkish soil against the foreign invader in 1915.[7]

---

7 The first two lines of the following poem by Necmettin Halil Onan are outlined in large letters made of white stones visible across the Dardanelles from the Çannakale side of the straits.

> Dur yolcu, bilmeden gelip bastığın,
> Bu toprak, bir devrin battığı yerdir.
> Eğil de kulak ver, bu sessiz yığın,
> Bir vatan kalbinin attığı yerdir! . . .

> Stop traveller, this ground on which you come
> and unthinkingly tread is the place of an era's founding.
> Bending your ear, this voiceless mound
> Is a place of a nation's heart pounding.

Even Gönül Çapan, my Turkish teacher of four years and no lover of the military, said that what the military had replaced was not democracy but anarchy. She and her husband Cevat Çapan, a poet and a towering figure in the literary world, had left Turkey judiciously for a brief period after the military coup. When they returned to academic life, Cevat was caught in the petty but miserably demeaning requirement to choose between his beard and his job at university. He rightly chose his job, but such a choice is intolerable. Judy taught English in the faculty of literature at the Beyazit campus of Istanbul University, and in theory was supposed to prevent women in all-embracing coats and headscarves from participating. In spite of these petty and in some cases truly demeaning excesses, I believe that Turkey did benefit from that particular military intervention and the subsequent reforms, preventing a continued slide into anarchy and mayhem in the 1980s. Unfortunately, even if you can forgive or even approve a military intervention, one cannot rely on it to turn out well, as Nigeria has so often seen. The present government of Turkey also regards, with some justification, the commitment of successive military governments to the maintenance of a strictly secular state and the prevention of all forms of public religious expression as oppressive. The different sides of this argument are well represented in France today.

In Turkey, as part of the civilian government's commitment to law and order and the defence of property, the government introduced a regulation that all companies with petroleum storage facilities deemed key to the nation should recruit and arm security guards. For some months I argued in vain that Shell was not a military organisation and that as far as I was concerned we did not and should not employ armed staff. I raised the spectre of some unfortunate accident involving the Kurdish population around our oil production facilities in eastern Turkey. Who would be responsible then? I was assured that if a community member was unfortunately shot the same procedure would apply as if they had been shot by a policeman. This was not regarded as a very serious argument against having armed staff. I finally had a discussion with the minister concerned. He explained to me that they had been through a similar argument with the banks. He pointed out that I had no doubt noticed

43

that outside every bank branch there was now an armed bank security person. I had indeed. The minister said that the banks had argued long and hard as I had done, but the problem had been solved by putting a couple of bank managers in gaol. A law was a law and business had to conform or take the consequences. I got the message and we commenced recruiting, training and arming our own security forces. Shell's security chief, a retired military man, enlightened me on rules of engagement and appropriate weapons. He explained that the most appropriate weapon for our security would be a low-muzzle velocity weapon. When I asked what that meant he explained that a typical low velocity weapon is a sawn-off shotgun. Unlike a high velocity rifle, such a weapon would neither penetrate oil tanks, nor injure unseen bystanders a mile or so away. Had the Voluntary Principles on Security and Human Rights been in existence then my life would have been easier and I would have been much better equipped to deal with such a situation.

Coalitions on corruption and conflict diamonds

Another coalition formed to address a particular problem is the Extractive Industries Transparency Initiative (EITI), which aims to reduce improper payments and the misuse of funds in the resources industry. This global initiative (see also Chapter 8 on Corruption) emerged from the 'Publish What You Pay' campaign, driven by Global Witness and the Soros Open Society Foundation. The EITI itself was launched at the Johannesburg World Summit on Sustainable Development in 2002 and involves cooperation between governments, companies and civil society organisations. The target was to get all oil and mining companies to declare all their payments to governments and to make the receipt of these by governments more transparent. There is also an important requirement for an independent oversight panel made up of members of civil society. The progress has been encouraging, but from the outset I have argued that while this was a reasonable objective it was only a first step. In many countries the magnitude of payments made quite legitimately was well known and discussed in the press in the country. The problem was what happened to the money after that. I recall a payment of $10 million made perfectly legitimately by Shell into the central bank of a francophone country in West Africa at the outset of an agreement—a so-called signature bonus. The payment was duly recorded but during a subsequent review by the International Monetary Fund (IMF) the funds were not to be found. The local press was full of articles asking what had happened to the money. Meanwhile the long-standing, and now late, president merely smiled enigmatically. There was no doubt in the public's mind as to the amount involved, it was the use to which it had been put which remained in doubt. Many years later, in conversation after a talk that I gave, I learned of the likely overseas destination of the funds. Or rather I learned of a purchase of an overseas property of about that value at around that time. The EITI process would have at least removed any doubt as to where the funds went missing.

In the case of the Kimberley Process (KP), which was devised to keep illegally mined diamonds out of the global supply chain, the role of governments is even more critical. Illegally mined diamonds are often controlled by warlords or participants in civil strife and indeed civil war. The Kimberley process is multi-stakeholder, involving both civil society and business. However, in the end it is crucially dependent on a certificate of origin from a producing country government. Other governments and the multi-stakeholder board are able to expel a government and thus invalidate its certificates. Having said that, governments are notoriously bad at questioning or confronting each other. The issue of the origin of diamonds from Zimbabwe is just such a contentious case.

If these coalitions are to have a lasting impact in strengthening the role of governments and building capacity, the involvement of host governments is essential. Yet the involvement of governments introduces delicate questions of sovereignty. No government likes to feel that they are being dictated to in some way from the outside. There is a clear requirement in the EITI process to have some form of multi-stakeholder oversight over the uses to which extractive revenues are put and over its distribution between central government, regions and communities. In many signatory countries, the very formation of an oversight panel with the necessary defences to ensure that criticisms can be voiced is a major step forward. Countries with long-established and functioning democracies such as Canada and the United Kingdom have resisted signing up to any form of process involving their own extractive industries. They argue that they already have functioning governance structures. This makes their enthusiasm for encouraging lower-income countries to adopt the EITI open to the argument that it is hypocritical and even somewhat colonialist.

For this reason it is laudable that Norway has itself subscribed to the process. This allows a well-established democracy with strong governance to examine how an EITI process can be made to work effectively alongside strong democratic processes. Even more importantly, it means that the danger of relatively ad hoc multi-stakeholder bodies being regarded as some substitute for a truly representative process is avoided. Civil society organisations often cite their membership as giving them a form of legitimacy. While indeed large numbers of individuals may be involved this bestows no more democratic legitimacy than do the hundreds of thousands of people who own directly or indirectly shares in major companies. Neither is a substitute for a mandate from an enfranchised population.

What seemed like a good idea at the time . . .

Companies are frequently well aware of the need to achieve consensus agreement with the communities with whom they interact and whose lives they affect. It is, however, not always easy to achieve this. In developing a large open-pit platinum mine in Limpopo Province in South Africa, Anglo Platinum was faced with the challenge of relocating a village of some 8,000 people to make way for a mine. This was an unusual challenge for a platinum miner as most platinum mines in South Africa are underground with less surface disruption. No one in any part of the world likes to have to move from his or her home, however much the alternative housing and land provided is an improvement on the existing arrangements. Furthermore, there is almost certainly an inevitable imbalance of power in commercial and legal sophistication between a large company and a rural community. Aware of this, Anglo Platinum worked to help the community set up an independent not-for-profit organisation to represent the community, and provided funding to this organisation so that it could get independent legal and financial advice. I had nothing to do with this arrangement, but interestingly the idea of corporate funding of independent advice had been one of the ideas mooted in the multi-stakeholder World Bank Group Extractive Industry Review under the Chairmanship of Emil Salim in which I also participated on behalf of industry.[8]

The arrangement worked fairly well for some time. Houses were carefully recorded and new houses allocated and constructed that were more than equivalent in area and of modern construction. Land was also acquired. There were some objectors who resisted relocation away from the mine, but this was not unexpected. However, the entire process took some years and at a certain point the community became unsatisfied or disenchanted with their representatives in the not-for-profit company. They requested that Anglo Platinum change the leadership, something that was of course impossible because the not-for-profit company had been carefully established so that it was legally completely independent to ensure that Anglo Platinum could not influence its management in any way. What had seemed like a good idea had become a source of dissatisfaction. With hindsight, the mistake was for Anglo Platinum not to have ensured that the governance structures of the community organisation were clear and fully understood by the community. In fact it is difficult for a company to play such a role in relation to a community. To achieve it a company would have to become closely involved with the very organisation and governance of the community. In such a case conflicts of interest are likely to occur or to be perceived and in any case such work is far from the core skills of almost any company. It is therefore much better to find a well-established civil society organisation, trusted by both sides, which can work independently with the community ensuring that proper structures are developed and truly functioning.

---

8 World Bank, *Striking a Better Balance: The World Bank Group and Extractive Industries: The Final Report of the Extractive Industries Review* (Washington, DC: World Bank Group, 2004).

Perhaps the most interesting example of a well-meaning attempt to constrain a government's freedom to spend extractive revenues as it sees fit has come from Chad and the agreement that was made over the Chad–Cameroon oil export pipeline. This is an example that illustrates not only the sensitivities of national sovereignty but also the difficulties of making progress unless a national government is genuinely committed to the process.

During the early 1990s, a consortium operated by Exxon, with Shell and Chevron[9] as members, was planning the development of significant

9 In 1993, Chevron decided to sell its share in the joint venture to the then partly state-owned French oil company Elf. As I recall, the agreed price was $20 million—very low given the amount of money that had been spent over the years by the partners. Shell and other partners decided to pre-empt the sale, as was permitted in the partnership agreement, and buy Chevron's share ourselves. We duly gave notice and asked the Chad government for permission for the transfer, permission that the concession agreement said in customary language 'would not unreasonably be withheld'. While this was in progress I met the President Directeur General of Elf, Loïk Le Floch-Prigent, at an opera sponsored by Elf. In the interval we discussed the pre-emption. I explained that while we would welcome Elf as a partner, they would have to buy the Chevron share at a higher price, given all that had been spent. Le Floch-Prigent replied that that was impossible; France simply would not permit it to happen. If the Chad government were to give permission for the pre-emption, French military support would be withdrawn, so it was not going to happen. In those days French paratroopers were stationed in many Francophone African countries to be called on in case of trouble. I was shocked at this extraordinary threat. My wife had to endure my quivering indignation all through the second act. But so it came to pass. The Chad government expressed embarrassment but said they were having difficulty approving our pre-emption. We reminded them of the standard clause that permission would 'not be unreasonably withheld' and they agreed that it was very awkward. In the end they said that they had found a reason: a clause in the agreement provided a let-out in case of 'national security'. The government said that this was unfortunately clearly such a case. One had to have sympathy with their view.

Some three years later, Le Floch-Prigent and his African fixer André Tarallo were indicted for embezzlement of tens of millions of dollars of Elf Funds. Both went to prison. Much of the money had been channelled to various African heads of state, apparently with the knowledge, and perhaps at the behest, of the Mitterand government. The long trial produced many lurid stories. None of this reserves of oil that had been discovered in Chad. Oil discoveries had been made earlier but exploration had been halted by the ten-year civil war during the 1980s. Under the government of President Idriss Déby it looked as though a commercial development could be possible. As Chad is land-locked, this would mean building a pipeline through neighbouring Cameroon to the sea.

International civil society and non-governmental organisations were vociferous in their opposition. They argued that this was just another Nigeria in the making. Much was made of the environmental dangers of building a pipeline through tropical forest to the sea. The industry is familiar with such objections and, while the record is not perfect, if construction and operation is properly executed such a project can be carried out with very limited environmental impact. The main argument put forward was that as Chad was one of the poorest countries in the world and as the oil is in the Doba basin in the south and the government is resident in N'Djamena some 400 km to the north there was likely to be friction. In summary, Chad was too poor and undeveloped to be able to handle the income from oil, so the oil should be left in the ground.

The idea that the outside world should decide that Chad should not develop its resources because of poverty or lack of organisation appeared somewhat arrogant to me. However, the scenario of misallocation of resources between government and the producing areas or indeed of little revenue being actually applied to economic and social development did indeed appear quite probable. The President was after all a northerner and a military man who had come to power by force of arms, both first defeating the Libyans in the field and subsequently making alliances with them. Surely there was a way of developing the oil to generate much-needed income while putting in place mechanisms to ensure that the money was spent on development and not, for example, arms and the army?

---

came as a surprise to those of us who had experience of competing with Elf in Francophone Africa. Elf subsequently merged with Total under Total management and the company is run on more conventional lines.

With the involvement of the World Bank an approach was devised that it was hoped would help resolve the issue. An agreement was made on the management of the revenue. This allocated 10% to a Future Generations Fund with 5% going for expenditure in the oil-producing region. Allocation of most of the remainder was to agreed priority development areas, with the whole arrangement embedded in law. A body with civil society participation, the Collège de Contrôle et de Surveillance des Ressources Pétrolières, was set up to review progress and advise the government on programmes to be financed. There was also an International Advisory Group to advise both governments, Chad and Cameroon, on implementation. In connection with this loans were made from the World Bank International Finance Corporation system to the government and the project.

The arrangement appeared to hold out hope for a new approach to the management of resource revenue. *The Economist* welcomed it in 2002 with a headline 'Useful stuff, maybe, for once' and a subtitle 'A novel scheme to extract oil without fuelling corruption or bloodshed'. The oil companies were happy because World Bank involvement had driven an agreement on how the government would spend the revenue, something that would be very difficult and even improper for a foreign company to demand. Furthermore, the involvement of the World Bank Group in loans meant that there was some multilateral leverage to ensure that the terms of the agreement were met.

I observed much of this from the sidelines as in 2000 Shell had withdrawn from the joint venture; Shell's share was taken up by Petronas. The reasons for Shell's withdrawal are of some interest. As surprising as it seems now, at that time it appeared possible that there would be another period of low oil prices such as had been seen only a couple of years before. The economics of the venture overall were poor when tested against a low price scenario in the $12–15 per barrel range. The fiscal agreement was such that at low prices the economics were perhaps acceptable to the company, but in such a scenario the government income would fall catastrophically. Such a situation would in our view almost inevitably cause the government to renegotiate the agreement. It is naïve to expect any government to hold to an agreement protecting a company's return in such a situation. So we withdrew in favour of others who, with hindsight correctly, had a more optimistic oil price outlook.

In the event the scheme was not a success. In the words of the World Bank's own most effective independent evaluation report

> The detailed agreements for Chad's use of oil revenues under-
> lying the World Bank Group involvement were too rigid and
> failed when oil revenues started accruing sooner and in higher
> amounts than anticipated. Slow efforts at capacity building
> were undercut by the rapid inflow of oil revenues. The latter
> also reduced the originally expected leverage of the WBG sup-
> port program.[10]

While a country may of its own accord develop a sound expenditure plan, doing so in response to outside arm twisting means surrendering a large degree of sovereignty. A country will only agree to that if there is no other way out. A government's heart will not be in it, and as soon as there is a way out, perhaps because of a windfall increase of revenue, a government will seize it. That started early in Chad. I recall before the formal agreement seeing about $5 million dollars worth of executive jet with 'Government of Chad' on the tail parked at Rotterdam Airport just after a payment had been made to the government. In the end the World Bank gave up and withdrew from the agreement. The ensuing criticism was I think unfair as the idea was not a bad one and the World Bank had worked hard to try and get it to work.

In my opinion the experience demonstrates that change brought about by outside pressure is likely to be illusory or temporary. Real change has to be built slowly from the inside coming from a dawning convic-tion that governance improvements and consultative processes are in the interests of a country and its government. For all the slow progress, that is the strength of the EITI. It is also the weakness of extraterrito-rial legislation or attempts at supranational legislation. In the absence of a global policeman such efforts are largely unenforceable within a

---

10 Independent Evaluation Group, 'Lessons from an Evaluation of the Chad-Cam-
   eroon Oil Development and Pipeline Program' (summary of the main findings)
   2009, web.worldbank.org/external/default/main?theSitePK=1324361&piPK=6
   4252979&pagePK=64253958&contentMDK=22389300.

country. Attempts to act as global policeman put us on a path that leads to Baghdad and should be avoided at all costs. That does not mean that we should not support such efforts as the International Criminal Court (ICC) to try egregious offenders when they can be brought to the court, although even then care is needed to ensure that the indictment is really supported by the people of the country concerned. Without that, national pride may well lead to support for the alleged miscreant within his country of origin. One irony is that the United States, the country most given to extraterritorial legislation, has refused to accept the role of the ICC, on the grounds that its own citizens and soldiers might be subject to spurious charges from such a court outside the United States.

So if outside pressures on a nation to improve its governance or its approach to such issues as corruption, human rights, the environment or working conditions have their limitations, do we as companies simply sit back and assume that nothing can be done? The EITI shows one way. Perhaps the largest of all multi-stakeholder corporate responsibility groupings, the United Nations Global Compact and its Local Networks, shows another wider approach and the next chapter considers its work.

Chapter 3

The United Nations Global Compact

In January 1999, in a speech at the World Economic Forum in Davos, the then United Nations Secretary-General Kofi Annan challenged the business community to adopt what he called a Global Compact. He proposed that business and the UN jointly initiate a 'global compact of shared values and principles, to give a human face to the global market'. The idea was that businesses would agree to conduct their operations in line with principles that were based on the major UN conventions on human rights, the environment and working conditions: the Universal Declaration on Human Rights, the Rio Convention on Environment and Development and the various conventions on labour. The following year the United Nations Global Compact (UNGC) was formally launched at the UN and there were some 40 international companies who, in letters to the Secretary-General, made a commitment to applying the principles in their day-to-day operations.

This was a brave commitment by Kofi Annan as he had no UN mandate for such an initiative. There was initially some grumbling by member states that he had gone 'off piste' with the initiative, although subsequently it has been regularly supported in General Assembly resolutions. The Secretary-General was able to point out that the initial nine principles were all based on existing UN Conventions (see Box 3.1).

One has to recall that up to that time the UN had had little engagement with business although various non-governmental groups were accredited to the UN, including the International Chamber of Commerce. By and large the UN was an intergovernmental body and any involvement with business was seen as potentially dangerous.

Box 3.1 **Global Compact: initial nine principles**

The initial nine principles were:

Human Rights

Principle 1: Businesses should support and respect the protection of internationally proclaimed human rights; and

Principle 2: make sure that they are not complicit in human rights abuses.

Labour

Principle 3: Businesses should uphold the freedom of association and the effective recognition of the right to collective bargaining;

Principle 4: the elimination of all forms of forced and compulsory labour;

Principle 5: the effective abolition of child labour; and

Principle 6: the elimination of discrimination in respect of employment and occupation.

Environment

Principle 7: Businesses should support a precautionary approach to environmental challenges;

Principle 8: undertake initiatives to promote greater environmental responsibility; and

Principle 9: encourage the development and diffusion of environmentally friendly technologies.[1]

---

1 www.unglobalcompact.org.

Part of the genius of Kofi Annan was to include civil society organisations and labour unions in the initiative from the outset. This has always been an essential part of the UNGC. While it is business-led, the participation of other sections of society in its work and all its elements is fundamental. There have been times in the history of the development of the UNGC when there was a choice to be made. On the one hand, it could be seen as a set of commitments made by business, with civil society standing on the sidelines as a sort of referee, pointing fingers when mistakes were made. On the other, it could be seen as a forum where business and other parts of society could work together to solve the problems that face us all. Fortunately for the future of the initiative, development has always been along the lines of the second alternative. The initial advisory group to the Secretary-General and the subsequent UNGC Board chaired by the Secretary-General has always had almost as many representatives of civil society and labour organisations as business people, with some major UN agencies represented.

Adding a tenth principle on corruption

Robin Aram, who played a key role in Shell's strategy unit in relation to civil society and thinking on the ethics of Shell, had had some insight and input into the draft of the Davos speech (Shell was one of the initial signatories). I understood that there was to be a paragraph on corruption in the speech. As I listened to the Secretary-General deliver the speech I noted that the paragraph on corruption had dropped out. The initial nine principles covered human rights, working conditions and the environment, but there was no principle on fighting corruption. There was at the time no UN convention on corruption. All the other principles were rooted in UN conventions, so the Secretary-General may well have been wise to omit it at that stage as being a step too far for the UN. However, it was a disappointment to me and to Robin Aram. Corruption is at the root of many of the other evils and in many ways is the most pervasive and corrosive of all evils. So when I was invited to serve on the initial Advisory Council to the Secretary-General I agreed on the condition that we should work to include a principle on corruption. It took several years to achieve this, with the key work being done by Transparency International led by Peter Eigen. Getting the 'Tenth Principle' agreed by signatories to the first nine, as was essential, was not an easy task. Many CEOs were nervous of creeping addition of further principles and were concerned at making *post facto* alterations or additions to the commitment to which they had initially signed up. However, there was by then a UN convention on corruption[2] and we made the argument that corruption was indeed a unique and pervasive issue that affected the other principles. Principle 10 states that:

> Businesses should work against corruption in all its forms, including extortion and bribery.[3]

We had to assure those who had signed up to the principles that the board had absolutely no intention of adding further principles. The principles are broad; with the inclusion of corruption the modus operandi should be to expand and develop on the practical implications of the ten principles rather than seeking to add more. This is indeed the way that the UNGC works. Through the exchange of experiences, companies, civil society organisations and labour unions develop guidance on the implementation of the principles in day-to-day operations. There are also working groups led by board members on human rights, on reporting on performance, on working conditions, supply-chain issues, the environment and so on. These involve representatives of companies as well as NGOs, labour organisations and academics.

I have been involved in the UNGC from the outset, both personally through the Secretary-General's Advisory Council and later as vice chairman of the board, as well as through Shell, Anglo American and other companies on whose boards I have sat. The present UN Secretary-General Ban Ki-Moon chairs the board. He has been enormously

---

2 The United Nations Convention Against Corruption was adopted by the UN General Assembly in 2003. There are now 167 parties to the Convention. It includes important provisions on the recovery of overseas assets that are the proceeds of corruption; much work remains to be done to implement these provisions.

3 www.unglobalcompact.org/AboutTheGC/TheTenPrinciples/principle10.html.

supportive from the moment of his appointment and takes a lively interest, promoting the Compact on his visits to countries. He attends the first hour or so of every board meeting and then generally attends a lunch to which he invites Permanent Representatives to the UN to meet the board. By his presence and his words he strengthens support and ensures that member states know what the Compact is doing. At the lunch we report back to the Secretary-General on the outcomes of the board meeting. I have come to appreciate his wisdom and self-deprecating sense of humour greatly. Quite contrary to some press reports, when he departs from his prepared script he demonstrates deep knowledge, sensitivity and humour.

Criticism of the Compact as a toothless tiger

The UNGC has grown to be far the largest organisation of companies committed to applying environmental, social and governance principles in their day-to-day work. There are currently almost 8,000 corporate signatories and a further 3,000 civil society organisations and other relevant entities engaged with the Compact.[4] Signatories are spread right across the world in 135 countries; signatory companies employ some 50 million people. Spain has the most signatory companies with nearly 1,000. There are about 1,200 signatories in France, Germany and the UK combined, some 300 in the United States, 250 in China, 150 in India, and over 400 in Japan and Korea combined.

The development has not been without controversy. As a movement to which companies make voluntary commitments the UNGC was criticised by some civil society organisations as being merely 'bluewash'.[5] There was a strong feeling that some companies signed up but actually did nothing. It was just words. There was certainly initial justification to this claim. However, when a company sends a letter of commitment to

4 unglobalcompact.org/ParticipantsAndStakeholders/index.html, last updated May 2013.
5 Bluewash is a derogatory term for a corporation seeking to gain credibility for its actions or principles by cloaking itself in the blue of the United Nations.

the Secretary-General, it makes a commitment within a fixed period to deliver a 'Communication on Progress' (CoP) to the UNGC Office and to make this public. This report has to show what steps the company has taken to implement each of the principles and to report on progress generally. These public reports allow the company to be held to account by its various stakeholders. Companies are responsible for the accuracy of their reporting and many have their reports independently verified. The reports and specific instances of behaviour are frequently challenged by stakeholders.[6] The UNGC has now gained credibility by a process of delisting companies who sign up but do not submit any Communication on Progress. Although over 2,000 companies have been delisted in this way, there is still strong growth in signatories. There is also a greater awareness at the point of signature that if you are not prepared to commit to the effort you had better not sign, so the number of companies delisted is now declining.

Governance of the Compact itself

As a bridge between the UN and business, the governance of the UNGC is complex. The UNGC Office is small with fewer than 20 people headed since its foundation by Georg Kell, a German with a lifelong commitment to the principles of the UN and a true example of an international civil servant. The staff members, almost all young and very enthusiastic, are employees of the UN. As such their salaries can only be paid by member states. The core office is funded by a Trust Fund to which various member states, initially mainly European, but now including countries such as China and Colombia, contribute. States will only contribute to

---

6 There are often calls for the UN Global Compact Office to verify the accuracy of Communications on Progress. The office checks that the report covers the required areas, but it has always been the policy of the board that it would be an impossible task for any one organisation such as the UNGC to verify or certify reports without a massive and unrealistic staff increase. Individual companies often have their reports independently verified and all reports are open to public scrutiny and comment.

a business-led organisation if there is financial support from business also. This is the role of the Global Compact Foundation,[7] an independent US-registered not-for-profit foundation, which I chair. This raises funds from signatories on a voluntary basis according to their size. The concept is to collect a large number of relatively small contributions, with no company having undue influence as a result of its contribution being dominant. Business is now rightly the main source of funding; signatory contributions, together with business support for initiatives and sponsorship is now a multiple of the government contribution. The Global Compact Foundation funds are used exclusively in support of and at the request of the Global Compact Office, for example, for travel of civil society representatives to meetings, for communication and publications, for major meetings, for consultancy work when initiatives are being developed and so on.

The Global Compact Office is a part of the UN organisation and as such the board cannot directly instruct the Global Compact Office to do anything, but it can advise its chair, the Secretary-General, to do so, so it is not without power. In practice the work is cooperative, with board members actively involved in leading and participating in various working groups. In addition there are two other important forums. The first is the Leadership Summit, held every two or three years and attended by CEOs and board members of signatory companies. Initiatives and strategies are presented and discussed at this gathering. Similarly, there is an annual gathering of representatives of the Global Compact Local Networks to discuss progress and issues that arise at the national level. The board is committed not to support major changes unless they have been aired and discussed at these two forums. The result is a complex and interlocking governance system, with an important further interaction with member states and the UN General Assembly. The contribution of Georg Kell in making this complex system work in practice with the minimum of bureaucracy has been, and is, fundamental. No less important has been his creative drive in support of the other critical initiatives of the UNGC.

---

7 www.globalcompactfoundation.org.

The UNGC Local Networks

The most important of these initiatives is perhaps the UN Global Compact Local Networks. In the end, progress on implementing the principles of the Compact depends not on talks in New York and Geneva, but on practical steps in each and every country. It is at the national and local level that things get done. No one company can achieve much on its own. It needs the collective action not just of business and industry in a country, but also of civil society and labour organisations working together. This is the role of the Local Networks that bring these sometimes disparate actors together.

There are now Local Networks in over 100 countries. They live or die by the activities of signatory companies in the country. They also depend very much on leadership from individuals taking the initiative. Probably about half of the networks are currently truly effective, with a quarter building up activities and a further quarter perhaps stalled or in retreat because of loss of leadership for one reason or another. The annual meeting of Local Networks is one of the liveliest and most stimulating meetings that I have attended. At a meeting in Geneva in 2013 the need for regional representation of networks was discussed. This clearly makes coordination simpler, but equally there is a need to respect the unique characteristics of each country and each network. Within the space of two days, over 150 network representatives and members had decided on the structure of the regions and elected regional representatives to a Local Network Advisory Group. Furthermore, the newly elected members of the Local Network Advisory Group had, after consultation with their regions, unanimously elected Matthew Tukaki, the Australian Local Network representative, to be the Chair of the Advisory Group with a seat *ex officio* on the UN Global Compact Board. Such speed of action and agreement across multiple countries is something that unfortunately the UN Member States can only dream of. Matthew Tukaki was able to attend a UNGC board meeting only a couple of weeks later.

Local Networks identify local priorities. Is the biggest issue in a particular country human rights, the environment, working conditions or corruption? Or, regrettably in some countries, all four? Are there practical things that can be done collectively, working with government where possible, to begin to make progress? It is not easy. It is important that these priorities are discussed and set by Local Networks themselves. When visiting a Local Network I am often asked what I think are the priorities. The answer has to be turned back to the Network itself. The centre may agree and support the priority, but the drive has to be local.

At a regional meeting hosted by the UNGC Local Network in Dubai, there was discussion of what the priorities should be in the Emirates and in the Gulf Cooperation Council countries. The two leading issues identified by the Network itself were working conditions for migrant labour and energy efficiency and consumption. These are indeed serious issues in the region. Low and subsidised energy prices coupled with a consumerist society have led to extremely high per capita energy use. How can a population wean itself off a consumption pattern that is ultimately unsustainable? Likewise, conditions of work for migrant labour, often from the Indian subcontinent or the Philippines, can be very bad indeed, with workers committed to work on a single basis for two-year spells in poor living conditions. Labour legislation is weak and frequently poorly enforced. While there are many responsible employers, the tail end is very bad indeed. In addition, the presence of large groups of migrant labour leads to a distorted work ethic in the citizen population. This issue is not new. Indentured labour in colonial times led to the ethnic Indian populations in the Caribbean and in Malaysia. Nor is it restricted to the Middle East; there are many jobs in Britain shunned by the indigenous population, which is content for migrants to do jobs in the agricultural or service sectors, preferring unemployment and support by the state to low-income jobs.

Both issues are excellent subjects for collective work by a group of responsible businesses who subscribe to the UNGC, working in coalition with NGOs to ensure, for example, proper, open communication with migrant workers in the absence of trade unions. Through such collective action government and other companies can be convinced that changes can be made in the norms of working conditions and energy usage without damaging the economy. Improvements are not just a cost, but frequently deliver improved business outcomes.

A few months after the meeting in Dubai I attended a gathering of the Bangladesh UNGC Local Network in Dhaka in Bangladesh. The first issue that they raised was that of migrant labour, but this time from the viewpoint of labour-sending countries. Workers need the employment. The wages, although low by international standards, can in the case of responsible employers allow significant savings to improve life for the family back at home. Bangladesh members were surprised to hear that the same issue had been raised by their fellow UNGC signatories in Dubai. There is clearly scope for cooperation.

The other issue raised in Bangladesh was the need to find employment opportunities for people with physical disabilities. There were excellent examples of companies finding ways of employing people with disabilities to great mutual benefit. Businesses working with relevant NGOs through the Local Network could make industry in Bangladesh aware of steps that allow employers to find loyal and industrious workers while at the same time having a positive impact on a disadvantaged sector of society. The attitude to disability begins to change: a family member with a disability ceases to be a burden on the family and becomes and active and contributing member. From such work the government can develop sensible regulatory frameworks. With hindsight, given the recent appalling fires and building collapses in Dhaka in Bangladesh, perhaps the Local Network should have identified as a priority steps to ensure that building codes were adhered to and fire precautions adequate. As in many countries, the relevant building codes and fire safety regulations exist but are not enforced, perhaps not least because of financial involvement of politicians in businesses in substandard buildings. In the aftermath of the Rana Plaza building collapse[8] two

8 On 24 April 2013, the Rana Plaza building in Dhaka collapsed. The upper floors of the building housed garment factories, while the ground floor housed a bank and some retail outlets. The day before the collapse, cracks had appeared in the building and government building inspectors are reported to have declared the building unsafe for occupation. In any case the upper four floors of the building were reportedly constructed without any building permit. The bank and retail outlets evacuated the building, but the garment factories continued to work, allegedly threatening their workers with significant pay stoppages if they refused to work. The bodies of 1,129 workers and children in a crèche on site were

major global unions, IndustriALL Global Union and UNI Global Union, whose General Secretaries, Jyrki Raina and Philip Jennings both sit on the board of the UN Global Compact, led a campaign to establish an Accord on Fire and Building Safety in Bangladesh. By May the Accord had been signed by some 40 garment companies, led by H&M, a UNGC signatory.[9] The Accord is binding on the signatories and provides for building and safety inspections, protection of workers while any remedial work is carried out and also for funding arrangements for such work. The Accord was not primarily an initiative of the UNGC, but is a good example of work by a multi-stakeholder group including UNGC members to address a specific issue. The tragedy is that the work was only triggered by catastrophic deaths.

In China, the Global Compact Local Network, which has over 300 Global Compact signatories as members, is chaired by Chairman Fu Chengyu of Sinopec, who is also a board member of the Global Compact. The Chinese Local Network, entirely on its own initiative, organised a workshop on human rights. The discussion of such matters in a Chinese context is very important[10] and is something that is increasingly possible, although as early as 2005 the Global Compact was able to hold a regional summit in China, with support of the government, at which working conditions, corruption and human rights were all discussed and which was attended by representatives of human rights NGOs and global labour unions.

I do not pretend that UNGC Local Networks around the world are already developing these opportunities to the full or that they are all

---

recovered and over 2,500 survivors were recovered from the wreckage of the building. The building's owner, Sohel Rana, and others have been arrested. Sohel Rana is alleged to have connections with the youth wing of the governing party in Bangladesh.

9 Although no UNGC signatory had workers in Rana Plaza in their supply chain, several have significant suppliers in Bangladesh. There is clearly much do be done through collective action to improve not just working conditions but the fundamental safety of places of work.

10 Such a meeting would have the tacit support of the Chinese government as many of the participants were state-owned enterprises and the Chinese government is also a supporter of the UN Global Compact Trust Fund.

working effectively, but they are potentially a powerful new way of working. Each network needs leadership and one of the big thrusts of the UNGC is to make sure that major global companies in the Compact adopt one or two local networks outside their own home country, providing some of the support needed to build a truly effective and inclusive Local Network. This is beginning to work and the annual meeting of Local Network focal points from around the world is one of the most stimulating of such gatherings. The future work of the UNGC will focus very much on the development of the Local Networks. Although the UNGC has almost 8,000 signatory companies, this represents less than 10% of the world's multinational companies. In addition, there are millions of national companies and small and medium-sized enterprises. It will only be possible to engage effectively with these through the Local Networks and thus change the face of business as a whole.

The PRI: investors and shareholders as drivers of change

If the UNGC is to expand rapidly beyond the current 8,000 or so companies employing some 50 million people in 135 countries around the world, experience shows that there have to be external drivers beyond the good intentions of the companies themselves. There are many such potential drivers—consumers, shareholders, campaigners and government regulation.

For this reason the UNGC has worked with the United Nations Environment Programme (UNEP) and a group of major pension funds to develop the Principles for Responsible Investment (PRI). Major funds with long-term investment horizons believe that if companies pay proper attention to environmental, social and governance factors their economic performance will be improved over the medium term and risks will be reduced. Signatories to the PRI undertake to take into account in their investment strategy and in their engagement with companies in which they are invested factors such as whether the companies have adopted the Principles of the UNGC. They seek to understand whether companies are integrating the Principles into their day-to-day operations.

To enable this they encourage companies to report publicly on their performance in UNGC-style Communications on Progress or by using global frameworks such as the Global Reporting Initiative. Signatories to the PRI now number over 1,000 investment funds and have some $34 trillion of assets under management (at April 2013).[11] This is work in progress and by no means all the signatories are as yet truly active. However, when 10 or 15 managers of major funds co-sign a letter to a Chairman or CEO enquiring on their company's approach to the Global Compact it gains more attention than a call from the UNGC Office. The company that I now chair, Hermes Equity Ownership Services, is owned by the British Telecom Pension Fund and is an active supporter of the PRI. The service that Hermes EOS supplies to its clients is engagement with a company board and management on strategy, environmental, social and governance issues on behalf of major pension fund managers.

Pension and investment funds are in turn accountable to members and clients for the way in which funds are invested. Individuals want a decent return on their savings but they also want to know that their savings are not invested in ways in which they would be uncomfortable or which are damaging to society at large.

A common cause for concern is the activities of companies in areas that are or have recently been subject to conflict. For this reason, a group of PRI signatories came together with members of the UNGC working group on Human Rights as well as other UNGC signatory companies to develop guidance that could be used by both UNGC signatory companies and PRI signatories in examining and evaluating the work of companies in such sensitive areas. I chaired a task force on the subject, which produced *Guidance on Responsible Business in Conflict-Affected and High-Risk Areas*.[12] The task force met in a number of different countries, including a workshop in March 2010 in Sudan organised by the Local Network. This workshop was supported by the then Government of National Unity in Sudan and was attended by several ministers.

11 PRI Factsheet, www.unpri.org/news/pri-fact-sheet.
12 UNGC and PRI, *Guidance on Responsible Business in Conflict-Affected and High-Risk Area* (New York: UNGC, 2010; www.unglobalcompact.org/docs/issues_doc/Peace_and_Business/Guidance_RB.pdf).

It was also supported by the China National Petroleum Corporation (CNPC) and other major oil producers in Sudan, as well as representatives of six major fund managers. These funds have indirect involvement in Sudan though investment in various oil companies such as PetroChina (which is a majority-owned subsidiary of CNPC but which does not itself operate in Sudan) or Oil and Natural Gas Corporation (ONGC) of India.

Under the umbrella of the UNGC the PRI investors were able to engage with CNPC and visit an operating area in Heglig, an area much impacted by the civil war that had raged between the north and south of Sudan before the peace treaty four years before. The investors were able to see the high standard of treatment of discharged production water (handled by a UK-based international contractor) and the use of that water for irrigation. They could see the nature of security and the relations of the largely Sudanese staff of the Chinese company with the local communities. They could also see a company-run hospital started ten years or so before by the Canadian company Talisman, which had earlier been forced to disinvest by public, Canadian government and investor pressure. The company hospital, run by a number of impressive Sudanese doctors, had operated right through the civil war providing outstanding free medical care to local people from very large distances around. The maternity unit, which was delivering six to eight babies a day, of which perhaps two would be by Caesarean section, attracted women from several hundred kilometres away.

Future directions of work in conflict-sensitive areas

Building on the work that produced the *Guidance on Responsible Business in Conflict-Affected and High-Risk Areas* there has been discussion with a number of Local Networks such as those in Pakistan, Colombia, Sri Lanka and Sudan as to how businesses and Local Networks can contribute to the development of peace in the country, to the benefit of both business and society at large. The Institute for Economics and Peace, founded by the Australian entrepreneur Steve Killelea, has demonstrated though its annual Global Peace Index, produced initially in collaboration with the Economist Intelligence Unit, that there is a strong correlation between the degree of 'peacefulness' in a country and economic development.[13] The Business for Peace initiative of the Global Compact aims to work with Local Networks to see how businesses in their country can contribute directly to peace while improving the local climate for business. The efforts are very country specific, involving, for example, efforts to reintegrate former combatants into employment in Sri Lanka, Colombia or Sudan or addressing the economic problems of Syrian refugees in Turkey.[14]

The dilemma of engagement

The direct local impacts of the CNPC operation in the local area was clearly positive in terms of employment, training and development of livelihoods both in the company's supply chain and outside it, as well as medical care. The area was clearly sensitive and without the sort of practical precautions and considerations spelled out in the guidance document there is clearly the possibility of exacerbating conflict—whether through impact of security, unbalanced employment, disputes over land or distribution of benefits. Provided this is handled carefully the main argument that critics can and do level at such operations is that, while the revenue does benefit the country, it also supports the state and its often suppressive security apparatus.

13 See www.visionofhumanity.org.
14 The Business for Peace initiative was launched by the UNGC and several Local Networks in New York on 20 September 2013. A list of participants appears at www.unglobalcompact.org/Issues/conflict_prevention/index.html. See also UN Global Compact and Principles for Responsible Investment with KPMG, *Responsible Business Advancing Peace: Examples from Companies, Investors and Global Compact Local Networks* (New York: UNGC, 2013; www.unglobalcompact.org/docs/issues_doc/Peace_and_Business/B4P_Resource_Package_company.pdf).

This argument came to the fore a year later in 2011 in relation to the events in North Africa, Egypt, Yemen and the Gulf countries with particular emphasis on Libya and Colonel Qaddafi. It is not new and was certainly in the minds of those attending the workshop in Khartoum.

Professor Elias Nyamlell Wakoson, State Minister for International Cooperation in the Unity Government of Sudan formed as a result of the Comprehensive Peace Agreement was one of the ministers who attended the entire workshop in Sudan.[15] He admitted that he had only planned to come to the opening but had found it so interesting that he stayed throughout. He made the point at the meeting that while security was indeed a major component of central government expenditure, the dream of a big 'peace dividend' as this security began to be gradually wound down was just that, a dream. Peace had been bought in many cases by paying militias to lay down their arms. However, this was a short-term solution; unless within a few years jobs could be created for former combatants the temptation to take up arms again would be very strong. Sudan desperately needed investment, including foreign investment, not just into the oil industry but also into agri-businesses and other enterprises.

The minister mentioned in his interventions the fact that in other parts of Africa what was first seen as illegitimate could be transformed over time into something stable and legitimate, without dwelling unduly on the past. In the UK we have after all seen something similar take place though the peace process in Northern Ireland, with extremists on both sides becoming leading members of the government.

Some months before the workshop, President Omar al-Bashir of Sudan had been indicted by the International Criminal Court for crimes against humanity (in my view, while this was just it was also counterproductive). Elias told of attending a meeting of African governments accompanying President Bashir shortly after the president had been indicted. After the opening ceremonies, Bashir had left the meeting, leaving Elias to handle the rest of the meeting on his behalf. Elias said that

---

15 Later Deputy Minister of International Cooperation in the new Republic of South Sudan.

the minute Bashir had left, the meeting spent hours debating the indict-ment, with arguments on all sides. The business of the meeting made little progress. Elias said that in the end he had to point out to all at the meeting that he himself had been an opponent of Omar Bashir in the civil war. However he was now a minister in a Government of National Unity and President Bashir was his President. He pointed out that Omar Bashir was like a man carrying a basket of eggs. If people kept jostling him, he would sooner or later drop the eggs and there would be broken egg everywhere. He felt that the time had come to get on with the busi-ness. Those were wise and moving words. In the subsequent referendum provided for in the Comprehensive Peace Agreement, South Sudan has overwhelmingly voted to split from the North; Omar Bashir has said that he would respect the outcome of the referendum and while the split has been contentious, and in some cases violent, full-scale war has been avoided. There are many issues on the movement of people, the shar-ing of revenues and the transit of oil to the north that still need to be resolved. Both parts of Sudan need support and investment now more than ever. There is an important role for responsible businesses investing in such difficult countries.

Voluntary approaches versus legislation

From the outset, the UN Global Compact has been a voluntary move-ment. Signatories take it upon themselves to embed the Ten Principles in their day-to-day operations. This is not a light commitment. They must have support at board level to make the commitment and when they sign they commit to reporting publicly on their progress. This exposes them to the scrutiny of the public—consumers, NGOs, the media, share-holders, their own employees and anyone interested in their operations and the way they go about their business. The contents of such reports are often verified by independent third parties, but even where they are not it would be a brave CEO to put in the public domain deliberately inaccurate information. There are many watchers and the power of con-sumer disenchantment or wrath is formidable.

In spite of this there is a significant body of opinion, particularly in parts of the NGO movement, which considers that legislation is necessary and, since one cannot trust national governments to put in place sufficiently tough regulation or to police and enforce it adequately, the legislation must be somehow be made international and be enforced through extraterritorial judicial processes.

I am not someone who believes that progress will be made simply by relying on the goodwill of people and companies to do the right thing. In all areas we need laws. The history of the development of laws governing working conditions is a case in point. Some enlightened employers such as the Quaker business people in the UK in the late-18th and early-19th century and pioneers such as Henry Ford who saw the need to pay his workers well, not only to keep them happy but also to turn them into potential purchasers of his products, began to improve pay and conditions for their workers. When coupled with many battles by organised labour and unions for better and safer working conditions, this demonstrated that such changes are beneficial to both the workers and the companies. Workers benefit from better working and living conditions, while the company benefits from improved quality and productivity. However, in each case, while such innovations are accepted by a few companies at first and are then followed by other companies who see the benefits, there are always a large number of companies that are unresponsive or even deliberately obstructive. It will always be necessary in the end to follow up with regulation and legislation to ensure that the recalcitrant tail is forced to adopt the new standards.

The place for such legislation is in the nation state, where it covers all companies, large and small, national and international. Attempts at international or extraterritorial legislation catches only the large international companies, which are often not the worst offenders.[16] This is

---

16 Studies show that pay and working conditions in international companies are normally superior to those of purely national companies, and that applies to many working standards as well. See, e.g. R.E. Lipsey, 'Home- and Host-Country Effects of Foreign Direct Investment', in R.E. Baldwin and L.A. Winters (eds.), *Challenges to Globalization: Analyzing the Economics* (National Bureau of Economic Research Conference Report; Chicago: University of Chicago Press,

not to say that international efforts that result in protocols and trea-
ties such as the UN Montreal Protocol on Substances that Deplete the
Ozone Layer (1989) or the (Land) Mine Ban Treaty (1997) are not valuable, but in the end it is national legislation that generally has to provide
for enforcement. Experience in the six decades since the acceptance of
the Universal Declaration on Human Rights, and in later international
agreements on labour standards and the environment, shows that the
challenges are in the implementation in individual companies and in the
day-to-day workings of companies and other organisations. In his excellent guidance on Business and Human Rights, the UN Special Rappor-
teur John Ruggie rightly puts the responsibility for the Protect part of
his Protect, Respect, Remedy trilogy firmly on the state, while focusing
the need for Respect and Remedy on companies (see Box 3.2).

Box 3.2 Protect, Respect and Remedy Framework

The Protect, Respect and Remedy Framework rests on three pillars:

· **Protect.** The State duty to protect against human rights abuses by third
parties, including business, through appropriate policies, regulation,
and adjudication

· **Respect.** The corporate responsibility to respect human rights, which
means to act with due diligence to avoid infringing the rights of others
and to address adverse impacts that occur

· **Remedy.** Both State and business responsibility to provide greater
access by victims to effective remedy, both judicial and non-judicial[17]

2004): 333-82; wage comparisons from page 345 onwards; individual chapter
available at www.nber.org/chapters/c9543.

17 Summarised from United Nations, *Guiding Principles on Business and Human
Rights: Implementing the United Nations 'Protect, Respect and Remedy' Frame-
work* (New York/Geneva: United Nations, 2011; www.ohchr.org/Documents/
Publications/GuidingPrinciplesBusinessHR_EN.pdf).

But what of the frequent laggard cases where local legislation is inadequate, perhaps obstructed by vested interests, or where legislation exists but is not effectively enforced, or where corruption of either the enforcers or the judiciary allows the unscrupulous to avoid the legislative constraints? To achieve an eventually satisfactory outcome the emphasis must be on working to improve national legislations and enforcement. This seems to many people to be an impossibly slow and quixotic task. The value of responsible international companies in such situations is that they can and do follow international standards, showing the way to other companies and encouraging the population by demonstrating that one can run a non-corrupt business with good working conditions and high environmental standards. This is where the UNGC Local Networks come in—both as a forum for exchange of ideas and practices and also as a coalition representing different sectors that can work with a government to improve standards, or try to push it into doing so.

Objectors argue that it would still be useful to have international or extraterritorial legislation to ensure that at least those international companies working in such laggard countries are forced to apply international standards. I believe that many of the so-called voluntary initiatives and standards are becoming in fact quasi-mandatory for global companies. Standards such as the Voluntary Principles on Security and Human Rights, or standards developed in order to prevent degradation of forests for agriculture, or practices developed by the International Council on Mining and Metals get picked up and incorporated into the Performance Standards of the World Bank Group. Through the Equator Principles, another multi-stakeholder initiative adopted by the banks that finance almost all private sector projects, companies seeking such project finance must adhere to these standards. Similar pressure will be exerted on a company by those of its shareholders who are signatories to the PRI. In this way international companies are pushed by a web of agreements into compliance.

Apart from consumer pressure on companies to ensure that goods sold meet certain standards in their production, it is possible to build environmental and labour standards into international trade agreements. However, efforts to do so tend to be strongly resisted. Many countries see this as richer countries seeking to build protectionism into trade agreements in a way that prevents lower-income countries from exploiting their competitive advantages. What we can and should do is to prevent the insertion into bilateral trade agreements of stability clauses that prevent a country from raising environmental and other standards in its legislation. The International Institute for Sustainable Development has done some pioneering and valuable work in this field, leading to the development of investment agreements that support more sustainable development.[18]

Having said all of that, would 'international legislation' or extraterritorial national legislation do any harm? For egregious crimes, there is already an International Criminal Court, although its record of bringing powerful individuals to trial is patchy and very slow at best. If such arrangements could be made to work, they would still suffer from the absence of a global policeman. While such a role was to some extent possible in imperial and colonial times, for instance in the role of the British Navy in the abolition of the slave trade, nations now quite rightly view this with great caution, particularly in the light of recent experience in Iraq and Afghanistan.

There are two very negative effects of the use in corporate cases of the US Alien Claims Tort Act, perhaps the most used piece of extraterritorial legislation. First, this Act has allowed cases involving alleged activities overseas, often in relation to non-US companies, to be brought to trial before a US jury.[19] In my experience this is normally largely motivated by a law firm's hope of earning significant contingency fees. A company is faced with the prospect of a long trial and a massive diversion of management effort in the process of discovery and deposition. In addition to this, there is the unpredictable nature of a trial before a jury whose members almost certainly have little or no knowledge of

---

18 International Institute for Sustainable Development, www.iisd.org/investment/law/contracts.aspx.

19 The use of the US Alien Claims Tort Act against non-US companies for actions committed outside the US has been somewhat restricted by a US Supreme Court decision in 2013 (*Kiobel v. Royal Dutch Petroleum, Co*, see www.business-humanrights.org/Documents/SupremeCourtATCAReview).

the circumstances on the ground at the time of the incident, which are normally a far cry from what one might expect in New York. This leads most companies to settle, certainly non-US companies that are unlikely to be viewed sympathetically by a US jury. This does not seem like sound justice to me. The notable exception in recent years has been Chevron, which has so far been successful in defending itself against claims.[20] Second, the more damaging effect is that, rather than encouraging companies to apply global standards in difficult countries, companies will simply gradually withdraw from such countries as, however high their standards and however careful they are in ensuring that these standards apply in their operations, there is inevitably a greater risk of something going wrong in such a country. Better to withdraw where possible and not run any risk. This deprives the country of a responsible operator and probably opens the way for those less constrained by such scruples. I see this happening and believe this to be the motivation, along with the business mantra of 'focus', which views such operations as distracting even if profitable.

If it is indeed so, it is a great pity. I believe that in conjunction with UNGC Local Networks, signatory companies of the Global Compact can be a force for good in many 'difficult' countries. That is why I continue to support the careful setting up and fostering of networks in such countries. There is a new GC Local Network being built in Myanmar. There were already Local Networks in Egypt and Syria.

---

20 In 1999 a Chevron oil platform offshore Nigeria was invaded by members of a community. Chevron claims that the platform was occupied for three days and staff held hostage (www.chevron.com/bowoto/background). The community claims that the occupation was peaceful. Two villagers were killed when the Nigerian security forces took the platform and ejected the villagers. A group of Nigerians brought a suit against Chevron in the US under the Alien Tort Claims Act. The charges were finally dismissed in 2010 and permission to appeal to the US Supreme Court was denied (www.business-humanrights. org/Categories/Lawlawsuits/Lawsuitsregulatoryaction/LawsuitsSelectedcases/ ChevronlawsuitreNigeria).

The next generation of business people

If we are to embed wider considerations than profit in businesses, we have to look to the education of future business leaders. A pioneer in this process has been the Aspen Institute's Business and Society Programme, founded and led since the late 1990s by Judith Samuelson. The programme has brought together leaders of business to explore value-based approaches to business and to work for the development of business leaders for a more sustainable society. In 1999, together with the World Resources Institute, the Business and Society Programme began a biennial ranking of business schools and MBA programmes with the title 'Beyond Grey Pinstripes' (now discontinued) looking at how well business schools integrate social environmental and governance issues and values into their curricula. There is no doubt that the interest generated by these rankings was a driver of change in business school curricula and there has been a steady increase in relevant material being included in business management courses. Judith Samuelson's persistence over more than a decade has contributed greatly.

In 2007, at the UN Global Compact Leadership Summit in Geneva, the UN Principles for Responsible Management Education (PRME) were launched.[21] The principles were developed by a task force of some 60 deans of business schools. There is oversight by a steering committee formed from eight international co-convening institutions, including the Aspen Institute's Business and Society Program. The secretariat is housed in the UNGC Office. There are now more than 500 participating institutions. Many of these are smaller institutions and it is valuable for them to be able to share teaching materials and ideas. Through this initiative there has been a progressive expansion of values-based business education and in the incorporation of ethics and values into the framework of the participating business schools. Over time this should make significant impact on how business is conducted around the world.

21 Principles for Responsible Management, www.unprme.org.

Does the Global Compact make a difference?

With almost 8,000 business participants employing some 50 million people, if all of the signatories work hard at the sometimes difficult job of implementing the Ten Principles in their day-to-day operation much progress can be achieved and the lives of many made better. If the principles can also be implemented throughout the supply chains of these businesses there would be further progress. As pointed out earlier, the Global Compact signatories represent less than 10% of the world's multinationals, and not all of the signatories are major international companies. Clearly to have a truly transformative effect there has to be a massive increase in participation. The UN Secretary-General Ban Ki-Moon has set a target of reaching at least 20,000 signatories by 2020—as an enthusiast for the UNGC he sometimes suggests that the target should be to achieve that number by 2015. Even that number would be less than a third of the growing number of international companies, many from countries whose companies are new to working internationally.

One of the most encouraging outcomes of the Rio+20 World Summit in Rio in June 2012 was not any declaration by governments but the output of the major three-day 'Sustainability Forum'. During this there were encouraging reports on progress from the some 2,000 companies, governments, investors and business schools that were present. Many of the companies present were not yet signatories to the UNGC, yet were working hard at issues covered by the Principles.

If we are to make significant progress, the hundreds of thousands of small and medium-size businesses need to be engaged. This is why perhaps the most important element of the UNGC is the Local Networks. Progress will be achieved country by country, with businesses of all sizes and types coming together with organisations in other parts of society to work on the most pressing issues in that country, be it related to human rights, working conditions, the environment or corruption. As in so many areas, this will require leadership on a country-by-country basis in business and government.

Chapter 4

Some alternatives in countries with military rule or human rights abuses:
Sanctions or withdrawal

The progress of reform from within each country is often extremely slow. This is true even when, as I advocated earlier, this is encouraged by coalitions of responsible companies, civil society organisations and other groups such as labour unions. While frustrating, we should perhaps remember that it took much of the second half of the 20th century to move Western societies from positions where the involvement of women in public life was limited, racial discrimination if not outright segregation was common, homosexuality was a criminal offence and much of the world was administered by colonial powers. The growth of institutions and embedding of what are now considered to be acceptable norms of behaviour in Europe and North America has taken decades. And yet we imagine that, given what we somewhat arrogantly regard as our good example, countries can cover in a couple of years what it has taken us half a century to arrive at.

None the less, many people feel that the process of change can be triggered by outside pressure of one sort or another. They also often feel that responsible companies should withdraw from any investments that they have in any country where the government is guilty of practices considered unacceptable to much of the rest of the world. The record of both such approaches is mixed. On the positive side, I believe that sanctions did play a role in achieving change in South Africa. The effective impact was on the morale of the white South African population, who found travel difficult and who found that their national sporting teams could not play internationally. The feeling of being treated as an international pariah undoubtedly had a major impact. On the other hand, in the absence of an effective naval blockade, the oil embargo was ineffective. The boycott did have an economic impact, but it stimulated a great deal of domestic creativity, whether in the manufacture of arms, in research and development of liquid fuels from coal or in other scientific developments. The country was not brought to its knees, but at least some of the ruling party could see that the apartheid policy was getting them nowhere and the prospect of a bloody civil war was increasing in spite of the oppressive mechanisms of the state. So the then President F.W. de Klerk took the critical steps to free Nelson Mandela and began the process of change. F.W. de Klerk, the country and indeed the world were fortunate that such a far-sighted, indomitable and forgiving man as Nelson Mandela was on the other side of the table. I attended a small gathering addressed by former President de Klerk and however much one might question the fact that he chose to join a party with such a misguided policy, I was impressed by his sincerity and approach. The long-lasting educational and other effects of apartheid are evil and they required evil means of enforcement. I found that the only question that de Klerk found difficulty in discussing was at what point he had decided to change his mind and the policy. Was it before or after the last election? The question is whether he went into that election having privately decided to start a process of change that he knew the white electorate would reject if he expressed it. His reticence on the subject is understandable; he is a man of strong religious conviction and the answer is one perhaps best left between the man and his maker. We should all be grateful that he did have the courage to commence the change.

In spite of calls for divestment, excoriating criticism in many public forums and indeed in spite of calls for a boycott of its products globally, my own company Shell remained in the country. The chief executive in South Africa spoke out against apartheid and the company advertised in opposition newspapers to provide them with income to help keep them alive. Within its operations the company practised non-discriminatory employment practices. While not directly involved in the breaking of sanctions by either the export or the import of oil, the company did process that oil in its joint venture refinery in Durban and sell the products in its stations. Shell was also involved in producing oil in countries where governments allowed the export of oil from their own share of the production through third parties to South Africa, without any Shell involvement. I never visited South Africa before the democratic elections of 1994 and was not involved in any decision-making in the early days, but I was on Shell's Committee of Managing Directors from 1991 onwards and supported the company policy. I sat with other directors on the platform at our Annual General Meetings while Sir Peter Holmes, Chairman at the time, arranged affairs so that we could have a period of concentrated discussion and questioning from opponents of Shell involvement in South Africa. I was also present at the first AGM after democracy when one of the most vociferous proponents of Shell divestment very graciously said that to his great surprise he now called for Shell to maximise our investment to get the South African economy going and generate the wealth necessary for progress. Such mild incongruities were common in an extremely complex situation. Shell sold its headquarters building in Cape Town to the African National Congress (ANC), which none the less kept the name Shell House. So at the time of disturbances in the run-up to the first free elections, television viewers saw footage of the ANC headquarters in 'Shell House' under attack by supporters of the alternative Inkatha Freedom Party.

The oil company Mobil chose a different route and sold their operations to Engen, an Afrikaner-led company. I do not believe that their withdrawal made any positive difference at all. Companies that remained and subscribed to working to improve conditions did help, although the picture was seldom unblemished. Companies were encouraged in this process of seeking change from within by the principles developed and progressively tightened by the Reverend Leon Sullivan. Sullivan was an

African American and one of the most impressive and persuasive people that I have ever had the privilege of meeting. When elected to the board of General Motors, Leon Sullivan undertook to visit its operation in South Africa and report on conditions. Being black, he encountered some resistance in South Africa. He told me that he had been strip-searched at the airport, a very demeaning experience. He was a giant of a man physically, with a calm but immovable resolve. Among many foolish things done by the apartheid government, this act, minor in comparison with many others, was a major mistake. Thereafter Sullivan worked pragmatically but with implacable persistence to get companies operating in South Africa to improve things; he also worked to end the apartheid regime. When Sullivan prayed uninvited at a meal or a meeting, I believe even atheists could feel the power of the spirit.

Anglo American, of which I was much later Chairman, was a South African company and withdrawal was simply not an option. Harry Oppenheimer, the son of the founder Sir Ernest Oppenheimer, was a remarkable man. I recall from my Shell days reading his very public arguments and statements against the whole apartheid system and being considerably moved by them. He was an opposition MP for ten years and, under his leadership as Chairman, Anglo American encouraged the formation of black trade unions in the early 1980s. Opposition newspapers were also part of Anglo American's extensive non-mining interests. Under the Chairmanship of Gavin Relly, Harry Oppenheimer's successor as Chairman of Anglo, a delegation of mainly Anglo American related companies met the then banned ANC in Lusaka in Zambia, to the fury of the Nationalist government in South Africa. There is no doubt that Anglo American was the leading liberal South African company working to eliminate and ameliorate the effects of apartheid and indeed the first ANC executive meeting in South Africa after the ban had been lifted was held at Anglo American's Vergelegen wine estate in the Cape. It is said that the ANC asked Anglo for help in finding a location that would not be bugged; so far as I know it was not. There are many moving photographs of the ANC stalwarts, black and white, who attended this historic meeting at Vergelegen. Having said that, Anglo's critics accurately point out that the core Anglo mining business in South Africa was based on single-sex hostels of migrant workers, to many the very epitome of the apartheid system. It is one of my regrets, as a subsequent Chairman of Anglo, that I never had the opportunity to meet Harry Oppenheimer, nor Gavin Relly, both of whom had died by the time I became involved with Anglo. There would have been much that I could have learned from both. Under Harry Oppenheimer's leadership Anglo did much to try and soften the long-term impacts of apartheid, and the social investment arm of Anglo, the Chairman's Fund, worked to improve educational and health opportunities for black South Africans.

The long-term damage of apartheid on black education is perhaps the most damaging and lasting legacy. I recall when I became Chairman of Anglo American in 2002, nearly a decade after the first democratic elections, I asked for some soundbite statistics to illustrate Anglo's impact. One of the most striking was that at that time nearly half the black students at university or technical college level were on scholarships or bursaries from Anglo-related companies or funds. I asked how many students this covered and was told almost 500. Impressive, until one realised that this meant that there were only about a thousand black technical students in a population of around 40 million. Such a heavily biased educational system will take years to repair. Progress has been slow in doing this, particularly in rural areas, with the distribution of books to rural schools recently being delayed in some cases by up to six months after the start of term. Much remains to be done and business support is still needed.

The practical palliative impact on the apartheid system of Anglo's efforts were clearly limited but none the less they had significant influence on thinking across the societal boundaries, and there is little doubt that some of the scenario work done by both Shell and Anglo did provide food for thought to all sides. Activity across boundaries in support of communities did soften attitudes. During an Anglo American board visit to Johannesburg while I was Chairman we arranged for board members to be briefed on the past and present activities of the Anglo Chairman's Fund. Among the Anglo board members present was Dr Mamphela Ramphele, a former Vice Chancellor of the University of Cape Town (the first black woman to hold such a position in South Africa) and a former Managing Director of the World Bank.[1] The presentation was given by Margie Keeton, who for many years led the Anglo Chairman's Fund's social investment activities most effectively and imaginatively. At the end of the presentation Margie Keeton produced a copy of a 1970's file note describing an application for funds from two young black South Africans for a project including medical facilities in the Eastern Cape. The note said that this was a most impressive pair and that the project was an excellent one. Although commenting that one might not agree entirely with the young man's politics, the note recommended that the funds be granted. The young man was Steve Biko and the young woman Mamphela Ramphele. Their son Hlumelo was born after Steve Biko's death at the hands of police while in custody. Dr Ramphele was not the only one close to tears at the end of the presentation.

The effects of sanctions

Sanctions only have an effect if they are likely, as in South Africa, to affect the morale and self-belief of those in power. Sanctions, if supported by the United Nations and not merely unilateral gestures by a small number of countries, can have an effect. This is particularly so if they are specifically targeted to affect the assets of the leading clique. For example, those targeted at Robert Mugabe and his close associates, preventing them from using overseas assets to acquire property and educate their children and grandchildren overseas, may influence their thinking. Sanctions are not, however, an effective weapon. If they are general, as in the case of Iraq, the effect can be negative. When enforced by an effective blockade they affect disproportionately the oppressed general population. In the case of Iraq, the undoubted damage that this did to the health and education of the general population led to the so-called Oil-for-Food policy, an attempt to ensure that food and drugs for the

---

1 Dr Ramphele has since left the board of Anglo American and other corporations and founded an opposition party with a very strong drive against ubiquitous corruption at high levels in government.

general population could be imported. The UN has been much criticised, particularly by the United States, for the way that this was handled. The problems were more a consequence of the way that the arrangement was set up by the countries concerned than the fault of the UN. For example, Saddam Hussein was allowed to choose which companies contracted with the Iraqi State Oil Marketing Organisation (SOMO). Shell and other major Western companies were never on the list approved by Saddam as this would have meant agreeing to pay a commission, which we were not prepared to do. Such commissions went straight to Saddam and the ruling elite. Some of the organisations purchasing crude and paying commissions have been brought to book since, but the system of commissions was no secret at the time.

The payment of commissions to be on a list to receive Iraqi crude was not the only flaw in the system. There were other easy ways for Saddam to make money through the Oil-for-Food programme. At the time Saddam's behaviour was apparently erratic. He placed strange conditions on the Oil-for-Food programme. There would be a build-up in the oil market of expectations that he was about to approve the lifting of his ban on exporting oil for food. Suddenly, and then for what did not appear to be rational reasons, he would reject the entire arrangement. The instant removal of a large amount of oil expected by the market would cause the oil price to jump. The reverse would also happen. I do not in general subscribe to conspiracy theories, but in this case it is clear that anyone outside Iraq who was informed of exactly when Saddam was going to make one of his unexpected announcements could make a great deal of money in the futures market for themselves and Saddam. This money would be made outside Iraq and would not be subject to any restrictions on its use. All that was needed was for Saddam to send a message of his intended move to accomplices outside Iraq.

Although there is no way of proving this I believe that more progress would have been made if sanctions had not been applied to Iraq and international companies had been allowed to invest. The result, over time, could have been an increase in the general wealth of the country. With economic liberalisation comes, however slowly, political liberalisation. Progress is slow and erratic, but at least it is home grown and rooted in the culture. This is the strength of such initiatives as the Extractive Industries Transparency Initiative (EITI), which requires governments to commit to putting in train certain institutional changes. Even with a great deal of backsliding and evasion, these steps gradually begin to change the culture and demonstrate from the inside that there is another way.

The strongest argument against dropping sanctions and adopting a 'change from within' approach is that of the danger of nuclear proliferation. There is no denying that this is indeed a serious danger. But is the response to every unsatisfactory regime with nuclear ambitions to be sanctions, bombing of facilities or military intervention? North Korea has demonstrated how such an approach carries the seeds of its own destruction; if you can demonstrate that you have some nuclear capability other countries stop threatening aggression. The product of such a policy is often an understandable desire to acquire a weapon to prevent aggression. From an Iranian point of view, Israel's well-known but unacknowledged possession of nuclear weapons is a stimulus to acquire a balancing counterforce. Acquisition of nuclear weapons by Iran is highly undesirable, but the arguments on the rationality of a regime or estimates of the likelihood of the actual use of weapons are inevitably subjective and subject to much cultural bias. The present very tight financial sanctions on Iran are causing great stress to the population. For example, foreign exchange is not available for the purchase of insecticides and fertilisers, causing a drop in agricultural productivity. The same may well be true of the availability of medicines. This undoubtedly deepens resentment in the population to those Western countries advocating this; meanwhile I am sure that such funds as are available are deployed in the areas chosen by the government, as well as in ways that strengthen their support, for example through funding militias. Economic sanctions against commercial investment may or may not slow Iran's undesirable nuclear efforts, but as always it certainly concentrates economic power in the hands of the ruling regime and their cronies.

The strategy of the West towards Iran over the last 20 years and more has demonstrated the failure of a sanctions policy. The US Iran and Libya Sanctions Act (ILSA) passed in 1996 was the culmination of several stages of unilateral US sanctions adopted from the time of the Iranian Revolution in 1979. During the early and mid-1990s, as the person responsible for Shell's exploration and production worldwide I had many discussions with the then Iranian Minister of Petroleum, Gholamreza Agazadeh. Initially the discussions went nowhere because we in Shell wanted a risk-bearing investment where our technology and capital would be rewarded according to its success. The Iranians on the other hand wanted Shell simply to apply technology and people in exchange for a fixed service fee. When I expressed frustration and said that I did not see how progress was possible given our respective positions, Agazadeh suggested that we should not give up. Why not put some young engineers on either side together and see if with fresh minds they could come up with some way round the difficulties? We did in fact devise a number of possibilities. At one point the Iranians suggested that Shell take over the Sirri offshore field development near the border with the United Arab Emirates. This was a field that Conoco had been planning to develop in conjunction with a field in the Emirates but had been prevented from doing so by the Clinton administration before ILSA was passed. We pointed out that it would be particularly provocative if such a field were to be developed by Shell. The Iranians were understanding of the argument and the field was in fact developed by Total of France, which had few assets in the United States and a rather different attitude to the subject.

An imaginative Shell idea was to develop a large shallow water gas field in the southern part of Iran, but to take the gas northward into the main Iranian oil-producing area for compression and injection into large oil fields. The economics of gas production in remote areas depends on the amount of hydrocarbon liquids or condensate that is produced along with the gas and condenses as the gas pressure is reduced. The liquid hydrocarbons have a higher value than the gas; a high content of natural gas liquids that can easily be separated from the gas improves the economics greatly. This particular field was a 'dry' gas field with very little liquid content in the gas. In order to prevent a reduction of ultimate recovery of oil, many large Iranian oilfields require the pressure to be maintained by the injection of gas. Failing this, or if gas from the gas 'cap' above the oil is produced, oil will move up into the part of the reservoir that formerly contained only gas. Some of this oil 'wets' the reservoir rock and the amount of oil that can be ultimately recovered drops rapidly. At the time of the Iranian Revolution in 1979 there had been major plans for gas compression and injection. These projects were delayed or cancelled due to the revolution and the subsequent Iran–Iraq war. In the proposed Shell project, we could demonstrate the massive benefits to the Iranian state from increased oil recovery over tens of years from a project to move the dry gas to the north for reinjection. The investment in gas production, transport and injection would be recovered easily, while as the gas from the field to be developed was 'dry' gas it was not a prime candidate for the export market. This seemed to be a real win–win project. Shell could be given an economic return on its investment, while the Iranian nation would benefit many times over and for many years out of increased production. The scheme unfortunately fell at an additional hurdle. The Iranian parliament, which was cautious about foreign involvement, had decreed that a foreign producing company could only be paid by the actual product produced, and not by the oil indirectly produced. Our technocratic Iranian counterparts in the oil ministry and the National Iranian Oil Company insisted that it was unwise to approach the parliament for any sort of exception as the results would be unpredictable.

Throughout the years of Shell discussions with Iran, the Iranians with whom we dealt were understanding of US sensitivities. We had an open arrangement with the professionals in the US State Department. Shell maintained a policy of 'no surprises', keeping the State Department fully informed of what we were planning and when it might become public. The Iranians were happy to vary programmes in line with any US sensitivities that emerged from this process. US counterparts admitted privately that the question of sanctions on Iran was a matter of US domestic political importance, with particular electoral sensitivities in the state of New York. In conversation one day my interlocutor in the State Department thanked me for the Shell 'no surprises' policy. I replied that we were happy to oblige but that frankly it was no great sacrifice on our part as I was confident that the US government would in any case be aware of what we were talking about from other communication chan-nels, among them intercepts from the UK Government Communications Headquarters (GCHQ) Cheltenham. While not disagreeing with this, my counterpart said that information we passed freely to them could be shared openly with members of Congress and indicated Shell's will-ingness to cooperate; information obtained by other more clandestine means could not be readily shared publicly with Congress.[2]

Although Shell did in the end redevelop two offshore fields whose platforms had sustained damage from the air in the Iran–Iraq war, the result was not very satisfactory from an economic point of view. Over the years, every time that work took place on a project and was then deferred or cancelled as a result of the indirect impact of sanctions, the technocrats in the Ministry of Petroleum and the National Iranian Oil Company lost credibility and the religious hard-liners gained ground. I feel that after many years of trying, we in the West have got the govern-ment in Iran that we deserve, having undermined the economic growth of a great country and simply concentrated economic power in the hands of the government. Economic growth and a more liberal approach would eventually have swept the extremists aside. Unfortunately, driven by sanctions and a hard line, the movement has all been in the other direction. Having said that, the current oil sanctions and the collapse of the Iranian Riyal is causing unrest and loss of credibility for the govern-ment. It does so at the cost of real hardship for the people and does not endear the West to them. There was a moment of hope in the early days of the Obama administration, but that stalled. The recent interim agree-ment with President Hassan Rouhani offers a new if faint hope.

In 1997, Gholamreza Agazadeh ceased to be Minister of Petroleum. He became head of Iran's Atomic Energy Organisation, a post he held until 2009, when he left, possibly due to disagreements with the govern-ment. I am sure that the greetings cards I used to send him there for the Iranian New Year or Nowruz were duly noted by the security services. I

---

2 The whole question of government surveillance of private communications has become a matter of public discussion since the revelations made in 2013 by former NSA employee Edward Snowden, but the practice was certainly no great secret in the 1990s.

wonder whether they also noted the delightful cards that I would receive at Christmas from Iranian colleagues in the National Iranian Oil Company or the government, with the inscription 'Greetings on the Birthday of the Prophet Jesus, Peace Be Upon Him'.

I am under no illusions about the sometimes malevolent intentions of the Iranian government and their support for terrorism in Iraq and Lebanon. I also do not welcome the thought of Iran having a nuclear weapon. At the risk of being reminded of Chamberlain and Munich and being called an appeaser, I do think that our policy of obstruction and isolation rather than engagement and offering carrots has had very unfortunate consequences. It is perhaps only the bitter experiences of Iraq and Afghanistan that prevent us from sliding steadily down a slippery slope to military intervention, a euphemism for war.

The lessons of Iraq

To me the lessons of Iraq are not that it was wrong ever to contemplate the removal of Saddam Hussein, or even that the invasion was predicated on inadequate or over-hyped intelligence on weapons of mass destruction that was used by the then Prime Minister Tony Blair to drive the case through parliament, suborning people and ministers such as Clare Short on the way. It is that we went into the war after years of neglecting the preparatory work in the region that would have won us support.

This is not a new view. In an interview in the *Guardian* on 11 January 2003, speaking of the expected invasion, Terry Macalister quotes me as saying

> I had dinner some weeks ago with people from Saudi Arabia and Bahrain, and they all agreed that the war and the protests on their streets would be over quickly. But all unanimously said it would lead into another ditch of deep, deep despair and deep feelings of injustice—and we all know what that brings. It's a recipe for disaster. It [the impact of conflict over Iraq] brings tears to your eyes. It's a part of the world that I am very fond of and I find the whole thing extremely worrying.

Macalister goes on to say correctly that 'he clearly has no love of Saddam Hussein—whom he firmly believes needs to be dealt with in some way— nor is he a pacifist' and again quotes me: 'You have to keep an army, and as far as I am concerned you want the best possible people involved in that army.' This last statement is in fact a repetition of a view often expressed to me by my wife Judy, who as a committed Quaker might be expected to be a pacifist.

The problem was that for years we had let the Israeli–Palestinian conflict fester without bringing the strong pressure necessary for a solution. We had progressively demonised countries such as Iran, culminating in George W. Bush's declaration in his 2002 State of the Union speech that Iran, along with Iraq and North Korea, were part of an 'axis of evil'.

At the World Economic Forum in Davos in January 2003, US Secretary of State Colin Powell made a speech giving the official US line on the pending invasion of Iraq. He made plain the need to deal with Saddam Hussein's persistent violation of UN resolutions and spoke with passion of the need to build trust and of the values that both he personally and the United States espoused. Before his speech, some of my NGO friends, who are normally extremely well informed, told me that there would be four questions from the floor allowed after the speech. One would be from the former Archbishop of Canterbury George Carey, one from the Secretary-General of Amnesty and one would be taken from a business person. Would I ask a question and say that war with Iraq would be bad for business? I said that I would be happy to say why I thought the invasion of Iraq was a very bad idea, but I could not simply say it was bad for business—war tends to have differential impacts on business. In the event, although I tried to ask a question, Klaus Schwab,[3] whom I have known for many years, either did not see me or choose to call on me. Judy accuses me of excessive bashfulness and lack of sufficient energy in standing up, waving my arm and generally calling attention to myself on such occasions. Whatever the reason I wrote a personal letter to Colin Powell after the Davos meeting (Figure 4.1).

3 The founder and Chairman of the World Economic Forum.

Sir Mark Moody-Stuart KCMG

9, Gun House,
122, Wapping High Street,
London E1W 2NL

Tel. 020-7702 4456
Fax 020-7265 1535
markmoodystuart@aol.com

General Colin Powell,
Secretary of State,
United States of America

By fax 1(202) 261-8577

1st February, 2003

Dear Mr Secretary,

Please forgive me for writing to you direct, but I take the liberty of so doing as I was one of the many business people in the audience at Davos for your moving and heartfelt address. I would like to make a suggestion as to a way forward in the Middle East. Given the opportunity I would have made it during the Davos session in the form of a question.

There is no doubt that the world owes a great deal to the United States for its values and for the way in which those values have been projected and supported around the world over many decades. There are over a billion people in countries from Algeria through Iran and Pakistan to Indonesia, very many of whom are no friends of Saddam Hussein nor respecters of Yasser Arafat. Many of these people aspire to values not far from those of the United States, seek greater popular involvement with government and would gladly educate their daughters. I had a private dinner with the then oil Minister Agazadeh of Iran just as the Taliban took Kabul and heard him in answer to my question describe the Taliban as barbarians, and he and his colleagues condemn the removal of girls from school and women doctors from hospitals as un-Islamic. He also remarked with foresight that the West would have great trouble with the Taliban in time. The point is that many of these people, together with those in the West who can empathise with them, are potential allies on the question of values, not enemies. The problem is that if a war with Iraq proceeds now, there will be a deep feeling of inequity in the hearts of these people, coupled with a further loss of trust.

This feeling of inequity or double standards comes, of course, from the situation in Israel and Palestine, which you addressed in your speech. As you so eloquently pointed out, the key to the way forward is trust.

There is a total lack of trust between the parties in the Israel-Palestine situation, with reasons good and bad on both sides. I believe that a solution can never be found when two parties are in dispute and one of the parties is also the referee of the dispute, and the judge and enforcer of the agreements. The situation in Northern Ireland made no progress while one of the parties regarded the British government – the referee and on the ground enforcer - as a party to the dispute and a biased one at that. Progress was only made by building trust through the intervention of the United

States and the Republic of Ireland, unpalatable as that was to many in Britain at the time.

In the case of Israel and Palestine a trusted, independent, on the ground force is needed as arbiter, removing Israel from the role of enforcer of the border and the occupied territories. The United States is the only country who can start this process. It would not be popular with the government of Israel. It might well have electoral risks for the Administration – although last year in Davos in New York I heard President Clinton muse that this might become necessary one day. It could cost lives of the enforcers on the ground. For reasons of trust and practicality, it could not be done by the United States alone. Israel owes its existence to the UN and a UN role in such a body would be justified, perhaps with forces from countries such as Turkey as well as the European Union.

If the United States could commence credible action in this direction before a war in Iraq, I believe the situation would be transformed. Trust would be built and many of those who would feel deeply concerned at an invasion of Iraq today would swing behind the United States and be supportive of justified action in Iraq. No one would expect an early solution, or complete peace, but in three to six months real progress could be made in the building of trust and an international framework within which an effective Palestinian Authority could begin to grow.

Such action led by the United States would transform the situation in the Middle East. I believe it would save lives, although it would not be without risk to lives. Feelings of injustice and accusations of double standards - so damaging to the spread of the values the United States holds dear – would be dramatically reduced. Trust would be built, a real basis for long term changes in the Middle East.

Mr Secretary, I do not expect a reply to this letter or to my suggestion. Please take it in the spirit in which it is offered, from a friend and admirer of the United States who has had long relations with people from all parts of the Middle East. Whatever the United States does, I thank you for the enlightened and principled role which you personally play in it.

Yours sincerely,

Mark Moody Stuart.

Mark Moody-Stuart

Figure 4.1 **Letter to Colin Powell, US Secretary of State, 2003**

2

The discussion with Gholamreza Agazadeh to which the letter refers was after a dinner of several courses of fish washed down with orange juice (a safe menu for Iranian officials if halal meat cannot be guaranteed) in Claridges in London in 1996. I asked Agazadeh what he thought of the situation in Afghanistan, where the Taliban had just taken Kabul. We had finished the dinner and also exhausted all our business discussions. The question was a delicate one for a businessman to a minister. He might well have thanked me for the dinner and left, but he launched into an attack on the barbarity of the Taliban and the fact that this did not represent Islam. He and his team clearly told each other horror stories in Farsi. I asked him who he thought funded the Taliban. He said, unfortunately accurately, that the Saudis were doing so. It was suggested that the Baha'i were probably also involved, to which I demurred saying that I had at least one good Baha'i friend, Jyoti Munsiff. Jyoti was the Shell company secretary and one of the most senior lawyers, and I said that I knew that Baha'i support for the Taliban was implausible as well as incompatible with their faith. Unfortunately prejudice against the Baha'i in Iran is very strong. Agazadeh's parting words to me were that the West often viewed Iranians as unreasonable, but that we had not seen anything yet—the West would have big trouble with the Taliban. In this he did indeed prove to be more prescient than many in the west.

The question of Israel and Palestine to which I refer in the letter is one that bedevils relations in the region. It is of course used by Iran and Arab regimes to divert attention from their own shortcomings, using an emotional external issue to divert attention from internal problems. However, it does require solution and I see little chance of it being solved when one of the parties, Israel, acts as both a participant in any agreement and also as the referee responsible for adjudicating any breaches of the agreement. However difficult it may be, third-party involvement is essential, with the necessary guarantees of the integrity and existence of both Israel and Palestine. The present situation is corrosive to the values of the state of Israel and is ultimately unsustainable.

I did get a response to my letter (see Figure 4.2), but it does not in any way address the question of the invasion.

In the case of Shell, there was another incident in 2000 involving Iran and the United States. At that time, transport fuel demand in Iran was

United States Department of State

Washington, D.C. 20520

FEB 1 1 2003

Dear Sir Mark,

Thank you for your letter of February 1, 2003 in which you proposed a way to reinvigorate the peace process in the Middle East. Secretary Powell's office has asked me to respond.

The United States remains committed to President Bush's vision of two states—Israel and Palestine—living side by side in peace and security. Our goal is to help the parties renew a political process that will bring hope to Palestinians and Israelis alike. The current atmosphere of violence and terror makes this increasingly difficult. Both sides must take steps to build trust and demonstrate that they are prepared to seek a peaceful resolution.

We believe that third party monitoring, such as you have suggested, could be useful if both sides agree to such a function. Previous statements by the Quartet noted that the U.S., United Nations, European Union, and Russia stand ready to assist the parties in implementing their agreements, including a third-party monitoring system. The Mitchell committee report also includes a role for monitors. Though nothing has been decided, we will continue to look at this issue with our partners in the Quartet.

We share your concern about the violence in the region. The road to peace is long and arduous, but possible. The United States will continue to work with all responsible parties to reach a solution that will ensure a lasting peace.

Sincerely,

David Satterfield
Deputy Assistant Secretary
Near Eastern Affairs

Sir Mark Moody-Stuart
    9, Gun House,
        122 Wapping High Street
            London, United Kingdom

Figure 4.2 **Reply to letter to Colin Powell, US Secretary of State, 2003**

increasing rapidly and the country's refineries were not sophisticated enough to convert a high percentage of Iranian crude into transport fuels. So Abadan refinery, which had once been one of the largest and most sophisticated refineries in the world, was producing large quantities of 'straight-run' fuel oil. This is crude oil that has only been lightly treated to extract the transport fuels. Since it has had valuable lighter products removed, such fuel oil is worth less than the crude from which it originates, yet when put through a very sophisticated refinery such as Shell's Pulau Bukom refinery in Singapore it can be upgraded to quality fuels at an attractive margin. Every ten days or so a Shell tanker would pick up a load of this straight-run fuel oil from Abadan refinery and take it to Singapore.

In April 2000 the Shell 300,000 ton tanker *Myrina* was loading such a cargo from the port of Bandar Mahshahr at the head of the Gulf in Iran. Due to water depth at the port, the cargo had to be shuttled out to the big tanker in smaller 60,000 ton tankers. One of these was a Greek tanker on time charter, the other a Russian tanker *Akademik Pustovoit*. As the Russian tanker was taking its last load to the *Myrina*, the US Navy ship policing the UN sanctions on Iraq approached the *Myrina* and told her to depart immediately without contacting the *Akademik Pustovoit* as the latter was about to be arrested for smuggling Iraqi fuel oil. The *Myrina* duly left for Singapore with her cargo, topping up at the Saudi terminal of Ras Tanura on the way.

At that time there was a well-established smuggling trade involving barges of Iraqi fuel oil being taken through Iranian coastal waters with the connivance or involvement of the Iranian Revolutionary Guard to Dubai, where the fuel oil would be sold into the international bunker market. Indeed, if the US Navy ship had refuelled in the Gulf, the chances were that she had some Iraqi oil in her bunkers. The US Navy took the *Akademik Pustovoit* to a southern Gulf port, naturally over the strong objections of the Russian government. We were told we could have the cargo back if we paid $2 million within a short time, failing which the cargo would be confiscated and auctioned. This was not a difficult decision to take as the cargo was worth a great deal more than $2 million.

I must admit that when I was informed of this, I assumed that the US Navy had some concrete evidence of a violation. Perhaps there were satellite pictures of the Russian tanker loading some Iraqi fuel oil from a barge for bunkers. We knew that the main product had been loaded in Iran; such things are carefully and independently witnessed for quantity and paired samples kept by buyer and seller in case of a dispute on quality. There was of course a great deal of adverse publicity about a Shell tanker being potentially involved in sanctions breaking. We soon discovered that the US Navy claim was that the entire cargo from Abadan refinery contained Iraqi oil. The conclusion was based on a quick analysis carried out on board the US Navy vessel. This seemed unlikely and became even less plausible when the Iranians, who were understandably indignant, offered to give us data on the exact diet of crude oils on which the refinery had been run and also samples of crude from any the Iranian fields involved for which Shell did not already have samples. As the Iranians do not normally volunteer a great deal of detailed information, it seemed probable that they did indeed have nothing to hide. After careful fingerprinting of all the crudes and the product, the conclusion of the Shell laboratories was that the product did match the Iranian crudes, although some of these are not unlike neighbouring Iraqi crudes.

Armed with this analysis, Shell requested a meeting with the US technical experts so that a comparison of results could be made and any misunderstanding clarified. However, we were told that the US technique was classified and could not therefore be disclosed, so scientific discussion was not possible. This was very unsatisfactory in the light of all the negative publicity Shell had received. After prolonged efforts, in the final days of the Clinton administration we did receive an official statement that Shell was in no way involved in any improper activity. This was some consolation, although I personally found the proximity to the infamous pardoning by Clinton of Marc Rich uncomfortable.[4] Of course the damage had been done. A quick search of the Internet will only give you the story that Shell was 'fined' $2 million in connection

---

4 Marc Rich was a well-known oil trader wanted in the US for tax evasion. He made significant donations to the Clinton Library and was pardoned by President Clinton at the end of his second term as President. Marc Rich Associates evolved into the trading house Glencore. Marc Rich died in Switzerland in 2013.

with the event. The $2 million has never been refunded, although I have suggested that if a refund was difficult it might be donated to charity.

There was a sequel. Some months later a Shell tanker involved in the same trade was stopped by the US Navy. A sample was taken of its Iranian cargo—also from Abadan refinery. An onboard analysis by the apparently classified technique was carried out and the cargo declared to be clear and to everyone's relief the Shell tanker was allowed to proceed to Singapore. A subsequent analysis by Shell laboratories produced a similar fingerprint to that of the originally offending cargo.

The case of Syria

Syria is another example of a country where I believe a different approach might have led to a different outcome. Shell was involved in the private-sector development of the Syrian oil industry, building production in the 1990s from the very low levels that had been achieved by the Syrian Petroleum Company, the national oil company, to some 400,000 barrels a day. This operation had originally been started by Shell Oil, the US Shell affiliate that, under a curious internal Shell arrangement, continued to operate largely independently even after the buyout of the minority shareholders. Shell Oil even had its own overseas exploration and production arm. Shell Oil's involvement in Syria came to an end under the pressure of US sanctions, and the operation was taken over and developed by the main Shell entity outside the United States. I was a frequent visitor to Damascus, as our operating agreement there was not without its challenges, both technical and political. One could see the positive impact of the slow and cautious opening up of the economy by President Hafez al-Assad after the collapse of the Soviet Union, of which Syria had been a client state. Mindful of the chaos that had resulted in the aftermath of the Soviet Union and doubtless of the destabilising effects of such liberalisation on his own regime, Assad was very cautious about further opening of the economy. An unintended consequence of the negative and sanction prone approach of the United States was to reinforce this cautious approach. I believe that, had the West wholeheartedly embraced investment in the Syrian economy, the resulting economic liberalisation would have spread to other areas of society. As it was, the economy as well as the security levers of power remained in the grip of the military and the Assad regime.

Initially, Hafez al-Assad's son Bashar al-Assad was considered by observers in the West to be much more liberal and indeed the economy did develop and normalise somewhat further. I believe that such normalisation was slower than it would have been in the absence of continued efforts by the United States to block foreign investment and to discourage foreign companies from participating in the Syrian economy. Economic power remained concentrated in the hands of individuals connected to the ruling group, including the military. This economic concentration has in itself been a source of protest. Wherever there has been extensive public protest it has been met by oppression. Levels of violence by government forces, including attacks on civilians and indiscriminate shelling and bombing of towns, have reached previously unimaginable levels beyond any conceivably acceptable norm. Opposition forces are divided and have also been guilty of human rights abuses. There is now a full-scale civil war. Clearly, any initial hopes of liberalisation by Bashar al-Assad have been completely dashed. It is not clear whether he is really in control of the government, but whatever the case he clearly bears responsibility. In the meantime there is little that the West is prepared to do except to step up various sorts of sanction. Military intervention would be much more difficult than was the case in Libya, although surely there must come a time when some action to mitigate the slaughter of civilians will have to be taken. This moment appeared to be approaching with the apparent use of chemical weapons by the Assad regime or its supporters. As a result of an apparently chance remark by the US Secretary of State and follow-up by Russia, an agreement has been reached to inspect and then destroy all Syrian chemical weapons. One wonders whether ongoing dialogue rather than continuous condemnation might not have led to an earlier and different outcome; the United States has not even had an ambassador in Syria for some years.

An International Criminal Court indictment of Bashar al-Assad is no more likely to have a positive impact on the situation than did that of

President Omar al-Bashir of Sudan; whatever the judicial arguments, such indictments simply increase the support within a country from those who feel that this is outside interference and increase the incentive of the person indicted to stay in power.

I have no solution to propose to the present appalling situation; the point I wish to make is that had a policy of economic and political engagement been followed for the last ten or fifteen years, as opposed to isolation and sanctions, the present situation might have been very different. Although it is difficult to prove, I do believe that an alternative approach could have led to a different outcome. Had there been more Western engagement and investment by international companies, the economy would have been further diversified and the economic concentration of the ruling elite somewhat diluted. There might still have been an autocratic regime in power, but with perhaps some hope of gradual improvement in governance and human rights with the economic liberalisation. Perhaps as a result the response to protest might have been different and the present tragedy averted. At any rate the situation could not have been worse than it is now, with millions of Syrian citizens having fled across borders to neighbouring countries. I am sure that a great majority of these greatly regret the collapse of the previous status quo, with its shortcomings.

Each case and country is different. Libya has been cited as a success of the pressure resulting in change. Colonel Qaddafi accepted the bargain of forgoing nuclear power in exchange for a lifting of sanctions. The resulting opening of the economy had started. However, such things take tens of years to have effects and at the time of the uprisings any effects had yet to be really felt. The overthrow of Qaddafi in Libya has been driven by Libyans internally. The outside world did lend essential military air support, which undoubtedly tipped the balance of power, but it has been the bravery and sacrifices of the Libyans that has delivered the changes.

Many would argue that Egypt has demonstrated that a supportive approach merely props up the existing regime. Was not the Mubarak regime corrupt and guilty of human rights abuses and apparently intent on simply entrenching the approach through nepotistic succession? That is certainly the case but, perhaps partly as a result of such a policy pursued over decades, when the population demanded change, the result, at least superficially, was very different. Again it is difficult to demonstrate cause and effect. And while there has certainly been change in Egypt it is too early to tell the final outcome. It is likely to take ten years or more before some of the necessary changes are embedded. An analogy would perhaps be the radical changes that took place over the years in Spain after Franco's death in 1975. In the meantime, in Egypt and elsewhere in the region I hope that responsible foreign and national businesses will be growing the economy and putting in place practices in their own operations and in their relations with society that support the changes needed.

In the case of Egypt, not only was the economy somewhat open to investment, but there was also massive support from the United States in the form of military and other aid. It does seem that, in the interests of stability, insufficient pressure was applied through conditions on the flow of aid. A careful balance of carrot and stick might be the most effective. As a business person, being part of the carrot is of course preferable. A balanced approach might be to encourage investment and opening of the economy while putting tough conditions on any aid provided. At the same time any sanctions should be very carefully targeted at individuals and in turn have clear conditions attached.

Although many would argue that the analogy is invalid and inappropriate, such an approach could be applied to Israel. Israel is a democratic country with many admirable and liberal aspects. Israel has ample cause to fear aggression by its neighbours, but Israel's continued building of settlements in the occupied Palestinian West Bank is an unacceptable block to any lasting and just two-state solution to the Israeli/ Palestinian problem. President Obama has demanded that there be a freeze on settlement building. Prime Minister Binyamin Netanyahu has equally firmly rejected Obama's demand. This rejection has done much damage to President Obama's credibility in the Middle East. Rationally it would seem that a demand to cease settlement building should have been clearly linked to the continued supply of the large amounts of military aid flowing from the US to Israel. Rational as such a proposal may be, for electoral reasons such a linkage is unfortunately very unlikely to be made by any US president seeking re-election. It is at least something that President Obama should be considering in his second term. There is a renewed effort at face-to-face negotiations, strongly promoted by Secretary of State John Kerry, but at the same time the Israeli government has just approved the building of more illegal settlements.

Relevance to Burma/Myanmar

Burma/Myanmar has been under one or other form of sanction for a number of years. The desire to apply sanctions, just to do something, is understandable. The regime is geriatric and inward-looking with a determination to hang on to power at all costs. They have responded to peaceful protest with violent oppression without any respect for the human rights of the protesters. The government response to the devastating cyclone that struck Burma in 2008 demonstrated its complete inability to provide basic services to its people; the only effective response came from international agencies, civil society organisations and companies. The military junta kept Aung San Suu Kyi, leader of the National League for Democracy (NLD), which won the 1990 elections, under house arrest for about three-quarters of the last two decades, in spite of her calm, determined non-violent approach in opposition. They refused to give her terminally ill husband a visa to visit her, insisting that if she wanted to see him she should leave the country, an offer she refused as she believed with good cause that she would then not be allowed to return. The military junta were trapped in a system and I believe saw little way out.

During much of the last 20 years Burma has been the subject of generally tightening sanctions from the United States and the European Union. The initial sanctions were related to arms but gradually spread to exports of other materials. The sanctions have always been opposed by the members of the Association of Southeast Asian Nations (ASEAN). During 20 years of isolation the Burmese economy has stagnated and ossified. Little had changed until very recently, although an optimist could point to a few signs of a modest movement towards liberalisation by the government. There were elections in November 2010 that were heavily criticised by the West and that were won by the Union Solidarity and Development Party (USDP); the NLD boycotted the elections. Aung San Suu Kyi was not allowed to take part. The USDP did not win all the seats, so although the military remain in effective control there are some seats held by opposition parties.

It is certainly legitimate to ask whether sanctions have been the right tool or whether the process of engagement and investment coupled with advice followed by the ASEAN nations has been the more productive. Have sanctions done more than make an isolated and reviled government more inclined to stay in power? In spite of the sanctions and campaigns against them some Western companies remained active in Burma in hydrocarbon production, the French company Total being the most notable. Total produces gas from offshore production and the gas is exported by pipeline to Thailand. Total has been under strident attack over the construction of the onshore section of the pipeline and the oppression by the military of the Karen tribes though whose homeland the pipeline passes.

Once it emerges from the sea, the pipeline from the offshore gas fields traverses a stretch of Burmese territory close to the Thai border and then crosses into Thailand where the gas is sold. The population of the areas is historically opposed to the central government, and partly because of this but partly because of the need for security on the pipeline (there was a fatal attack on contractors working for Total) there is a significant military presence in the area. There is no doubt that the security forces have conscripted villagers to carry military equipment and requisitioned carts from the villagers. Although they do not consider themselves the cause of the malpractices, Total have paid compensation, making it plain to the villagers that they do not support this behaviour. Furthermore, they say that these incidents occurred mainly in the initial stages of the operation. In 2000, Total were early supporters of and signatories to the Voluntary Principles on Security and Human Rights, which as I described in Chapter 3 was developed by human rights organisations, responsible businesses and governments. The work in Burma predated the development of the principles, but it is exactly the kind of situation that the Voluntary Principles were developed to address.[5]

In the early 1990s, Shell did have an exploration programme in the onshore areas of Burma. At that time, through indirect contacts with the opposition groups, we understood that they did not object to this activity (before the recent liberalisation moves they had subsequently apparently expressed opposition to the offshore gas project). The Shell exploration onshore was unsuccessful and the permits lapsed. We did, however, examine the possibility of involvement in the offshore gas developments and considered the issue of the onshore section of the pipeline in Burma. Some of my colleagues considered that the risk of building a pipeline in heavily forested areas, whose population had historically been in opposition if not rebellion against the central government, was perhaps too high; I confess that I personally considered these risks manageable. In the event, we collectively decided against involvement because of commercial issues related to the potential gas sales contract to the Thai state company. Reading the published material, although there were clearly unfortunate and unexpected incidents in the early stages of pipeline construction, I think that Total's work is what you would expect a responsible company to do. Had the Voluntary Principles been developed at the time, perhaps even the early incidents could have been avoided. I think that the presence of Total and the community projects that they initiated even before construction began is a contribution not just to the physical well-being of the communities in the area but also supports their organisation and governance, building the means to decide on what priorities need to be addressed.

It now looks as though the government of Myanmar is at last embracing change. Elections have been held and Aung San Suu Kyi is free to

---

5 A very full report on the project and the work that Total does in relation to communities in the area is available on burma.total.com. A highly critical report from civil society groups is on resources.revenuewatch.org/fr/node/398. An excellent and independent web resource is available on www.business-humanrights.org/Categories/Individualcompanies/M/MyanmarOilGasEnterpriseMOGE. The Business and Human Rights website publishes in an impartial way both criticisms of businesses in the human rights field and also the responses of businesses.

travel. The United States and the European Union are re-engaging and sanctions are being eased. I even recently saw an interview with a government minister of the ruling faction extolling the principles of the UN Global Compact. All is not yet well and there are intractable ethnic conflicts in some areas, but I believe that there is hope for progressive change. I believe that there is a clear role for responsible companies in building the economy, operating to principles such as those of the UN Global Compact.

Some may claim this as a success for Western sanctions and isolation. Personally, I believe it is much more the product of trade and engagement with neighbouring countries in ASEAN and a desire of the government to participate fully in ASEAN growth and development. The ASEAN countries have been engaged and cooperative and yet have never hesitated to give critical advice. History will be the judge of which approach has been more effective.

Sudan, Talisman and changing views

To anyone interested in the rights and wrongs of companies operating in countries with unattractive regimes, the history of Talisman Energy in Sudan marks something of a turning point. Talisman was formed in 1992 out of BP's operations in Canada. As an independent company, Talisman expanded rapidly. In 1998, it acquired through Arakis Energy a 25% interest in an operation in Sudan. The other partners in the venture, the Greater Nile Petroleum Operating Company (GNPOC) were the Chinese state oil company China National Petroleum Corporation (CNPC) and the Malaysian state company Petronas, with a small Sudanese government share. Sudan at the time was in the grips of a civil war between the north and the now independent Republic of South Sudan.

There is no doubt that serious human rights abuses were committed by government forces attacking civilian populations as the war raged across many of the oil-producing areas. A report in 2000 by the Canadian Assessment Mission on Human Rights in Sudan makes miserable reading in detailing the human rights abuses inflicted on communities in the area and on the forced relocation of populations.[6] Although the oilfield facilities were used by government military aircraft, these were removed when requested by the oil companies. There is no evidence of any direct involvement by Talisman in such abuses, as was claimed by some NGOs who referred to the bombing of churches and the murder of civilians. Whether or not Talisman's purchase of an interest in an operation in such a disturbed area was wise, I have no doubt that, once there, the efforts of Talisman in supporting community development and medical care and in engaging constructively with the government had some ameliorating effects on a bad situation. Talisman was certainly more open to engagement and cooperation with civil society organisations than some of their Asian partners, reporting publicly on their activities. In the end, as a result of continued pressure by NGOs on investors and also continued pressure from the Canadian government, Talisman withdrew from Sudan in 2003 and sold its interest to the international arm of the largely government-owned Oil and Natural Gas Corporation (ONGC) of India.

Both Talisman and the international oil and gas industry have learned much from this episode. Talisman became involved at an early stage in the development of the Voluntary Principles on Security and Human Rights, which address so many of the issues of engagement with government and other security forces (see Box 2.1). Talisman is also an active signatory to the UN Global Compact. In that context, in a meeting in the UN Human Rights Commission held as part of the information-gathering process of John Ruggie, the UN Secretary-General's Special Representative on Business and Human Rights, I heard a representative of Talisman ask the assembled representatives of all the large human rights NGOs whether anyone had done a study to see whether the withdrawal of Talisman from Sudan had been beneficial or not. No one had done a study, but it was clear that no one from the NGO movement thought that Talisman's withdrawal had been beneficial. In a difficult situation it was clear that Talisman was open to constructive engagement and also did provide ameliorating actions. Probably for this reason, NGO calls

6 publications.gc.ca/site/eng/372916/publication.html.

for withdrawal in such situations are now fewer and the focus is more on what positive actions can be taken.

Shell also had operations in Sudan, but entirely in marketing and refining. The Port Sudan refinery dates from the early 1960s, a period of major global refinery construction in Shell, with refineries in Port Dickson, Malaysia and Karachi being part of the same wave. One day, when I was Chairman of Shell, I was rung by the late Sir Geoffrey Chandler[7] of Amnesty UK. He said that Amnesty, together with Pax Christi in the Netherlands, understood that Sudanese government helicopter gunships and Antonov bombers were being refuelled by Shell at Khartoum airport and that these aircraft were guilty of grave human rights abuses in the South. Furthermore, he felt that the separatist army probably had the greater justification on their side. My reply was that I thought it most unlikely that Shell was refuelling such aircraft, although I knew that we did have a facility at Khartoum airport that refuelled many relief and World Food Programme flights. I thanked Geoffrey for the warning and promised to enquire into the facts and to come back to him with an answer.

By the late 1990s, the Shell marketing operation was entirely run by Sudanese. I knew the Shell Country Chairman Mohamed Elshafie, a long-serving Shell employee. Mohamed had triggered some controversy with the mayor in Khartoum by employing young women as well as young men to serve at the pumps in service stations in Khartoum. There had even been a comment that Shell was using sex to sell its products. I had asked Mohamed whether he had taken this action because of Shell's equal opportunity principles or whether he did it because as a Sudanese

---

7 During his time in Shell as 'Trade Relations Coordinator', which later morphed into the more conventionally named Head of Public Affairs, the not yet knighted Geoffrey Chandler had been the architect in the 1970s of the original Shell 'General Business Principles'. After retiring from Shell he was a founder of Amnesty's business section. He made a great contribution to thinking in Shell. He was someone whom I knew and for whom I had a great deal of respect. In many ways his Shell career demonstrated the remarkable impact that a principled individual who is not at the very top of a company can have on that company, always assuming that colleagues and the leadership of the company are willing to listen and act. (See Chapters 11 and 12.)

and a Muslim he felt that it was the right thing to do. He reassured me that it was definitely the latter—the young women needed employment and they were good at the job. I knew that Mohamed had been engaged with the British Council in Khartoum in running workshops on human rights and on corruption. I considered Shell Sudan to be an outstanding example of a Shell operating company working in difficult circumstances and had said so at a Shell Annual General Meeting.

When I raised Geoffrey Chandler's accusation with Mohamed, he too was confident that it did not happen, but in his turn said he would investigate. After checking he confirmed that there was absolutely no instance of Shell's aviation operation in Khartoum fuelling Sudanese military aircraft. However, he said that we did have a contract to supply bulk fuel to the Sudanese government. He discovered that some of this fuel was being loaded onto barges and shipped to the South. There was thus every likelihood that it then found its way into military aircraft.

In discussions with Geoffrey Chandler we had agreed that Shell was not a pacifist organisation. I pointed out that in many countries the fact that the local Shell company supplies the military is a source of great pride to many Shell people who are nationals of the country. The question was therefore not one of the supply to the military, nor indeed any opinion as to which side in a civil war might have the greater justification. The question was whether or not the military concerned were guilty of systematic human rights abuses. Even on a quick read of the available information it was clear that serious abuses had taken place and appeared to be ongoing. Mohamed agreed that we did not want Shell fuel finding its way into aircraft that might be involved in abuses. He said that time was needed to achieve this and that if NGOs publicly paraded Shell's withdrawal this could rebound on Shell Sudanese staff, itself a human rights concern.

The NGOs involved agreed that there would be no publicity and indeed there was none. I reminded Sir Geoffrey that Shell ending the contract with the Sudanese government did not mean that the aircraft would suddenly be short of fuel, a reality that he readily acknowledged. In fact, with domestic oil exports growing, a new partly government-owned refinery was being developed and the government oil company was only too happy to take over a government contract from Shell. Disengagement was quick and relatively easy, which is by no means always the case.

It seems to me that this kind of interaction between a company and NGOs is a goal we should strive towards. NGOs will often become aware of issues before a company and the possibility should be there of raising it at a senior level, in a spirit of openness and reasonable mutual trust. The facts and the principles involved can then be discussed and a way forward agreed. In this case, this was clearly made easier as Sir Geoffrey Chandler had been the person who some 30 years before had drafted the first formal Shell Business Principles.

The discussion as to whether companies should remain engaged in a country is now much more nuanced. Many more people have come to recognise the benefits of responsible companies remaining engaged and the contributions that such companies can make. I believe that the UN Global Compact has a significant role to play in this, as discussed earlier, through the Global Compact Local Networks and initiatives such as the Principles for Responsible Investment (PRI). The Local Networks bring together large and small companies, domestic and international as well as civil society and labour organisations. In difficult and stressed countries they provide a principled framework for addressing complex issues, with some neutral cover provided by the UN connection. Furthermore, they provide a means for investors who are signatories to the PRI to see for themselves conditions on the ground and to assess the risks. The Ruggie Framework, with its three pillars of Protect, Respect and Remedy, is a valuable contribution to ensuring that all involved in this process, whether government, civil society or business, are aware of the challenges and responsibilities (see Chapter 3, Box 3.2).

I recently attended a small dinner at which Neil MacGregor, the Director of the British Museum, spoke with passion of the role of the Museum in building cultural ties across boundaries. The unifying love and respect for cultural objects, whatever their background, is something that unites not just academics and curators but people of all backgrounds across nations and ethnic groups. The Museum's excellent training programmes for museum staff from various countries helps to build this network through which communication continues even in times of diplomatic and political difficulty. The impact on relations of the loan of the British Museum's 2,500-year-old Cyrus Cylinder to Iran was considerable. This loan was arranged in spite of the diplomatic tensions and fears that once in Iran it might never be returned to the British Museum (although the Cylinder was originally found in the ruins of Babylon in modern Iraq and not in present-day Iran). This artefact of a great Persian king, with all its implications for freedom and respect for people, restoration of shrines and rebuilding the walls of a conquered city, is of great cultural and historical significance; the concepts resonate greatly with the founding narrative of Persia all the way to modern Iran.

A somewhat similar process can be seen when business people of different backgrounds get together. The enthusiasm for enterprise and recognition of what it takes for business relationships to flourish are uniting factors across the world. Just as in the case of the British Museum, whose right to hold items acquired at various points in history from different countries is questioned, so too the legitimacy of business to operate in certain areas is questioned. In spite of these controversies, there is a link through business that transcends politics. Properly regulated and conducted in a responsible and ethical manner, business provides something that every society needs, just as every society needs a cultural and artistic life. A recent example quoted at the Business for Peace launch meeting, at the UNGC Summit in New York in September 2013, by Diana Klein of International Alert is of companies from different countries in the Caucasus region getting together to build peace and to market sustainable products as 'Caucasus Products', regardless of their national origin. They adopted the slogan 'When we say Peace, we mean Business'.

Chapter 5

Dining with the devil:
Engaging with those guilty
of human rights abuses

Some time ago, I sat next to the late Mo Mowlam at a large public dinner, I think in the Mansion House in London in 2001. She had been
Northern Ireland Secretary at the time of the signing of the Good Friday Agreement in 1998, although she was replaced the following year
by Peter Mandelson. Because of her involvement in the negotiations in
Northern Ireland, we spoke of the challenges of relating at a human level
with people whose activities you personally find repugnant. In Northern
Ireland there were those on both sides of the negotiations to which this
would clearly apply. Somewhat to my surprise, Mo Mowlam said that
the Sinn Féin leader she could relate to most easily was Martin McGuinness. This surprised me because I had always, from a position of no
great familiarity with the details, regarded McGuinness as a hard man
who had in all probability been more directly connected to terrorism
than, for example, Gerry Adams, whatever their respective responsibilities might be. It had always seemed to me that Adams, at an intellectual
level, had been more nuanced in his approach and had indeed at times
taken some considerable physical risks from some on his own side. Mo
said that, on the contrary, while she could relate to McGuinness at a

basic human level, with him taking an interest in small, personal things, she found it difficult to penetrate Adams's cold reserve.

We agreed that in order to have any influence on a person, it is essential to establish a connection on an individual and human level. To sit stiffly emanating disapproval is simply a barrier to any progress.[1] While there can be no compromise on fundamental principles, in order to earn the right to express differing opinions, there has to have been human contact and, if not friendship, at least human empathy with some things that are important to the individual. Such things could be language, culture, the history and heritage of a country, or longer-term economic or societal goals. One cannot do this without any compromise at all; even such minor compromises can be stressful. This is what I term 'dining with the devil'—the mere proximity is potentially contaminating. Furthermore, as some people who had relatively close relations with Colonel Qaddafi in the period of détente before his brutal attempts to crush the popular uprising in Benghazi discovered, their probably good intentions can take on an unfortunate appearance with hindsight.

The fundamental question is whether a company, or indeed individuals within a company, can operate in a country without being forced to abandon their own principles or deviate from their own values. Even within my own country of Britain there are values that are quite pervasive in society, and at times in government, to which I do not subscribe. This only becomes a problem if the legal framework forces an individual to act against his or her principles. Recent examples in the UK include a couple taking overnight lodgers in their own home being prosecuted for not accepting single-sex couples, or adoption organisations run by the Catholic Church being refused licences due to unwillingness to accept that single-sex couples should be considered suitable adoptive parents. Personally, I have some difficulty with these examples of intolerance, but the line is difficult to draw. The recent controversy over gay marriage is a similar example. There are many people who are entirely in favour of single-sex civil partnerships and are indeed supportive of

---

1 Although I was not aware of it at the time, Martin Luther King is reported to have said, 'You have very little morally persuasive power with people who can feel your underlying contempt.'

such unions being blessed in church, but for whom the term 'marriage' remains something which by definition is heterosexual.

In the 1990s, Shell had a major operation producing oil in Syria. The late President Hafez al-Assad presided over an authoritarian government. As Shell's production in a Shell-operated joint venture with the state oil company increased, it was necessary to establish a relationship with the president. When discussing sometimes controversial contractual or regulatory issues, it was always prudent to enquire politely whether the government approach had been cleared by 'higher authority'. There was no need to mention the president by name, a simple roll of the eyes towards the ceiling sufficed. The reply would often be 'yes, by the highest authority' accompanied by a similar upward roll of the eyes. I recall a discussion with a minister with whom I was not only friendly, but for whom I had a great deal of respect. In Syria, listening devices were ubiquitous. The minister always had an official note-taker present in our discussions. In view of the listening devices, this seemed somewhat redundant to me, so one day I asked him why he bothered take notes—accompanying this with a roll of my eyes towards the chandelier. The reply was 'So that I have my own record', accompanied by a similar gesture.

Over time I became aware of many instances in which information clearly came from overall surveillance. Such systems generate so much information that they have their flaws. On arrival in a corporate jet at Damascus airport, I would be met by someone from the minister's office. Incidentally, I believe corporate jets are only worth the expense for places such as Damascus where one can leave Europe on Friday evening, work on the days following the Syrian Friday 'weekend' and be back in the office on Monday. They also enable the negotiating trick of announcing one's immediate departure and avoiding the counter-ploy of stretching negotiations until the imminent and unavoidable departure of the commercial flight. Being met by a government official speeds immigration, although when I asked how they knew the first names of my father and mother, as required on the landing card, the reply was always 'We just put Miriam and Abdullah'. I was always accommodated in the same room of the same hotel. The unnecessary suite had a large bathroom with a Jacuzzi, alongside which was a huge mirror. Being someone who prefers a shower, I always wondered, as I soaped and washed myself with a rather inadequate hand-held shower head, who might be watching from the other side of the mirror. Certainly private conversations were best conducted against a background of extremely loud television in Arabic, wandering in the delightful byways and small streets of Damascus, in the Umayyad Mosque with its stories of the heads of both John the Baptist and the Shi'a Imam Husayn ibn Ali, or contemplating the tomb of Salah ad-Din, the 12th-century Kurdish nemesis of the Crusaders on the Horns of Hattin. Apart from privacy, such places give one context and subjects of conversation for meetings.

At my first of several meetings with President Hafez al-Assad I was warned by the government protocol officer that I had an appointment of exactly 30 minutes. I mentioned to Assad that when I had lived in Malaysia I had been surprised to find both orthodox and catholic Suriyani Christians, whom Judy and I knew of from visiting Mardin in south-eastern Turkey. Assad said that he was familiar with the long-standing community of Suriyani in Kerala in southern India, traditionally said to have been founded by St Thomas. It is moving to hear a Suriyani liturgy in Aramaic, the language of Christ. For 45 minutes, we discussed various Christian sects and schisms. Assad was much amused by the nature of the schisms but well acquainted with the theology of groups ranging from Copts through Maronites to Suriyani. Although we spoke through an interpreter, Assad plainly spoke excellent English. This was revealed when he was explaining that the so-called monophysite heresy, to which the Suriyani adhere, is all a question of the composition of Christ's body. As the interpreter struggled with the words 'material' and 'composition', Assad interrupted with the English word 'substance', showing a remarkable familiarity with the formulation of the Christian Nicene Creed, drafted precisely in order to put an end to such differences of opinion by defining one side of the discussion as heretical.

After 45 minutes on such matters I was nervous that I was going to be ejected without having made a single point of relevance to the business. I need not have feared. A couple of hours later, to the chagrin of the officers of protocol, we were still at it. The former UK Foreign

Secretary Sir Malcolm Rifkind has said that one of his most unpleasant experiences was meeting Hafez al-Assad, who although he occasionally smiled with his lips never smiled with his eyes.[2] This was absolutely not my experience. Assad had not only a lively sense of humour, but a very large intellect behind his towering forehead. This is not to in any way forgive or forget the massacres of Hama some years before where an almost inconceivable 20,000 people are believed to have died. Hama was shelled as a rebellion by the Muslim Brotherhood was brutally suppressed. The secular Assad regime was as opposed to the Muslim Brotherhood as was the Mubarak regime in Egypt. Hama is a beautiful city with ancient water wheels lifting water to irrigate gardens along the banks of the Orontes River, known in modern Syria as 'the rebel' as it flows south to north in contrast to the other major rivers in the region such as the Tigris, Euphrates and even the Jordan. The tragedy is that Bashar al-Assad, the son of Hafez, has led a government even more prepared to use indiscriminate force against civilians and which has developed in a way that makes his father's actions seem almost restrained in comparison.

There were two issues that I raised every time that I had a meeting with President Assad. The first was the question of salaries for Syrian engineers working for the 50/50 venture between Shell and the national Syrian Petroleum Company (SPC). During the exploration phase, work was conducted by a company fully owned and operated by Shell. We were free to pay Syrian engineers in this company at reasonable rates. These would not be as high as salaries for similar experience in the Gulf, but as many Syrian engineers preferred to stay in their own beautiful country in contact with their families and able to benefit from the high-quality and long-established educational system, this was not a competitive necessity. On the other hand, the bulk of the Syrian engineers in the production company came from SPC and were paid essentially on Syrian civil service scales. Expatriates from many different Shell operations around the world were paid international rates. The result was that a

2 M. Rifkind, 'An Economic Blockade Can Defeat President Bashar al-Assad', *Daily Telegraph*, 14 February 2012.

young Syrian engineer fresh out of university would work for the joint venture company for three or four years, gaining experience and training at international levels unachievable in SPC and then, just as they were really valuable and needed for more senior jobs, they would leave and get a job in the Gulf. I would point out to the President that we needed to pay able Syrian engineers and geologists about five times as much as the civil service scales and approach permitted. The President would then explain to me that neither he nor the public had any difficulty with private-sector salaries being much higher than the state sector. For example, there were a few state-run shops, but he acknowledged that these were hopelessly inefficient and unattractive and of course the private sector paid more in this area. Retail was generally regarded as being a private-sector activity in Syria, even if there was the odd state outlet. Oil, however, was different. This was a national asset and it was not generally accepted that this could be a private-sector activity. Furthermore, if the salaries of young engineers were raised, the next day the professors who had taught them at university would be in his office saying that surely they should be similarly paid. Shortly after that he could expect the school teachers. One could certainly see the problem—such are indeed the strains of a market economy—but I pointed out to the President that a Syrian engineer could go to Egypt and work for the Shell joint venture there and be paid as an expatriate. At the same time, an Egyptian engineer working for the Shell joint venture in the Western Desert, which suffered from a similar inflexible structure, could work as an expatriate for Shell in Syria. Some simple adjustments would keep both at home and contributing to their own national development.

It was only possible to take small steps towards resolving the issue. The President suggested that we send promising engineers for training internationally and pay them good allowances. I said that we already did that, knowing that in two or three months of technical training in the Shell research laboratories in the Netherlands an engineer eating a decent lunch provided on the job and living carefully could save allowances probably amounting to a year's salary. But this did not solve the problem—the engineer was then even better qualified for a job outside Syria. At this the President admonished the minister present to ensure that the full force of the law be applied to people breaking their contracts. This led to a discussion on the free movement of people and the fact that we in Shell did not use unwilling conscripts. At such times the basic control system of the regime showed through, as it did when a minister whom I knew well and respected remarked to me that if I made a mess of my job, I would be fired, while if he made a similar mess he and his family would lose a great deal more.

The other regular topic of discussion was the development of the economy. Syria had been a client state of the Soviet Union and many senior people had been trained in Russia. With the end of the cold war, Soviet support and investment in projects such as a major power station had collapsed. There was however a cautious liberalisation of the economy. The first steps were freeing up the imports of electrical white goods and the like. One could sense the stirrings of economic growth and activity together with some increase in freedom of expression. As in many such economies, if there was a good harvest this also had a visible positive impact on the economy. When one commented on such changes, the president took obvious delight in the feeling that economic progress was being made. However, that progress was very modest; much of the import activity came via the military in Lebanon, benefitting mainly senior officers. Removal of stifling government bureaucracy was glacially slow. I suggested that, although one could see changes, unless progress was accelerated, when peace at last came to the region through some progress in the Israeli–Palestinian (and of course Syrian) situation and borders were opened, neighbours such as Jordan and eventually Israel would be in much a better position to benefit. Liberalisation of manufacturing was needed, as was foreign investment in areas other than simply oil. At this President Assad would always point to the collapse of the Soviet Union and the chaos that resulted if markets were unleashed and changes made too quickly. In his view, better to have incremental change than chaos. This is a strategy that works unless change is so slow that widespread frustration breaks out and demands faster and much more radical change.

Did these conversations with President Assad have any effect? I would like to think so, even if small. The growth of production from the Shell joint venture to 400,000 barrels a day during the period, compared to the some 100,000 barrels a day that came from SPC's historical stand-alone operations meant that we certainly had the President's attention. A highly intelligent and analytical person such as President Assad must surely have pondered on what might make the difference between an essentially Soviet and totalitarian approach as opposed to a liberal free-market one, given that both were largely carried out by Syrian nationals with similar educational backgrounds. The caution on the danger of chaos was ever present, coupled no doubt with an underlying dynastic concern linked also to the preservation of the dominance of the Assads' Alawite minority group. Such caution is increased if there is an impression that the world is seeking to isolate your country, hold back its development and seek its downfall; such an impression is naturally heightened by any sanctions, and there had been sanctions of one sort or another on Syria for many years.

There was one occasion where I think that I did have an effect. The oil minister, Dr Nader Nabulsi, with whom we had worked for a long time, was removed and placed under house arrest. Dr Nabulsi was an able engineer who had been chairman on behalf of the government of the Shell joint venture and had then been appointed minister. He was a very effective man and was always supportive of efforts to raise efficiency. The apparent cause of his removal and arrest was an issue related to foreign exchange. There was no doubt that there had been serious mis-application of foreign exchange regulations, but it was also clear that, if he had any part at all, Dr Nabulsi's involvement would have been minor. It was obvious to anyone interested that there were clearly other actors who had played a major part and benefited greatly financially. These people remained untouched and apparently immune.

Somewhat similar to the system in the former Soviet Union, in Syria there were many laws, often conflicting with each other. In both systems this meant that almost every individual could be demonstrated to be guilty of breaching some law. There is no doubt that with government salaries being extremely low many public servants had various other forms of income. But certainly as far as our joint venture was concerned Dr Nabulsi shared our own standards in relation to transparency, proper award of contracts and conflicts of interest.

On a visit to Syria just after this sudden change had happened, President Assad asked me what I thought of the change of minister. Dr Nabulsi had often been present at my meetings with the President. I replied that it was the Syrian government's sovereign right to change ministers and that that was not for me to comment on. I did, however, say that I thought that both Syria and Shell owed a great debt to Dr Nabulsi. Without his efforts and guidance, the target of 400,000 barrels a day would never have been reached. To this President Assad asked whether therefore Dr Nabulsi should be allowed to retire in peace. I said that this was indeed an excellent idea. The President then said that the problem was that Dr Nabulsi was a very active man and he might not wish to retire in peace. I said that I was quite confident that if the President suggested it, I was sure that Dr Nabulsi would indeed retire peacefully. Although Dr Nabulsi was then released and allowed to travel, it was still a great loss, as he was a very effective engineer and a good minister.

In our relations with the Syrian government there were often long, unresolved differences of opinion. For example, there were continued disputes on cost recovery under the terms of the production-sharing joint venture, with the government reserving its position in spite of repeated third-party audits by international audit firms. Under the terms of the agreement we were actually systematically reimbursed for the expenditures as they occurred, but subject to subsequent revision; however, long after an oilfield was in production for all to see, potential claims for hundreds of millions of dollars of capital expenditure would be outstanding. These claims were kept on one side, as if in a cupboard, while work went on as normal. If things went well, a few claims would be taken out of the cupboard and settled. If the government wished to show displeasure, a claim would be taken out of the cupboard and the heat of the argument turned up a few notches. In a discussion with Dr Nabulsi's predecessor, the minister remarked how well everything was going. Production was rising, the oil price was good and the rains had meant a good crop and the weather was beautiful. What could be better? Why did I keep worrying about these outstanding claims? After all, we were being paid. To this I said that although everything appeared normal, the situation was in reality untenable. I promised to bring the minister a present of a picture by a well-known Dutch artist on my next visit. At this, a Dutch colleague living in Syria began to laugh as he guessed to which artist to whom I was referring. On my next visit I brought the minister and several other members of the government presents of framed prints of different examples of M.C. Escher's 'impossible realities', showing people walking up and down stairs on ramparts in impossible continuity, or the continuous waterfall or the morphing of fish into ducks. I think only Dr Nabulsi actually hung my present on the wall of his office.

In 2000, Hafez al-Assad's 30-year rule came to an end with his death and he was succeeded by his second son Bashar, the elder son and heir apparent Basil having been killed in a car crash in 1994. There was much hope that Bashar, who had been a medical practitioner in the UK and not being of a military turn of mind, would progress liberalisation of both the economy and of society. Clear initial steps in this direction faltered. The Arab Spring in Tunisia and Egypt in early 2011 encouraged demonstrations in Syria as well. The response has been a brutal and continued suppression of protests in cities all over Syria. It was not initially clear whether Bashar al-Assad was in control or whether the oppressive actions were effectively forced on him by powerful people around him. This placed the Shell joint venture in an increasingly uncomfortable position.

I ask myself whether the approach that we in Shell and I personally took in the 1990s made the present situation more or less likely. I believe that the growth of the private-sector oil economy, the financial benefits that it brought to the country as a whole as well as the infrastructure and capacity building which it contributed to were beneficial. As I have written in earlier chapters, I believe that if the world, and the West in particular, had encouraged continued trade and economic liberalisation, this could have been linked to and encouraged political liberalisation. That is the conclusion I have drawn from observing such developments over the years, but I freely admit that it remains a matter of opinion rather than of provable fact.

So what should Shell do in such circumstances? I hasten to say that I was not asked for advice, but there is little point talking about the lessons of the past if one is not prepared to try and apply them to the present. I am sure that the management and board of Shell are trying to do just that.

If a company has an operation in a country with an increasingly unacceptable regime, there are a number of questions that need to be asked. The first is whether the events in the country as a whole are impacting on the company's ability to maintain its own standards in relation to the people in the company, their families and the operation. Clearly, if one were prevented by the government from respecting the legitimate rights of the employees and their families, or from maintaining standards of health and safety, this would be a factor in considering whether to discontinue operations. Failure to do so could lead to the company becoming, or being perceived to become, complicit in abuses. A factor in the decision would be whether such discontinuation would simply make matters worse.

The second question would be whether the company has unequivocally, preferably publicly but at very least in private, expressed profound disagreement with the oppressive actions taken. This may not be easy, and will undoubtedly be unpopular with the government, but it is essential. There is no denying that a company with major operations in a country has the connections to do this and may have built sufficiently solid connections with a government to offset the negative impact of a critical statement. Total has a company policy of non-involvement in party politics, but they have made public statements in relation to the detention of Aung San Suu Kyi in Burma/Myanmar and also in relation to the Syrian government's initial actions of violent suppression of dissent. In 1997, Shell had added such a principle to the published list of responsibilities of Shell Group companies: 'To Society—to conduct business as responsible corporate members of society, to observe the laws of the countries in which they operate, to express support for fundamental human rights in line with the legitimate role of business . . .'. In fact, the first two principles of the UN Global Compact are: (1) Businesses should support and respect the protection of internationally proclaimed human rights; and (2) make sure that they are not complicit in human rights abuses.

The third question to be asked relates to the company's own employees. Every company has responsibilities to its own people. These responsibilities are often forgotten by the world at large (and indeed may too often be forgotten by a company itself). I recall listening to a BBC report from Kinshasa at a time of uncertainty and civil war in what was then called Zaire at the end of President Mobutu's rule. The reporter said that the international agencies had removed their international staff and that the international NGOs had also pulled out. He remarked that there were only one or two commercial people left—the implication being that they were just there in order to continue making money. In fact, I knew that they were still there to make arrangements for the Congolese staff, who unlike expatriates cannot simply leave the country, their homes and wider family. Of course, such arrangements also have implications for the continuity of the business when things return to normal, but that is a benefit to employees and society as well as to the company. I was proud when I learned that just before the fall of Saigon at the end of the Vietnam war, my predecessors in the management and board of Shell had readied a supply boat with an offshore barge with helicopters in Brunei, across the South China Sea from Vietnam, so that Vietnamese staff working for Shell in Saigon could be evacuated. As Shell was a major supplier of fuel to the military, such staff would have been vulnerable in the aftermath of the war. In the event the arrangement was not necessary, because the people concerned were evacuated in the US operation that is familiar from so many graphic images of the fall of Saigon. There was no publicity about this and in fact I only learned of it some years later from one of the pilots involved. The question that needed to be asked was what impact would withdrawal or cessation of operations have on the nationals running that operation? The answer was that they would inevitably be at risk from the incoming regime.

Lastly, there are events and actions of those outside the company, including governments, to be considered. The United States and Europe may apply sanctions against the use of oil produced in a country, or sanctions may be agreed by the United Nations, although such global agreement is rare. Clearly, UN sanctions must be respected. However, some countries may not apply sanctions, and in the absence of an effective naval blockade oil will find a way to such countries. The role of a company operating in a sanctioned country becomes increasingly problematic. The government of a sanctioned country, such as Iran, will want to export oil to any country willing to buy it, and in the absence of UN sanctions it may be difficult for a producing company to argue that this is illegitimate. The same applies to a refining and marketing company in an oil-importing country under sanctions, as was the case in South Africa. All of these factors need to be taken into account and it is the job of the management and the board, and the company's shareholders and home government, to ask these questions and to take the answers into account. Cases are very individual. My advice to the management and the board when making a decision—a decision that will in any case need to be continuously revisited with changing circumstances—is to listen to the range of outside views carefully. In doing so, it is wise not to pay undue attention to those who see the picture in simple black and white and who are generally in favour of ceasing operations and pulling out immediately. It is also wise not to pay too much attention to the views of lawyers, who are often under the misapprehension that if something is not illegal it is acceptable to go ahead and do it. In the event, both Shell and Total were forced by European Union sanctions to close down their operations in Syria. As the production companies are joint ventures with the Syrian Petroleum companies, the operations would have continued with essentially the same employees. I have no doubt that the Syrian staff would have been very distressed at seeing the foreign partners withdraw; many of those staff will now unfortunately be caught up in the horrors of the civil war.

The difficult thing about giving advice to tyrants is that, to stand any chance of being listened to, the advice has to come from someone who is not perceived as an opponent on all counts, although there may be disagreements in some areas. As a business person I have often found it easy to cooperate with NGOs who acknowledge that business can play a positive role, but who nonetheless may be critical of certain actions. It is, however, difficult to work with those organisations who regard business and commerce as the root of all evil and whose ambition is that you and your company should cease to exist. I suspect the same is true of your average despot. Unless one makes a human connection at some level, one is unlikely to be able to have any influence. Equally, it is necessary to demonstrate that there are some benefits or something that could be admired in a change of behaviour. Over 350 years ago George Fox advised the fledgling Quakers to

> Be patterns, be examples in all countries, places, islands, nations, wherever you come, that your carriage and life may preach among all sorts of people, and to them; then you will come to walk cheerfully over the world, answering that of God in every one.

Those of secular inclination might prefer to replace 'preach' with 'be an example to' and perhaps 'that of God' with 'humanity', but it remains excellent advice.

So I have some sympathy with those who are now criticised for having addressed Muammar Qaddafi civilly and built relations with him in spite of his known failings. I suspect that they did not always find the process a comfortable one. Dining with the devil is not likely to be comfortable, but it may be worth a try. Brian Anderson was Shell's chief executive in Nigeria during Sani Abacha's rule. I have known Brian for many years and I have a great respect for him. Brian was born in Nigeria and has a deep knowledge and love of many Nigerians and things Nigerian. He told me that he found his meetings with Abacha deeply uncomfortable. They would involve waiting around for hours or even days before being admitted to his presence in the early hours of the morning, to conduct a conversation with the television tuned to CNN in the background. From a personal point of view I am sure that Brian wished to have absolutely nothing to do with Abacha. But he continued to have the meetings, as it was important for the thousands of Shell's Nigerian staff and for the business to maintain some connection and perhaps exert some positive influence. The impact of the Abacha regime on Nigeria and on Shell is discussed further in Chapter 11.

In 1987, during the time that I was living in Malaysia, the then Prime Minister Mahathir Mohamad used the Internal Security Act at a time of heightened racial tension to arrest over a hundred people of different backgrounds, among them a Shell employee: Hilmy Mohd Nor. Hilmy is a Christian. He had been brought up in Sumatra in Indonesia where the concept of a Malay Christian is not quite such a contradiction in terms as it is in Malaysia.

The background to the racial tensions that led to Dr Mahathir invoking the Internal Security Act was complex. It started with a dispute over the Malaysian government's handling of appointments of teachers to Chinese schools. These schools deliver excellent Mandarin education and are very important for the preservation of Chinese culture in the country. There were meetings to protest the appointments and a large rally. Given Malaysia's history it was perhaps inevitable that this would provoke a Malay counter-rally. By a terrible coincidence, a mentally disturbed Malay soldier on leave shot two Chinese passers-by in an area of Kuala Lumpur. The present Prime Minister of Malaysia Najib Tun Razak, who was then Chairman of the United Malays National Organisation Youth (UMNO Youth) and also Minister of Youth, Sports and Culture, led the Malay UMNO Youth Rally of some 10,000. In my opinion, this was extremely unwise. Intemperate language was used on all sides. Another major UMNO rally was planned, ostensibly to celebrate an anniversary. The situation was very tense and there was fear of a repetition of the terrible racial riots of May 1969. Chinese shopkeepers closed their shops and I recall that many Chinese Shell staff in Kuala Lumpur stayed at home. They were often in communication with their Malay colleagues in the office and returned to work when they were assured by them that the streets were quiet.

At that point Dr Mahathir banned the planned rally. In an effort, I believe, to cool tempers and perhaps balance things somewhat, he invoked the notorious Internal Security Act (ISA) and arrested about a hundred people from a wide range of backgrounds. Dr Mahathir has always pointed out that the ISA, which allows arrest and detention without trial of anyone who threatens the security of the state, was a practice inherited from Britain as the former colonial power. Detention is initially for 60 days but this can be extended for up to two years. The original colonial order was intended for use against communists in the Malayan Emergency, but as we know from the Britain of today efforts to legislate on the holding of suspected terrorists for prolonged periods on security grounds are rightly controversial. And this is so in Malaysia also.

The people arrested were of many backgrounds and religions and included all races. The police sweep to round them up was symbolically named Operasi Lalang, after the Malay word for the tall and very sharp grass that invades roadsides and any untended plot in Malaysia. Most political parties, including, it must be said, members of the government party UMNO, were represented in the group arrested, as were representatives of civil society organisations and individuals. Some newspapers were also banned. Personally, although I am not a supporter of the ISA, one could have some sympathy with the combined action of banning a large provocative march and at the same time removing from the scene for a week or so a collection of people, many of whom either had, or were perceived to have, contributed to the rise in inter-communal tension. The situation was extremely dangerous and could well have spiralled, as it had before, into bloody racial riots in which hundreds if not thousands might have died. In fact at the time many thought that a number of other prominent individuals should have been added to its list. Such selections are by their nature arbitrary and prolonged arbitrary detention without trial is unacceptable in any country, but in my opinion a short sharp shock to avert violence by removing some actors may be acceptable.

Caught in this net was Hilmy Mohd Nor. The argument was that by being a Christian he was threatening Malay culture. The Malaysian constitution actually defines a Malay as someone who speaks Malay, is a Muslim and practises Malay culture. I suspect that Hilmy was included on the list as a sop to more radical Malays, as several of the opposition Malay Islamic party were on the list as well. Talking to his Malay colleagues in the office, none of them appeared to feel culturally threatened. Hilmy's Christianity and his background, as well as the fact that he and his Chinese wife May Lee held church groups in their house, were well known in the office and so far as I know no one had any objections.

I expected Hilmy to be released rapidly, but his detention dragged on for well over a year. The religious affairs department demanded that Shell cease paying Hilmy's salary, which we refused to do. I discussed this with the then Chairman of Petronas, Tan Sri Azizan, a person of great integrity and wisdom. Azizan simply said 'Just ignore them.' I did raise the case with Dr Mahathir, explaining that, in my opinion and from observation, Hilmy was absolutely no threat to security. Shortly after that Hilmy was released, which may or may not have had any connection. He returned to work in Shell. After some time he left the country and went to Canada. On a visit to Malaysia some ten years later I had a phone call from Hilmy. To my surprise he was back in Malaysia working for a church. I did ask him whether this was really wise, and I was much relieved recently to get a message from Hilmy saying that he was now in Sabah working for the church. This seems to me to be a potentially more fruitful outcome, as there are many Christians in Sabah of different indigenous groups so there are fewer sensitivities.

It is naïve of major companies, particularly major oil, gas and mining companies, to pretend that they do not have frequent access to governments and private opportunities to offer advice in a constructive form. In the 1980s, when I was in Malaysia, Shell had a major and long-established production operation in Sarawak as well as a major gas liquefaction and export plant. Shell was also constructing with partners a pioneering plant for converting natural gas to high-quality liquid fuels. So we undoubtedly had access to the state government and vice versa. The Chief Minister of Sarawak at the time was Taib Mahmud. In fact he has now remained in that position for some 30 years. His tenure has not been uncontroversial, but I know from observation and conversations with him his skills in leading a multi-ethnic government and his strong commitment to development. This has also led to his critics saying that this development has too often ignored the costs to the environment. During his tenure there have also been many accusations of corruption. Suffice it to say that his family is very wealthy; there are now clear signs that he has outstayed his welcome as Chief Minister.

At one point Taib Mahmud approached me in an indignant mood. He said that several Shell employees in Sarawak were actively campaigning against his party in the local elections. This was no way to build a supportive relationship and would we therefore please fire them forthwith. Frankly, I am not sure whether he really expected us to act on his request, but Sarawak politics can be extremely robust. The outcome was that we had a long discussion. I explained Shell's principles in this matter, but also pointed out that regardless of the principle, even if we did it (which we would not) it was unlikely to be to his advantage. There would be all sorts of negative publicity that would be used to great effect in the communities in which Shell operations were based. Taib eventually accepted this, but asked that we prevent them from campaigning. This too was impossible, particularly if they had accumulated leave. We agreed that to give people extra leave to support a campaign could be seen as a political act, although if an employee wished to stand for election themselves it would be reasonable to grant them the flexibility needed to do this. By going through a discussion on the principles, a conclusion was reached that satisfied Shell principles while the Chief Minister was somewhat mollified and did not press his demand further.

In all situations like this, achieving any progress depends on trust. Trust can only be developed by establishing human and friendly contact. This is difficult if one uses the 'long spoon' recommended in the proverb on dining with the devil. More appropriate in such close encounters is a Kevlar vest of very clear and well-rehearsed lines of principle, which are plain and which cannot be crossed. Having said that, I have never met someone whom I have regarded as being the devil incarnate; some had that of the devil in them, but they also certainly had a bit of what George Fox called 'that of God', even if they kept it well under wraps.

Chapter 6

Markets are essential, but they cannot do everything

I am a strong believer in the power of markets. They are essential to offer choice and to encourage the efficient allocation of resources. Even where attempts are made to eliminate them, such as in communist societies, people develop them. Whether it is in the bartering of goods outside a collectivised state system or in the exchange of favours and advantages in a supposedly equal communist society, some kind of market mechanism creeps in. Yet there is probably no topic more likely to stir up emotions in discussions, whether on the effects of markets in the delivery of public services or in the setting of levels of pay.

There is also a tendency to link the operation of markets with capitalism. Markets can and do operate regardless of the source of capital. For example, I enjoyed serving on the board of Nuffield Health, a commercially run not-for-profit owner and operator of hospitals and fitness centres. The capital had all been raised originally by charitable donations or generated internally from profits retained as there were no shareholders requiring dividends to remunerate their capital. The model can work well but expansion is limited by internally generated funds and the loans, with the latter clearly being limited by the assets of the organisation. There is no mechanism to raise further capital from shareholders as there would be with a public company. I once had a discussion with Muhammad Yunus, the Nobel Peace Prize laureate and pioneer of microfinancing. He is a person for whom I have a great respect and he is also a great believer in the power of markets. He argued that he could relatively easily raise patient loan capital[1] for his various Grameen ventures, which avoids the need for social entrepreneurs to turn to the conventional capital (and capitalist) markets. Given his reputation, it was clear that he could access such patient funds from public-spirited wealthy individuals with surplus funds. One does not, however, escape capitalism by this route as these individuals had in the main generated their wealth in the capitalist system. I should add that I am not only a great believer in the power of the markets and the benefits that they can bring, but also in capitalism and the power of shareholder capital. They are, however, separate issues.

To make them work properly, markets need certain regulatory frameworks, as indeed does shareholder capitalism. In my experience, business people are paranoid about regulation, particularly business people in the United States. The paranoia is generally well founded, as we often suffer greatly from over-regulation or the wrong sort of regulation. Unfortunately, the paranoia leads business people to instinctively oppose regulation in areas where it is clearly needed, either for the effective functioning of the market or where the market on its own will not deliver the benefits that society seeks.

Even those who are ideologically opposed to markets will normally readily concede that a market where consumers can choose from a variety of fruit and vegetables, or food and drink, is good in that it offers the opportunity for consumers to select the product that they want and to compare prices. It also offers producers a chance to test demand for a new product, and if the product is popular, to adapt their business to produce more of it. This will probably lead to some other less popular product being replaced, or being only available in reduced quantities. Equally, even those adamantly opposed to regulation will accept that even such a basic market will need some regulation on weights and measures, and probably also on minimum quality to prevent people

---

1 Capital that does not require a high degree of remuneration, if any, or rapid repayment.

being poisoned or defrauded. Adam Smith's hypothetical baker in the *Wealth of Nations* would probably have accepted the need for regulation to prevent competitors or suppliers adulterating their flour with chalk, and his customers would certainly have approved. For markets to operate fairly for all participants, transparency in pricing is needed. It is also prudent to ensure that players are not allowed to combine to dominate the market on either the sellers' or the buyers' side.

It is possible for markets to operate without regulations where participants know and trust each other. In the early 1990s, Shell had a business in what was then Zaire (now the Democratic Republic of Congo), which had been ruled by Mobutu Sese Seko for some 30 years. The Shell business consisted essentially of marketing oil products, although there was also a minority stake in a small oil production venture operated by another company. As Zaire was a notoriously corrupt and chaotic country, I made a visit to see whether it was possible to run our business in line with our standards.

Since 1990, Judy and I have had a connection with a Congolese couple who ran an excellent project that trained young women, some from the streets, in sewing and basic business. They also provided accommodation for them and sometimes for their babies. In 1990, Judy had met Bakamana Mouana, the husband, at an international Quaker gathering in the Netherlands and had assisted in the supply of sewing machines, as well as helping to sell some of the products in Europe. I am glad to say that 20 years later, after all the confusion and civil war in the country, the family and the project Action pour la Jeune Fille are still in action. For a while one outlet for their work was a contract to make the uniforms for staff in Shell petrol stations, and they also had a sales outlet for their goods in a Shell station, a tiny example of the impact of corporate supply chains. Through this connection we had some idea of life in the tougher areas of Kinshasa. Judy has visited Kinshasa several times over the years.

On the visit I did not meet Mobutu, who was already quite reclusive. I had no wish or need to do so. I did, however, meet the Prime Minister Kengo Wa Dondo, an urbane and able individual with a law degree and I believe a doctorate from the University of Louvain in Belgium.

The Prime Minister had a reputation as a person who at various times in his career tried to introduce reforms in government, clearly not an easy job with Mobutu as president. I explained that my concern was whether Shell could operate to our own standards. Kengo Wa Dondo treated me to an analysis of all the ills and mistakes that had affected the country. He explained how inflation had reached several per cent an hour on occasion, the consequences of which I had observed when walking down the main currency exchange area of Kinshasa, known to some as 'Wall Street', where the women pavement traders dealt with wheelbarrow loads of notes, sometimes weighing rather than counting them. In such a market the lower denomination notes were worth more than the newer higher denomination notes, which were subject to counterfeiting. The Prime Minister explained to me that control of the money supply was difficult in an environment where the (reportedly Lebanese) suppliers of the bank notes printed three copies of every serial number and only delivered two to the government. I presumed that one of these had been for the Central Bank and the other for Mobutu. At one point during our discussion, the Prime Minister noted that I had on three occasions referred to the maintenance of standards and that frankly he was in the same boat—his problem was also standards. I pointed out that although in the same boat, he was actually in charge of the national boat, which I was not.

In fact, although in the same country, we were not in the same boat. The Shell manager in the country at the time was a Dutchman for whom I had a great respect and who loved the country with all its manifest faults. The company performed an essential role in the supply of imported fuels in a reliable way, without which the economy could not operate at all. Our own people were paid regularly and had reasonable working conditions. This was certainly not true of the bulk of those in the country, but Shell's withdrawal would make it worse, not better. The operation was profitable, but in no way material to Shell.[2] The very

2 Shell has more recently sold marketing businesses in many countries in Africa. I believe that the rationale was not in general a lack of profitability, but rather to reduce management stretch and focus on larger operations elsewhere. The arguments are complex and I am not party to all the current background, but it

operation of the business was dependent on trust between Shell and other business participants in the economy. Without that, even the reliable supply of products would be difficult. At a lunch with some of the foreign business community, including the Citibank and Standard Bank managers and the Heineken manager, it was explained to me that foreign currency rate-setting and clearing between importers and exporters was done on a morning radio call entirely on trust. The Zairois Citibank manager remarked that one should perhaps view Zaire as the ultimate experiment in a laissez-faire economy as there was effectively no government. Those round the table agreed, but then modified this to say that there was in fact a government that manifested itself from time to time as a large hand that appeared and tried to empty your pockets on some pretence. Clearly these business people knew each other and assisted each other in difficult circumstances.

My point is that it is possible to operate a market economy in the absence of regulation, if there is trust. However, proper regulation is highly desirable to ensure that no group conspires to take advantage of others.

The creativity and power of a competitive and free market frequently takes the world by surprise. Very often this is not a result of the large incumbent players, but comes from a myriad of experiments by start-up companies, many of which fail, but some of which hit on an idea or a model that has wide appeal to consumers or gives them a significant advantage over their competitors.

We are all familiar with the creativity and complexity of the mobile phone and tablet market, where in the space of months the never-ending competition between different handsets and tablets plays out, with the winners determined by consumer choice driven by a complex mixture of convenience, design, utility and fashion. In the case of web search engines or social media start-ups, the ability to attract advertising or recommendations from users becomes in the end the driver of survival, inextricably linked with the number and nature of the users. In the

---

is something that I rather regret. Withdrawing on grounds of focus from a profitable part of a core business providing an essential service to society could in the end be short-sighted.

competition around the world to grow mobile telephone networks, it has often not been the big legacy owners of the fixed-line networks who have won. In Africa and Latin America it has often been the player with the regional knowledge and understanding of the local consumer who has beaten the large international group. In Africa, it is the African mobile phone companies that are introducing payment methods by mobile phone, thus extending basic secure cash transfer methods to people who do not have bank accounts.

The speed and power of market responses is not limited to these relatively modern areas. In the comparatively capital-intensive field of oil and gas production, apparently dominated by major oil and gas companies and the state-owned companies of the major resource-holding countries, the same phenomenon is true. Throughout the 1990s and well into the 21st century, there were repeated forecasts that production in the minority of the resource-holding world outside the major largely Middle Eastern countries that were members of the Organization of the Petroleum Exporting Countries (OPEC) would decline. That minority of production was delivered by free-market players, both large companies and a myriad of small companies, particularly in the United States. Time and again this free-market production has surprised on the upside, both in finding new sources and in responding to fluctuations in demand. Large predictive models of production growth tend to seriously underestimate the power of the thousands of individual actors who make up this free-market segment.

Indeed the creation of OPEC and the closing of many of the major petroleum resource-holding countries to the capital and inventiveness of the free market meant that that capital and technology sought other outlets. In the 1970s and 1980s the capital and technology flowed to the North Sea and the North Slope of Alaska. Added to this, the oil price rises driven by OPEC enabled the development of production in harsher and more costly environments. Many of the big projects in the northern North Sea, which were developed in the 1970s with large and complex production platforms built to survive extremely harsh weather and wave conditions, experienced the major cost overruns that nearly always afflict pioneering and frontier projects. This results from the optimism and vision that are needed if you are to pioneer something, coupled with the fact that such projects inevitably involve the first application of technologies, with all the unpredictable failures and difficulties that that involves. Without the cost rises imposed by OPEC, many of those major projects, which often cost almost double the original estimate, would have been in financial difficulty. The actions of OPEC created their own competitor. Such is the response of the market.

An even more striking example is the development of shale gas extraction. Some relatively small and independent companies had experimented for years with applying techniques and equipment well known in the industry around the world to fracturing shales to stimulate the production of natural gas. Similar techniques of fracturing rocks (what geologists call 'fraccing'—now popularly known as 'fracking') using fluids pumped at high pressure to create fractures are common in the industry, along with wells drilled horizontally to give a borehole greater exposure to a hydrocarbon-bearing rock sequence and thus increase the productivity of the well. The application to shale was new. When the technique, coupled with the drilling of a large number of closely spaced wells, proved successful, a rush was on. The combined power of many actors, large and small, became apparent, with the bigger latecomers acquiring their smaller and faster-moving peers who had specialist knowledge of different areas. Natural gas production increased dramatically and as a result the price in the United States dropped. The effect on natural gas supply in the United States has been remarkable and the race is on to replicate this achievement around the world and extend it to the production of oil in a somewhat similar way. As with many technological revolutions, there has been a reaction to it. There are accusations of polluted aquifers and questions asked about the toxicity of some of the chemicals used. As is so often the case, the industry was confident of its own ability to handle the negative side effects and so has been slow in addressing the understandable worries of the public. Clearly, there needs to be proper regulation, taking into account risks when significant aquifers are in close proximity to the producing horizons. There is also clearly a need to ensure high standards of operation. Given that regulatory framework, I am confident that the market will have delivered access to an important source of low-cost and relatively climate-friendly energy. This energy will be important in many countries as we build sustainable energy sources to replace finite fossil fuels. In the end it will be up to sovereign nations as to the extent that this technology is applied, but the speed of adoption seen in the United States is unlikely to be replicated elsewhere for two reasons. The first is that in the United States, unlike in almost every other country, it is the private surface landowner, and not the state, who also owns the rights to subsurface minerals. This alignment of benefits with the area of production means that there is less local resistance, although nationwide campaigns against the technique flourish. The second difference is the remarkable free-market economy in the United States, where thousands of small companies, often local, can call on abundant suppliers of oilfield services to assist in the execution of projects.

One of the most striking demonstrations of the power of the market is the development in the United States of the capacity to make ethanol from corn (maize). This demonstrates how the market and creativity can be stimulated by a regulatory framework; unfortunately, it also demonstrates that with the wrong framework the market can work to send thousands of players haring off in a direction that is not beneficial to society as a whole.

If in 2002, someone would have suggested that five or six years later enough manufacturing capacity would have been created to convert about half of the United States corn crop, which in turn is about 40% of the global corn (maize) crop (in 2012), into ethanol it would have been regarded as a wild flight of imagination. Yet, stimulated by tax breaks, subsidies and mandates to increase the percentage of ethanol in US gasoline, that is just what happened. Thousands of farmers were attracted to the idea and investments large and small were made in capacity to convert corn to alcohol. The idea behind the policy was that a fuel made from domestic agricultural produce would not only be renewable and result in lower greenhouse gas emissions, but it would add to energy security as well. To this must be added that the policy was also partly driven by members of Congress from Corn Belt states such as Ohio who thought that the policy would be beneficial to their constituents.

Unfortunately, calculations show[3] that due to the energy used in the manufacturing process, the net effect on greenhouse gas emissions is negligible, and indeed, if the power used in manufacture comes from coal-generated electricity, the effect is strongly negative. At the same time, corn prices rose sharply and as a result, in Mexico, for example, there were protests at the sharp increase in the basic raw material for the staple tortilla. There are statistical arguments that the rise in food prices was not caused by the increasing use of crops to make fuel, but in the case of corn in the United States and Mexico the circumstantial evidence appears strong.

So, the good news is that, when stimulated, the market will deliver significant changes in investment and usage of materials. The bad news is that in this particular case the policy was a very ill-conceived one. Markets are complex and the use of subsidies to encourage the adoption of particular production methods can often lead to perverse results.

What the market will not deliver

Unless stimulated or driven by a policy framework, the market will not, in general, result in an increased demand for things that do not benefit the individual consumer when making his or her choice of purchase, even though that choice will benefit society as a whole and therefore the individual consuming member of society.

Consider the example of the catalytic converters on the engine exhaust pipes of vehicles, which are now mandatory in many high-income markets. A catalytic converter on the exhaust of a vehicle adds two or three hundred dollars to the cost of the vehicle and is of no immediate value to the driver or owner of the vehicle, although it does benefit the person in the car behind, pedestrians, city-dwellers and indeed society at

3 D. Koplow, *Biofuels: At What Cost? Government Support for Ethanol and Biodiesel in the United States* (Winnipeg: International Institute for Sustainable Development, April 2006; www.iisd.org/gsi/sites/default/files/Brochure_-_US_Report.pdf). See also work by the IISD's Global Subsidies Initiative, not only on biofuels but on all energy subsidies, at www.iisd.org/gsi.

large. On a recent visit to Tehran I was struck when walking the streets that, although the traffic was not much worse than in many other major cities, the smell of unburnt fuel was oppressive, very noticeable and undoubtedly unhealthy. The difference was due to the fact that vehicles in Iran are not fitted with exhaust catalysts. While a small percentage of public-spirited citizens might have installed the devices voluntarily, it is only through regulation (and an enforcement of regulation) that the undoubted benefits to society have been achieved. In spite of the cost, the legislation has been generally accepted by consumers and voters without complaint, although the automobile industry was initially opposed to it on grounds of cost.

Another example is the legislation banning the use of lead additives in gasoline. This was opposed by the refining industry on grounds of cost. Less creditably, the industry went to great lengths to fund work with the objective of denying or minimising the negative health impacts of lead in the atmosphere.[4] As is fairly typical in such cases, the initial estimates by industry of the total probable costs proved to be much higher than the actual cost. In my opinion, this was not due to the industry wilfully exaggerating the costs, although many would certainly suspect this, but rather due to the workings of the market. Once the legislation mandated the removal of all lead by a certain date, the market effects of competition and pressure to reduce costs kicked in. Ingenious ways were achieved to reduce the costs and also to find substitutes that would attract the owners of older cars, whose engines would be damaged by the removal of the lead additive.

The example of auto catalysts demonstrates that regulation is necessary to deliver some benefits to society that the market on its own will never achieve. However, it is also a good example of a common shortcoming of regulation. Under the regulatory framework, a particular model of engine has to be tested with a particular catalyst application. The testing programme is extensive and expensive. This means that once an engine manufacturer has received approval for a particular catalyst

4 For an account of the arguments, see H.L. Needleman, 'The Removal of Lead from Gasoline: Historical and Personal Reflections', *Environmental Research* 84.1, September 2000: 20-35.

for a particular series of engine, for example, based on platinum, it is not easy to switch to an alternative catalyst, such as palladium. The regulation thus specifies not just the level of emission control required, but also fixes the exact make-up required to achieve it. This is inflexible and means that once the initial approval is gained, the benefits of competition and invention are frozen out. Anglo Platinum, largely owned by Anglo American, produces about 40% of the world's platinum and is also a significant producer of palladium. About half of the market for these metals is essentially driven by regulatory requirements. Given the considerable relative price changes between platinum and palladium, it is undoubtedly frustrating for manufacturers to be tied in to one or the other for their current products, although it is probably advantageous to producers of platinum and palladium. A much better approach is to specify the required outcome and leave it to the ingenuity of the market to find the most effective and economical method of delivering the required result. Far too often, whether in relation to auto catalysts, building regulations or health and safety, regulators specify not only the required outcome, but also the precise means of achieving it. This takes all the fun out of the game and seriously inhibits the creativity of the market.

Business people should support sensible regulatory frameworks instead of instinctively arguing against all forms of regulation. Close involvement of business in framing sensible legislation is necessary, but to prevent special pleading it is advisable to have input from other business sectors as well as civil society. A good business leader should be able to take off the 'corporate hat' and put on a 'citizen hat'. Too often business people from one sector are reticent about commenting on nonsensical regulation in another sector, perhaps out of an unwillingness to be seen to interfere in the business of other sectors. We are all affected by inefficiencies and market distortions, so we should not be afraid to bring our general business skills to the discussion.

There is probably no area where this is truer than the issue of climate change and what needs to be done about it, something I look at in the next chapter.

Chapter 7

Oil, gas and climate change

Throughout my career, the oil and gas industry has often been the subject of controversy. Up until the 1990s, these controversies mainly involved environmental issues, with both human rights and corruption issues sometimes arising. As you can see from earlier chapters in this book, I believed, and continue to believe, that the industry has an important role to play in economic development. Oil and gas provide the world with an economic, reliable and convenient form of energy that has underpinned the growth of the world's economies. So, while acknowledging the challenges and the many mistakes that we have made, I remain proud of my involvement with the industry.

However, from the 1990 publication of the First Assessment Report of the Intergovernmental Panel on Climate Change (IPCC),[1] there began to be serious questions asked about the impact on the climate of carbon dioxide generated by the burning of fossil fuels. The potential impact became more apparent with the publication of the IPCC's Second

---

1 Intergovernmental Panel on Climate Change, *Climate Change: The IPCC Scientific Assessment* (Contribution of Working Group I to the First Assessment Report of the Intergovernmental Panel on Climate Change; ed. J.T. Houghton, G.J. Jenkins and J.J. Ephraums; Cambridge, UK: Cambridge University Press, 1990; www.ipcc.ch/publications_and_data/publications_ipcc_first_assessment_1990_wg1.shtml).

Assessment Report in 1995.[2] None of this was entirely new, of course. The greenhouse effect of earth's atmosphere was well known, and reading the Club of Rome's *Limits to Growth*[3] when I was working in Borneo in 1972, I remember being particularly struck by the increases of atmospheric carbon dioxide recorded over the years by the observatory on the volcano of Mauna Kea in Hawaii. Being a geologist, I assumed that this was probably connected with some longer-range volcanic cycle. We now know that the contribution of volcanoes is probably relatively small in comparison to the human effects. Given the enormous orogenic, environmental and climatic effects playing out over millennia that we geologists study, it is still a source of wonder that man's relatively recent efforts could have such a global impact, but the accumulating evidence does appear compelling, even though there is much we still do not understand completely.

So here was an effect that suggested that the use of our products derived from fossil fuels, beneficial though they might be in terms of economic development, was having an adverse climatic effect. As a geologist, one is all too aware that fossil fuel resources are finite, but energy sources evolve and my assumption has always been that we are unlikely to use the last of our oil before other energy sources are developed. Furthermore, hydrocarbons are far too valuable a chemical feedstock simply to be burnt. We started the 20th century with wood and coal being the dominant sources of energy, with oil being in its infancy. It has been pointed out to me that at that time there was in fact another major energy source, namely the oats that fed the horses pulling the carriages and carts that still formed a major part of the transport fleet. Since the mid-19th century, changes in energy supply and use seem to have taken place in cycles of thirty to a hundred years, driven by technology and

---

2 Intergovernmental Panel on Climate Change, *Climate Change 1995: A Report of the Intergovernmental Panel on Climate Change* (Second Assessment Report of the Intergovernmental Panel on Climate Change; Geneva: IPCC, 1996; www.ipcc.ch/publications_and_data/publications_and_data_reports.shtml).

3 D.H. Meadows, D.L. Meadows, J. Randers and W.W. Behrens III, *The Limits to Growth: A Report for the Club of Rome's Project on the Predicament of Mankind* (New York: Universe, 1972).

convenience. After the rise of steam and coal in the 19th century, in the first half of the 20th century motor transportation developed, fuelled by gasoline and diesel. At the same time the heavier parts of the oil barrel, fuel oil, began to be used to power trains and ships.

After the Second World War, oil companies began to sell lighter fuel oil for domestic use in central heating and for use in power stations. But in the late 1950s and 1960s in Europe and somewhat earlier in the United States, large accumulations of natural gas had been found in the search for oil. On the back of the discovery of the enormous Groningen field in the Netherlands, my forebears in Shell developed with the government and others the pipeline and reticulation system to bring this natural gas to factories and homes across Europe. This valuable fuel had previously been regarded as almost a waste by-product of the production of oil and a source of disappointment when only gas and not the more useful oil was found. The development of natural gas introduced a direct competitor for the oil companies' own fuel oil and with the switch to more convenient natural gas, the market for fuel oil was greatly reduced. Confounding those who say that oil companies will never compete against themselves, they did just that. Technology found a way of cracking and adding hydrogen to the molecules of heavy oil and the now surplus fuel oil, creating lighter transportation fuels. A modern refinery now produces virtually no fuel oil, and a major power station burning fuel oil is rare. Many of the coal mines that powered the industrial revolution of earlier centuries in Europe have been closed, not because the seams were exhausted, but because more efficient power sources had been found or because coal is imported from more efficient mines in other continents. By the end of the 20th century a wide range of other sources of power were available, from nuclear to various types of renewable energy. We were also beginning to develop modern and more efficient methods of using biomass than feeding it to transportation animals, or simply burning wood.

The threat of human-induced climate change meant that instead of letting the evolution of energy sources be driven entirely by the market, another form of stimulus was needed. With energy supplies changing only slowly in response to technological developments or demand for convenience, it appeared that it might become necessary to agree frame-works to guide the market in certain directions. In April 1997, in the Shell Annual Report approved by the board, Shell formally acknowl-edged the threat of anthropogenic climate change, stating 'There are still many uncertainties about the impact of increasing atmospheric con-centrations of man-made carbon dioxide on global climate. However, there is now sufficient evidence to support taking prudent precautionary action.' Shell also supported the Kyoto Protocol, which was adopted later that same year.

At that time, I had several discussions with John Browne (later Lord Browne of Madingley), then Chief Executive of BP, on the subject of cli-mate change and on what we energy companies should be doing about it. We were both enthusiasts for market approaches to the issue and both BP and Shell developed internal trading systems to ensure that emission-reducing investments were made in the most effective way. Shell also introduced at that time a shadow price of carbon, rising as I recall to $20 per ton of carbon dioxide. Internally we required this penalty to be included in the economic analysis of every significant investment. This did not in fact have a great impact on the economic calculations, result-ing generally in only a few decimal points of reduction in the earning power of projects. It did, however, have a big impact on the thinking of the engineers working on project design. In order to put a meaning-ful number into the economic analysis, it was necessary to look at the relative carbon efficiency of different types of equipment. In my experi-ence, once engineers begin to take something into consideration, they normally work to optimise it. So a shadow price for carbon helped to change mind-sets.

John Browne and I also discussed[4] the question of withdrawal from the Global Climate Coalition, an industry financed think-tank and lobby group. It was becoming increasingly clear that the group was adopting

4 John Browne and I would have quite frequent discussions on environmental or climate matters. Although such matters are not really the subject of competi-tion, each company maintained its independent public stance, and differences in expression of views often reflected the nature and history of the company concerned.

a position of lobbying against any consideration of action on climate. Many NGOs regarded such membership as hypocritical and criticised both Shell and BP. As always in such cases, the argument is whether to stay in the group and try to change the policy or to leave. BP left the group in 1997 and Shell in early 1998. In the case of the American Petroleum Institute (API), which also sometimes took positions we did not agree with, neither company withdrew. The API is an important industry standard-setting body and not essentially a climate lobby. In an interesting twist, I note that in 2010 Shell decided to continue to support the US Climate Action Partnership, a coalition that calls for US reductions of greenhouse gas emissions, while BP, a founder member, decided with some other companies to withdraw given all the other pressing economic issues in the United States and the industry.

In May 1997, John Browne made an excellent and thoughtful speech at Stanford University setting out BP's position on climate change and the actions they planned to take. The speech rightly attracted much attention[5] and is often described by commentators in the press as the first acknowledgment by a major oil company of the threat of climate change and as having caused great consternation in the rest of the industry. It was indeed an excellent speech and quite rightly gained much attention, but in relation to Shell neither of the common descriptions by commentators is accurate. As noted above, Shell had in fact formally recognised the threat and accepted the need for precautionary action in its Annual Report published a month earlier.

In my opinion, one of the tragedies of the 1997 Kyoto negotiations was the deep suspicion with which the Europeans regarded US proposals for the use of market mechanisms. The US had of course useful experience in the use of trading systems to achieve reductions in sulphur emissions, but Europe, perhaps because the idea originated from the biggest emitter of all, was not at all keen. I sometimes think that had the US approach been more welcomed, the general approach to carbon trading would have been simpler and more practical. As it was,

5 See www.thefreelibrary.com/British+Petroleum+CEO+John+Browne+delivers+s peech+on+global+climate...-a019423206.

under the United Nations Framework Convention on Climate Change (UNFCCC) we got a very bureaucratic international Clean Development Mechanism (CDM). Europe went its own way and developed the European Union Emissions Trading Scheme (EU ETS). This scheme is a pioneering move in the right direction, but it has suffered from the complex negotiations and inevitable political gaming of the initial permit allocations that brought the initial cycle into disrepute. Furthermore, there has been some blatant fraud in the handling of permits.[6] Ironically, this has made the United States suspicious of trading schemes. In fact, although slow to develop, the European scheme has provided valuable working experience in spite of its flaws. For a while it looked as though a series of regional schemes might develop—not just in Europe, but also in Australia and in the United States. Certainly, at a federal level a US scheme seems improbable at present; proposals for the contentious Australian scheme were revived, but proved so unpopular with industry in that coal and natural resource dependent country that they have been shelved once more.

It has to be said that part of the blame for the delays and confusion rests with business. After all, if two of the world's largest oil companies had already acknowledged the threat in 1997, the lack of progress on international framework agreements needed to drive change is disappointing. In business, we have been bad at giving simple explanations of how a cap-and-trade scheme works, and we have tended to omit references to the essential cap without which there would be nothing to trade. Even in Shell, an energy company that might be expected to

6 There has been electronic theft of permits in the markets involving some €28 million of credits stolen. See S. Carney, 'EU Carbon Market Suffers Further Setback', *Wall Street Journal*, 28 January 2011, online.wsj.com/article/SB100014 24052748703956604576109272255053468.html. There have also been gains from the over-allocation of permits and utilities passing the full costs of the permits on to consumers. See Committee on Climate Change, 'Carbon Markets and Carbon Prices', Ch. 4 in *Building a Low-carbon Economy: The UK's Contribution to Tackling Climate Change* (First Report of the Committee on Climate Change; London: Committee on Climate Change, December 2008; www.theccc. org.uk/publication/building-a-low-carbon-economy-the-uks-contribution-to-tackling-climate-change-2).

quickly implement a trading scheme, it took a long time to get the base-lines established and the mechanisms set up. And in Australia, Anglo American had much work to do to build a picture of the costs of various steps to reduce carbon emissions. If you do not know the costs to your own business of avoiding emissions, you cannot operate effectively and economically in a carbon-emission trading scheme.

Ideally, a scheme should work like this. The baseline emissions for each plant covered are established and capped. The cap on each plant is then reduced by, say, 10%. This means that the sum of total emissions of all the plants in the scheme will also fall by 10%. It is this reducing cap that is vital to the effective operation of the scheme. This is where the European scheme met problems because in some cases the baseline allocations were too high and some organisations were able to profit from the sale of permits that they did not need, without reducing emissions. This was exacerbated by the reduction in energy use caused by the financial crisis and recessions connected with it. It is of course always probable that some plants will find it easier and cheaper than others to reduce emissions, particularly if plants of different industries are covered. A company with a low cost of reducing emissions can make a greater than 10% reduction and sell the extra permits to a company for whom a 10% reduction is more expensive, or even perhaps impractical. The targeted reduction is thus made in the most efficient way and at the lowest cost to the economy as a whole.

At successive China Development Forums organised in Beijing by the Chinese government, I have had animated discussions with the Nobel economics laureate Joseph Stiglitz, who to my surprise tended to favour carbon taxes in place of cap-and-trade schemes. I would have thought that the efficient allocation of resources driven by a cap-and-trade scheme would win the day for an economist, but Stiglitz argues that there is merit and clarity in simplicity. There is also the evidence of a malfunctioning European scheme to consider, although in the real world there is as much gaming, avoidance and corruption in taxation to require transparent application of both. In practice, there may be merits in a scheme that uses a tax to set a predictable floor price for a cap-and-trade scheme. This is being tried in the UK,[7] with varying concerns on its impact.

In October 1999, David Anderson, then just appointed as Minister of Environment for Canada, invited David Runnalls of the Canadian International Institute for Sustainable Development (IISD), of which I was later a board member, and myself to join the Ministerial pre-meeting in the run-up to the sixth Conference of the Parties of the Kyoto Protocol—in the world of intergovernmental climate discussions one becomes used to long titles and acronyms. The minister thought that it might be useful to inject a bit of business thinking into the discussions. The meeting was held in the parliament building in Ottawa in impressive surroundings. There was much discussion of market mechanisms. In Shell we had a number of ideas on how we could participate constructively in the Clean Development Mechanism of the Kyoto Protocol and as Chairman I was interested to see how this might work. The idea of the CDM is that investment in approved projects in the developing world could earn credits that could be used as offsets in the countries committed to reductions under Kyoto (so-called Annex I countries).

Initially I found the Ottawa meeting encouraging, as there was a wide range of ministers engaged in the discussions. The United States was present, although not at secretary level. Gradually my concern mounted. There was a strong group of ministers from Europe who felt that projects should not be allowed CDM credits if they were 'economic' in any case. This is the so-called additionality principle. The definition of 'economic' is problematic. A company normally has many projects that

7 The Carbon Price Floor came into effect in the UK on 1 April 2013. See HM Revenue and Customs website, www.hmrc.gov.uk/climate-change-levy/carbon-pf.htm. The floor is set initially at £16 a tonne as opposed to a price on the EU ETS market of around £4 a tonne. The floor is aimed to rise to £70 a tonne by 2030. As it does not apply Europe-wide, proponents believe that it will attract low-carbon industry to the UK while opponents are concerned that energy-intensive industries will migrate to other countries where there is no floor. Clearly, a Europe-wide scheme would be preferable. For a simple explanation of the possible floor price mechanisms in relation to the EU Emissions Trading Scheme, see Sandbag Carbon Floor Price Briefing, www.sandbag.org.uk/site_media/pdfs/reports/CarbonFloorPriceBriefing.pdf.

it could do that earn at least a return equal to the cost of its capital. As the supply of capital is constrained, only the most profitable projects on the list, or those that offer most opportunity for future growth or building future business, are likely to win in the internal competition for capital. Thus a project that is 'economic' in terms of meeting the cost of capital may well not be implemented unless there is an additional incentive. The incentive might be that it opens an opportunity to develop new markets, or it might be an economic incentive in the form of earning carbon credits.

Apart from this concern, there were then those ministers who felt that an absolute limit should be put on the quantity of projects accepted. There were many points made on other conditions. The representatives of low-lying small island states (among whom was John Ashe representing the island of my own birth, Antigua) pointed out that it was probable that many of the projects would be done in major economies such as China and India, as in general companies are more likely to have existing operations in large and emerging economies (this was indeed prescient). The small island states pointed out that they were likely to be major victims of sea-level rises and should therefore benefit from a stream of income from credits earned elsewhere. For a businessman this made the outlook rather depressing. I pointed out that if a project was truly uneconomic it was unlikely to become so simply because of carbon credits, although credits could move a project up the list of planned projects. In the unlikely event that anyone was going to commit to an uneconomic project, people were talking of applying limits to the process even before a single project had been implemented. And if a project was undertaken, the proposal appeared to be that it would effectively be taxed to create a stream of income for small island states. It seemed to me unlikely that many projects would make it through this list of hurdles, particularly as there would also be a great deal of measurement and reporting needed. Perhaps a more flexible approach should be taken on an experimental basis, at least initially?

In the end the number of hurdles and the heavy administrative burden of getting projects approved have indeed meant that initially there were few projects undertaken. Many major companies gave up and abandoned their proposals in frustration. China has led the way in the use of the CDM, attracting projects involving the investment of several billion dollars. Some of these have justly been criticised as involving emissions controls on new plants, which in most countries would be covered by basic environmental legislation. There are, however, encouraging signs that after initial delays and mistakes, what is essentially a worthwhile scheme is becoming more streamlined and practical. From a low base in 2006, thousands of projects have been registered under the scheme. By 2011, according to the IPCC, the value of projects registered and undergoing certification was over $100 billion, a major investment in greenhouse gas reduction. This again demonstrates the power of market mechanisms. Properly designed and implemented trading systems operating in a well-regulated framework can stimulate thousands of projects. There have certainly been failures in the operation of the CDM. As suspected at the outset, almost half the projects are in China, with a further 20% in India and with Brazil a distant third with around 5%. It remains true that it is only through the action of markets guided by regulatory frameworks that we will achieve the changes in energy patterns at the rate that we need to address the challenge of climate change.

Towards the end of my tenure at Shell, I was asked to co-chair a G8 Task Force on Renewable Energy. My fellow co-chair was Dr Corrado Clini, the Director General of the Italian Ministry of Environment.[8] We were appointed by the G8 with a call in the Communiqué issued at the end of the G8 meeting in Okinawa in 2000 to form a multi-stakeholder task force 'to prepare concrete recommendations for consideration at our next Summit regarding sound ways to better encourage the use of renewables in developing countries'. There was also a 'call on all stakeholders to identify the barriers and solutions to elevating the level of renewable energy supply and distribution in developing countries'. Given the interest that both Shell and I personally had in the development of renewable energy, I was pleased to have the

---

8 Clini was later appointed Minister for the Environment in the unelected 'government of technocrats' under Mario Monti.

opportunity to learn more about the development of sustainable energy. In the event I also learned a great deal about the functioning of the G8 and intergovernmental relations, some of which was not entirely encouraging. Fortunately, Corrado Clini was well versed in such matters and I was also fortunate to have Scott Gegan seconded to Shell from the UK Ministry of Environment to assist in the process. The Okinawa meeting was in June and by August we had put together a task force with members from every continent and region, including people from civil society, business and international agencies. Many, such as Professor José Goldemberg from the University of São Paulo in Brazil, had deep experience in the development of biomass, wind, solar and hydro power. As we had to report to the G8 meeting in Genoa in mid-2001, there was no time to waste. We had also been asked to have the report ready for submission three months before the actual meeting, reducing the time available still further. We extracted a solemn promise that the time would not be used to edit our report in any way.

At an early meeting of the Task Force we had to address the delicate issue that our brief marching orders from the G8 referred to 'developing countries' in three places. The members from developing countries very reasonably asked why the G8 countries did not want to use renewable energy themselves, given that they were concerned to promote such use in theirs. We got round this by making it clear in the Task Force Report that it was only in the developed economies that power markets and opportunities were large enough to allow the development of renewable energy to come down the classic cost development curve that comes with the learning from increasing volumes of applications. Without work in the large developed markets, progress would be minimal.

Some time in September or October, some of the G8 governments enquired as to how they should nominate their representatives to the Task Force. Corrado and I explained that we had already appointed members from around the world and had commenced work weeks before. We pointed out that, as they had appointed us as co-chairs, we thought that the composition of the Task Force was our responsibility. Surely G8 countries could be as effectively represented by people from business or civil society as from governments? In the end we agreed that each government that had not already done so could nominate one task force member, who like all other members should attend in person without supporters. Our last actual government appointee joined around the following March. Some governments move very slowly.

At the beginning of the process a group of major NGOs including Greenpeace and Friends of the Earth had submitted a lengthy list of recommendations that they thought should be included in the task force report. The Task Force did not discuss the list but started from first principles. When I did a cross-check at the end of the report, I found that the report in fact included in some form essentially all of these recommendations. I sent a final draft of the report to the NGOs who had given us the advice so that they could prepare their response to its publication, pointing out that we had in fact covered effectively almost all the points that they had made. Their public statements on the report were very positive. I think that the regret that we all have is that there has been only limited progress since.

Drafting such a report is extremely difficult and we were lucky to have Rick Sellers from the International Energy Agency seconded to do much of the detailed work. The report found that the barriers to the introduction of renewable energy were cost, including the fact that while the running costs are low, the upfront costs are high and so upfront financing mechanisms are important.[9] The report also addressed the lack of human capacity, inconsistent policies and weak incentives. There were 19 recommendations to overcome these barriers. The main recommendations addressed the need to reduce costs by expanding markets, particularly in the larger developed markets so that technologies could move rapidly down the well-established experience curve, reducing costs. There was much emphasis on developing markets and using market mechanisms, as well as recommendations on the mobilisation of finance.

Although the report was, I believe, generally well received, we hit a major snag at the end. The Okinawa G8 meeting in mid-2000, which

9 G8 Renewable Energy Task Force Report, 2001, www.g8.utoronto.ca/meetings-official/g8renewables_report.pdf.

set up the Task Force, was in the last year of the Clinton administration in the United States. Throughout our work, the US administration had been supportive, both from departmental policy and in the attitude of individuals. However, by the final Task Force Meeting in March 2001, the Bush administration was in place, although the process of staffing the relevant departments was still under way—it starts from the top and works down. The people we had dealt with were sufficiently high level to be subject to political appointment, so there was effectively a vacuum. The only official US government representation at the meeting was therefore someone who was not sufficiently senior to have been replaced in the process of political change and I suspect he was not feeling particularly secure. He was also not formally a member of the Task Force.

The result was a somewhat bizarre series of events. The final Task Force meeting was in Tokyo and, as we were discussing and approving the final draft, most members were present. At the outset of the meeting, when we were considering the introductory section of the report, the US representative announced that he had a copy of a version approved by Vice President Cheney and Secretary of State Colin Powell and he suggested that we replaced the draft that we had developed with that version. Frankly, I very much doubt whether at that point in the administration either the Vice President or the Secretary of State of the United States had had an opportunity to pay any attention to the work of our Task Force, or indeed were even aware of it, but that is what the individual said. He also said that the Task Force draft text was far too long. Most of the Task Force Members were stunned into silence, in particular those from developing countries. The situation was saved by one of the American members of the Task Force, who suggested that as we were at that time only talking about the introductory paragraphs of the report, it might be possible to merge the two versions. He also helpfully pointed out after a quick count that the US version was in fact longer than the current Task Force draft. So with that we set about a bit of collective drafting paragraph by paragraph, never a very constructive process. The meeting at that point was being chaired by my co-Chair, Corrado Clini, but while the discussions were going on I could see that the individual who had presented the US proposal was not involved in general discussion about the text but talking to different members of the Task Force, including those from the International Finance Corporation (IFC) and the World Bank. I therefore asked him publicly to share anything he had to say with all of us. His reply was that it was generally accepted practice in international negotiations to conduct bilateral discussions during the meeting. This unfortunately is true, to such an extent that if you are in a major UN meeting, with those impressive tiers of country representatives, the background noise of conversation in the assembly is often so loud that if you do actually want to hear what the speaker is saying you have to use the earphone system through which the translation comes, even if the speaker is speaking in your own language. In my opinion, it is a bad practice, although perhaps it is necessary in such major meetings. I pointed out that this was a Task Force and not an international negotiation, and we had established clearly different rules. He was extremely angry, and in the following coffee break he asked me whether I really wanted the United States to reject the whole report. I said that it depended on the reason. It would be better to have the report rejected than to modify it for bad reasons. I said that I was sure that any rejection would be judged on its merits.[10]

Corrado Clini and I had been invited to go to Genoa and present to the heads of government at the G8 meeting. The individual concerned may have had more influence than I imagined, as we were informed just before the meeting that the invitation had been withdrawn at the request of the United States. The reasons given were that the report was unacceptable to the United States, in that it did not place sufficient emphasis on market mechanisms and also suggested simply throwing money at the problem. In fact, of the four groupings of recommendations in the report three were headed 'Reduce technology costs by expanding markets', 'Build a strong market environment' and 'Encourage market-based

10 For contemporary comment on the report and the US position, see C. Church, 'Leaked Report Shows G8 Task Foce Report Lays Global Blueprint for Renewable Energy but the US and Canada are Blocking G8 Summit Conclusions', 15 July 2001, groups.yahoo.com/neo/groups/localsustuk/conversations/topics/1062?var=1.

mechanisms'. The fourth, on 'Mobilising financing', did not suggest any additional government money, although it did propose some realignment of funding.

Clearly my diplomatic skills had let me down. However, I suspect that it was more a matter of the new administration being uncomfortable in its early days with a report in the preparation of which their predecessors had been supportively involved but with which they had not had time to come to grips. We had put a successful example of wind-energy development in Texas as the third of some 25 case studies in the report in the hope that this would attract favourable attention, but to no avail. Had the timing been different, I would like to think that the Bush administration would have been more interested in the findings. In the event, although not presented to the leaders at the Genoa G8 summit, the report was published by the G8. I believe it did have some impact on the policies of individual governments and on the practices of the multilateral financial agencies.

After the report was submitted, in the light of our experiences I wrote to the Prime Minister, Tony Blair, with the following suggestions for any future G8 Task Force.

> In spite of the diverse nature of the Task Force, because of the very focussed subject, the main outlines of what needed to be done became clear relatively rapidly. Without constraining people, realism is injected into the discussion if the target is to produce useful recommendations that will stand some prospect of being listened to by G8 Governments. So the calls for billions of dollars of additional aid died away fairly rapidly with the agreement of all Task Force members. After 3 day-long meetings and a lot of consultant work over six months we had a report which most people could be happy with.
>
> A problem occurred in the final meeting. A number of G8 government representatives began to push what they perceived to be their home government lines. In the space of half an hour the Task force degenerated into a G8 intergovernmental negotiation (with bilateral discussions during the meeting). As it stands I believe the report represents a genuine consensus of Task Force views, but the intergovernmental negotiation on detail could have continued for months.

For any future Task Force on a global issue, I believe it is essential for the G8 Heads to define very clearly their requirements. Do they want a report from a responsible but independent Task Force, drawing on experience from outside government and the G8 countries, with clear recommendations which G8 governments may then either individually or collectively accept or reject? This is the assumption our Task Force was working on. An alternative would be to have an intergovernmental report with merely advisory input from others. Both are possible, but there should be absolute up front clarity. And if it is the former, the role of 'government' representatives needs looking at (for their own peace of mind!). Their insight into the thinking and sensitivities of their own governments is very useful to Task Force members in general, but it should not be over riding. If the latter approach is chosen, there is a clear two tier body, with the responsibility on the government representatives. This is workable, but I do not think you would get the same enthusiastic involvement from the 'outsiders'.

The support from various departments of the UK government [the then Department of the Environment, Transport and the Regions and the Department for International Development] both in approach to the Task Force and in funding for consultant and developing country travel support was very positive and none of the above remarks apply to those involved on the UK government side.

As I have said, I believe that the concept and implementation of the Task Force reflected well on the G8, although it nearly came unravelled at the end after an excellent start. I hope that the above thoughts are useful should the G8 be thinking of any further Task Forces. Thank you for the opportunity to participate. I believe that we have produced a useful report, and if the recommendations are followed we could reach the aspirational target of supplying in the coming decade renewable energy to an additional billion people, mainly in developing countries, including a large number of those who currently have no access to the modern energy so essential for development.

In the deliberations of the Task Force, we did not discuss nuclear energy, and because of the controversy over large hydro schemes we also left them out of our deliberations. This was not just out of a desire to avoid controversy, but because the whole thrust of our report was that the choice of technology should be made by the market and not by governments, although within a regulatory framework approved by governments, including carbon pricing mechanisms. Both nuclear power and large-scale hydro schemes should have a place, subject to market factors, once they have passed regulatory examination on health and safety, and, in the case of large hydro, the impacts on large areas of land and on the rights of the present occupiers of the land that will be flooded. Given a proper independent body to determine the life-cycle carbon impact of any technology, coupled with market-based carbon pricing, the market will deliver the most cost-effective solution. The judgement of the other environmental, health and wider risk factors will then be for countries to choose through their own societal and governance mechanisms. The outcome will undoubtedly vary from country to country, as we have seen and are seeing with the usage of nuclear energy.

There is one technology I will however comment on as a geologist and someone who has dealt with fossil fuels all his life, and that is carbon capture and storage (CCS). As a geologist I am convinced that the technology is both safe and feasible, although there is much work to do to gain public acceptance of this. We have been safely injecting large volumes of gas, including carbon dioxide, into rocks for years. The industry knows a lot about the technology involved. In my opinion the problem is not feasibility or safety, but cost and scale. Depending on the point of collection, it would appear that a reliable carbon price approaching $100 per ton of carbon dioxide will be needed, at least initially. For public purposes, large-scale demonstration projects will be needed and these will have to have some sort of government support if they are to proceed. All of that will be sorted out in competition with other technologies within the regulatory and market framework that is needed to allow the right technology choices to be made.

To me the interesting aspect of this technology is its ability to deliver low-carbon use of fossil fuels, whether hydrocarbons or coal. If energy demand is not constrained by significant increases in efficiency of use, the additional supply of energy is likely to come from the most easily expandable source of energy, which has been coal up to now, although the advent of shale gas through fracking technologies in the United States and elsewhere may change this and provide a much less carbon-intensive alternative to coal. For this reason the capability to sequester carbon dioxide may be critical. It is not the technological challenge of doing this that is the issue; it is the scale that would be required to have an impact that worries me. In a talk to the International Geological Congress in Oslo in 2008, I pointed out that to have a significant impact we would have to create an industry similar in size to the current global natural gas industry.

To capture the emissions from 100 gigawatts of coal-fired generating capacity (approximately this amount of capacity has sometimes been installed in a single year in China) would require the capacity to inject of some 350 billion cubic metres of carbon dioxide per annum or volu-metrically about half of the current North American gas production capacity. To achieve CCS on the scale envisaged in most low-carbon energy scenarios would require essentially recreating the current global gas or oil production capacity by 2050. The figures are not strictly comparable as gas production involves treatment and processing of the gas but limited compression, while in all cases compression will be required for CCS. However, this does give an idea of the scale of pipeline systems and injection plants required, quite apart from separating the carbon dioxide from other gases, which is probably the biggest technical challenge. Depending on your viewpoint, and on the market rewards for sequestering carbon dioxide, creating systems to handle such volumes of carbon dioxide is either a great economic opportunity to build a new business or an impossible economic challenge.

In the last decade, progress in the evolution of the energy landscape has been slow, but there has been undeniable progress. Market-driven private-sector capital investment in alternative 'clean' energy has climbed to some $150 billion a year, although it has faltered somewhat since the financial crisis. To put it in perspective, estimated oil and gas capital expenditure in 2008 was some $400 billion. To achieve a real breakthrough and rapid change will require the market to be channelled by a sensible regulatory framework that is supported by consumers and voters. In 2004, in a presidential address to the Geological Society of

London, the world's longest-established Geological Society, I suggested what was required to achieve this. For a variety of reasons we are still some way off achieving those conditions. To achieve real progress we need a measure of agreement between groups sitting as it were at the three corners of a triangle. The three groups are government, the consumer/voter, and business. Although the linkages and interdependencies between the groups are clear, the problem is that the three constituencies tend to pass the buck to one another.

Consider the positions of each of the three groups in turn, perhaps in caricature, but not so far from the truth.

Passing the buck: the business position

Let us start with business. Business tends to shift the buck to consumers, with sideswipes at government regulation. Major energy companies, for example, work successfully on the energy efficiency of their own operations. They set targets for themselves well in excess of the Kyoto agreement (although this on its own would certainly not deliver anything like the reduction in greenhouse gas emissions that the IPCC considers desirable, if not essential). However, these targets addressing their own internal consumption ignore the much larger impact of fossil fuels in the hands of their customers. Energy companies also offer choice and advice to their customers to improve their energy efficiency and to allow them to make lower-carbon choices. Several of them have growing renewable energy businesses or are working on transitions to biofuels or even hydrogen. However, the very essence of business is to meet the demands of customers—we cannot sell what customers do not want. This is what might be called the 'Bill Ford dilemma'. Bill Ford, Chairman of the Ford Motor Company and great-grandson of Henry Ford, has stated publicly that he does not think that large four-wheel-drive vehicles are a good thing environmentally. Several of his shareholders pointed out that those vehicles are popular with customers, Ford is rather good at making them and that is where the biggest margins are made. So Bill Ford found himself trapped in an uncomfortable dilemma. In general in businesses, the buck is quietly passed to consumers. The industry (and Ford) is now addressing this dilemma by making more-efficient hybrid versions of the same large vehicles, thus giving the consumer the choice of making a move towards greater efficiency, but the underlying issue remains.

There are also encouraging signs in the retail industry of businesses finding new ways of engaging with their customers. In 2007, the major UK retailer Marks & Spencer (M&S) launched its very thoughtful 'Plan A' programme with the declared intention of becoming the most sustainable retailer by 2015. The programme is a mix of commitments to targets in its own use as well as offering consumers more sustainable choices. They committed to making all their UK and Irish operations carbon-neutral by 2012, maximising their use of renewable energy and using offsetting only as a last resort. At the same time in the area of energy use they offer their customers tips on energy saving or renewable energy use, giving them also a possibility to make a personal commitment online to an action such as using low-energy light bulbs. I am sure that the programme as a whole has been beneficial, both in informing employees and customers on more sustainable approaches and giving them a feeling that they are doing something positive. This will undoubtedly have had wide impact and benefits, but understandably the great majority of the population is driven by considerations of cost, convenience or image. In the case of M&S, in 2012 their website showed that only around 20,000 people had signed up to individual commitments, although there is no doubt that millions will have bought their more sustainable products. Achieving effectively universal use of, for example, more energy-efficient appliances or vehicles requires regulation. This may not be popular with either businesses or consumers.

As I said in Chapter 6, business in general is paranoid about regulation. This is because of bitter past experience of the cost of unnecessary or overly prescriptive and bureaucratic regulation, which in the end drives business into the ground. Bureaucracy is an anathema to business. However, if you ask business people whether they really think regulation is unnecessary, you will soon extract an admission that it is essential to the sound working of markets—regulation on transparency, on quality, on competition and so on.

Passing the buck: the consumer position

Consumers, who in democracies are also voters, have considerable power. Where a negative view becomes generally held, a company or government can be destroyed. Polls suggest that in many countries, including the United States, consumers believe that climate change is a potential problem, even if it is not fully understood. However, after an increase in awareness we may now be seeing some weariness with the topic. In countries all across the world, I have found consumer attitudes very similar. People want instant, economic and reliable energy. Where they do not get it—whatever their level of affluence—they go to great lengths to acquire it, whether it be through expensive and inefficient generators, or by lugging lead acid batteries on a bicycle miles to be recharged, a dangerous, environmentally unfriendly process. Such is the demand that the very poor are prepared to spend a disproportionately high share of their meagre income to acquire energy. It is also true that although people demand energy at almost any cost, they tend not to worry about the environmental impact, both local and global, of their own individual actions. The demand for personal transportation is also similarly global. We sometimes forget in our world the great social and economic liberation brought about by personal transportation some decades ago. That liberation is occurring in China and India, as people progress from bicycles via motor scooters to cars, allowing them to bring goods to market and take themselves to a more remote place of work. As a result, demand for transportation fuel in these markets is booming way ahead of GDP growth. Equally, whether in Mumbai or Beijing, people worry about the consequences of increased personal mobility—its traffic jams and its local pollution. For both power and mobility the consumer is normally well aware of the problems, particularly the more immediate local impacts of pollution, but is normally loath to forgo any personal convenience to address the problems. That is something that consumers think 'they' should do something about—'they' being government or business.

Passing the buck: the position of governments

And what of governments? They are certainly fearful of offending the consumers, their voters. They therefore fall back on exhorting businesses to develop solutions, to spend more on research and development and so on. To be fair they often try to do their best through both taxation and regulation, the two main levers available to them given that governmental exhortation is generally ineffective. In regulation they tend to fiddle at the edges in things that are often costly to business, but whose price impacts are not directly visible to consumers. In taxation, fearful of the wrath of consumers, they also try to act in areas somewhat remote from their voters. Governments are generally nervous of attracting criticism from businesses for supposedly damaging the economy or destroying jobs, neither of which governments have any desire to do. The temptation of allying government with consumers for a bit of business bashing, particularly where the costs are hidden or can be blamed on business, is usually there and governments sometimes succumb to it. Given its lack of votes, business in turn defends itself with the best weapon at hand—the argument that international competitiveness will be lost.

A three-cornered approach?

Given all this potential for buck passing between business, government and consumers, is there genuinely a chance of a three-cornered approach that will encourage us down energy paths that are more likely to deliver a low-carbon outcome?

I think any successful approach needs to have the following elements clearly and openly expressed:

First, it is essential when delivering mobility and energy alternatives that utility to the customer is maintained and the cost is not noticeably increased. Consumers are happy to use renewable energy as long as it is reliable, it is available all the time and it does not cost a great deal more than traditional forms of energy. In transportation, consumers will not give up personal mobility (or will aspire to it if they do not have it) except in city locations where public transport gives clear advantages. Despite its sometimes poor operation, I believe this is so in central London, where the London Underground will almost always beat surface transport for speed if not comfort, although I am reminded of a friend of my daughter's who once said 'When my Dad says he's using public transport, he means a taxi.' In personal transportation, I believe people want reasonable performance and space. A European environmental minister once asked me how to get people off their love affair with the motor car. I believe we should not even try to interfere with that love. It is deeply imbedded and interfering with other people's love affairs is normally unproductive. But the love is for personal movement and space, and the freedom that it brings, not the internal combustion engine per se. This means significant investment in public transport, particularly urban public transport and work on low-carbon vehicles.

Second, this is a case where the market on its own will not deliver solutions; we need a framework to guide it. The market is an unsurpassed mechanism for allocating resources to deliver goods and services. Through the market, technologies compete and are optimised or discarded, which opens the field for creativity in competing businesses and for consumer choice. For markets to work well they do require regulation on transparency, quality and defences against monopoly. I am a strong believer in the power and value of markets, but like most things, they have a failing. Without regulation to channel their power, markets will not on their own deliver things that are of no immediate benefit to the individual consumer making a choice, even though they may be beneficial to consumers collectively, in other words society. For example, in the United States in the past 20 years there has been a radical improvement in the efficiency of automobile engines, delivering more power for less input. Every bit of this gain in efficiency has gone into larger and heavier vehicles, with consumer decisions in part driven by a feeling that you are safer than your fellow road users if you drive a heavier vehicle. US history demonstrates this quite graphically. In response to the last significant increase in oil prices in the 1970s, when prices in the equivalent to 2012 prices climbed to $55 per barrel in the 1973–74 oil crisis and climbed again to $99 per barrel with the Iranian revolution in 1979 and the Iraq–Iran war, efficiency of the US light auto fleet climbed quite dramatically up to the mid-1980s. In response to price and the US Corporate Average Fuel Economy (CAFE) standards enacted by Congress in 1975, light-vehicle fuel efficiency almost doubled, from 12 to 21 miles per gallon, until the oil price crash of the mid-1980s and the relaxation of the CAFE standards.[11] As is well known, the picture is distorted by the growth of 'light trucks' not properly covered by the regulation.

From the early 1980s, and in particular after the oil price crash in the mid-1980s, all the gains in engine efficiency went into the increased power needed to drive ever heavier vehicles together with an increase in acceleration—a gain of 4 seconds in accelerating to 60 mph or 100 km/hour. Such are the priorities of affluent societies around the world. Now, with the impact of the financial crisis coupled with actual and expected high oil prices we can expect significant increases in energy efficiency, particularly if governments adopt policies to drive the markets in that direction. There are encouraging signs that the Obama administration has put in place tough efficiency mandates for the automobile industry.[12]

Economists have a ready answer to influencing consumer choice: use price signals in the market by internalising costs through taxation. In many societies, consumers react in a very negative way to this, certainly above a certain price threshold. The fuel tax protests and the blockade of refineries by lorry drivers in the UK in 2000 forced the then Prime Minister Tony Blair to reverse the policy of automatic fuel tax increases above inflation, intended to dampen fuel demand. The wrath of the consumer voter is something democratic governments rightly fear. At a certain level of tax-imposed price increases there will be a rebellion,

11 For illustration, see G. Maring, Cambridge Systematics, 'Surface Transportation Funding Issues and Options', PowerPoint presentation to the National Surface Transportation Infrastructure Financing Commission, June 2007, www.docstoc.com/docs/805187/Surface-Transportation-Funding-Issues-and-Options.

12 The new standards mandate average fuel economy of 54.5 miles per gallon by the 2025 model year, with 35.6 by 2017; see B. Vlasic, 'US Sets Higher Fuel Efficiency Standards', *New York Times*, 28 August 2012, www.nytimes.com/2012/08/29/business/energy-environment/obama-unveils-tighter-fuel-efficiency-standards.html?_r=0.

perhaps through the ballot box, perhaps through direct action. Such a protest may often have much popular support, at least in the short term, and leaves governments fearful of the electoral backlash. Indeed, there is much to be said for the argument that consuming countries should adopt a variable sales tax on energy, reducing it when the market drives energy prices high and increasing it when market energy prices fall, thus delivering a more stable consumer energy price.

Unfortunately, increasing prices, the standard economic solution to controlling demand, have very undesirable social effects in all countries and hit low-income and rural populations particularly hard. It is therefore much more desirable to achieve the same results by regulatory frameworks that clearly tighten efficiency requirements over time. These encourage the market to find solutions to delivering the same utility at increased levels of efficiency. While it is important to use such frameworks to accelerate reductions in energy intensity in the industrialised world where energy usage is already high, it is even more important to ensure that the strong growth of energy-consuming stock in the rapidly industrialising parts of the world is invested in the most energy-efficient alternatives.

The unintended consequences of the uneven impact of increasing fuel prices through taxation, with its negative impacts on poor or rural communities and knock-on effects on prices through increased delivery costs, can be avoided by regulations mandating vehicle efficiency. This affects all consumers equally and is generally seen as 'fair'. Competition to meet consumer preferences for power or space would still take place within the efficiency mandate, but there would be a non-fiscal premium on efficiency that would benefit all. In other areas where demand is driven purely by regulatory frameworks, such as in regulated requirements for seat belts, airbags and catalytic converters, the market continues to operate, driving higher efficiency, lower cost or greater utility. There is sometimes an increased cost through requirements for additional mandated equipment, but the cost is hidden from the public, which generally accepts the requirement in the interests of safety or health. In the case of fuel efficiency, there is an additional direct consumer benefit to the individual consumer through lower fuel usage.

There is a curious reluctance of governments to place a general upper limit on the fuel consumption of any personal vehicle, or indeed to mandate efficiency levels in domestic appliances. We see an increase in transparency in demonstrating the energy efficiency of vehicles and appliances, with the hope that consumers will exercise rational or socially beneficial choice. There seems to be an underlying assumption that we have an inalienable individual right to choose an inefficient solution that is manifestly not in the interests of society as a whole and thus not in the end in our own interest. As well as labelling vehicles and appliances with their efficiency levels, it seems to me that it would be sensible to progressively raise the lower limit and ban the production and sale of less efficient units. The market would then compete to deliver the characteristics most attractive to consumers within that framework. In transportation different sections of the consuming public are attracted by speed and acceleration, elegance of design, space and comfort or different combinations of these attributes.

I know from my own experience that there is surprisingly strong opposition to frameworks mandating minimum mileage efficiency levels. In a BBC television programme in 2008 I proposed such a solution. In the interview I did not in fact specify a particular level of mileage efficiency, but the BBC's environment correspondent Roger Harrabin picked 35 miles per gallon as the cut-off and it was reported as though I had recommended that level.[13] As that is not a particularly aggressive target, I did not contradict the report. The successive Toyota Priuses that my wife and I have been driving from 2001 (at that time I was still Chairman of Shell and we have passed the older models on to the rest of our family where they are still in service) do above 50 mpg even if you drive fast and aggressively. Although much of the reaction to the report was positive, there were many objections from motoring enthusiasts and motoring correspondents, linked with accusations of hypocrisy because of my career with Shell and the fact that both Anglo American and Shell use corporate jets. I also incidentally own a 50-year-old Aston

13 R. Harrabin, 'EU "should ban inefficient cars"', BBC News, 4 February 2008, news.bbc.co.uk/2/hi/science/nature/7225451.stm.

Martin, which like current Astons is a beautiful piece of engineering. I was neither suggesting that all existing vehicles should be banned, nor a restriction use of either aircraft or vehicles that can carry large families or even small numbers in comfort. In delivering that utility, however, we should make sure that the means of doing so meets mandated minimum fuel efficiency standards.

I also do not think that hybrids are unequivocally the answer to vehicle efficiency. There needs to be a common and well-established basis for determining the 'oil-well to wheels' consumption of energy of a vehicle, including all the energy used in its manufacture. It is important to have a reputable and independent scientific body to determine this and not simply depend on advertisers' claims.

Perhaps my views on the use of regulatory frameworks rather than relying on price signals came from my early personal experience of the effects of emission control. When as a ten-year-old I first came to London from the West Indies in 1950 to go to boarding school, I lived during the holidays with my two of my father's sisters, who were spinsters of the First World War generation. We lived in a flat in which space and water heating came largely from coal fires, supplemented by coal-generated town gas. One of my duties in the school holidays was to call down the service well at the rear of the flat and ask Mr Monday, the porter, to send up a couple of hods of best anthracite for the water boiler and a hod of Welsh nuts for the living-room fire. These I would dutifully unload and if permitted shovel into the boiler or coal scuttle. The electricity was of course also supplied by large coal-fired power stations such as those at Bankside (now elegantly converted to the art gallery Tate Modern) or the iconic Battersea Power Station, a listed building derelict for years while a suitable use for it is sought. In fact, I can remember the fourth and final chimney on Battersea being completed in the 1950s. Battersea is reputed to be the largest brick building in Europe and both it and Bankside were designed by the architect Sir Giles Gilbert Scott, who also gave us the classic red London telephone box.

As a result of the combustion of all this coal, the atmosphere in London in the 1950s was choking. Thick sulphurous fogs were relatively common in winter and on occasion were so thick that buses took the wrong turning on their routes. I can also remember people walking in front of cars and buses to guide them. The worst event was in 1952 when several thousand people were reported to have died. The health effects were certainly severe and in the end the Clean Air Act of 1956 (and later in 1968) made London a smoke-free zone. One could only use town gas or 'smokeless fuels' burned in especially efficient stoves. I suspect that I agreed with my aunt that the inability to toast crumpets in winter in front of an open fire represented the beginning of the end of civilisation as we knew it, but within a few years we all blessed the result. The point about this is that it was regulation that applied to all, forced the habits of all to change and equally benefited all. There was no effort to use the market (although the market has of course delivered since many different heating solutions and even 'flame effect' fires in front of which you could toast crumpets should you wish). There was no allowance for the residents of the more affluent London boroughs of Kensington and Chelsea to pay a bit more, keep their open fires and generate a bit more pollution for the rest of London. If you ride a sub-urban train into one of the south London main-line stations you will see the serried ranks of quite small terraced houses with five or six chimneys on each house unit dividing wall. Each of these had the capacity to emit clouds of choking smoke in winter. The change was dramatic and far-reaching. Within a relatively short time the air in London became cleaner and over the years the blackened and corroded buildings have been cleaned and restored. My aunts lived to bless the regulation.

It may therefore be more acceptable to increase overall energy efficiency through regulatory frameworks that drive the market towards efficiency—through building regulations, transport efficiency standards, industry-sector efficiency standards and so on—rather than relying on pricing that can have unintended side effects. Most societies already have regulations covering non-energy-related matters: for example, building regulations to ensure earthquake safety and various emission standards. Although these have a cost, they are generally socially acceptable, provided the population can see the overall benefit. Major changes have been achieved through such regulations—examples are not just exhaust catalysts on vehicles, removal of lead from gasoline, seat belt and airbag regulation, but also mandating certain fuels for public transport in city centres such as New Delhi, elimination of chlorofluorocarbons (CFCs) through the Montreal Protocol and so on. Unlike most of these initiatives, which cause a permanent increase in cost, many energy-efficiency frameworks actually deliver positive net present values.

In the case of climate, it is of course not just a matter of ensuring more efficient energy use, but of constructing a framework that drives the market to develop less carbon-intensive energy sources. This does mean establishing a price for carbon and globalising carbon pricing as much as possible, allowing transfer of finance and technology to where it has most impact. Europe already has a carbon-trading scheme. It does not look likely at present that the United States will introduce a national scheme, although there are movements within several states. China is now experimenting with carbon trading schemes. The UNFCCC Clean Development Mechanism already allows for the transfer of technology and finance to developing countries. All of these schemes would, however, benefit from harmonisation and improvement. International carbon trading will be important in allowing the transfer of funding from developed countries to developing countries such as China and India, where the impact may be greatest. This would also be a contribution to breaking the international deadlock on whose responsibility it is to move first on abatement measures. It is important not to confuse carbon pricing with pricing of energy overall. In the UK, for example, much of the price of a litre of petrol (gasoline) is made up of tax and duties. Should a price of US$50/ton of CO_2 be introduced it would be equivalent to only an additional £0.07 a litre on an overall price currently at around £1.30 per litre. This is within the short-term price variations that we have seen in the last year. So, even if a carbon price of $100 per ton of carbon dioxide was required to effect real change, the price impact would be painful, but not completely unacceptable.

A rational approach to the issue of climate change that also has some chance of achieving public acceptance is to accept:

- That we have to continue to provide consumers with the utility that they expect, that they must not feel that they are being unnecessarily burdened financially or forced to accept a reduction in the utility that they have come to expect

- That a broad regulatory framework driving efficiency is necessary to guide the market as well as a framework to establish carbon cap and trade schemes, and

- That the creativity of the market is necessary to find solutions, to provide choice and to guide the allocation of resources

It is encouraging that China, with its very rational government, has set itself energy-efficiency targets overall. I have had many discussions on the subject with Chinese planners and ministers over the years and I believe that it is not impossible that they will begin to apply the regulatory framework needed to drive efficiency. There is, however, the problem that in China regulations are often ignored. I believe that the Chinese government can see that they have an opportunity to develop their motor industry, which is already probably the largest in the world, in a direction that produces lower emissions and uses energy more efficiently: for example, by using hybrid technology or building electric vehicles. Given the size of its market and industry, China could become a world leader in the production and export of low-carbon-intensity vehicles, reducing a large energy import bill that is a source of growing concern to the government. To establish a carbon pricing system will undoubtedly take longer in China.

There will certainly be those who argue that we need radical changes of lifestyle in order to achieve emission-reduction targets. I do not believe that drastic changes in lifestyle are saleable politically in wealthy democracies. I think it is also wishful thinking to hope that consumers in developing countries will be satisfied with a standard of living any lower than we have in the West, and indeed why should they? This is a matter of delivering the same high standard of living and utility but at radically greater levels of resource efficiency and reduced carbon intensity than is possible at present. If it is guided by the right framework, I am confident that the market can deliver this over time. It is of course possible that those who say that a radical reduction in the global average standard of living is needed are in fact correct, but I doubt that it would happen unless a crisis, such as a war, is manifestly at the door. It may come to that, but I suspect that the boiling frog analogy is uniquely apt in this context.

It is of course also possible that there is some long-term cyclical effect that we do not as yet understand that is going to cause the earth to cool instead of warm. After all, only a few decades ago many people thought from the study of trends that we might be going to enter another ice age. Those who cite this as an argument for doing nothing, or who claim that there may yet be some factor that climatologists have not properly taken into account, should remember that there is no reason why these unknown effects or trends should lead to cooling to offset our human effects. They might just as well be additive and make the situation worse. Even if one is of a particularly sceptical bias, it would appear wise to take serious precautionary steps now to use resources much more efficiently and to find energy solutions that will be necessary in the long term, regardless of arguments on climate change.

To address the challenge of climate change and of excessive resource utilisation, we need to emphasise that we will deliver the same for very much less—a classic challenge for business. And there will of course be many in businesses who also say that that is impossible. That is quite normal. In any business when a cost or efficiency target is first raised, the cry is always that it is impossible. Surprisingly, when the arguments over the theoretical level of the target cease and creative minds are focused on practical implementation, the targets are often exceeded.

There will be arguments from enthusiasts for one or other technology who will insist that their particular enthusiasm represents the holy grail—whether it be solar photovoltaics, wind, nuclear, hydrogen, geothermal, carbon sequestration, hybrid vehicle technology or tidal power—and that that technology should receive special attention or even subsidy. I do not know which of these technologies will win, and I am not confident that anyone else knows either. The frameworks we need to guide the market should be technology-blind. It would probably be best to use carbon intensity as a framework rather than a broader area such as renewable energy, but I would accept some modest mandating of different broad power sources as a first step.

Finally, I would not like to give an impression that the consumer should be inactive in this process. Consumer choice is vital and is not always based on economics. If that were so, many designer labels would be put out of business by their functionally equivalent utilitarian competitors. Similarly, the urban four-wheel-drive or sport utility vehicle would not have gained such popularity, for in terms of utility they represent high capital outlay followed by higher operating costs due to fuel consumption. People flock to drive them because of the image, the feeling it gives them and perhaps a feeling of security due to the tank-like construction. I believe we need to harness the market. The image of these vehicles is indeed beginning to change. We have to make eco-efficiency as fashionable as four-wheel-drive vehicles. We need to use the powers of social pressure and the attraction of beautiful engineering. This is not hair-shirt environmentalist stuff—we should rather call it eco-hedonism: taking pleasure from both comfort and operating performance as well as eco-efficiency.

The challenge of climate change is something that no section of society can address on its own. There are many energy sources, each with its limits.[14] The approach that I have outlined is one where I believe it might just be possible to get wider alignment around. Whether or not this is so, I remain convinced that, unless we can develop a genuinely three-cornered approach, acceptable to governments, to the consumer and to business, there is little chance that we will take the necessary timely steps.

14 For an extensive discussion of energy sources and policies, see Daniel Yergin, *The Quest: Energy, Security, and the Remaking of the Modern World* (New York: Penguin Press, 2011).

Chapter 8

Corruption:
The biggest market failure of all

It is often said that climate change is the result of the biggest market failure of all time. I would argue that corruption is in fact an even greater distortion of markets and to date has done much more economic damage than climate change. Corruption is a pervasive evil. While some would say that so-called facilitation payments, small payments that encourage officials to do something that is their duty, are not damaging, I would disagree. This is merely the most common form of a very infectious disease that slides readily into making a payment to encourage an official to neglect his or her duty. However, it is true that the major damage comes not from facilitation, but from the award of contracts on the basis of corruption. In those cases, not only is the price of purchase inflated by kickbacks, but also the product or service delivered is often useless or in a location designed purely to win political favours.

A key question—have you ever bribed anyone yourself?

Given my opposition to corruption, I have often been asked whether I have been involved in the payment of bribes or personally paid a bribe. In 2010, I was asked this on a BBC World Service broadcast during a discussion on corruption.[1] I am pleased to say that both Shell and Anglo American both had very strong anti-bribery policies throughout my career with them. The same is true of the other companies on whose boards I have served. HSBC, Accenture, Saudi Aramco and Hermes EOS all hold unequivocal positions on corruption. On numerous occasions I have refused requests for bribes, both personally and on behalf of the companies for whom I worked. However, I have twice personally paid a bribe. I still feel guilty about it, but the circumstances illustrate what leads people to take the line of least resistance.

On one occasion, I was returning by road with my family from a camping holiday in northern Nigeria, Mali and Burkina Faso. We were almost back to our home in Warri when we drove through the city of Benin. Two of our children had chicken pox and we were all hot and dirty from camping. In the city I did a left-hand turn across the traffic at traffic lights. A policeman stopped us and accused me of doing an illegal turn. No amount of argument on the niceties of the Nigerian Highway Code helped and, while most Nigerian officials are sympathetic to cases of family illness, this one insisted that chicken pox was just heat rash. In the end I agreed to buy a case of beer for the upcoming policemen's Christmas party, and duly did so and delivered it. On parting friends with the constable, I asked him to give my regards to the local state Chief of Police, whom I knew by name. He remarked that had I said before that I knew his Chief there would have been no problem, but to me that would have been a more offensive form of corruption.

You might ask why I did not report the demand for money to the Chief. Some time before, we had had a major oilfield fire and the Shell fire-fighters had been assisted by the municipal fire-fighters. As a thank-you gesture from Shell we arranged to give the fire station a collection of armchairs and a television set for their recreation room. To avoid the probability of a cash donation being diverted at higher levels, my Nigerian colleagues and I decided that the goods should be purchased by Shell and delivered directly to the fire station, where it was received with

1 J. Melik, 'The Dilemma of Bribes: To Pay or Not to Pay', BBC News, 15 December 2010, www.bbc.co.uk/news/business-11957514.

great delight. To my horror, I later heard that the State Commissioner of Public Works had purloined the goods from the fire station and replaced them with similar but older goods. A short time later at a reception I saw the Commissioner talking to the Chief of Police. I went up to him, full of indignation. He greeted me warmly, thanked me for the generous gift to the fire station and immediately went on to say, without any shame, that as the goods were far too good for the fire crew, he had put them in his own house and replaced them with his older material. I added him to the mental list I keep of people I have met who should be in jail,[2] but the Chief of Police's attitude indicated that this was not something that was likely to happen soon.

The second occasion on which I was personally involved in bribery was when my wife Judy and I were planning with my seven-year-old daughter, a Welsh friend Carole and a Malaysian colleague Ibrahim Ahmad to drive our Toyota Land Cruiser back across the Sahara from Nigeria to England. As the vehicle had been bought and heavily taxed in Nigeria, the plan was for another friend to use it to drive back from England to Nigeria. To achieve this we needed a certificate that would allow the re-import of the vehicle to Nigeria. Given the licence documents of the vehicle, this should have been a relatively simple matter. When Judy went to the relevant office in Lagos, she was approached by an agent at the door who asked if she would like him to do the paperwork for her. She declined, saying she would queue and do the work herself. The official viewed the papers and said that all was in order. He then asked where the vehicle was, and on learning that it was several hundred kilometres away in Warri, he smiled the smile of one about to play a trump card, and said that he needed to see the Toyota himself. There was no way that this would have been possible before we had to leave and so at that point Judy asked him to wait while she consulted her friend (the agent) who for about five pounds swiftly handled the processing of the paper.

---

2 I have another mental list, alas somewhat shorter, of those whom I have met who did subsequently go to jail.

I still feel bad about these two breaches of my own principles. They do, however, demonstrate that even people opposed in principle to any form of corruption may succumb if the alternative seems difficult or impossible, or affects their family. In many cases, given time and persistence in a steadfast refusal, payment can be avoided. On one occasion, returning to a country with my family, I did not have the necessary resident re-entry stamp in my passport, although I did have a letter from the ministry saying that I should be permitted to re-enter. After an hour and a half of argument, during which the immigration official had initially threatened to put me back on the plane to London, we discussed why Shell would not pay a small sum to avoid this greater expense. I filled out many forms to accompany our confiscated passports to the ministry. The official finally realised that sending our confiscated passports to the ministry would simply involve more work and bring no benefit and so he capitulated. I could have our passports back and we could tear up all the forms. The airport was nearly empty and all the other officials had gone home. We had got to know each other quite well, and as I left the officer asked me whether I still had nothing to give him. I have subsequently regretted that I rather piously still refused. He had after all long since let Judy and the children through. We had both quite enjoyed the argument, and in the end the fault was not his personally, but the system in which he worked and which was probably routinely late in paying his salary. With hindsight, a small gift of friendship to buy himself a meal or a drink would not have done much harm.

About ten years later, when my son Douglas was going to spend a year driving with three friends down through Africa to Cape Town, I gave him advice for crossing borders. Be patient, absolutely polite and respectful, and if in doubt apologise profusely for your very existence. He later told me that it was the best advice I had ever given him. He added that on days when they were going to cross a border, he always put on a clean shirt and had a shave. In this way they had crossed numerous remote borders. As he pointed out, it is just a matter of showing proper respect to officials doing an important job, often poorly or erratically paid.

'Grand corruption' and the involvement of governments

In 1997, my eldest brother George published a book with the title *Grand Corruption: The Problem of Trade and Business in Developing Countries*,[3] an analysis of corruption and its impact on development. The book was an expansion of an earlier 1994 paper[4] that he prepared for the recently formed organisation Transparency International. George was a founding member of that organisation, which was the inspiration and passion of Peter Eigen. Peter was determined to do something about the evils of corruption in the world, which he had seen during his work with the World Bank. George had spent a lifetime working in sugar and various agro-industries in developing countries, living in the West Indies, Kenya and Fiji, and was Chairman of the UK Chapter of Transparency International.

It was a delight to both George and me that we received awards from the Queen at the same investiture, just as some 80 years earlier in 1918 our father and uncle had both received Military Crosses from the King. I believe they were the first brothers to do so at the same investiture. George's award was an OBE with the citation 'for services to the fight against corruption'. Mine was for 'services to the international oil industry'. I always felt that George was more deserving of the knighthood.

George was particularly interested in what he called 'grand corruption'.[5] This is the most damaging form of corruption at ministerial or head-of-state level, which distorts entire economies and does not just inflate the cost of a project but often lumbers a country with an ineffectual and unnecessary white elephant. He pointed out that there were certain industries and types of project that were particularly prone to attracting corruption on a grand scale. First, the projects had to be

3 G.H. Moody-Stuart, *Grand Corruption: Problem of Trade and Business in Developing Countries* (New Delhi: World View Publications Paperback, 1997).
4 G.H. Moody-Stuart, *Grand Corruption in Third World Development* (Working Paper; Berlin: Transparency International, 1994).
5 Nihal Jayawickrama credits George with coining the phrase 'grand corruption' in A.Y. Lee-Chai and J.A. Bargh, *The Use and Abuse of Power: Multiple Perspectives on the Causes of Corruption* (Philadelphia, PA: Psychology Press/Taylor & Francis, 2001).

large and require a quantum of funding that would be attractive to a minister or head of state. Second, corruption was most likely in complex projects where it was difficult to make comparisons on a single element of performance. This allows for discretion in choice and hence opens the opportunity for corruptly influencing the choice.

George pointed out that these conditions are perhaps most effectively met in the arms industry, where the performance of, for example, different types of aircraft is often difficult to compare on a like-for-like basis, depending on which characteristic is emphasised. Furthermore, military sales have the advantage that the analysis can be cloaked in secrecy due to 'national security'. He might have added the condition of where there is an element of perceived national interest, such as supporting a strategic industry in the home country of the seller, otherwise honest people suspend their normal ethics. This is just an extension of the argument for committing unethical acts in the course of espionage for national security.[6] This element was certainly a factor in the appalling behaviour of the French oil company Elf in West Africa in the 1990s,[7] for which the then President Directeur General of Elf Loïk Le Floch-Prigent was later rightly convicted and sent to prison. In fact Elf, was merely being used by the Mitterrand government as an arm of French foreign policy. Not for nothing was Jean-Christophe Mitterrand, the son of President Mitterrand and his adviser on African affairs, known in West Africa as Papamadi ('Papa m'a dit' or 'Daddy told me'). From judicial enquiries in the 1990s it appears that the same was also true of Agip, a part of the

---

6 For a detailed, thoroughly researched and depressing review of corruption in the arms industry in many countries at all levels, see A. Feinstein, *The Shadow World: Inside the Global Arms Trade* (London: Penguin Books, 2012).

7 Elf under Le Floch-Prigent made corrupt payments to various Francophone West African governments, interfered in internal politics and used military support, or the threat of its withdrawal, to influence government actions. See also Chapter 2. (He has since [September 2012] been deported from Côte d'Ivoire to Togo and charged with being an accessory to fraud—the outcome is unclear.) Le Floch-Prigent is someone who is on both my lists referred to earlier in this chapter. See also J. Henley, 'Gigantic Sleaze Scandal Winds up as Former Elf Oil Chiefs are Jailed', *The Guardian*, 13 November 2003, www.guardian.co.uk/business/2003/nov/13/france.oilandpetrol.

Italian state enterprise ENI. And, lest one is tempted to think that this is merely something that is practised by continental European countries, we should not forget the UK's own scandal over the suspended prosecution of BAE Systems over alleged corruption in relation to sales to Saudi Arabia. I recall being appalled when a British High Commissioner to Malaysia said to a group of business people that businessmen did not mind corruption as long as the rules by which it was played were clear. I challenged him strongly on this statement both personally and on behalf of Shell. I realised, however, that at that time in the 1980s his views would have been shaped by the fact that most of his connection with business would have involved arms sales.

The United States was a commendable early mover in legislation against corruption with the passage of the Foreign Corrupt Practices Act (FCPA) in 1977, stimulated by a number of overseas corruption scandals, including that of Lockheed military aircraft sales to various governments. For 20 years or more the FCPA was the only piece of national legislation covering the bribery of foreign officials. Years later, foreign bribes were still tax-deductible in some European countries. The UK was embarrassingly slow to pass the Bribery Act 2010, which puts its national legislation on a par with or in advance of the US FCPA and meets its legislative obligations under the requirements of the OECD Anti-Bribery convention of 1997 and the subsequent tightening of these requirements in 2009.[8] However, even the United States is not proof against the temptations to promote national interest over transparency. I am personally aware of two cases, one in Bangladesh and one in Nigeria, where the United States used diplomatic channels to overturn awards made to non-US companies after transparent bid processes. On one occasion, when in a meeting with the president of the country concerned I complained about the abandonment of a transparent award

---

8 OECD Convention on Combating Bribery of Foreign Public Officials in International Business Transactions (see www.oecd.org/daf/anti-bribery/oecdantibriberyconvention.htm). The suite of documents covers the 1997 Convention, the 2009 Recommendation of the Council for Further Combating Bribery, and the 2009 Recommendation on the Tax Deductibility of Bribes to Foreign Public Officials.

process, the president said that he had been pressed by a phone call from the US Secretary of State to make an award to a US company. I have no reason to believe that this was untrue as the president was clearly very uncomfortable with the situation.

I have been critical of the slow progress of the UK government in introducing effective legislation covering overseas bribery and believe that the UK government does not have entirely clean hands in relation to arms sales. So when in the late 1990s I received a request to meet the then UK Trade Minister Brian Wilson I was concerned as to what subjects might be raised. I enquired within Shell as to what issues might be current and relevant, and soon became aware of a major offshore contract in Nigeria that was about to be awarded. I immediately feared pressure to award the contract to a British company. As it was neither in my power nor in line with Shell's principles to comply, I was not looking forward to a pleasant meeting. I was favourably surprised that when the subject of the contract came up, all that the Minister asked was that the proper and transparent procedures should be followed. The Minister was well informed that the process was under considerable pressure from elements in the Nigerian system to distort the process and I was delighted to be able to assure him that should such pressures become irresistible we would abort the whole process and accept significant delays on the project rather than accept a distorted outcome. I am happy to say that the Minister's behaviour was impeccable.

The ingenuity of corruption and of countermeasures

Corruption comes in very many forms, and approaches to corruption are as varied as countries themselves. There is an almost infinite variety of ingenious methods. The argument put forward that in some countries corruption is simply an accepted cultural norm is flawed. To say that corruption is rife does not mean that it is accepted as legitimate by the population at large, although it may well be by the beneficiaries of the corrupt practices. When faced with the argument that in a particular country a particular form of corrupt payment was culturally acceptable, my brother George suggested that if a payment were to be made the details should be published in the papers. He pointed out that potential recipients who argue that payments are culturally acceptable in their country are never prepared to have details of corrupt payments made public. Such payments are generally only considered reasonable by the recipients, not by the population at large who pay the price. This 'newspaper test' is a useful check in cases of doubt.

I recall many years ago a young Dutch engineer in Brunei who considered that there was evidence of collusion in the submission of bids from a group of local Chinese contractors. He called them all in and said that he suspected collusion. He announced that he was going to re-tender the job and he expected better behaviour in future. The new bids came in at satisfactorily reduced prices. The engineer was satisfied and gained credit for his actions. I suspect that the second set of bids had also been agreed in the local coffee shop. The contractors knew that the engineer could not be corrupted with money. Instead they gave him a result that not only gave him credit in the eyes of his superiors, but also made him think that he had got the measure of the contractors and so he would hopefully reduce his vigilance in future. One effective way forward would have been to bring in additional contractors who were not part of the ring. Unfortunately, this is not always practical, so other means have to be tried. The battle against corruption equally requires ingenuity on the part of those issuing contracts. I was reminded of this particular incident when I read in the press of a legal battle that the US government had had over the construction of a new embassy building in Tokyo. The legal battle was won and the contractors guilty of collusion were fined. However, this was a somewhat Pyrrhic victory, as I understand that it was accepted that the contractors could agree among themselves how to allocate the fine.

There are many indirect forms of corruption that can be difficult to detect. When I was responsible for operations in the Western Division of Shell's Nigerian operations in the late 1970s we had a problem with imports through the newly built port of Warri. Shipments of oilfield goods were repeatedly held up in the port and large amounts of duty levied on them, in spite of the fact that they were mostly not dutiable. In addition, the taxation arrangements between Shell and the government were such that all forms of tax were aggregated and then topped up until an overall rate was reached. So it made no difference to either Shell or the government whether tax was collected as duty paid at the port or as tax in the later rounding-up process. This was explained repeatedly to the chief of customs in the port, but none the less he insisted on levying millions of dollars of duty on goods coming through the port. This resulted in a large amount of administrative work all round and, much worse, delayed equipment essential for oil production. Apart from extra work and delays, the financial effect for both the government and Shell was negligible, so the intransigence of the chief of customs appeared inexplicable, unless he had found some method of diverting the payments to his own advantage. I puzzled over this for a long time, but investigations showed that the payments could be tracked though the correct routes to the central authorities. This continued to puzzle me until one day I saw in the newspaper a photograph of the head of Warri Port customs receiving an award for being the officer who collected most customs duty in all of Nigeria. As essentially all of this duty came from Shell, there was no need to collect duty from anyone else, opening a potentially lucrative path for accepting payments from others to avoid duty. After all, who would investigate an officer who was so clearly highly industrious in collection of duties? I was full of admiration for the ingenuity, whether or not there was actually any malfeasance involved.

Ingenuity in corruption requires ingenious countermeasures. One of the most ingenious was designed by my successor as Chairman at Shell, Phil Watts. When Phil was in Nigeria in the early 1990s during the appalling regime of General Sani Abacha, the arrangements for the Nigerian Liquefied Natural Gas (LNG) export scheme were being negotiated.

The Nigerian LNG scheme had had a long and chequered history. It had first been mooted in the late 1960s, at the same time as the pioneering Brunei LNG scheme. At that time I was an exploration geologist working in Brunei and we were finding much of the gas offshore in neighbouring Sarawak that subsequently fed the Malaysian LNG schemes. So I watched the Brunei LNG scheme being built and come onstream in 1972. Unfortunately, the Nigerian scheme suffered repeated delays, initially because of the Nigerian civil war and its aftermath, but subsequently due to disagreements over the formation and terms of the joint-venture partnership and also the availability of funds for the Nigerian equity in the project.

As with many major projects that carry risk of various sorts, LNG projects are funded partly by equity capital put up by the shareholders and partly by project financing from a consortium of banks. To convince the banks that the project is viable and worth lending money to, a series of complex agreements is needed: first the producer's assurance that the reserves are there (normally with independent verification of reserves to ensure a 20- or 30-year project life); then the winning bid from the contractors who will build the actual LNG plant specifying the construction costs; then contracts for chartering or more often actually building the ships that will transport the gas to markets; and lastly long-term purchase contracts from the utility customers in Japan, Korea or Europe who will actually buy the gas. As a separate exercise, the banks have to be convinced that the shareholder equity is also available, as it is this equity that acts as a first cushion for the banks against the risks of the project.

All of these contracts are negotiated in advance and on one fateful day they are all signed together. If one piece is missing, the whole financing structure will fail. The process is not unlike the traditional method of buying a house in the UK where the mortgage money is only made available when all the surveys have been done, contracts exchanged, and the prospective owner's part of the purchase price is safely in the hands of the lawyers acting for the parties.

In the case of the Nigerian LNG scheme, the equity for the scheme was to come from the main partners in the scheme, Shell and the Nigerian National Petroleum Corporation (NNPC). Although over the various incarnations for the project from the 1970s to the 1990s money for the required Nigerian share of the equity had been set aside by NNPC, the problem was that, when it came close to being needed, the special account built up from oil revenue had been found to be empty. A generous interpretation would be that the funds had been applied to some other purpose. A less generous interpretation would be that they had been stolen.

The senior officers of NNPC were well aware of this danger, particularly given the particularly kleptocratic nature of the Abacha regime. They had no wish to see funds they had carefully built up for the NNPC equity share misappropriated. They therefore sensibly suggested that both the NNPC equity funds and the Shell equity funds be paid into an escrow account with a reputable bank, such that the funds could only ever be released to be spent on the LNG project. This was a pretty good idea, but it had one disadvantage for Shell. If the project did not go ahead or was delayed interminably, several hundred million dollars of Shell money would be stuck, along with the Nigerian money, in the escrow account. Although by the 1990s it did really look as though the project would go ahead, there was clearly a chance that the money might be stuck irretrievably for another decade or so, given that the gestation period so far had been some 30 years.

It was at this point that Phil Watts and his team came up with what I thought was a very ingenious and practical idea. The money would indeed be put by all parties into an offshore account with a reputable international bank. This was called the 'glass box'. Unlike a normal escrow account when the money can only be withdrawn for the intended purpose, any of the partners could put their hand into the box and remove their share of the money. However, if this happened, the independent bank was charged with making a global press release that would name the party that had withdrawn its funds and also announce that, because of this, the entire project was cancelled. We were confident that even the most corrupt government would not dare to put a hand into the box and be publicly revealed to be the cause of the cancellation of what was a prestige national project. So we proceeded towards the exchange of contracts and the launching of what has indeed proved to be a truly successful Nigerian project, a major source of income for Nigeria and a valuable outlet for gas that would otherwise be wasted or unused.

This was in 1995. Ken Saro-Wiwa and his colleagues were executed by the Abacha regime just shortly before the signature of the whole package of LNG-related contracts was due. The background of the unfair trial and tragic execution of Ken Saro-Wiwa and his fellow Ogonis and Shell's involvement is covered in Chapter 11, but there was global outrage. It was clear to everyone that to sign a multi-billion-pound LNG contract with a Nigerian government-owned entity as partner almost immediately after these appalling events was almost unthinkable. All the parties involved agreed on a delay and the construction contractors were persuaded to extend the validity of their bids for some months.

When General Abacha was informed of this decision he declared that, if Shell insisted on any delay at all, he would announce that by this action Shell had breached the terms of the agreement and caused the cancellation of the project. All parties would then be free to withdraw their money from the 'glass box'.

The implications were clear. If the project were delayed, a major project of benefit to Nigeria (and indeed Shell) would be cancelled and several hundred million dollars of funds from the account would be stolen by Abacha. He had found a route into the 'glass box'. We got the World Bank to issue a statement saying that the project was highly desirable from a national development and environmental viewpoint. Furthermore, it was clear that there would be no direct income benefit to the Nigerian government for many years, by which time the government would almost certainly be a different one. Faced with a choice between on the one hand Abacha cancelling the project and stealing the money if we delayed and on the other hand Shell being pilloried for gross insensitivity if we went ahead, we decided to go ahead. The decision was taken in full knowledge of the consequences. We were indeed excoriated in the press, redoubling the outrage that had initially naturally accompanied the execution. It is not the kind of decision that I would wish on anyone else, but I believe that in the long run it was the right one. The Nigerian LNG project is an outstanding success for Nigerians and Nigeria, a source of justifiable national pride, a bright light in the troubled Niger Delta. The plant, largely run by Nigerians, has never failed to load a cargo of LNG on time because of a plant failure or technical problem. Ironically, one of the main gas pipelines flows unmolested through Ogoniland. Abacha was dead long before any Nigerian government reaped the benefit of the income from the plant, but future generations of Nigerians will continue to do so. I still think that the 'glass box' was a good and ingenious idea to foil corruption, although we were not ingenious enough to think of all possible consequences.

Ingenuity is not always enough. In some cases it needs the determined and persistent actions of a government. At one point in the 1990s in Brazil, the major oil companies became aware that through an ingenious scam involving the paper export and improper re-import of Brazilian petroleum products, the Brazilian government was being defrauded of well over a billion dollars a year in tax revenue. Furthermore, as this product was much cheaper than properly taxed product, the independents were taking market share away from the major companies, further compounding the loss to the state and rendering honest businesses unprofitable. The government agreed with industry that action was needed to stamp out the practice. However, it took two years or so to achieve it. Perpetrators would be brought to regional courts, but judges would be bribed to dismiss the cases or find the perpetrators not guilty. A billion dollars a year of illicit revenue gives ample ammunition and incentive for corruption.[9] In a democracy, quite correctly, corrupt judges cannot simply be fired; due process has to be followed. Persistence and ingenuity on the part of government is required.

Practical steps to beat corruption

If corruption is to be beaten, it needs a concerted effort by different elements of society. An organisation such as Transparency International focuses on forward-looking action, using the sins and shortcomings of the past as lessons in how corruption can be prevented in future rather than seeking ultimate justice. They have developed many ingenious

9 This is part of the problem with the illegal theft of crude oil or 'bunkering' in Nigeria. As described in Chapter 1, the proceeds of this activity are at least some $1.8 billion a year, and probably much more; sums that can buy a great deal of delay and inactivity, if not actual support.

collective approaches, bringing together companies and civil society to see how the issues can be addressed in various ways and lobbying governments to improve legislation and then to enforce it rigorously. Transparency International UK also provides excellent anti-bribery training material on its website.[10]

However, there is absolutely no doubt that from a corporate point of view the place to start is within the corporation. That requires not just an uncompromising attitude towards any form of corruption, however minor, but also great care in sending the right signals from the top. Sending the right signals involves talking about corruption openly and giving examples of consequences, including being very open when contracts are lost or access is denied through refusing to pay a bribe. People within a company are more convinced by a good concrete example of where taking an ethical line actually lost the company a contract or cost money than they are by any number of talks on the theory of corruption and the applicable laws.[11] Discussion and training needs to include as many practical 'war stories' as possible. Setting an example in relatively minor things includes being careful about hospitality and gifts both offered and accepted at a senior level.

It is useful in a company to distinguish between outgoing bribes and incoming bribes. Outgoing bribes are within the control of a company. If a company does not want to pay a bribe, it does not have to, even though there may be severe damage to the business as a result. For any company to survive it has to have sound accounting systems so that it is clear what the money is being spent on. Developing and operating such systems is a core skill for a corporation. For that reason it is just nonsense for the senior management to say that they were quite unaware of systematic payments made over a long period. Either the management is lying, or they are woefully incompetent. How could a company such as Siemens pay out well over a billion euros improperly without being aware of it? Siemens is rightly now taking the lessons

10 www.transparency.org.uk.
11 See also the discussion in Chapter 12.

seriously to heart and is to be commended for it.[12] That is not to say that a country manager may not at some point, perhaps in what might be regarded as a fit of misplaced enthusiasm or an effort to improve performance, make an improper payment. In my Shell career I know of one such case. A country manager arranged for a political payment to be made for campaign expenses and disguised it as an advertising or information technology contract payment. Proper financial controls from the finance function and internal audit will normally reveal this. The country manager in question, an otherwise effective individual, left the company, and everyone knew why. However, it is much better to try and ensure that such things do not happen in the first place.

In contrast, incoming bribes are less in the control of a company. A decision by another business to try to distort a bidding process by attempting to bribe an employee is not something that management can control directly. One simply has to be aware of the possibility and to put in place processes in which decisions are not in the hands of a single individual but require input or agreement from others. Likewise in a country where small payments as an encouragement to do your job are common, vigilance is needed to ensure that a receptionist is not receiving small tips to ensure delivery of employment applications. Such practices are not easy to control. Clearly, development of an overall ethos will help, along with pride in company standards, but it would be wise to make sure that there is a functioning and trusted communication route to report irregularities that is available both to company employees and

12 In a settlement in 2008 with the US Justice Department and the Securities and Exchange Commission, Siemens pleaded guilty to violating accounting provisions of the Foreign Corrupt Practices Act, which outlaws bribery abroad. The company received fines of some $1.6 billion in fines and fees in Germany and the United States and will spend more than $1 billion for internal investigations and reforms. See www.nytimes.com/2008/12/21/business/worldbusiness/21siemens.html?pagewanted=all&_r=0. At the same time, in an agreement with the World Bank, Siemens agreed to spend $100 million in supporting anti-corruption projects around the world. See www.siemens.com/press/en/pressrelease/?press=/en/pressrelease/2010/corporate_communication/axx20101225.htm. A small portion of that money is being spent in supporting UN Global Compact Local Networks in anti-corruption work.

to suppliers or contractors to the company. Sometimes the disappointment that a representative of a major contractor was prepared to offer a bribe to company staff, perhaps even in the form of a bundle of notes left in a bag, is offset by delight that the company employee concerned reported it immediately. Saudi Aramco, the Saudi state oil company on whose board I sit, works hard on the development of such an ethos, with encouraging results. The document 'Doing Business with Saudi Aramco' makes plain that companies do not require an agent to deal with Saudi Aramco but can deal directly with the company.[13] At the same time all suppliers and contractors must sign a Supplier Code of Conduct and are given a confidential contact point within the company to raise any issues or concerns in relation to corruption. The company is also extremely tough on delisting contractors and suppliers who attempt to bribe staff or engage in corrupt behaviour, and major Saudi and Western companies have been suspended or delisted from doing business with the company for offences. Western companies are often more cautious about taking such action, at least overtly, as they are more likely to be subject to legal challenges in different jurisdictions if they attempt to apply global bans to suppliers and contractors.

---

13 'Doing Business with Saudi Aramco' is on the Saudi Aramco website (see www. saudiaramco.com/en/home.html#doing-business-with-us%257C%252Fen%25 2Fhome%252Fdoing-business-with-us.baseajax.html). This includes reference to the Supplier Code of Conduct, which states: 'Saudi Aramco is committed to conducting its business in an ethical manner. Saudi Aramco requires its Suppliers and Contractors to share these commitments and, therefore, has established the Supplier Code of Conduct. All registered vendors, manufacturers, contractors, and sub/contractors with which Saudi Aramco conducts business are required to acknowledge, and agree to abide by, the policies and principles set forth in the Code of Conduct to continue doing business with Saudi Aramco. This is also applicable to all new potential vendors, manufacturers, contractors, and sub-contractors. We also expect our Suppliers and Contractors to provide this Supplier Code of Conduct with all Employees within their organizations who are involved in conducting business with Saudi Aramco. Our business relationships are founded on trust and we understand that it is essential that all parties involved in supply-chain procurement activities feel confident in the fairness and transparency of the related process.'

In Shell an important control instituted was part of a normal 'letter of representation', signed by the country manager, which attested not just to the fact that two books of accounts were not being kept but that no bribes had been paid. Most country managers cascaded this system down the company so that those reporting to them signed similarly. More important was the institution of the so-called 'face-to-face' interview between the country manager and the managing director or executive committee member responsible for that region. This discussion covered the whole state of corruption in the country concerned. Grey areas could be discussed. Did the placing of a traditional seasonal gift of chocolates and fruit from the company by the stand of the policemen stationed at the intersection close to the office constitute a bribe? In my opinion this is marginal, but I think nowadays it has been so deemed. I recall Jacques Gueneau, a long-time colleague and friend and at that time country manager in Congo Brazzaville telling me in his face-to-face interview that in the year he had paid an Angolan soldier, who was part of an invading force supporting a scandalous coup, five hundred dollars to allow a third-country national and his family to go to the airport because he deemed them to be at risk of violence. Jacques said to me that he thought it was money correctly spent. I agreed with him. Our country manager in Yemen told me that he had fired two finance staff for collaboration and malfeasance and reported them to the police. He heard shortly after that the police were using violent methods to determine which was the guiltier. He had had to rush to the police station and withdraw the charges as he correctly decided that protection of human rights was more important than punishment for defrauding the company. Every year would bring a number of examples of business lost or grey areas discussed, which provided valuable and real practical examples from around the world that could be used elsewhere in training and discussion. Generally this was not a matter of legal discussion but of human common-sense as to where to draw boundaries. The annual face-to-face discussion would also cover the issue of incoming bribes. What was the general atmosphere in the country? Were there likely to be cases undetected? Was the company hotline or whistle-blowing system in place in the local language and was it open to both staff in the company and to contractors who felt that a staff member was looking for some benefit? Was there trust that identities would be protected and that there could be no retaliation?

The complexities of corruption and conflicts of interest

There are obvious pitfalls to be avoided in preventing outgoing bribe payments. The fixer who explains that the president's wife has founded a society for the preservation of the national culture that just happens to have a bank account in Switzerland is unfortunately a relatively common approach. I recall the case of a US citizen, James Giffen, operating very effectively in Kazakhstan controlling or brokering access to the President. His suggested methods could not be reconciled with Shell's principles. He was eventually arrested in the United States in 2003 for offences under the US Foreign Corrupt Practices Act in what was dubbed Kazakhgate, but I believe that all the charges against him were eventually dismissed by 2010.

When I was in Turkey in the early 1980s, the effective mayor of Istanbul was Bedrettin Dalan. His declared ambition was to clean up the Golden Horn, the inlet of the Bosphorus that divides the city, at that time heavily polluted by sewage that poured untreated into the restricted waters of the Horn through Byzantine and Ottoman drains. He famously declared that by the end of his period of office the waters of the Golden Horn would be as blue as his eyes, and as he came from the Black Sea coast, his eyes were indeed blue. He achieved much of his objective by digging two interceptor drains along each shore of the Golden Horn. These cut through Byzantine, Venetian, Genoese, Greek and Ottoman drains and collected their muck before it hit the waters of the Golden Horn. By bulldozing and dredging he created a series of spaces for gardens along the waterfront. This incurred the wrath of conservationists when a couple of fine Venetian houses were bulldozed. It incurred equal wrath of environmentalists as there was not enough money for a treatment plant and the collected sewage went into the Bosphorus, injected into the deep north flowing current that took it into the euxinic waters of the deep Black Sea. This was not a perfect solution by any means but I think it was a commendable practical start and visitors to Istanbul today will see the results of his efforts in the cleaner waters of the Golden Horn and the gardens that line its shores.

At that time Shell had an old oil product depot site on the Bosphorus that had been closed by government orders to avoid any possibility of pollution of the waterway. It had been converted into a very pleasant staff recreation site. In the hot summer, families could perhaps swim in the Bosphorus, but the waters were insalubrious and the currents were dangerous at that point. The answer was to build a swimming pool. So we applied for planning permission. The Mayor let it be known that planning permission would not be a problem if Shell adopted one of his new garden sites along the Golden Horn. This could be appropriately branded as Shell and would surely be a good way of Shell showing civic consciousness as well as gardening skills. I explained to the disappointed staff that the planning permission should not be linked to some other benefit. Planning permission had its own legal processes and regulations. Both sides were intransigent and we never got our swimming pool. The staff thought me frankly unreasonable, and perhaps I was, although the message on zero tolerance for corruption has to be clear and unequivocal, whatever the cost. On returning to London to work some ten years later I was astonished to find that a similar approach had been enshrined in the British planning process. Planning permission may be granted if sufficient 'planning gain' is included in a planning application under Section 106 of the Town and Country Planning Act 1990. Public spaces and elements of social housing count towards this. To my distress it appears that the amount of additional work is at the discretion of planners and is not simply a fixed quantum. Allowing judgement in such matters that are difficult to measure objectively is, in my opinion, an open invitation to corruption. If one wanted to devise a system to facilitate corruption, difficult-to-measure benefits and large amounts of discretion would be high on my list of desirable characteristics. Bedrettin Dalan was perhaps a pioneer in more than cleaning up polluted waterways.

Sometimes the cost of corruption is much higher than a matter of planning permission. Since the inception of the gas supply from the Soviet Union to Europe, the main pipeline system has crossed Ukraine, then of course part of the Soviet Union. The construction of this system, bringing gas from giant West Siberian fields such as Urengoy, was a major technological achievement. It is often forgotten that at that time the United States refused export permission for the huge compressors necessary to compress and pump the gas to Europe, so that the compressors had to be built in the Soviet Union or acquired from more sympathetic European suppliers. The development and construction was handled by the Soviet gas company Gazprom, which was probably the closest thing in the Soviet Union to a Western corporation. Gazprom at the time was efficient and had its own pride and ethos.

Shell, itself a major gas supplier with partners Exxon and the Dutch government from the giant Groningen field in the Netherlands, had relatively close relations with Gazprom. The two sources, Gazprom and the Netherlands joint venture Gasunie, were the major suppliers to Europe, with Norwegian gas being later added as a major source.

As the Soviet Union broke up, Ukraine split off and became independent in 1991. The pipeline system across Ukraine began to suffer from a lack of maintenance and upgrading of compressors. Furthermore, a certain amount of gas was taken off the system for Ukrainian domestic use. This was not always with the agreement of Gazprom, the owners of the gas. The issue of 'leakage' arose. Gazprom wanted to buy the lines from Ukraine, but the price could never be agreed. This was an emotional business. As the then Chairman of Gazprom, Rem Vyakhirev, pointed out to me, he had built the lines and regarded them as Gazprom's in any case, so paying for them was unpalatable. There was also the question of Ukraine's relationship with Russia. In Ukraine I was often told the joke about a Russian and a Ukrainian finding a ten-rouble note lying on the ground. As they fought over it, each holding one end, the Russian says, 'This is ridiculous, why don't we split it like brothers.' To which the Ukrainian replies, 'No, let us just split it fifty–fifty.'

With the knowledge of Gazprom, Shell made an offer to make a major payment—some $1,500 million—to Ukraine for a share in the pipeline. The idea was a three-way Ukraine/Gazprom/Shell joint venture, with the Western partner playing an independent role between the other two parties. All three had a critical interest in the pipeline. The funds injected would be used to upgrade the pipeline and ensure that all offtake in Ukraine was properly regulated and measured. The proposal also included a plan to upgrade and develop the compressor manufacturing capacity of Nikolaev, the former Soviet centre for compressor manufacturing where the original compressors for the pipeline had been made, which happened now to be in Ukraine. For Shell's part, we were prepared to evaluate compressors made by Nikolaev, which were advanced, and possibly use them in Shell operations as a step towards a major manufacturing export marketing thrust by Ukraine. It seemed to me to be a plan with great benefits all round.

I made repeated visits to the then President Leonid Kuchma in the beautiful city of Kiev, redolent of tragic wartime and post-war history where so many Soviets and Germans had died, including many prisoners in the post-war period. We discussed the advantages of the proposed arrangements. I pointed out that unless there was a stable route through Ukraine for the Russian gas, eventually other routes would be found through Poland and elsewhere. Ukraine would lose volumes of transit gas and a source of income. President Kuchma was always enthusiastic and promised that the team we needed to inspect the state of the pipeline (and check on the 'leaks') would be granted access. In the days and weeks following each meeting such access would always be blocked. There were clearly vested interests making much money out of the existing situation. The then Prime Minister Pavlo Lazarenko was opposed to the arrangement.[14] In August 2006, Lazarenko was convicted and sentenced to prison in the United States for money laundering, wire fraud and extortion. According to the official count by United Nations, approximately $200 million was looted by Lazarenko during 1996–97 from the government of Ukraine. He is said to have had a business connection with United Energy Systems (UES) of Ukraine, which was the

14 Lazarenko was one of those on my mental list of people whom I have met who should be in jail, and on the shorter list of those who did indeed eventually go to jail.

main importer of gas from Russia. The state of the pipeline and the number and nature of offtake points was clearly a sensitive matter, and perhaps for that reason a survey by a Western company was not desired. The Chief Executive of UES at the time was Yulia Tymoshenko, said to be one of the wealthiest women in Ukraine. She subsequently came to fame politically in Ukraine's 2004 'Orange Revolution', appearing a picture of innocence with her traditional plaited hair and supporting the democratic cause. She was Prime Minister briefly in 2005 and from 2007 to 2010. She is currently in prison in Ukraine after a very controversial trial relating to alleged abuse of office in relation to a much later agreement with the Russians on gas supplies.

It is tragic that the issue of reliable gas transit across Ukraine has never been resolved. Gazprom and Russia have always been stymied by the fact that they cannot cut off supplies to Ukraine without affecting supplies to Europe. In the short term, Ukraine thus had a strong hand. However, the game is playing out just as one long expected it would, with alternative pipeline systems being built across the Baltic, across Poland, across Belorussia, and southwards though Turkey. While some multiplication of pipelines was necessary and desirable, it is a tragic waste of resource where this is driven by short-term obstruction for personal or political gain.

What if the cost of saying no is simply too high?

Simply saying no is a luxury that a large international company such as Shell or Anglo American can afford. I recall encouraging Owen Bavinton, the head of exploration in Anglo American, to set up an exploration office in the Democratic Republic of Congo, for it is only by having eyes and ears on the ground that one gets a true picture of opportunities and risks. Owen pointed out that to set up an exploration office one needed maps. From his observation, the only way of acquiring the basic maps was to bribe the local survey office and he was not prepared to do this. He was of course right and the results potentially costly. Either the company did not have an office on the ground, meaning that opportunities might be missed, or it would be necessary to set up an office without all that was needed to be effective. The amount of time required for a patient and persistent approach that would allow progress without corruption was quite unpredictable. In some cases refusal to bribe means that a competitor gets the business, but in others you actually get there in the end by expensive and frustrating patience and persistence.

Such an approach may not be easy or even possible for a small company. A manager of a small company awaiting payment for a major contract successfully delivered in a corrupt country would find it tempting on a lesser-of-two-evils basis to make a small facilitating payment in order to free up the main payment rather than laying off large numbers of staff for lack of funds. Telling such a person that a prudent company would never put itself in a situation where it is wholly dependent on payments from such a country is not really helpful, although it may be true. Equally, companies often argue that their competitors in the business corrupt the bidding process.

Transparency International has developed a practical collective approach to overcoming this problem. Often, companies feel that they are pushed by competition, or by those tendering contracts, to enter the ultimately self-defeating process of offering inducements of various kinds. Yet many of those companies involved regard this as an undesirable practice that they would like to avoid. Likewise, governments or individuals within governments are often also trying to clean up their bidding processes. Transparency's approach is to try to capture the desire for improvement in 'Integrity Pacts'.[15] An Integrity Pact is a bit like a peace treaty with monitored disarmament clauses or an arms embargo. It has to start with willingness on the part of an agency to run a transparent bidding process. Of course, most countries and agencies profess that they do so, but when it comes to agreeing transparent monitoring procedures they may have second thoughts about entering into the process. Equally important is an agreement by all bidders that they will refrain from paying bribes and commissions and that they too will agree to an independent and transparent monitoring process. It is

15 www.transparency.org/global_priorities/public_contracting/integrity_pacts.

essential that the bidding agency remove from the list of acceptable bidders any company that does not agree to sign up to the pact. As part of the pact there are agreed penalties for malfeasance, such as the loss of bid bonds and exclusion from future bid rounds. The process is not easy, but it can be effective. The likelihood of such processes being agreed is now being further increased by anti-corruption legislation in the home countries of many of the major companies that bid for international construction contracts.

A similar collective approach to address corruption and the misuses of funds in the oil, gas and mining industries is the Extractive Industries Transparency Initiative (EITI) (referred to in Chapter 2). This developed out of the Publish What You Pay campaign and was led in its early stages from 2002 by the UK government and Transparency International. The secretariat was subsequently established in Norway. The strength of the EITI is that it requires countries to commit to undertaking a number of steps to improve the transparency of and accountability for payments by companies and their receipt by governments. Agreement from the national government is essential to prevent legislation or confidentiality agreements being used as an excuse to avoid the publication of payments. Countries seeking to join the EITI, and the companies which support it, commit within a certain time frame to ensuring independent auditing of all payments by extractive companies to governments and equally and separately independent auditing of the receipt by government. In addition to this, countries agree to set up an independent panel with the involvement of civil society organisations to oversee the process. As of October 2013 there are some 40 implementing countries that have committed to the process, with 25 of those countries having reached the stage of being considered 'compliant'. There are a further 16 candidate countries and 3 countries whose status is currently suspended for failing to meet some requirement. There is no doubt that this thorough process is significantly strengthening capacity for the control and management of funds in many countries with extensive extractive industries. The initiative has addressed over a trillion dollars of government revenue. While sovereignty and control of the process still clearly rests with the national government, the EITI and its multi-stakeholder board ensures that the required standards are met in the process and that commitments are also honoured. The board includes representation from implementing governments of countries in which the extractive companies are domiciled as well as civil society organisations, extractive companies and investors. In my opinion this is a much more thorough process than the extraterritorial activity of the US Dodd–Frank legislation requiring extractive industry companies with US connections to make very extensive declarations of payments. This requires no commitment from the country concerned and unlike the EITI does not address the issue of what happens to the money paid. In addition, Dodd–Frank only applies to one group of companies involved in a country (those registered with the US Securities and Exchange Commission) and does nothing to address the others. In the worst case it might provide an excuse for a country to do no more. In summary, like so much extraterritorial legislation it will have little impact in the real world on the ground—it will just make a few people feel that they have achieved something.

Some dilemmas of exposing corruption at high levels

Any business person operating internationally at a high level will inevitably become aware of cases involving distortions of processes and corruption. An individual and a company may conduct business with impeccable integrity but will still be aware of failings in the system, although they themselves are not involved. They may also be well be aware of individuals who have actually asked them for bribes that they have refused. What is the business person's responsibility in such a case? The act may not be damaging to the company's own business, but it is certainly damaging to the economy of the country as a whole.

On one occasion, a new minister asked that he be granted the same arrangements or payments as his predecessor had enjoyed. It was explained to him that there were no such arrangements with his predecessor. This led to embarrassment on both sides. Having made the request the minister clearly felt compromised. I was concerned that the impression of corruption with the former minister might be more widely shared, so contact was made with the country's ubiquitous security service. We were assured that they knew that there were no corrupt relationships with the previous minister and that the president was also aware of this. You may ask why we did not expose the new minister's request to the government or the president. There were two reasons. First, such an accusation in the end comes down to one person's word against another. More importantly, if the authorities accepted the charge and decided to act on it, it was probable that the actions taken would not have been in line with generally accepted human rights principles.

Drawing the line of responsibility is difficult. I once had a discussion in London with a minister of a country in which the company I worked for played a major role. He asked me to intervene with the head of his government to try to stop the irregular activities of certain people who were earning large amounts of, at best undeserved and in all probability downright dishonest, income from the country. We had, as a matter of deliberate policy and principle, avoided any connection with their activities and the minister himself knew it. The government as a whole also knew it because I had discussed with them the undesirability of any link and my views on one of the projects that this group proposed. When I pointed out to the minister that this was no concern of mine, that it was not my country or my government so why me, he replied that when it all went wrong I could guess whose fault it would be seen to be. At first this seemed to me to be grossly unfair. But was it really so unfair? We were long-standing friends and partners of the country. Had the issue been a natural disaster, or even a social issue for the nation, we would have immediately offered to play our part. Is it the act of a friend to avert your eyes and walk down the other side of the street when a crime is being committed, just because it is not your business? So I pondered the wisdom of entering into what would have been controversial discussions. Telling a friend that in your opinion another friend of his is a crook is in any society a high-risk strategy, even if you think that you have a relationship of trust. Your motives may be questioned. In the event, before I had come to a conclusion an unrelated but accidental event occurred that caused a review and termination of all those relationships.

It is sometimes possible to take a somewhat roundabout route. Consider the case of a well-functioning and profitable mine in Venezuela. A few years ago the government suddenly cancelled permits covering reserves around the mine, alleging breach of contract. In discussions with the ministry to resolve the issue it was made plain that for $35 million in a certain bank account the problem would be resolved. The demand was clear, but it was not clear from what level it was coming. Was it the minister, or was it from freelancers in his office? In either case the answer was going to be no, but it was important to try and establish where the request really originated. After much effort a meeting was arranged with the minister with non-nationals also present; the meeting was cordial and promises to investigate were made. In the antechamber after the meeting the demand was again made by a couple of very smooth professionals. When it was refused, they said that in any case $2 million was already owed for arranging the meeting with the minister. This was also refused. While we knew that the Chavez regime was in no way pro-business, I had hitherto not thought of it as inherently corrupt. We attempted to see or phone President Chavez without success. At that point I adopted a different tactic. In London there are frequent diplomatic receptions to celebrate the National Days of different countries. At these, and even at the Venezuelan reception itself, ambassadors of Latin American countries would be present. I told anyone interested the full story of the demand with details of the country concerned and that we were not going to pay because we never did. I was reasonably sure that this would get back by some route to the President Chavez. I still do not know the extent of ministerial or even presidential involvement. The mine continued to operate for some years and no payment was made.

I think this experience suggests that the advice that I used to give to Shell country representatives on major bribery demands was accurate. The advice was in case in their country they received a high-level demand for a corrupt payment, with the threat that the company would lose its entire business in the country or that the expatriate country representative would be expelled. They should do two things; first, say no, and, second, report it to the centre at the highest level. Should the threat be implemented, they could be certain that the corrupt demand would be made public. I think that it is most unlikely that many governments or presidents would be willing to face the questions that their own people would ask. It is also a good argument for never engaging in such practices. Once you have done so it will weaken your ability to cry foul in the case of threats. I have seen examples where competitors paid for grants of licences and received them more swiftly than we did. But when the time comes, as it almost inevitably does, that the demands have escalated to a point where it is not worth paying, both bribers and non-bribers have similar difficulty in getting the permits. The non-bribers can at least complain loudly.

The beneficial effects of transparency—and its limitations

There is no doubt that transparency is a great disinfectant for the disease and infection of corruption. When there is transparency, the general public can find out what is happening to flows of money and can demand explanations and correction where necessary. This is further reinforced where there is a lively free press. This is unfortunately not always the case. Sometimes it is disappointing that when corruption is exposed, the public reaction is remarkably forgiving. The populace does not rise up and demand resignation or punish the offenders in the ballot box. At present this disturbing trend is visible in South Africa, where members of the ruling party who appear to be at very least involved with those found guilty of corruption do not seem to lose their positions. It is encouraging that the South African judiciary continues to pursue such cases in an independent way. Such surprising tolerance has also been seen in Italy in the case of the repeated re-election of Silvio Berlusconi and it is not entirely absent elsewhere in Europe or the United States. The cause is not clear. Is it due to a cynical view of all politicians, or due to pragmatic acceptance that although an individual has clear moral failings none the less he remains a proven effective performer? Or is it tolerated by one part of the population because the individual is seen to be delivering benefits or protection to them? In such circumstances one can only take comfort from the recent events in the Middle East that show that even after many years of apparently passive acceptance of corruption, in the end the population responds collectively and effectively. Perhaps this, together with an increasing web of legislation against corporate corruption, gives hope that in the end there will be appropriate retribution for the perpetrators. As Henry Wadsworth Longfellow put it in 'Retribution', a 19th-century poem derived from earlier sources:

> Though the mills of God grind slowly;
> Yet they grind exceeding small;
> Though with patience he stands waiting,
> With exactness grinds he all.

May it indeed be so!

Chapter 9

Enterprise solutions to poverty and development

The existence of millions of people living in grinding poverty, without access to clean water or modern energy and subject to the ravages of diseases that are relatively easily prevented or cured, is an affront to all of us. In spite of tens of billions of dollars of overseas development assistance (ODA) and the efforts of many non-governmental organisations—often acting as delivery agents for government aid as well as for charitable donations—the problem persists. That is not to say that there has not been progress, particularly in countries such as China or Brazil, but these have been largely as a result of concerted and well-planned government efforts rather than external action.

Clearly, some poverty results from natural disaster such as floods or drought, but much persistent poverty is simply the result of poor governance or a lack of capacity in governments, coupled with a dearth of significant economic activity or sustainable livelihoods. ODA is essential to assist in overcoming temporary problems, or to help build economies through support for education, healthcare or infrastructure, but only the growth of economic activity can provide a more permanent solution. In the case of states coming out of conflict, for example, quite often considerable sums of money have been spent to disarm militias and collect guns. However, the ex-militia cannot live on hand-outs forever; unless they can find sustainable means of livelihood they are likely to revert to their old practices.

There is much that can be done by responsible companies even in very poor countries. It is not just through providing employment and growing local businesses and introducing them into their supply chains. It is also through building the capacity of local entrepreneurs who operate as dealers and stockists. Through this, people learn the basics of business, such as stock and cash control and basic book-keeping. This gives them the capacity to start up in business on their own. In many countries around the world I have met wealthy business people who have told me that their first job in life was running a Shell station, before they branched out on their own into whatever successful business they were now running. I would joke with them that this must have been because Shell had been too generous in the split of the profit margin with dealers.

Efforts by the UN Global Compact to grow sustainable business

In any country, businesses need other businesses to supply services. A kind of business ecosystem is required that functions for businesses large and small. One of the first dialogues that we set up in the Global Compact in 2001 was to try to address this issue and see if we could build coalitions of businesses in the poorest countries of the world, with the involvement of civil society and labour organisations. We had a concern that at the then upcoming UN World Summit on Sustainable Development in Johannesburg in 2002 we would have two groups of people who would pass each other like ships in the night without communication and without the recognising the need for and benefits of cooperation. Some civil society organisations focused on the need to address poverty by increasing overseas development assistance from governments, along the lines of what developed into the 2005 Make Poverty History campaign. This focus on development assistance often included a feeling that business, at least big business, was part of the problem. The other group consisted of business people who felt that the reason for poverty was a lack of economic activity and in turn the reason for the lack of economic activity was due to the inhibiting investment climate in the country concerned, often coupled with concerns about security and corruption. Many business people were also somewhat sceptical about the effectiveness of development aid.

Each of these positions has some merit. It is certainly true that the only sustainable way to lift people out of poverty is by developing livelihoods and economic activity. Furthermore, this activity has to be scalable; otherwise people remain at subsistence level. Equally the role of development aid in building capacity and developing educational and healthcare systems is vital, as is the construction of infrastructure to connect communities and indeed whole countries to markets for their goods. What is needed is closer connection between the two, with development assistance having as part of its goal the creation of the conditions and the capacity in a country for businesses of all sizes to grow. There should also be cooperation on the provision of the infrastructure that is necessary for an economy to grow. Until the rapid expansion of Chinese involvement in Africa, too often basic infrastructure was neglected as an object of development assistance. There is much potential benefit if the infrastructure necessary for activities such as resource extraction, which rightly should be funded by the private sector, is none the less integrated into an overall national infrastructure plan. There are synergies in such integration, not least in the fact that the private sector generally has more capacity for managing major infrastructure construction projects and for doing so in a way that prevents the undesirable leakage of funds.

Although it is important to increase economic and business activity in countries, it is preferable that it should involve responsible businesses. This makes the Global Compact a natural home for such an initiative. As discussed in Chapter 3, signatories to the Global Compact are committed to implementing the principles of the major UN conventions on human rights, the environment, working conditions and the fight against corruption in their day-to day-business and to reporting publicly on how they are doing this. Furthermore the Global Compact involves both civil society and labour organisations, so the opportunity to bridge the gap between differing views in an environment of mutual trust is present. So, we started an initiative under the banner of Growing Sustainable Business in the Least Developed Countries, holding workshops in New York and London to see how we might progress the work.

There are 50 countries defined by the UN as Least Developed Countries (LDCs). The list starts with Afghanistan and Angola and ends with Uganda and Zambia. Two-thirds of these 50 are in Africa. They have been evaluated on three groups of criteria defined by the UN Economic and Social Council (ECOSOC). These criteria take into account income (generally well below $1,000 per capita per annum Gross National Income); human assets (nutrition, health, infant mortality, adult literacy, etc.); and economic vulnerability (dependence on a single source of export income, vulnerable local economy, susceptibility to natural disasters and so on). Over the past two decades, few of the countries in this group have managed to progress out of the group. A notable exception is Botswana. In many of these countries economic activity is very limited. Georg Kell, the Executive Director of the UN Global Compact Office, would often say of them that the problem is not business, it is 'no business'.

That is not in fact strictly true. In any of the poor countries of sub-Saharan Africa you will find the local affiliates of many multinationals active and managing to do business. There are those selling transport fuels (such as Shell, Total and Agip), those dealing with the necessities of life (Procter & Gamble, Unilever and Nestlé), the beverage companies (Coca-Cola, Heineken and Diageo), telecoms companies (MTN, Ericsson, Airtel and Zain), the banks (largely Chartered Bank and Standard Chartered), pharmaceutical companies and the tobacco companies. All of these companies have networks of dealers and representatives who are essentially small entrepreneurs with a high degree of control over their own business. I know from Shell in the late 1990s that of some 34 operations in Africa, only four were extractive; the rest were marketing petroleum products from bottled gas to diesel. The operations were generally profitable although from time to time a disputed election or some other problem would cause a country to shut down and business to fall. In these cases business in neighbouring countries often increased proportionately.

The management and control of such businesses is difficult. In Shell they were grouped into clusters so that a small core of specialists could serve several countries. Many of these specialists were from the region, working outside their own country. Away from the pressures and demands of their extended family and communities they could measure their own performance against an international benchmark. Although small, the profitability in terms of return on capital was generally above that in Europe, for instance. Yet I found that in Shell there was often internal pressure to withdraw. This was partly because of the undoubted difficulty of maintaining standards in clusters of countries, concern about 'management stretch', and the problems of communication and so on. Travel between countries in Africa is difficult; it is often easier to return to a hub such as London, Paris or Johannesburg rather than try to fly direct. Added to these difficulties is the undoubtedly higher risk of something going wrong with consequent damage to the corporate reputation. It always seemed to me that the contribution to the country in terms of capacity building, the inherent profitability of the businesses and the pool of talented staff of all nationalities that enjoyed working in challenging circumstances offset the risks and allowed a global company to be just that, global. It also allowed the development of new customers as the economies grew. I suspect similar discussions were held in the boardrooms of the different types of businesses. Yet all of these different businesses needed each other to do business—for reliable communication, transport fuels, financial services, healthcare and necessities. Each was also vitally interested in improving the business climate, making sure that they had a supply of trained and educated staff, battling to eliminate corruption and improving governance. Working together with civil society organisations and labour would build trust and give the grouping a greater opportunity to deliver the improvements that are needed. This was not philanthropy, but growing business, including, hopefully, new business models of the kind that could serve the 'bottom of the pyramid' as ably illustrated by the writings of the late C.K. Prahalad and Stuart Hart.[1] The then Administrator of the United Nations Development Programme (UNDP), Mark Malloch-Brown, was enthusiastic and the then UN Secretary-General and original convenor of the Global Compact, Kofi Annan, was also very supportive. On behalf of the Global Compact, I wrote to the chief executives of major companies who had businesses in the LDCs asking them to list those countries in the LDC grouping in which they did business and whether they could nominate one country in which they might take the lead in a coalition with other companies working there. We had modest success. Pilots were started in Ethiopia (Shell), Madagascar (Total and EDF) and Tanzania (ABB and Ericsson), with plans to start in a few other countries.

Perhaps rather too early in the process we decided to launch the idea at the World Summit on Sustainable Development in Johannesburg in 2002. Tony Blair's office expressed interest in supporting it and Tony Blair himself said that he would encourage Jacques Chirac, the then President of France, to attend. The event gradually grew and before long six presidents or prime ministers had agreed to participate. Unfortunately it was not a great success; in some ways it was extremely comical, but in others tragic. At first we were going to have a panel discussion over lunch, but at the last minute protocol said that heads of state could not eat while there were television cameras in the room in case of mishap. So we got no lunch. The event and the concept were ably and briefly introduced by Kofi Annan. Mark Malloch-Brown chaired the panel. It had been agreed that I should give a five-minute introduction to the concept. Apparently it is not normal to illustrate a talk to heads of government or states with PowerPoint slides, but I explained that they were needed if the message was to be got across in five minutes, so we went ahead. The agreed programme stated that each president or prime minister would then speak for three minutes, after which there would be a general discussion bringing in the CEOs of the many businesses present. To his credit, Tony Blair spoke for three minutes exactly, absolutely on the subject. Jacques Chirac spoke for somewhat longer and managed

---

1 See e.g. C.K. Prahalad and S.L. Hart, *The Fortune at the Bottom of the Pyramid: Eradicating Poverty Through Profits* (Philadelphia, PA: Wharton School Publishing, 2004).

to get in a reference to the West African gas pipeline. This set President Obasanjo of Nigeria off at some length on resource-related matters. Prime Minister Jean Chrétien of Canada followed this up in similar vein for about ten minutes or more. By this time the meeting was getting a bit out of hand and well over time. President Abdoulaye Wade then gave a lengthy talk on development in Senegal and finally President Abdelaziz Bouteflika of Algeria spoke from a prepared text for 17 minutes without once touching the subject of the meeting. I learned much later that this was not his fault as he had been given the wrong text. At one point I asked Mark Malloch-Brown, who was sitting next to me and chairing the meeting, whether there was not some way of stopping speakers, but he pointed out that it is not possible in the UN to cut off heads of member states in mid-flow. The Secretary-General left at the appointed time, as did Tony Blair. When the speeches had finished and the national leaders had left, we were able to have a brief discussion with the remaining CEOs on the subject. We also got some lunch. There is a saying that actors should beware of appearing with children and animals, as the actor will probably lose control of the situation. I learned that the same is true of trying to orchestrate heads of government.

The follow-up activities were housed in the UNDP, which has resident representatives in many developing countries. UNDP involved Richard Sandbrook in the project. Richard was an enormously respected proponent of sustainable development, having been involved in and leading the International Institute for Environment and Development (IIED) for more than 20 years and having played a key role in several initiatives that brought NGOs and business together to drive improvements. One of these was the Mining, Metals and Sustainable Development Initiative, which led to the formation by leading mining companies of the International Council on Mining and Metals (ICMM) with the aim of improving sustainable development performance in the global mining industry. The then CEO of Rio Tinto, Bob Wilson, was instrumental in this. Richard was thus supportive of the idea of coalitions of major companies working together to grow their own businesses in a sustainable way in developing countries, in the process contributing to the creation of a business ecosystem in which small businesses could also flourish.

He and I both resisted the tendency for the Growing Sustainable Business initiative (GSB) to slide more in the direction of corporate philanthropy through businesses assisting in projects and development of small businesses in areas not necessarily related to their own businesses. The essence of the idea was to get businesses to assist each other in growing their own businesses in a sustainable way, in the process helping smaller businesses grow in their supply chains and related areas. By working in coalition with others, including civil society, they could work to improve the general business environment in such a way that any business, large or small, could more easily flourish.

Tragically, Richard became ill and died in 2005. He made a remarkable contribution to the growth of thinking on sustainable development for over more than 30 years. Having been a founder member of Friends of the Earth, which nowadays is one of the organisations that tends to regard business as a barely necessary evil, Richard was one of those people in the green movement who worked readily with businesses and could see that profit was not incompatible with increasingly sustainability, and also that business and economic development are essentials if the parlous state of many poor nations is to be addressed. To achieve real improvements business had also to be responsible, thoughtful and mindful of the needs of the wider societies of which they are a part. I believe that if Richard had lived, the original concept of GSB would have had greater impact. As it was, the initiative was gradually incorporated into UNDP's Inclusive Market Development (IMD) programme, which focuses much more, as its name suggests, on smaller businesses and their inclusion into the market. There are some 15 countries in which the GSB cum IMD is active in Africa, Latin America, Asia and Eastern Europe.

The business environment is like a natural environment in that its health depends on ecology. For a business ecosystem to be healthy it needs businesses of all sorts and sizes to be able to find their niche and thrive. Businesses are interconnected and depend on each other for services as well as on the health of society at large from which their customers are drawn. Governments play an important part in setting the conditions in which business works. In a difficult or stressed business environment it is often only one particular kind of business that can flourish. It could be state-owned business, small traders, large international businesses, family-owned conglomerates or corrupt or illegal businesses such as the drugs trade. Whichever group it is, if the ecosystem is not able to develop in a way that allows all businesses to flourish, the environment will be unhealthy and often slow to grow or evolve. This is one reason why I think the Local Networks of the UN Global Compact have such potential, bringing together large and small businesses, international and national businesses, civil society, labour unions and sometimes governments. By their varied membership they will support actions and policies that benefit all and help to grow a healthy business ecosystem. Because of their varied membership they will be more trusted when they advocate economic policies; the same varied membership helps keep all members honest and prevents them from being excessively self-serving in their efforts. Not just in poor countries, but in countries of all sorts, a Local Network provides a mechanism to influence the business environment positively and to work for the benefit of wider society.

Efforts by individual companies: health and job creation

Collective efforts take time and energy to get going. For this reason there is an understandable tendency for companies to carry on doing their own thing, only joining and supporting wider efforts as these are developed. There are positive sides to this. Individual company efforts, even in non-competitive areas, stimulate competition and encourage emulation. Where a company has success with an approach that wins it outside praise, motivates staff and creates societal value, others will be inclined to emulate the approach.

Many such initiatives may appear to be philanthropic, but in fact they are closely linked to the needs of the business or to mitigating stresses on the business. They may be recognised as having significant benefits to society, but in fact there is a business driver. This is part of the reason why they are successful. Purely philanthropic efforts by companies are likely to vary with the financial health of the company, and indeed with the tolerance of its shareholders towards what *The Economist* has called 'borrowed virtue',[2] in other words philanthropy at the cost of the shareholders. Where there is a clear business driver, the activities are much more sustainable.

An example of what might appear to be philanthropic activity yet is often inextricably linked to a company's operations is the HIV/AIDS pandemic in Africa. Through the pioneering work of Anglo American's Chief Medical Officer Brian Brink, Anglo has had a concern about HIV/AIDS since the late 1980s. At that time Brian Brink attended a conference in Paris on the disease. He could see the threat to South Africa. Through his efforts the Chamber of Mines organised tests on some 35,000 miners, something that would be difficult to do nowadays. The incidence of HIV was very low—a fraction of 1%, with the highest incidence being in a small cohort of migrant miners from a country north of South Africa. Prompted by Brink, Anglo has had an HIV/AIDS coordinator since the early 1990s and has generally adopted leading education and prevention strategies including making condoms and testing widely available.

In spite of adopting what I believe were industry-leading approaches to the HIV/AIDS issue, the rate of infection grew inexorably, so that by the beginning of the 21st century HIV prevalence rates were in some mines above 20%. It was little comfort that prevalence in some communities outside the mines, where programmes did not reach, were even higher. Had we known then what we know now, and had today's techniques and treatments been available then, the story might have been difficult. Brian Brink has been tireless in extending the lessons to other countries to prevent a repeat of the same situation, as has what was initially the Global Business Coalition (GBC) for HIV/AIDS, later going on to also deal with malaria and TB and now becoming GBC Health.

Just before I became Chairman of Anglo American in 2002 and involved in the GBC, Anglo American under the leadership of Tony Trahar as Chief Executive took the decision to make antiretroviral

2 In *The Economist*, 'Profit and the Public Good', 20 January 2005, www.economist.com/node/3555259. *The Economist* has since become more favourably inclined towards what is sometimes called corporate social responsibility.

therapy (ART) available to all staff. At that time studies showed that, depending on the assumptions made, the costs of doing this ranged upward from something that might be just about bearable commercially to a company-destroying burden. Tony Trahar told me that he did not believe that further analysis would reduce the uncertainty and that in the end he felt that the decision to go ahead was simply the right thing to do. It was thought that there were three things that would reduce the cost. First, the cost of the drugs needed for the treatment would come down rapidly. This has indeed proved to be the case and the cost of drugs is no longer a significant barrier. Second, that others including donor governments would support the programmes. To be effective, programmes have to cover wider communities, not just employees and their families as covered by the Anglo American programme. This is coming, but coming slowly, and of course at the time of Anglo's decision in 2002 the South African government was still largely in denial on the causes of HIV/AIDS. The then President Mbeki was extremely sensitive on the subject of HIV/AIDS, its causes and consequences. On one occasion at the end of a meeting, I asked the President whether there were any unresolved issues with Anglo companies that we should talk about. He replied by saying that he had had reason to take issue with an Anglo company that reported 'deaths from HIV/AIDS'. He had pointed out to the company, which had indeed been forced to agree, that the deaths were not in fact from HIV/AIDS, but from TB or other secondary infections. Although the Anglo programme was welcomed in the South African parliament, the then Minister of Health opposed it. The third and saddest factor likely to reduce the cost of the programme was that experience everywhere in the world had shown that take-up of treatment was slow and costs of treatment therefore rise only slowly. That proved to be the case also in South Africa.

HIV/AIDS is clearly a business issue. Although not an industrial disease, it decimates workforces and also affects customers. It is manifestly in the interest of business organisations to join with others in the fight against it. Indeed within a relatively short time after the introduction of the Anglo programme, Brian Brink was able to demonstrate that the cost of the programme, the largest component of which is now the cost of the medical services delivering monitoring and treatment rather that of the drugs themselves, was largely being offset by the reduction in absenteeism caused by the infection and the treatment of other diseases that multiply as a result of reduced immune systems. The benefit to families of the lives of breadwinners being saved or prolonged for some years is impossible to express in financial terms.

In my experience, HIV/AIDS is unlike most business issues in that the problem is not susceptible to the straightforward application of analysis and logic. Deep emotions and fears complicate solutions. Before the introduction of ART programmes in Anglo, it was often argued that the take-up of testing programmes was low because people might feel that there was little point in being tested if no treatment was available. Of course there was also undoubtedly the suspicion in the minds of some that confidentiality of any testing programme run by the company could be compromised and that the results might influence decisions on employment. I recall visiting a coal mine shortly after Anglo started supporting treatment and talking to the nursing sister who was delivering the programme. Her eyes sparkled with excitement as she told me of the six miners who had been suffering from full-blown AIDS who now with treatment were healthy and back at work. Everyone in the mine would have been aware of this, and from what illness those six miners were suffering; they would also have seen their remarkable recovery. I naïvely assumed that everyone would now want to be tested. In fact it took some time and real leadership by mine management, unions and worker representatives and involvement of the local community, including traditional healers and even the local sex workers, to build the necessary trust. I recall a meeting at a mine involving all the stakeholders where the traditional healer said that while she agreed that her medicine would not treat HIV effectively, if she told workers to take their pills consistently they would do so. First, the smaller coal mines, and later the larger underground platinum mines, achieved the present state where effectively everyone is tested voluntarily every year. What remains surprising is that, in spite of everyone knowing their status as well as being fully aware of the means of transmission and the precautions necessary to avoid infection, some new infections still occur. What is not surprising is that the cooperative programmes necessary to arrive at this point of effectively universal testing has improved trust and communication in the mines such that many other things are positively affected—productivity, industrial safety, industrial relations and so on.

Enterprise development

One of the potential contributions of resource companies to a country's economy is employment. Apart from the construction of major plants and projects, much of the labour for which often comes from other parts of the country or the world, oilfields and mines are not great direct employers. In general, mines provide greater direct employment than oilfields, but modern mining is also increasingly automated so needs progressively fewer people. Furthermore the educational standards required for the workforce may not be initially available in the local community. One of the main ambitions of a community that is host to a major operation is for employment for its sons and daughters.

Clearly it is in the interests of a long-term operator of a mine or oilfield to invest in education in the community so that there are community members who can meet the necessary educational requirements. The hope is that community members would not just meet the minimum standards but in due course could aspire to highly skilled and professional jobs in the industry. This is the basis of the long-term educational programmes that Anglo American and others have run for decades. This is sometimes not just a matter of educational deficits in a remote local community, but may also result from an entire part of a population being historically disadvantaged. As I have already said in Chapter 4, when I became chairman of Anglo American in 2002, I was shocked to find that there were only a thousand or so black South Africans studying to fill engineering and technical jobs. This highlighted the real long-term damage of the apartheid system; one can abolish discrimination by legal action, but a wickedly skewed educational balance takes much longer and is much more difficult to address. To his enormous credit, apart from his long-standing and very public opposition to the apartheid system, Harry Oppenheimer, Anglo's Chairman until he retired in 1982, had focused a great deal of his personal attention and that of Anglo on black school education in maths and science, supporting both students and teachers as well as ensuring that appropriate classrooms were built.

Educational projects are inevitably relatively long-term. In 1989 Anglo started a fund, called Anglo Zimele, to help black entrepreneurs in South Africa to set up their own businesses. Some of the initial businesses were in the Anglo supply chain, often with the involvement of someone who had left Anglo to set up the business. Gradually, the businesses were increasingly from sectors unconnected with Anglo, or certainly those that had markets well beyond Anglo. For example a business initially focusing on maintenance of underground mine railway systems was able to expand and serve South African Railways.

The model is to support entrepreneurs in a commercial way through a, say, 20% equity investment. All relations with the invested companies are on a purely commercial basis, except for help with the business plan and guidance to the management. The investments are based on a business plan such that after three years or so the entrepreneur can buy out Anglo's stake, so that the money is returned to the fund. This makes the fund relatively self-financing except for the initial capital, which was quite modest.

Anglo Zimele has been recognised by the World Bank International Finance Corporation as a leading-edge practitioner in this field.[3] Anglo Zimele now runs three additional funds—a mining fund, a small business loan fund and a fund for women entrepreneurs. Although the approach of taking an initial equity stake in a business is effective and encourages close involvement, it also requires a heavy investment in the amount of time required. This inevitably restricts the approach to larger investments. In 2007 Anglo added the concept of small business hubs not only in South Africa but also in other parts of the world.

The impact of these initiatives is considerable. In Anglo's 2009 Report to Society a figure is given of 17,200 jobs having been created in various

3 Described more fully in the 'The Anglo Zimele Model: Practice Notes on a Corporate Risk Capital Facility Experience' compiled by the IFC and Anglo Zimele; see commdev.org/content/document/detail/2329.

Anglo enterprise development projects around the world.[4] I suspect that the actual figure is much higher because for many years the records kept of jobs created by companies that had their birth in Anglo Zimele and had subsequently become independent were rather poor. However, this is by no means the largest or most important contribution that a company such as Anglo makes to societies and economies, particularly in the developing world.

Civil society critics of major companies often regard them as delivering benefits only to shareholders through dividends. Similarly, governments often look at investments in their country purely through the lens of corporate taxes delivered. Neither view gives a true picture of the balance of benefits.

Consider the figures from the Anglo American Annual Report and Report to Society for 2008. Net income was $5.2 billion, with dividends to shareholders of $2.3 billion and $0.5 billion in interest to the other providers of finance, the banks. $6.6 billion was reinvested in the business. Taxes paid were $3.0 billion plus a further $1.2 billion collected and paid to governments on behalf of employees and in value-added taxes and the like. Half of this amount was paid in developing countries. Salaries and wages to 104,000 employees amounted to $3.0 billion, almost two-thirds of which ($1.8 billion) was in developing countries.

Viewed in the light of the way that the wealth was generated, the split does not appear unreasonable. Equal amounts went to shareholders and employees while, taking into account indirect collections, governments received somewhat more. What is more important is the impact on local economies. The almost $2 billion paid to employees in developing countries goes straight into the local economy in the form of food, housing, education and services, generating employment and local service enterprises. Outweighing this is the over $13 billion paid to suppliers, over $8 billion of which was in developing economies. Much of this in turn goes to employees and to the supply chain of the suppliers, generating local multipliers. So in a single year, apart from taxes, one large

---

4 In a speech before she stepped down as Anglo American Chief Executive in 2013, Cynthia Carroll stated that over 40,000 jobs had now been created

company put around $10 billion into the economies of developing countries through employee remuneration and payments to suppliers with significant impact on the development of the local economy and local enterprises. This is a more direct and immediate effect than tax revenue. If tax revenue is spent wisely the money goes into education, healthcare and infrastructure, all of which of course have important longer-term impacts. That $10 billion from one company compares with the $154 billion of ODA in 2010 (according to the UN Millennium Development Goals). The $76 million in social investment projects that Anglo reported in the same year is also important, but remains small in relation to the impact of the core business.

Rio Tinto also gives a breakdown for 2011 of taxes paid in relation to gross revenues and payments to other stakeholders such as employees, shareholders and suppliers.[5] Perhaps as importantly, they give a very detailed breakdown of all payments in whatever form made to governments by level of government, whether central, regional or local, in each country in which they operate. This should allow the citizens of the country to track the use of payments in a way that should contribute to accountability and the reduction of corruption. It also allows citizens to see whether the tax paid by a company is commensurate with their activities in a country and thus highlight cases of avoidance or of aggressive use of tax loopholes.

The Shell Foundation was established in 2000 to provide a vehicle independent of the corporation that could nonetheless work with the business to apply its skills to sustainability solutions. After much consultation, it was established with an endowment of $250 million so that partners would regard it as an organisation independent of the business cycle, which inevitably potentially impacts initiatives funded from ongoing corporate profits, although the Foundation has always received annual injections of funds from Shell. The Foundation was led initially by Kurt Hoffman from its conception and design in the late 1990s until 2008 and then by Chris West.

5 www.riotinto.com/sustainabledevelopment2011/economic/tax.html.

In 2005 the Shell Foundation produced a seminal report entitled *Enterprise Solutions to Poverty*,[6] which reviewed the Foundation's efforts over its first five years and argued that, necessary as development aid and charitable support are, the only solution to poverty elimination is the growth of sustainable business. Although much of the trillion dollars spent globally in the last few decades on poverty alleviation had indeed had a temporary effect, it was clearly not a sustainable solution. The report argued that businesses, especially large businesses, have three 'assets' that are invaluable in the creation of sustainable businesses in poor communities. The first asset is the intrinsic business 'DNA' and business skills built into such enterprises and which could be transferred. The second is the convening power, the ability to approach other actors such as banks easily and enrol them in the effort using commercial arguments. The third is the specific industry-based knowledge, which in Shell's case was specifically energy related. The Foundation is thus not just a grant-giving body, but one that is committed to the growth of sustainable businesses. Indeed if there is not potential for a sustainable business the Foundation is unlikely to be involved, other than for purposes of research.

The report presented four case studies—on indoor air pollution, on solar home systems in India, on small-scale infrastructure funding and on small-scale energy funding in Africa. None of these problems or issues was new. All had attracted previous aid or donor funding. What was perhaps new was the relentless business-based approach. If there was not a business proposition in there for someone, it was not going to work.

Five years later, in 2010, the Shell Foundation produced another review entitled *Enterprise Solutions to Scale*.[7] This report emphasises

6 Shell Foundation, *Enterprise Solutions to Poverty: Opportunities and Challenges for the International Development Community and Big Business* (London: Shell Foundation, 2005; www.shellfoundation.org/download/pdfs/Shell_Foundation_Enterprise_Solutions_to_Poverty.pdf).

7 Shell Foundation, *Enterprise Solutions to Scale: Lessons Learned in Catalysing Sustainable Solutions to Global Development Challenges* (London: Shell Foundation 2010; www.shellfoundation.org/download/pdfs/FINAL+Shell+Foundation+(Full+Copy).pdf).

that the successful efforts to grow enterprises to scale all involved cooperation on a new model, with Foundation involvement from the outset and a willingness of the entrepreneurial partner to focus entirely on the project and commit significant personal resources to its success. The model is basically one of venture capitalism with a focus on developing economies and a willingness to commit patient seed capital.

Approaches to intensifying and scaling up agriculture

The issue of 'going to scale' is of particular importance in agriculture. In many developing economies agriculture is of enormous importance; it is also often very inefficient. As far back as the 1970s, when I worked in Nigeria, Shell put much emphasis on trying to improve the productivity of agriculture around operations. A particular focus was cassava, the staple food of the Delta. The company ran a very effective agricultural outreach service delivering high-yielding and blight-resistant strains to smallholders to improve productivity and prevent loss from bacterial blight. We also started a programme of developing fish farms in the Delta. Although the fish farm project had the potential to go to a larger and more industrial scale, in common with many of the programmes run by progressive companies in the 1960s and 1970s, the Shell programmes of the time essentially improved subsistence farming. There is no doubt that this approach delivered real benefits to farmers, and indeed it is the basis of the current NGO programmes that encourage people to support the donation of livestock or improved seeds. These programmes mobilise resources from individual donors in the wealthier parts of the world and increase awareness of the issues. They do deliver real value and are commendable; they lift low-grade subsistence farmers to a higher level and deliver increased and more secure income. The final outcome remains, however, subsistence-level farming that will never be enough to lift populations out of poverty.

If we are to be able to feed a population that will, on almost any estimate, reach 9 billion by 2050, it will be necessary to radically increase the efficiency and productivity of global agriculture. In a 2011 report,[8] Oxfam suggest that by 2030 overall food production will need to be increased by some 50% from 2005 levels to feed a global population of just over 8 billion. Given that agricultural productivity in the high-income parts of the world has almost doubled over the last quarter-century (and is now relatively intensive) while that in sub-Saharan Africa has stagnated, most of the productivity gains will have to be achieved in developing countries.

To achieve this there is no doubt that there will have to be an intensification of agriculture as well as radical improvements in the collection and preservation of crops. The question is how to do this without disenfranchising the present subsistence farmers and their families. This is no mean challenge. It is also one where there is polarisation between the extremes of those who have a somewhat idealised view of smallholdings and those whose vision is more one of intensive and mechanised large-scale farming. The more sustainable path lies between the two extremes. As occurred in Europe and the United States in the 19th and 20th centuries and China in the 20th century, this will inevitably involve a degree of migration to the cities.

One company that has been working on such improvement of agricultural productivity and products is Nestlé. For more than 60 years it has worked with farmers in emerging markets on milk production, providing advice on animal husbandry and improved breeds while gathering the milk and processing it for onward distribution. This is a powerful development model, providing an effective outlet for increased production and lifting hundreds of thousands of farmers out of subsistence poverty. This process, which I have heard described by third parties as the 'Nestlé Development Model' has not received the recognition it might otherwise have because of the controversies on the marketing of infant formula that originated in the 1970s and have been astonishingly persistent ever since. This is ironical as in 2011 Nestlé was the only company to meet the FTSE4Good Breast Milk Substitutes marketing standards,

8 L. Wegner and G. Zwart, *Who Will Feed the World? The Production Challenge* (Oxford: Oxfam, April 2011; www.oxfam.org/en/grow/policy/who-will-feed-world).

the criteria for which had been developed in consultation with many stakeholders. I have the feeling that many people have invested so much energy into demonising Nestlé over decades that almost nothing could persuade them to believe that the company is not only responsible but makes a significant contribution to development. Unilever also has some outstanding programmes through which they assist in the development of more intensive agricultural production in rural areas of developing countries, ensuring that the produce can get to a much wider and more affluent market, while at the same time ensuring that there is produce available for local markets and consumption. Similar work has been done by SABMiller on sourcing supplies for beer in Africa. All of these are of great benefit to communities, while building reliable and cost-effective supplies for an international company.

One of the challenges of intensifying agriculture in developing economies is to ensure that the processing and preservation of food for sale in more remote markets, whether in towns in the same country or for export, does not deprive the local rural population of easily accessible and low-priced basic foodstuffs. Any attempt at increasing agricultural productivity and raising incomes must address this issue; the matter is further complicated by the fact that often much of the fuel use in poor rural areas is provided by the unsustainable use of wood or charcoal, which also has very negative side effects on respiratory health and eyesight.

An innovative approach to addressing all of these problems is the CleanStar Mozambique venture,[9] developed by the Danish company Novozymes, CleanStar Ventures, ICM and Bank of America to produce ethanol for domestic stoves. The use of charcoal for domestic cooking in Maputo, the capital of Mozambique, is rapidly depleting forests in the country; the price of charcoal has therefore doubled in the last few years. The burning of charcoal also damages lungs and eyesight through indoor air pollution. Most approaches to this problem have focused on the use of more efficient stoves for combustion, usefully both reducing air pollution and fuel consumption. The alternative is to encour-

---

9 www.cleanstarmozambique.com.

age switching to more expensive kerosene or bottled gas. Novozymes is a company specialising in the production of enzymes for industrial use. Novozymes and its partners have focused on producing an ethanol-based fuel from cassava, a good example of a company applying its core skill or technology to a problem.

At first sight, this might be seen to be converting a food crop, cassava, into fuel and therefore placing pressure on food supplies for both the rural and urban poor. At present farmers tend to cut down forests for charcoal that can be sold as cash crop. The resulting land is underutilised because of a lack of market access. The CleanStar project appears to address this problem by co-locating facilities for processing and transporting food crops to market, while converting some of the crops to make fuel. This provides an alternative and better livelihood for the farmers than cutting forest to make charcoal and provides a commercial outlet for their other crops, increasing their income all around. At the same time, the supply of the alcohol fuel to Maputo reduces the demand for the charcoal that, as is common in many African cities, makes up most of the fuel used currently by the population.

The long-term success of this promising project will depend on three main things. First, the market acceptability of the alcohol-based fuel and the Swedish-designed stoves in which it is used; the stoves do indeed appear to be accepted as an attractive and convenient alternative to charcoal. Second, the ability of the project to process and deliver the fuel to the city at a price competitive with charcoal and below that of competing hydrocarbon fuels of kerosene and bottled gas. Third, the long-term sustainability of the project in terms of land use and food supply. It is likely to take some time to determine the long-term economic and social impacts of the project. At this stage it looks to me to be an interesting and attractive commercial development that addresses a number of complex problems.

A group with agricultural projects at a somewhat earlier stage is Phoenix Africa Development and its Lion Mountains project in Sierra Leone and other projects elsewhere. The essence of this proposal is to form joint ventures with local communities to introduce modern, more intensive agriculture on currently underutilised but cultivable land. This is also linked to efficient collection and processing of the crops. Unlike the Mozambique project, the aim here is to produce food crops with currently no fuel component. Apart from any commercial agricultural aspects the success for the project will depend on the ongoing acceptability and durability of the joint venture agreements with the local communities. This in turn will depend very much on the governance structures on the community side, making sure that all the community stakeholders feel empowered and engaged and that the community leaders really do represent them. It is the dissonance between the visible and apparent authority structures and the real feelings in the community that has caused so much stress in the resource industries in the past, not least for Shell in Nigeria. It is essential, apart from the commercial work, for any commercial organisation to have a deep and preferably independent insight into the structures of the community. It has often proved wise to have a trusted independent intermediary to assist in this process. If indeed truly independent and trusted by the community, such an intermediary can help the community develop its own governance structures and through this reassure the company on the robustness of the decision-making behind any longer-term agreement.

Another interesting approach to the need to intensify and industrialise agriculture is that taken by the major private commodities firm Louis Dreyfus Commodities. Its approach is to enable communities to have the regular income that comes from supplying industrial-scale processing for export on the basis of long-term agreements as well as to have independent production for local consumption. The latter may also require investment, but this can be enabled through the long-term agreement, with the control and decision-making remaining entirely in community hands. This approach allows the community to maintain independence and ownership of the land while accessing the capital necessary for upgrading and intensifying agricultural methods.

Other approaches: public–private partnerships

Many issues, whether it is the growth of enterprises or matters of health-care, cannot be addressed by one section of society alone. They require cooperation and partnership.

For example, much as businesses can work on growing other businesses in their supply chain or outside it in areas adjacent to their operations, it often requires action by government to create the conditions in which a business, large or small, can flourish. This was recognised in the report of the Commission for Africa in 2005,[10] which supported the idea of forming a public–private partnership to improve the investment climate for businesses in Africa. The Investment Climate Facility for Africa (ICF)[11] was supported by the G8 in 2005 and formally launched in 2006 with Benjamin Mkapa, former President of Tanzania, and Niall Fitzgerald, formerly Chairman of Unilever, as co-Chairs. The private sector co-Chair is now Neville Isdell of Coca-Cola. The idea was to have a body run on private-sector principles that could assist African governments who were seeking support in improving the climate for investment in their country. The ICF is funded by private-sector donations (Anglo American was an early donor), governments and international financial institutions. The Facility assists governments in such areas as property rights, business registration, taxation and customs, financial and labour markets, competition and not least the fight against corruption. It has projects in 29 countries and about ten projects have been completed. For example, in Burkina Faso they report that, thanks to close collaboration between government agencies, the Chamber of Commerce and local businesses, it now takes just 19 days for a construction permit to be issued, instead of 208 days and the cost is US$480 instead of US$2,270.[12] In Rwanda, it now takes two days to register a business instead of 16 and the cost has fallen tenfold to US$43. The

10 Commission for Africa, *Our Common Interest* (London: Commission for Africa, 2005; www.commissionforafrica.info/2005-report).
11 www.icfafrica.org/page/about-us.
12 See ICF website for projects: www.icfafrica.org/area/business-registration-and-licensing.

National Land Centre has been digitalised, reducing the number of days to register property from 371 to 55 and the cost from 10% of a property's value to 0.4%. Changes of this sort make a real difference, not just to big businesses but also to small businesses that do not have the capacity to deal with prolonged and excessively complex administration.

In the field of health, one of the challenges to the fight against malaria is the build-up of resistance in mosquitoes to the common insecticides. No new insecticide for control of mosquitoes has been developed in the last 30 years or so. This is particularly worrying as resistance builds because of the two main insecticides, synthetic pyrethroids and DDT,[13] only the pyrethroid-based insecticides can be used to impregnate mosquito nets. The use of impregnated nets has been a major element of many anti-malaria campaigns.

The lack of new mosquito-control insecticides has two linked causes. First, while originally public health insecticides came from research into crop-protection insecticides, the properties that make a product desirable for the two uses are now different. Insecticides for crop protection need to degrade in a matter of days to prevent ingestion of toxins by human consumers; in addition, crop research has focused very much on systemic insecticides. In contrast, to be useful in impregnated nets or for the spraying of hut walls insecticides need to remain effective against mosquitoes for as long as possible—preferably for years. Thus the chance of a crossover to public health use from agrochemical use is now lower. The second reason for the lack of development is the small size of the market for public health insecticides. To develop, test and license an insecticide nowadays is likely to cost at least $70 million. Yet the total market for public health insecticides is only $200 million in revenue—a sum that has to cover manufacturing and distribution. I have heard a higher figure quoted for the total market for insecticides needed to keep golf greens in pristine condition, which reflects rather sadly on our social priorities (before one gets too excited about golf greens, it is worth remembering that the market for pet-related products

13 DDT (dichlorodiphenyltrichloroethane) is banned in many areas of the world, but it will remain an essential WHO-approved tool in the fight against malaria in many countries until alternatives are developed.

in Europe is of the same order of magnitude as the total global aid budget). These two factors combined have led to a dearth of research on new insecticides for mosquitoes.

It was to address this problem that the Innovative Vector Control Consortium (IVCC) was put together. This brings together major academic institutions in Europe and the United States led by the Liverpool School of Tropical Medicine,[14] whose Director Janet Hemingway was a driving force behind the organisation. The IVCC has been funded in two tranches of $50 million each by the Bill and Melinda Gates Foundation, as well as other foundations. This is typical of the strategically targeted funding of the Gates Foundation, where money is used to seed what become hopefully sustainable efforts.

In this case the IVCC involved major pharmaceutical and agrochemical corporations in a partnership with the objective of using grant money to lower the initial costs of insecticides for diseases borne by insect vectors (carriers). Major companies such as Bayer or Syngenta have large libraries of chemicals that have been synthesised in the past. The agreements with such companies provide for the IVCC to fund post-doctoral scientists to screen literally hundreds of thousands of compounds in these libraries, which are made available free of charge by the companies. The companies also provide lab and office space for the work. The work is steered by IVCC advisory committees of eminent scientists from institutions around the world. Standard intellectual property agreements provide that any promising results from this work are available for the public health market and can be produced either by the company concerned, if it wishes, or by a generic manufacturer. Should other uses in the agrochemical or veterinary field emerge, these remain the intellectual property of the company. The IVCC also works with

---

14 I had the honour to be President of the Liverpool School of Tropical Medicine from 1997 to 2008 and Chairman of the IVCC from its formal incorporation in 2008. Both positions give fascinating insight into the work of these two great institutions and I have learned a great deal about some unfamiliar fields. In both I have played the part of supporter and occasionally facilitator. Others, in particular Janet Hemingway, have led the work and delivered the results, for which I take absolutely no credit

companies, other organisations and the World Health Organisation to streamline the testing and licensing of any new or adapted compounds. The advantages and costs are carefully negotiated and balanced, but the companies also gain intangible benefits. Interestingly, a major factor in company thinking is not the actual costs, but the opportunity cost of diverting highly skilled researchers from the company's main line of commercial research.

This ingenious approach has been remarkably successful, first in developing agreements with almost every major company in the field and secondly in the results. In only five years there are already at least three promising formulations being tested that overcome mosquito resistance and three completely new molecules showing promise.

Chapter 10

Lessons from China on poverty eradication

Much is written on the remarkable and sustained economic growth of China and the disparity between the coastal regions and the west of the country. Perhaps not enough is heard of the thoughtful policies put in place to lift tens of millions out of poverty. This success has been as a result of creating jobs and employment and not through hand-outs. For three and a half decades since Deng Xiaoping launched the process of 'reform and opening up' the disastrous policies of the Mao era have been progressively deconstructed. Agriculture has been decollectivised, entrepreneurs allowed to start businesses and a massive programme of infrastructure building commenced. I am not qualified to comment on all of the details of the extraordinary experiment covered by the enigmatic phrase 'a socialist market economy with Chinese characteristics', but given the challenges of poverty in large parts of the rest of the world, it is worth looking to see if there are specific lessons on poverty eradication that can be drawn from China's approach to its own enormous challenges.

My own knowledge of China is relatively recent, starting with visits in the 1990s in relation to Shell oil and gas exploration activities and discussions on the major Shell investment with China National Offshore Oil Corporation (CNOOC) in the Nanhai petrochemical project in Huizhou municipality in Guangdong Province. Since 2000 I have also been a regular attender at the annual China Development Forum first on behalf of Shell, then Anglo American and most recently for the UN Global Compact. This event gives a remarkable opportunity for foreign business people to interact as a group with the Premier, Vice Premier and many ministers as well as hearing the views of Chinese academics and business people, all conducted in a remarkably open way. In addition I have for some years attended annually the China Council for International Cooperation on Environment and Development (CCICED), which also discusses and focuses very much on sustainable development and whose papers make recommendations and suggestions for Chinese policy-makers. The Minister of Environmental Protection, Zhou Shengxian, not only chairs these meetings but also takes an active and lively interest in the discussions. Taking into account HSBC board visits, I have been in China at least twice most years for one reason or another.

The movement of people and the *hukou* system

Discussions on the major joint Shell and CNOOC petrochemical plant in Guangdong Province took a number of years. Petrochemical plants are complex and it is important to optimise the product slate, which can be extremely varied. At times the Chinese side would become very impatient with Shell. One issue of concern was not on products or engineering, but on the need to relocate some 8,000 villagers. In a country where 1.2 million people were moved to make way for the Three Gorges Dam this appears to be a minor problem, particularly in the light of the Chinese estimates that over 300 million people will move from the country into towns and cities in the next 25 years or so. This is the equivalent of more than the populations of France, Germany, Italy and the United Kingdom combined. Nonetheless, moving 8,000 people was of great concern to Shell. Chinese officials repeatedly assured me that the relocation of villages was a matter for the Chinese authorities and should not concern Shell. My reply was that, while we fully acknowledged that it was the responsibility of the authorities, it was of concern to Shell because the products of the plant would be marketed internationally and international or World Bank standards and conditions should apply to the relocation. We received reassurance on how the villagers would be rehoused. While I was still fretting as to whether the villagers would indeed be content with their new lot, I was assured that I could be absolutely certain of that. The villagers would be reclassified under the Chinese *hukou* or residence-permit system as town dwellers. As this was the desire of almost every villager in China due to the greater job and education opportunities, I could be certain that they would be very content.

The *hukou* system controls the movements of people in China. It not only prevents people living with their families where they wish, but it can lead to migrant workers being severely disadvantaged relative to those who are residents of the areas to which they migrate. For this reason it is a source of great controversy and criticism in the West. I recall that at a meeting of the China Development Forum some years ago an elderly Chinese professor made a moving speech in the presence of a minister in which he said that in his opinion the *hukou* system was an offence against human rights and that he was ashamed of it. However, he went on to say that he had visited Brazil and seen the favelas and shanty towns surrounding large cities there and in other parts of the world. That too in his opinion was an offence against human rights. If China abolished the *hukou* system before there was adequate provision of infrastructure in the cities, the result would be similar to that in other countries with similar conditions developing. Therefore with regret he concluded that, undesirable as such restrictions are in principle, he felt that restrictions on mass movement were necessary until such time as the infrastructure could accommodate them. In this I confess I tend to agree with him. Although there are undoubtedly many injustices in relation to the status of migrant workers that need to be corrected, it is just too simple to assume that free movement of population is paramount. Even if conditions for migrant workers are very far from ideal, history may show China as a country in which the mass migration of people from rural areas to the cities was not accompanied by the development of the slums that have accompanied every such migration elsewhere, including the UK.

Five-year plans and evidence-based policies

China is unusual as a country in that its economic and social policies tend to be evidence-based and that its policies are framed in five-year plans. A third differentiator is that its ministers tend to be technocrats—often engineers or scientists. I believe that the Chinese practice of basing policies on solid evidence and experiment is a great strength. On the whole I have not been a great fan of five-year plans, whether for a corporation or a country. Perhaps this is just a prejudice based on the manifest failures of the Soviet centrally planned economy and its disastrous five-year plans. In China, the system of using a five-year plan to set an agenda and a direction for a period appears to have worked, certainly in the last two cycles.

The 11th Five-Year Plan covering 2006–10 was the first one to which I paid real attention. From the plan and from the discussions around it seemed to me, and indeed to those attending the China Development Forum, both clear and admirable. The two overarching goals of the plan were summed up in the phrases 'harmonious society' and 'scientific development'. As someone who has tried to steer a global business, I have been impressed by the frequent use of these phrases in conversation and speeches, often to indicate that whatever was being proposed was in fact in line with these overall principles. In this way, far from being the shallow slogans that some in the West might regard them as, they are actually useful shorthand for broad principles. The general thrust was to continue the emphasis in the 10th Five-Year Plan on spreading development from the eastern seaboard to the western interior, reducing the income gap. This would certainly contribute to a more 'harmonious society'. It was not just an aspiration; there appeared to be a clear strategy on how this was to be achieved.

Exports would continue to be important, but there would be a shift towards higher value and more complex exports, as well as an increase in service industries. This would free the manufacturing capacity of consumer white goods and household electrical appliances to feed the increasingly affluent domestic market. However, this was not going to work unless the market demand and consumer spending power was there, and this was inhibited by the very high propensity of the people to save. There would of course be the changes in consumption coming from the high rate of movement from the countryside and agricultural jobs into the towns and urban jobs, but the high savings rates of individuals were driven in part by a high level of 'precautionary savings'. Precautionary savings are accumulated by families to cover costs of education, provide savings for retirement and for medical emergencies. For this reason as well as for social reasons the plan included targets over the five years for the provision of basic pensions to urban workers and the provision of basic health insurance to the rural population, as well as increasing the provision of education to nine years. There were also ambitious environmental targets such as reducing the amount of energy per unit of GDP by 20% and reducing both emissions and water use. I believe that one of the reasons that China responded rapidly and effectively to the financial crisis was that there was already a plan in place on which a stimulus package could be based. It was only necessary to accelerate expenditure in some areas.

Although the 11th Five-Year Plan itself might be excellent, there were certainly serious concerns at the outset about the ability of provinces and municipalities to put in place the pension and healthcare changes as well as to enforce some of the environmental provisions. I remember it being pointed out in 2006 by Shengman Zhang[1] that compliance with regulations in the construction industry in China was very low; it was suggested that only 5–10% of the buildings in China and only 10% of its steel plants complied with the environmental regulations. The second statistic is interesting in that China is undoubtedly the only country that builds enough steel plants to form a large enough statistical sample. In a subsequent discussion session with a deputy minister, I asked why he thought that compliance was so low. Was it lack of inspectors, inspectors with inadequate checklists or was it because it was cheaper to pay a fine than to comply? I did not mention the possibility of corruption, but everyone present would have realised that that would be a real pos-

---

1 Shengman Zhang had recently stepped down as a managing director of the World Bank after some ten years of service, having previously served in the Chinese Ministry of Finance.

sibility. I did not get a full answer to my question as the minister in his answer focused on the fact that compliance was probably higher, perhaps more like 30% or 35%, which he appeared to think would answer my question. Whatever the precise figure, it was clear that compliance was a problem.

I therefore took the opportunity in a group meeting with Premier Wen Jiabao of raising the issue. I had met him some years before when he was Vice Premier and we had discussed mutual interests in geology; not only is his academic background in geology but he practised geology in the Gansu geological bureau for more than a decade in his early career, afterwards becoming a Vice Minister in the Ministry of Geology and Mineral Resources. I had also several times since been in groups that had met him and been very impressed by his thoughtful responses to questions. So I asked him how he envisaged raising the levels of compliance so that the strategies outlined in the 11th Five-Year Plan could be delivered. Would this be by picking a few leading issues and taking a tough line? Or would it be by training and exhortation? Or would there be incentives to comply? His reply was that compliance was indeed essential for the delivery of the plan. He gave his reply in three parts. First, he said that it was essential to establish the rule of law. This sounded to me like getting tough and in China sometimes laws can be enforced with draconian penalties. He immediately went on to say that there would be no deviation from using market forces and incentives. These could be used to encourage compliance also. He had elsewhere spoken of developing systems of performance appraisal of provincial officials, with rewards in the form of promotion and central support, or the opposite (his second point). But it was his third point that I found most interesting. He said that in order for the plan to be delivered it was essential for the government to build the trust of the people that the government would deliver on the few things that it was important for a government to deliver, namely education, healthcare and social security. These had to be delivered if the plan was to succeed. He suggested that I return in five years to see whether this had been successful. I have done so every year and while there are clearly still major problems, the progress has been remarkable.

The 12th Five-Year Plan (2011–15) has continued to build on this progress. In the preamble it declares that

> The 'fundamental end' of economic transformation is to improve people's lives, which could only be achieved by improving the social welfare system, giving priority to job creation, providing equal public services to every citizen and stepping up reform of the income distribution system.[2]

To this end, while proposing a somewhat lower rate of economic growth at 7%, it envisages shifting the economy towards higher value-added production and an increasing service industry, moving away from industry dependent on low wages with increases of the minimum wage by at least 13% a year. At the same time the coverage of medical insurance is to be increased, with the differences between urban and rural residents reduced. Pension schemes should by the end of the period cover all rural residents and some 350 million urban residents. The global challenge of climate change is acknowledged and a 16% reduction in energy and a 17% reduction in carbon dioxide per unit of GDP targeted. Combined with what was achieved in the 11th Five-Year Plan, this would bring the carbon intensity of the economy down by 40–45% from 2006 levels by 2015. A reduction in water usage by 50% per unit of industrial production is also proposed. These are steps towards achieving the dream of a 'circular economy' in which all resources are reused and recycled.

These are remarkable objectives for an economy that, although large, is still relatively low in per capita income. There is probably no other country that has set itself such rational targets and furthermore China has a track record of achieving its targets. This is not to say that all is perfect. China has a very poorly developed legal system and its treatment of citizens can be capricious, with draconian punishments for those who are perceived as stepping out of line. The suppression of the voices of those who criticise the government is common and unacceptable. Such matters as the common use of the many executed criminals as sources of organs for transplant causes revulsion in other societies, particularly

---

2 British Chamber of Commerce in China translation; see www.britishchamber.cn/content/chinas-twelfth-five-year-plan-2011-2015-full-english-version.

those in which capital punishment has been abolished, albeit only in the last 50 years or so. In addition, there is corruption in both the education and healthcare systems, with additional side payments being expected to ensure delivery of services to which people are entitled or which should be covered by health insurance. These very real defects sometimes cloud perceptions of the remarkable achievements in many other areas.

The issue is one of control by the party, supported by the People's Liberation Army, which has provided a stable framework for the delivery of the economic and social benefits and is paranoid about the consequences of losing control. While one may be critical of this as an organisation simply wanting to prolong its hegemony, we should bear in mind that experiences from other countries where such systems have collapsed rapidly have produced some very undesirable social results. I believe that the authorities are well aware of the challenges and stresses in society, but are concerned how to achieve change progressively and in an orderly fashion. This may lead to differing conclusions on the direction that change should take.

As an illustration of this I listened with fascination once to a discussion in a very open forum between Chinese academics and representatives of the government, including people of ministerial rank. The subject was the source of community disturbances that destroyed the 'harmonious society' and what should be done to prevent them. Interestingly, all agreed on the basic cause of the disturbances. Consider the example of land used by a rural population for agriculture being converted to use for housing or industry. In such a case, the business acquiring the land, which in China is not owned individually but by the state, will pay compensation to the municipal authorities for the land. The problem is what happens to that money. It is only a slight caricature to suggest that the first use of the compensation money is the construction of municipal buildings, including those marble-floored 'guest houses' in which foreign visitors are so often welcomed by Chinese officials. The respective groups are seated in rows of armchairs on either side of the main protagonists, the mayor or governor on one side and the senior foreign dignitary on the other, all accompanied by cups of green tea. After construction of a suitably imposing 'guest house' and municipal offices, should there be funds remaining these may be used for transportation. The result is that the former occupiers of the land, seeing the mayor in his new Mercedes, throw rocks at the vehicle and a disturbance ensues. All parties agreed readily that this was the kind of scenario that caused disturbances; the answer is clearly to ensure that the compensation paid by the business goes to those who were previously occupying the land and using it productively. To the Chinese academics the solution was quite simple: distribute ownership of the land to those who are currently using it. For the government, such a solution would take the party and the state out of the chain, so that the preferred solution was to regulate matters properly so that the municipal authorities passed the compensation on to those to whom it was due. From my own experience, the outcome for a responsible foreign company may effectively be that the compensation may have to be paid twice: once to the authorities and once to the justly aggrieved previous users of the land.

I believe that history will view the achievements during the ten years that Wen Jiabao has been premier positively. He has taken a cooperative and consensual approach, with great humbleness of manner, while at the same time not being afraid to be outspokenly critical of failings. At the time of the People's Congress in March 2007 he famously declared that 'China's economic growth is unsteady, unbalanced, uncoordinated and unsustainable', a statement that he has often repeated, and which is often quoted. One cannot imagine any Western leader making a similar criticism of the direction of economic development in his or her own country. The shadow that hangs over his period in office is the great growth in corruption, including stories of corruption by leading families, and indeed of Wen's own family. Whatever the facts relating to Wen's family and the allegations of the use of insider information by family members, there is no doubt that corruption as a whole has grown greatly, further increasing income disparities.

Perhaps because of his geological background, Wen Jiabao has also taken an active interest in mine safety. This was also of great interest to Anglo American as we endeavoured to grow operations in China in line with international standards. In 2003, Tarmac, which was part of Anglo American, acquired the Yang Quarry in Huzhou, Zhejiang Province, in order to supply Shanghai with construction aggregates. It is a limestone quarry that was formerly worked by five different small-scale operators with a poor capital investment record and 12 to 15 fatalities annually. With the support of the Zhejiang Provincial Government, Tarmac acquired the consolidated quarry and in fact was allowed to hold a 100% interest, which was unusual in China.

It was necessary to invest significant sums to get the quarry into safely workable condition. The vertical face had to be cut back to benches to prevent catastrophic collapses of the working face and drilling equipment acquired. When I visited the quarry while remediation was being undertaken I heard many stories of the previous operators having people abseil down the face with drills to drill shallow holes for the explosives. The same drillers charged the holes that they had drilled. The resulting explosions sent rocks flying through the air into the neighbouring villages. When Tarmac was ready to make the first major blast the villagers remained concerned, as they knew that the amount of charge was much greater than had ever been used before. However, when the blast occurred, as the shot holes were deep, the result was merely a tremor in the ground; the deeper holes ensured that the blast energy went into breaking up the rock rather than escaping to the air taking rocks with it. Moreover, in the first two years of Tarmac operation, producing 1.4 million tons of aggregate per annum, rather than having the 25 fatalities that would normally have occurred in the period with the former five small operators, there were only two minor lost time injuries. Furthermore, in 2007 the Yang Quarry won a prestigious mining environmental award. The Chinese quarrying industry is never going to be dominated by foreign companies. Indeed there is some doubt as to whether much expansion will be allowed. However, there is no doubt that the authorities have regarded the Yang Quarry as a valuable learning and demonstration exercise, as indeed did Anglo. The quarry has now been sold to another operator.

China's progress in fighting poverty

The publication *Eliminating Poverty Through Development in China* by Wang Xiaolu, Li Shi and Wang Sangui, produced by the China Development Research Foundation under the Chairmanship of Wang Meng Kui, former President of the Development Research Centre of the State Council, throws interesting and honest light on China's efforts to reduce poverty.[3] The authors argue for a significantly more rigorous criterion for identifying poverty than China's official rural poverty line of around ¥ (yuan) 700 ($100) per annum, favouring a measure that takes into account income distribution and access to healthcare and education needs above subsistence. Even using the dollar a day criterion, China's progress has been impressive. In 1981 China's poor constituted 43% of the global population in poverty; by 2001 the Chinese component had reduced to less than 20%. The current progress in reduction of global poverty is largely attributable to programmes in China. No other country has made progress on a similar scale. The achievements in Brazil are also encouraging but, perhaps surprisingly, they have been based more on direct state intervention or subsidy. An exception may be the impressive extension of access to electricity, for which consumers pay commercial rates, with the cost of access infrastructure borne by the state.

China's policy approach to issues is analytical. Wang *et al.* demonstrate with statistics and correlations the impact on poverty of infrastructure construction. You cannot lift a village out of poverty unless it is linked to the market by a road and has reasonable access to power and communication. The difficult social issue of relocating communities from villages in areas of poor resource opportunity that cannot be economically connected by road is not ducked. The link between poverty and family ill-health is demonstrated as well as the need for primary and secondary education if poverty reduction is to be sustainable. The authors also stress the vital role of sound governance in policy implementation.

3 Wang Sangui, Li Shi and Wang Xiaolu, *Eliminating Poverty Through Development in China* (China Development Research Foundation; London: Routledge, 2008).

The government response to these requirements has been impressive. The provision of rural infrastructure in the form of highways and roads is familiar to any visitor to rural China, but there has been equally impressive progress in other areas, often first methodically piloted before being rolled out more widely. So it was with education, starting with school fee exemption in the western provinces in 2006, with supplements for books, and later in 2007 rolled out to nine years of compulsory free education nationwide. The book charts the deterioration of the original revolutionary medical system to the point in 1998 when over 75% of the population was not covered by a medical care system. Access to medical care and basic health insurance is expanding and is a current government priority.

As the bulk of China's poor are in rural areas where agriculture is the main source of income, improvements in this area have been fundamental. Starting with experiments in 2004, the central government took the radical step in 2006 of abolishing agricultural taxes nationally, and incidentally reforming the somewhat mediaeval method of tax collection by party cadres. These taxes had taken the form of highly regressive land and animal husbandry taxes, and their abolition put an annual ¥125 billion ($18 billion) straight into the pockets of farmers.

The book's impressive statistics have a very human face, which I was able to see in 2007 on a visit to Zhashui County in Shaanxi Province with Lu Mai, the Secretary-General of the China Development Research Foundation, who plays a key role in organising the China Development Forum. Shaanxi is not a particularly poor province, but Zhashui County, located in the southern mountainous area, has an average annual per capita income of ¥1,300 ($188). The villages we visited were poorer than average. In Xiaoling village we visited a Mr Huang. Five years before his annual income was ¥1,000 ($145). He was in his late fifties with two sons, both working not far away, and a daughter-in-law. He had started keeping pigs, with government advice on methods, and now had 20 pigs. They were in a barn across the road with a clean concrete floor and piped water. He had sold a total of around 100 pigs since he started. He bought the maize for food locally from other farmers with more land. His wife also made bean curd for sale. Mr Huang now earned ¥20,000 ($2,900) a year. As with many of the villagers, Mr Huang had a biogas generation system from human and animal waste. For this a subsidy of ¥2,000 was available from government. Mr Huang estimated that his system, including the cooker and piping had cost him ¥3,200 to build. These systems are clearly an excellent idea, improving hygiene, reducing greenhouse gas emissions and providing free gas for cooking and lighting.

Lu Mai and I discussed what had enabled the dramatic change in Mr Huang's fortunes five years ago from the abject poverty that he had suffered during all of his previous life. He had been relocated from his remote house up the valley to a house on the paved road, enabling him to get produce in and out easily. Probably because his land holding was small—unoccupied land being in short supply—he was encouraged to start on pigs. The abolition of the specific agricultural tax was a major contributor to his change in circumstances. The subsidised biogas system also reduced his expenses and advice from the government had enabled him to run his pig business successfully.

The next house we visited was a less happy story. The house, almost a neighbour of Mr Huang, was not in good condition. The family consisted of six—a grandfather and grandmother, the owner and his wife, and his two children. The owner had had a major brain operation for a tumour some time ago that had cost ¥60,000, which the family had had to pay, draining extended family resources dry. He still required medicines but now he had government health insurance that paid for about 40% of the costs. Had he had this health insurance earlier the operation would not have been such a family catastrophe. His father had also suffered from paralysis for much of his life. He and his father got a disability allowance from the government of ¥60 ($8.6) a month. They had some income from growing maize on their land. There was a foot-powered sewing machine in the house on which his wife had used to make clothes for the villagers, but there was no longer any demand due to the availability of cheap modern factory-made clothing.

The two examples illustrate the importance of communication for market access and the vital role of healthcare provision. But what of the next generation and education?

We visited the Xiaoling lower middle school, which had 600 pupils, studying 60 in a class. Half the students boarded in the school. The boarding block had been demolished as being unsafe—probably from poor construction perhaps due to corruption—and was being rebuilt. In the meantime the 15 boarding boys in each class slept in bunks in the back of the class. The girls slept in a separate classroom completely converted to a dormitory with 60 girls in one room, all two to two-tier bunks and tightly packed.

Feeding for the boarders was very basic. The government subsidy was ¥1.5 ($0.21) a day per student and this meant that there was only vegetables and tofu, no meat, cooked on site and served in polythene bags. Lu Mai was interested in the issue of food supplements, as the China Development Research Foundation has been doing systematic research on the impact of nutrition and on the most effective and low-cost method of feeding schoolchildren in poor areas. China has 30 million boarding students in education, three-quarters from rural areas in middle and western China. The Foundation has conducted controlled programmes of improved nutrition on 2,000 students in Guangxi Zhuang Autonomous Region, giving the control group equivalent benefits in clothing and other support in lieu of food supplements. The experiments demonstrated the considerable improvement in physical and learning development if food supplements were increased from the very low levels to ¥2.5 or ¥5 ($0.35 and $0.70) per day. As a result of their report the government has now increased daily supplements to ¥3 per middle school student and ¥2 per primary student.

In spite of the large classes and difficult conditions, some of the students in Xiaoling spoke good basic English and the textbook of a student whose favourite subject was mathematics dealt with quadratic equations and the binomial theorem, as well as statistics. According to the headmaster, some 15% of students went on to university—equivalent to Britain in the early 1960s when my wife and I went to university. The introduction of nine years of universal free education has been of great help. A university student living away from home would spend about ¥10,000 ($1,400) p.a. on tuition and living, which is clearly a significant barrier to poor rural families. Government loan systems are being introduced; students can also get a free university education, which is then repaid by teaching in rural areas.

As a follow-on to the work on food supplements Lu Mai and the China Development Research Foundation is doing some outstanding work on early years' education in the ten western provinces. This is to ensure that not only the children, but in some cases their parents who are involved in the process, learn to speak the national language necessary for employment, instead of just their local or ethnic dialect.

Although there is clearly much still to do, China has made enormous strides in poverty reduction. Not only developing countries but also more wealthy ones, including the UK, would do well to absorb the lessons. The analytical process, followed by methodical experimentation and final roll-out of successful approaches is impressive and, given the emphasis on sound early education, the successes should prove sustainable.

The balance of progress

There are many in the West who criticise China on the grounds that the remarkable economic progress has been achieved at great environmental cost. They argue that as a result of weak legal protection and strong suppression of dissenting opinions, individuals suffer great injustices and that in the long term society will pay the price. It cannot be denied that there have been and still are some very negative consequences. From my experience the Chinese government is well aware of this and is making progress in addressing the main issues. Progress is slower than it might be due to two things. First, there are the problems of ensuring that central initiatives and policies are in fact implemented in the provinces and counties of China. This question of compliance is one that has always been an issue in China with the well-known explanation: 'the mountains are high and the emperor is far away'. Progress is being made in compliance, but it remains a problem. The second issue is more fundamental and existential. How does China make changes to its political system that will allow greater and more formalised participation by the population at large without a breakdown in stability and order, which would be in no one's interest? This is particularly difficult in an age of widespread Internet access and growing interaction through the social media. One might see Singapore as a possible model, and I suspect the Chinese government observes those developments with interest. Singapore is in essence a single city-state, so there is nothing like the same issue of compliance. In spite of being close to a one-party state, Singapore has had recent electoral shocks that have prompted significant resignations of long-standing government ministers and changes in policy to demonstrate greater connection and responsiveness of the government to the people. This has been achieved with much anxiety, but without disruption. The economic and social model has responded, but essentially continues its uninterrupted progress. I believe that achieving the same in China is difficult, but not impossible. I also believe that on any rational analysis the great Chinese experiment of the last three and a half decades has been hugely positive for the people of China, in spite of its areas of shortcoming. Other countries can learn a lot from adapting some of these Chinese approaches to their own situations.

Chapter 11

1995: Shell's *annus horribilis* and its consequences

1995 was a very bad year for Shell as a result of two unconnected events: the attempt to dispose of the storage and tanker loading buoy Brent Spar in the deep Atlantic and later in the year the execution by the Nigerian government of Ken Saro-Wiwa, who had been involved in many protests against Shell's activities in Ogoniland in the south-east of the country. The public outrage at these two events caused us in Shell to examine our principles and policies. The review, and the consultation process that preceded it, led to some modifications to Shell's long-standing Business Principles, but equally importantly had a significant impact on Shell's whole approach to engagement and consultation with the public.

The Brent Spar

In 1976 the Brent Spar was installed as an innovative and unique solution to transporting oil from the recently discovered and developed Brent field in the northern North Sea to shore without building a pipeline. Oil from the production platform was produced into the Spar, a floating cylinder 147m from top to bottom and 29m in diameter. The Spar displaced 66,000 tons and had accommodation and a helideck on top of it. At regular intervals tankers would moor to the buoy and load the crude oil for transport to shore. The installation served in this way for some 15 years.

Brent Spar had been constructed in the horizontal position in Britain and then towed to a deep-water location and upended. The original plan had been to dispose of the buoy by reversing the process. However, it was feared that during the initial upending process for installation the structure had been somewhat over-stressed and might have been weakened, increasing the risk of break-up if the process was reversed. Furthermore, during operation there had been further stress. A valve had been incorrectly closed, isolating a storage cell and the differential pressure caused by the cooling oil had damaged the cell. I had always heard that one of the crew on board had closed the valve in an effort to stop the annoying and sleep-depriving rush of air in and out of the cell as the buoy moved in the waves, but this may well be apocryphal.

When disposal options were considered, onshore disposal was rejected because of concerns for human safety and environmental damage if the Spar broke up while it was being rotated from the vertical to horizontal. After much deliberation, it was decided that the storage tanks should be flushed through with water and the installation sunk in the deep waters of the Atlantic to the north-west of Scotland. In Shell we thought that we had consulted all relevant parties, including fishermen. We had made the necessary notification to the Oslo and Paris Commission for deep-water disposal, waiting the prescribed time to ensure that there were no objections from any other state. We had had permission from the UK government. We were all ready to go ahead with what we thought was a responsible and relatively uncontroversial operation. Little did we know what was in store for us!

Greenpeace commenced a truly brilliant publicity campaign against the method of disposal. One of the most telling advertisements by Greenpeace was an image of a supermarket trolley in a village pond, focusing on the social irresponsibility of not recycling waste. Greenpeace occupied the platform and the images of fire hoses most inadvisably used to prevent further boarding and harass the occupiers made great television and presented the dispute as one between David and Goliath. There was much public outrage, particularly in Germany where a boycott of Shell had considerable impact. Shell stations in Germany were also fire-bombed and attacked. Requests to the German government to condemn this met with the response that this was unnecessary as German citizens knew that such behaviour was illegal. The German government formally requested the British government to withdraw the disposal permission. Although the financial impact was not material in the context of the whole event, the boycott did result in a loss of market share that took two or three years to recover.

Greenpeace made much of the allegedly toxic contents of the Spar. They also pointed out that the disposal site might well be the home of delicate cold-water corals, *Lophelia pertusa*, which would be obliterated. Needless to say, corals are always emotive in the marine environment and to be fair Shell also pointed out that in the Gulf of Mexico platforms such items as old tyres were often dumped in the sea to provide habitats for fish and corals. Neither argument was particularly relevant.

After some time, the protesters were removed from the platform by the authorities. The UK government remained supportive and indeed both the Prime Minister John Major and Tim Eggar the Energy Minister felt that to halt now would be to give in to threats, simply encouraging future illegal activism.

Once the platform was back in Shell hands and preparations for the tow to the North Atlantic complete, I had a call from Chris Fay who was Chairman of Shell UK at the time (I was at the time the Shell Managing Director with overall responsibility for oil and gas exploration and production—the 'upstream' in Shell terminology). They were about to cut the anchor chains on the Brent Spar and commence the tow. Once this was done, there would be no going back as there would be no means of anchoring the Spar in open water again. Chris just wanted to check that we were still OK to go ahead. In what was probably not one of the best decisions of my Shell career we agreed that we should go ahead and cut the chains. With hindsight, we should have paused at that point and taken the Brent Spar into a Norwegian fjord (deep water was required) and done further extensive analysis and consultation.

As Brent Spar was being towed to the final disposal point in the Atlantic, she was reoccupied by Greenpeace activists. At this point the activists on board put out a detailed report that they had physically dipped the tanks on board and from the measurements taken they calculated that there were some 5,000 tons of oil sludge on board, as opposed to the 50 to 100 tons that Shell believed. Chris and I knew that this could not be true as the tanks had been flushed through with sea water that was pumped into a tanker. We spent time trying to work out how such a conclusion could have been reached and came up with some complex scenarios. There were also far-fetched allegations based on a sworn affidavit from an alleged witness that toxic waste from another rig had been transferred to the Spar. Protests continued unabated and if Brent Spar had been sunk at that point the accusation of Shell misinformation on a significant scale would have hung over us unresolved for ever.

It was decided to abort the sinking of the platform. The Norwegian government agreed that the Spar could be stored in a Norwegian fjord while alternatives were considered. In addition an independent survey was commissioned from the respected Norwegian classification firm Norske Veritas find the truth of the allegations. In the event, some three months after the main allegation and just as the inspection was about to begin, Greenpeace withdrew the allegation, stating that the measurements had been mistaken and apologising for the 'minor mistake'.[1] It may well be correct that a mistake was made in calculation, but I suspect that in the days immediately before what appeared to be the inevitable destruction of the evidence, those on board were, to say the least, cavalier in their calculations, knowing that they could never be proved wrong. The subsequent independent examination also showed that there was no evidence of the alleged toxic waste and the witness was manifestly unreliable. I have a considerable respect for Greenpeace

1 'Greenpeace UK's head of science, Susan Meyer, said the organisation was obliged to own up as soon as it discovered its error: "I still feel extremely comfortable about the stance Greenpeace took against dumping this structure at sea," she said. "We're owning up to minor mistake."' (N. Schoon, 'Greenpeace's Brent Spar Apology', *Independent*, 6 September 1995, www.independent.co.uk/news/greenpeaces-brent-spar-apology-1599647.html).

and have since appeared in support of some of their policy events. I do not for a moment think that the erroneous measurements were planned at management level, but Greenpeace, like Shell, is an organisation of many humans, and I think, like Shell, Greenpeace cannot always be sure that every action of all its staff and campaigners is responsible.

Even at the moment of taking the decision to abandon the sinking of the Spar, we in Shell were not particularly adept in our public affairs management. At the very moment of the announcement John Major and Tim Eggar were in the House of Commons defending the decision to continue with the deep-sea disposal. John Major was understandably furious and I do not think he ever forgave us in Shell.

Once Brent Spar was safely in the Norwegian fjord, watched over by a Greenpeace boat, an exhaustive consultation and review process was undertaken. Eventually, the most acceptable solution was deemed to be to cut up the Spar and reuse the resulting rings of steel in the wharf of a Norwegian ferry terminal. This cost tens of millions of dollars more than the deep-sea disposal route, but such decisions are choices for society as to how best to allocate resources.

Our 50–50 partners, Exxon, had managed to keep out of the limelight and their name out of the press. This was reasonable, as Shell was and always had been the operator of the venture with responsibility for both operations. The name of Exxon was never really associated with the event. In fact, ironically, because the installation was called Brent Spar and did not have Shell in its name, the general public in the UK has difficulty separating one oil company from another. This was confirmed in a survey of a cross-section of the British public some months after the event. I was able to ring my competitor and industry colleague John Browne at BP and tell him that the good news for him was that the brand recognition of BP was as high as that of Shell; the bad news was that as many people associated Brent Spar with BP as with Shell. Exxon, the 50% partner, hardly registered.[2]

---

2 On the other hand Exxon is forever linked to the *Exxon Valdez* disaster in 1989 because of the inclusion of the brand in the tanker's name. The same is true of the *Amoco Cadiz* disaster in 1978. From the pioneering first bulk tanker, the *Murex*, built in Marcus Samuel's day early in the 20th century, Shell tankers

Ten years after the event, Greenpeace's magazine *Greenpeace Business* asked me whether I would write a piece for them on what the impact the Brent Spar event had been in progressing sustainable development. I wrote them the piece shown in Box 11.1, which they did not publish.

Box 11.1 **Article requested for *Greenpeace Business***

Ten Years after Brent Spar

Brent Spar taught us all lessons. We in Shell learned that not all problems can be solved simply by technical analysis. Many views, including intuitive feelings, have validity—we need to listen to them and address concerns. Greenpeace probably learned that they have as much responsibility for checks and controls to ensure the validity of information generated by their front line troops as we do in business. And everyone learned of the power of public outrage once unleashed, including the unintended consequence of several Shell stations in Germany being firebombed and one even being sprayed with bullets.

For me a critical point was when a Scandinavian minister of the environment said that he believed that Shell's analysis was technically correct, that the environmental impact would indeed be negligible, but he felt that the deep sea disposal was just wrong. How could he teach school children to recycle their rubbish if they saw such an example on television?

In Shell, once deep sea disposal had been halted, an extensive and very open process of public consultation and reanalysis of the contents of the Spar was carried out. Out of this we learned the truth about the 'thousands of tons of oily waste', the 'radioactivity' and even the 'bags of toxic waste' said by sworn affidavit to have been taken to Brent Spar and cemented into hidden compartments for disposal.

Meanwhile, the tragic execution of Ken Saro Wiwa in Nigeria, helped to launch Shell into global public consultations on the responsibilities of

---

have always been called after seashells, perhaps in respect for the origins of the 'Shell' business. Tankers of one design all have seashell names beginning with the same letter. Anyone in the business will know immediately that this is a Shell tanker and of which class.

major global corporations. From this came revisions of Shell principles to address human rights and sustainable development, with in turn comprehensive consultation and reporting through the Shell Report. Open reporting of performance against principles and targets, using for example the Global Reporting Initiative, is critical in building more sustainable development into the day to day activities of companies. For Shell, the experience of Brent Spar was certainly part of the trigger for this activity, but in my view the event itself teaches us more about the power of public outrage than about sustainable development.

The last irony is Lophelia pertusa. Remember her? She was the threatened deep water coral whose family would be extinguished by the descent of Brent Spar and its toxic contents on their heads in the deep sea. When the analysis of the biota of Brent Spar was made in a Norwegian fjord she was found happily living stuck to the hull. She ended up entombed with sections of her erstwhile habitat the Spar in a Norwegian ferry terminal.

They published instead a more amenable article by my friend and colleague James Smith, who at the time was Chairman of Shell UK. They explained that they were really looking for someone more current in the Shell scene. There is a copy of James's article on the Shell Brent Spar Dossier site as an endpiece.[3]

The execution of Ken Saro-Wiwa

In November 1995, after the Brent Spar events of the summer of the same year, Shell was hit for the second time by public outrage, this time in connection with the tragic and unjust execution of Ken Saro-Wiwa by the Nigerian military government of Sani Abacha.

Ken Saro-Wiwa was born in Bori in what is now Rivers State in southeastern Nigeria. Bori is in the centre of the Ogoni area. He won a scholarship to study English at the University of Ibadan, at that time the

3 s02.static-shell.com/content/dam/shell-new/local/country/gbr/downloads/e-and-p/brent-spar-dossier.pdf.

pre-eminent university in Nigeria. He was a talented and multifaceted man. Somewhat controversially as someone born in the east of Nigeria he supported the Federal side in the Biafran war. He became a Federal Civil Commissioner in the east and was also a Commissioner in the Rivers State government during the period of General Gowon's government after the civil war.

He was a successful businessman, a prolific author and writer of a very popular satirical television series. He became quite wealthy and his children went to boarding school in England. His push for autonomy for the Ogoni region started back in the 1970s.

In 1990 the Movement for the Survival of the Ogoni People (MOSOP) submitted the Ogoni Bill of Rights to the Federal Military Government of Ibrahim Babangida and followed this up in 1991 with further material. The thrust of the documents was first a demand for autonomy for the 500,000 people of Ogoniland, with access to revenues, representation at federal level and control of resources. The preamble states that the Ogonis demand

> political control of Ogoni affairs by Ogoni people, control and use of Ogoni economic resources for Ogoni development, adequate and direct representation as of right for Ogoni people in all Nigerian national institutions and the right to protect the Ogoni environment and ecology from further degradation.

The argument was put forward that these rights had been removed from the Ogoni by British colonisation and should have reverted to the Ogoni at the end of that period rather than being usurped by the majority ethnic groups of Nigeria.

The second demand was for compensation for the oil produced since the discovery of oil and compensation for environmental damage. This was aimed particularly at Shell operations in several oilfields in the area. There was also reference to genocide committed by the 'multinational oil companies under the supervision of the Government of the Federal Republic of Nigeria'.

The situation became progressively more heated and potentially violent. In 1993 Shell withdrew all staff from oil-producing operations from the Ogoni area and closed in the wells. They have not been operated since, although it has taken many years to gain access to plug them properly and in a tamper-proof way. I flew over the area in a helicopter in the mid-1990s and could see that everything moveable had been removed by the community.

In 1994 four Ogoni leaders were murdered in intra-Ogoni strife. It was for alleged incitement to this crime that Ken Saro-Wiwa and eight others were tried by a military court. Shell was not involved in the trial in any way, nor did any of the charges involve Shell or its operations. I believe that the trial was unfair. At the time Shell publicly stated that Ken Saro-Wiwa had a right to express his views and should receive a fair trial and have access to proper medical treatment. When the nine were found guilty by the court, my colleague and Chairman Cor Herkströter wrote to Sani Abacha, who by that time had assumed power as President, asking for clemency.

Serious though it was, I had assumed that the death sentence would not be carried out. All the knowledge and advice that we had was that the matter would drag on for some time and eventually be resolved. That was what had happened with the sentence passed on former President Obasanjo who had been accused and found guilty of treason. In an interview in December 2011, Ken's daughter Noo Saro-Wiwa also said that the family had never expected the regime to carry out the sentence.[4]

So why was the sentence in fact carried out on 10 November 1995? A senior Nigerian who at the time had the unenviable task of representing the very unpredictable Sani Abacha to the outside world told me that Abacha felt aggrieved that he had got no credit or thanks for releasing former President Obasanjo after many representations from abroad. The Commonwealth Conference was coming up and he simply thought that he would pre-empt any complaints. In fact, Nigeria was subsequently suspended from the Commonwealth. This account has a kind of twisted dictatorial logic to it. If true, it is appalling to think that the lives of nine humans can depend on such whims.

4 *Mail & Guardian*, 'Activist Ken Saro-Wiwa's Daughter Remembers Her Father', *Mail & Guardian*, 31 December 2011, mg.co.za/article/2011-12-31-activist-ken-sarowiwas-daughter-remembers-her-father.

In 1996 a civil suit was brought under the Alien Tort Claims Act in New York against Shell and Brian Anderson, who had been the Managing Director of Shell in Nigeria at the time, with accusations of complicity in the executions. These accusations are quite untrue. I referred in Chapter 5 to Brian Anderson and his distaste at having to meet Sani Abacha. I have known Brian since the 1960s and worked with him when he was representing Shell in Nigeria. He was born in Jos in Nigeria and I know him to have a deep love and understanding of Nigeria and Nigerians. At the time he was deeply concerned about the plight of Ken Saro-Wiwa and the other Ogonis.

This case dragged on for years. Eventually, long after I had retired from Shell I was in fact deposed by the claimant's lawyers in London, and I would have been fully prepared to give evidence in court. The deposition involved hours of questioning, mainly on the corporate structure of Shell with the intent of establishing the United States as an appropriate forum for such a case under the Alien Tort Claims Act. I recall being asked whether I had known that the trial of Ken Saro-Wiwa was held under military regulations with no appeal. I replied that I had certainly known that the court was a military one, but that I could not recall whether I knew that there was no appeal possible. I added that although I am not a legal expert I had since frequently discussed the process with lawyers; I understood that the closest analogy to the Nigerian military court conditions were those of military trials in Guantanamo Bay. This reply pleased the human rights lawyer who was present, but her more commercially minded colleague had it struck from the record. I never had to appear in court. In 2009 Shell reached a settlement with the plaintiffs for some $15 million. According to Shell 'this included money for a trust fund to benefit the Ogoni people and a compassionate payment to the plaintiffs and the estates they represent, as well as covering plaintiffs' costs and fees'. Given the time that had to be spent in court this was probably a sensible commercial decision, but I still felt disappointed that a claim that I consider to be without any basis could result in any payment that might be interpreted as an admission of fault in the case, however much this is covered in the wording of the agreement. Unfortunately many claims in the United States under the Alien Tort

Claims Act end up being settled in this way for similar reasons. This is doubtless why they are popular with the lawyers who end up getting fees in any case, more or less regardless of the merits of the case.

I never knew Ken Saro-Wiwa, although I have several times since met his son Ken Wiwa, who is a journalist who has written movingly about his complex relationship with his father. Many of my Nigerian Shell colleagues and their families knew Ken senior. Ken did not make a secret of the fact that involving Shell was his way of gaining international attention for the Ogoni cause, which otherwise would have never drawn great attention on its own. While I think the claims of environmental devastation against Shell in Nigeria are exaggerated, all is certainly not perfect. When it comes to revenue sharing, Ken certainly had a point. Shell has for decades supported the idea that a greater share of the petroleum revenue should go to the oil-producing states and communities. Indeed this has steadily increased over the years. However, the percentage share is not the necessarily the main problem. Whether it is 1% or 13%, as it later became, it has no effect if the money is absorbed on the long route from the federal coffers through the individual states and eventually to the communities. Much gets lost on the way through corruption and to meet other demands. That is why it is so important for states such as Nigeria to fully implement the requirements of the Extractive Industries Transparency Initiative (EITI). Nigeria is one of the countries that has subscribed to the EITI and has gone through the process of being recognised as a 'Compliant Country'. This means that all payments to the government, from any company whether private or state-owned, international or indigenous, must be independently audited on both the company and the government side and there must be a credible multi-stakeholder panel in place to oversee and advise on increasing understanding and transparency of the revenue flows.

Calls by MOSOP and the Ogoni Bill of Rights for political autonomy and control of revenues for the Ogoni people enter a controversial area. I well recall a banner headline in a Nigerian newspaper referring to the Ogoni demands with the single word 'SECESSION!' Given the Nigerian history of the secessionist Biafran War in which at least a million people died, demands for political and revenue autonomy are bound to stir up strong emotions. Ken Saro-Wiwa and MOSOP made clear that they were seeking autonomy within a Nigerian state, not independence, but the difference is likely to be lost on many.

In the years since 1995 I have often asked myself and been asked whether we in Shell should have acted differently. Going back 15 years or so before 1995 to the time that I worked in Nigeria I do think that there are things we could have done differently, mainly in relation to the way in which we interacted with communities, making sure that the authorities that we dealt with were indeed really representative and working with others to ensure that we had the capacity to listen more carefully to communities and involve them in the delivery of needs. These are lessons we have learned since. However, in relation to the specific events leading up to the execution I do not actually think that we could have done more. We did call for a fair trial and for fair treatment and we supported Ken Saro-Wiwa's right to express his opinion. We did call for clemency. Withdrawing from Nigeria either in fact or as a threat would have made no difference; the operations were largely run by very able Nigerians who could not simply have left. In any case a multinational company has serious ongoing obligations to those who work for it in any country. As described in Chapter 8, our actions in relation to the announcement of the Nigerian LNG project contract increased global outrage, as we knew it would. In historical terms the decision on the LNG investment was right; not only did it prevent the theft of hundreds of millions of dollars by Abacha, but also it meant that what has proved to be a truly great Nigerian project came on stream without further delay.

The impact of the events of 1995

The impact in close succession of the events of Brent Spar in the middle of 1995 and the execution of Ken Saro-Wiwa in November was massive; not the financial impact, but the impact on reputation and morale. The Body Shop, a UK-based international retail chain founded by the late Anita Roddick selling beauty products, ran a very effective campaign across their network excoriating Shell. Both Anita and her husband Gordon were strong supporters of the Ogoni cause. In general the reputation of Shell, particularly in Europe, suffered greatly. In many ways the greatest impact was that on Shell employees and their families. Having always had a great pride in the company and the work that we did, this was being called into question. What had gone wrong? There was also potentially an impact on future employees and the willingness of talented young people to work for the company.

Apart from this great reputational and morale impact, the financial impact was not material. We had lost market share in Germany because of Brent Spar, but largely not elsewhere; the market share in Germany recovered in due course and in any case the marketing earnings in most European countries were not large. The onshore disposal of Brent Spar and the exhaustive consultations connected with it took time and cost a lot more money but the bottom-line effect was less than the variability on a major oilfield development project. I can honestly say that I did not spend much time worrying about the financial effects.

On the other hand we had always regarded ourselves as a responsible company. The Shell General Business Principles that had been promulgated in the 1970s through work by the late Sir Geoffrey Chandler were ground-breaking in their time. Although the word 'stakeholder' was not used, those principles recognised that the company had obligations to many different constituent interests and not just to shareholders. The principles recognised an obligation 'to protect shareholders' investment and to provide an acceptable return'. Responsibilities to employees, to our customers, to those with whom we do business and to society at large were recognised. No exclusive or excessive focus on shareholder value there! There were strict injunctions against the payment of bribes or making political payments. As a result of years of working with the Business Principles and processes where all those joining the company received them, these principles were quite well embedded in the organisation; people knew about them and were proud of them. In most communities Shell was well regarded and anywhere in the world when one said that one worked for Shell the reaction was generally positive.

After the events of 1995 this changed. At very best, those who supported us and knew of our approach to business thought we had handled the publicity badly. Many others regarded our behaviour as unconscionable. In fact, even to this day some of Judy's fellow Quakers will ask her sympathetically what it is like to be married to someone who was involved at a high level in a major oil company like Shell.

Perhaps because so many Shell people have a scientific or engineering background, the corporate mind-set tends to be analytical and logical in relation to problems, an approach that also resulted in charges of arrogance. In the aftermath of 1995, Shell embarked on systematic global consultation process. The programme had the broad title of 'Society's Changing Expectations'. We thought that our principles were sound, yet plainly many people in society felt that we had fallen short of their expectations. Had expectations changed and if so what were society's expectations of a major global company?

Phil Watts had overall responsibility for Planning and External Relations and Karen de Segundo was head of External Relations, so they led the programme. Ian Henderson and John Williams in the same department were also involved. The consultation part consisted of round-table meetings and interactions in over 20 countries of the world. The format of the round-table meetings was the same everywhere. About 12 Shell people from a cross-section of the company met about the same number of representatives of NGOs, the media, academics, politicians and others. Each round table had a different composition on the Shell side and of course on the external side, so that we got a view from right across the world in many languages and from many different national cultures. The format was generally some hours of discussion followed by a dinner. The question asked of each group was 'What are the expectations of a major global company?' Given the question and the open way in which it was asked, we had almost no refusals in principle to engage with Shell. On the Shell side, tens of people from across the company had an opportunity to engage with a wide cross-section of outside people and hear their views.

I attended a round table in the Netherlands. I fully expected to be subjected to waves of criticism. In the meeting I attended, many of our interlocutors already had contacts with Shell and were aware of the positive as well as the negative so the emphasis was very much on what changes in society were needed and what Shell's potential role in this should be. In fact the general response from people was that no one had asked them the question before; they were not sure that they knew the answer but were happy to discuss it. We talked in terms of the pre-existing Shell General Business Principles document and what changes or additions might be needed. We promised to report back to them all at the end of the process.

Arising from this process, three significant changes were made to the Business Principles (see Box 11.2). First, we had for many years said that we would not be involved in politics and not make political donations. It was pointed out that as a major economic actor and player in economies across the world Shell could not avoid being involved in politics. The wording was clarified to prevent engagement in partisan politics but went on to say:

> when dealing with governments, Shell companies have the right and the responsibility to make their position known on any matter which affects themselves, their employees, their customers, or their shareholders. They also have the right to make their position known on matters affecting the community, where they have a contribution to make.

This is not just a matter of semantics; I think there is an important underlying principle. We should be willing to speak openly but in a non-partisan way on subjects, sometimes in alliance with others. This might be unpopular with a particular government or a system of government, but it is an important role of responsible business. I had long encouraged Shell people to take off their corporate Shell hat and discuss the overall merits of issues or of different approaches in fields where we had expertise or where the interests of society as a whole are concerned. When that is done, the corporate hat can go back on and one can approach the matter from the commercial viewpoint of the company. If we can successfully do this we will not only be more useful members of society, but we will build trust.

The second change was to make references to human rights. A company clearly has prime responsibility for the human rights of its own people and this was specifically addressed. But there are wider responsibilities to society as a whole apart from merely obeying the law. A specific responsibility 'to express support for fundamental human rights in line with the legitimate role of business' was included. These may seem relatively minor changes, but they do empower people to act. For example, given the strong admonitions in the previous principles against political involvement, there was an understandable tendency for Shell people to keep their heads down. If they spoke publicly against some practice and a government reacted negatively, might that be regarded as becoming involved in politics? The combined changes in the principles on politics and human rights meant that people were empowered to use their own judgement as to when it was likely to be constructive and helpful to speak in private or in public. Nigeria in periods of military rule would be a good example of this. Many people had in fact used their initiative before and raised issues of human rights with governments, but this codification led to wider understanding and, most importantly, to the discussion of examples.

The third change was to include commitments to conduct Shell's business in line with the principles of sustainable development. I often say that we did not really know what we were committing ourselves to; this is by far the most difficult of the three changes to truly apply in depth. Robin Aram, who was greatly involved in the redrafting of the principles and with whom I had many long conversations on difficult subjects when I needed clear independent thinking, says that we did know. Perhaps he is right, but since then I have time and again seen companies commit to the Ten Principles of the UN Global Compact and then only gradually come to realise how difficult it is to truly embed them in their company's operation.

Box 11.2 **Shell's revised General Business Principles, 1997**[5]

Principle 1: Objectives

The objectives of Shell companies are to engage efficiently, responsibly and profitably in the oil, gas, chemicals and other selected businesses and to participate in the search for and development of other sources of energy. Shell companies seek a high standard of performance and aim to maintain a long-term position in their respective competitive environments.

Principle 2: Responsibilities

Shell companies recognise five areas of responsibility:

To shareholders

To protect shareholders' investment, and provide an acceptable return.

To customers

To win and maintain customers by developing and providing products and services which offer value in terms of price, quality, safety and environmental impact, which are supported by the requisite technological, environmental and commercial expertise.

To employees

To respect the **human rights of their employees,** to provide their employees with good and safe conditions of work, and good and competitive terms and conditions of service, to promote the development and best use of human talent and equal opportunity employment, and to encourage the involvement of employees in the planning and direction of their work, and in the application of these Principles within their company. It is recognised that commercial success depends on the full commitment of all employees.

To those with whom they do business

To seek mutually beneficial relationships with contractors, suppliers and in joint ventures and **to promote the application of these principles in so doing. The ability to promote these principles effectively will be**

5 The main changes to the text of the Principles are shown in bold. The Principles have been revised several times since 1997; see Shell Global website: www.shell.com/global/aboutshell/who-we-are/our-values/sgbp.html.

an important factor in the decision to enter into or remain in such relationships.

To society

To conduct business as responsible corporate members of society, to observe the laws of the countries in which they operate, **to express support for fundamental human rights in line with the legitimate role of business and to give proper regard to health, safety and the environment consistent with their commitment to contribute to sustainable development.**

These five areas of responsibility are seen as inseparable. Therefore it is the duty of management continuously to assess the priorities and discharge its responsibilities as best it can on the basis of that assessment.

Principle 3: Economic principles

Profitability is essential to discharging these responsibilities and staying in business. It is a measure both of efficiency and of the value that customers place on Shell products and services. It is essential to the allocation of the necessary corporate resources and to support the continuing investment required to develop and produce future energy supplies to meet consumer needs. Without profits and a strong financial foundation it would not be possible to fulfil the responsibilities outlined above.

Shell companies work in a wide variety of changing social, political and economic environments, but in general they believe that the interests of the community can be served most efficiently by a market economy.

Criteria for investment decisions are not exclusively economic in nature but also take into account social and environmental considerations and an appraisal of the security of the investment.

Principle 4: Business integrity

Shell companies insist on honesty, integrity and fairness in all aspects of their business and expect the same in their relationships with all those with whom they do business. The direct or indirect offer, payment, soliciting and acceptance of bribes in any form are unacceptable practices. Employees must avoid conflicts of interest between their private financial activities and their part in the conduct of company business. All business transactions on behalf of a Shell company must be reflected accurately and fairly in the accounts of the company in accordance with established procedures and be subject to audit.

Principle 5: Political activities

Of companies

Shell companies act in a socially responsible manner within the laws of the countries in which they operate in pursuit of their legitimate commercial objectives.

Shell companies **do not make payments to political parties, organisations or their representatives or take any part in party politics.** However, **when dealing with governments, Shell companies have the right and the responsibility to make their position known on any matter which affects themselves, their employees, their customers, or their shareholders. They also have the right to make their position known on matters affecting the community, where they have a contribution to make.**

Of employees

Where individuals wish to engage in activities in the community, including standing for election to public office, they will be given the opportunity to do so where this is appropriate in the light of local circumstances.

Principle 6: Health, safety and the environment

Consistent with their commitment to contribute to sustainable development, Shell companies have a systematic approach to health, safety and environmental management in order to achieve continuous performance improvement. To this end Shell companies manage these matters as any other critical business activity, set targets for improvement, and measure, appraise and report performance.

Principle 7: The community

The most important contribution that companies can make to the social and material progress of the countries in which they operate is in performing their basic activities as effectively as possible. In addition Shell companies take a constructive interest in societal matters which may not be directly related to the business. Opportunities for involvement—for example through community, educational or donations programmes—will vary depending upon the size of the company concerned, the nature of the local society, and the scope for useful private initiatives.

Principle 8: Competition

Shell companies support free enterprise. They seek to compete fairly and ethically and within the framework of applicable competition laws; they will not prevent others from competing freely with them.

Principle 9: Communications

Shell companies recognise that in their view of the importance of the activities in which they are engaged and their impact on national economies and individuals, open communication is essential. To this end, Shell companies have comprehensive corporate information programmes and provide full relevant information about their activities to legitimately interested parties, subject to any overriding considerations of business confidentiality and cost.

When we reviewed the revised principles with our interlocutors at the round tables of the 'Society's Changing Expectations' programme, it was generally acknowledged that the revised principles were indeed excellent. However, it was pointed out that they were but a set of words: we needed to demonstrate that we were really behaving in line with the underlying principles.

So Shell issued its first Sustainability Report covering the activities of 1997. It had the subtitle 'Profit and Principles—Does There Have to be a Choice?' In preparing the report Shell had much advice from John Elkington of SustainAbility. Preparing such reports is a difficult job. It is essential wherever possible to use standardised indicators and to make sure that these cover all the activities of the company, wherever they are in the world. Over the years the Global Reporting Initiative[6] has made a major contribution by developing reporting guidelines and standardised indicators, both those that can apply to all businesses and also sector-specific approaches. The power of the GRI is that, like the UN Global Compact, it involves not just businesses but civil society and labour

6 I served on the board of the Global Reporting Initiative from 2002 to 2007.

organisations as well. All the GRI guidelines go through an extensive consultation process. GRI reporting guidelines can also be used by UN Global Compact signatories when making reports for their Communications on Progress.

One outcome of this phase of consultation was that it became common practice for Shell to have open consultations with others in society. The listening process that had been started had to become part of normal business. The task in the subsequent years was to make sure that the principles and values that they represent were thoroughly embedded in the day-to-day operations of all parts of the company. This is a major and ongoing task for any company. In addition, during this process, Shell had instituted a major and professionally run survey that involved thousands of face-to-face and telephone interviews carried out by an independent organisation. This allowed us to build up an honest picture of how the world saw us and how this differed from our own impression of ourselves. This provided an invaluable baseline; by returning to the same people we could measure whether the things that we were doing were having an effect. The results of the initial survey showed that Shell was admired as a competent and professional company, but that the company was seen as being somewhat arrogant, and less caring about the human and environmental issues of society than it should be. Our communications were seen as being technocratic and cold. Opinions did vary substantially across the globe, with people in Asia, Africa and Latin America generally being much more favourable than those in Europe or North America. There was clearly much work to be done.

Chapter 12

Embedding values and principles

A major global company cannot be run simply by referring to a rule book. Situations vary enormously from country to country and furthermore can change rapidly. No rule book could cover this and if it attempted to it would be voluminous; in any case it almost certainly would not be read. It is therefore essential to try to embed values and principles in a way that they are absorbed by people in the organisation wherever they are and whatever their background, race or religion. In this way an individual can respond rapidly and confidently to situations on the ground. However, that does not mean that individuals are on their own. They should be able to refer to other people in the organisation to discuss difficult issues and thus draw on the experience of the whole group. This will only be possible if conditions have been created where real-life past problems have been discussed freely and people know that it is not a confession of weakness or failure to discuss a dilemma.

There is an analogy with the values to which a family subscribe. At best these encompass all members of a family: parents, grandparents, brothers, sisters and children. There are established patterns of behaviour that are known and accepted by all as part of membership of the family group. They are not codified, but established by example and behaviour. They are also subject to adaptation. The situations encountered by children and grandchildren are different from those experienced by their parents and grandparents and inevitably changes in behaviour and response will be needed, but hopefully the underlying values remain the same.

If this is difficult to achieve in a family, it is even more difficult in a global corporation. The essential first step is a willingness to discuss and debate. One of the reasons why I continued to work for Shell for so many years is that it was always acceptable to say 'that does not seem quite right to me'. You would not simply be told to get on with the job, but people at any level would engage in a discussion as to why it did not seem quite right or fair and what could be done about it. Although I have been involved at a different level in other companies such as Anglo American, HSBC, Accenture and Saudi Aramco, I have found the same broad approach. The inclusion of Saudi Aramco on this list may surprise some, but, although the company operates in a totally different national, social and political environment, I have found the same to be true. If it were not I would not remain on the board. This does not mean in any of those companies that no compromises are made, but they are compromises based on open discussion and clearly recognised as such.

Can values in a global company be genuinely global?

People often question whether, given the great diversity of cultural, religious and political backgrounds in different countries, it is possible to have a universal set of values in a global company. Does the mere act of having common values not require the imposition of a particular set of cultural norms, presumably reflecting the national origin of the parent company? There is no doubt that the nationality of the parent company may influence the values that are given priority, but these values can nonetheless be applied around the world in ways that adapt with the culture.[1]

---

1 Some of the implications of corporate structure on the challenge of ensuring that that national operations are seen as part of local society while adhering to uniform standards are discussed in Chapter 13.

If one reads the published values or mission statements of many companies, respect for people is extremely common. There is no doubt that ways of behaving with respect to people will be very different in Europe, North America, Japan or Saudi Arabia. It might be quite acceptable to call your boss Bob in the United States or the UK, but in Japan he would be Yamamoto-san and in Germany probably Herr Doktor Schmidt. In a global corporation all three individuals would probably welcome being addressed in the fashion common in whichever country they were in. But what of the treatment of women, which varies greatly in different countries? Respect for people would mean that individual women in an office in, for example, Saudi Arabia could decide whether to wear head coverings or *abayas* or how they should work together with men. The result is that within an office there is a mixture of dress. Where I have seen this in both Shell and Saudi Aramco offices in Saudi Arabia it appears to work very well, with women with different degrees of covering working happily together both with each other and with men. Of course, in Saudi Arabia, it is a national requirement for women to wear an *abaya* and head covering in public, but this does not extend to the office. There was a time in Riyadh where the official interpretation was that similar rules should apply within an office and that men and women should be separated; this was subject to occasional inspection by the Mutawa, unofficial or volunteer religious police, although this interpretation has been officially overturned as a result of work by women in the Jeddah Chamber of Commerce. At the time when the rule was considered to apply, it was respected in the Shell Riyadh office at the time of an inspection only, with a suitable system being put in place to announce any arrival of inspectors and for men and women to return to their separate work areas. If this put Shell in a state of non-compliance with national law, which I do not think it did, I am sure it was the correct decision. In the case of Saudi Aramco, from my observations over more than 20 years, I do not believe that strict dress or separation rules were ever applied in offices.

What is practised in businesses in terms of behaviour and governance does have some effect on society as a whole, both positively and in some cases, regrettably negatively. For this reason, I believe responsible companies should be positively encouraged to invest and develop business in countries in which regrettable behaviour or government policies are common. This applies not only to resource and extractive companies, but also to companies sourcing and manufacturing products in such countries as well as to companies marketing products. It is important, however, that in these activities companies take responsibility for the standards of companies in their supply chain, and do not hide behind a veil of independent suppliers.[2] As I have said in earlier chapters, I believe that the very presence of decent standards, and the economic growth and engagement that they generate, contributes more to positive change than programmes of sanctions and other exclusionary approaches. The question for a company operating in any country is not whether the government or general approach in that country to such matters as human rights, equality and corruption is in line with the principles and values of that company, but whether the company is able to uphold its own principles, within its own operations and in relation to its own staff and those outside with whom it interacts, including companies in its supply chain. In my experience it is almost unknown for laws or government policy in any country to make it impossible for a company to apply its own global standards within its own operations.

Over the years I have found that, perhaps somewhat surprisingly, the area where corporate principles are most likely to come into conflict with national policies is employment. Responsible companies work hard to remove all aspects of discrimination in their employment practices. At the same time most governments do apply some sort of regulation to employment. The most common regulations apply to work permits for foreigners to encourage preferential employment of nationals over foreigners. In some cases this extends to differentiating between ethnic groups within a country, which can collide with company's policies

---

2 For this reason, the UN Global Compact has a Working Group on the Supply Chain. Local suppliers are an important lever of economic development, but they must meet the standards of the company they supply. Local suppliers are often not initially able to do so and for that reason it is necessary, if local supply is considered appropriate and advantageous, to put in place programmes to help suppliers to achieve the required standards.

on non-discrimination. Moves to balance employment and to provide opportunities for previously disadvantaged groups in the interests of fairness and social stability are worthy of support, but you do not have to go as far as the distorted extremes of South African apartheid policies to run into conflicts. The most common example is perhaps the treatment of ethnic Chinese in countries of South-East Asia who, in spite of having lived and worked in countries for several generations, may find that government policies discriminate against them. There are many other current examples around the world of discrimination in society on grounds of ethnicity, gender or sexual orientation and within my working life such discrimination was also common in countries where it is now illegal; such practices would be against company codes of conduct, but hard work is needed to ensure that they are truly eliminated in behaviour.

The second area of concern is the treatment of migrant labour, both cross-border and within a country. In these situations very open discussion within a company and between the company and the authorities are necessary to ensure that companies truly live up to their principles.

A good example from the non-business world of the same value being implemented differently in different parts of the world, while preserving the essence of the value, is the question of what constitutes a fair trial. Almost all societies, at least nominally, regard a fair trial for a suspect as an individual right. In the UK, a fair trial is often regarded as being one with the involvement of a jury. I myself am a strong supporter of jury trials and felt affronted when jury trials were suspended in Northern Ireland at the time of the IRA troubles to avoid the intimidation of jurors. I have lived for many years in the Netherlands where people regard the idea of trials involving 12 more or less randomly selected non-expert members of the public with some amusement. To them, a fair trial involves appearing before a panel of professional judges. As a result of history and the way the legal system has developed the system is quite different, but I am confident that in each country the system that has evolved does in fact deliver a fair trial.

The consequences of not living up to professed values

It is essential that the practices of a company are seen to be aligned with its declared values. Nothing induces greater cynicism than a management that through its actions does not reflect the values of the company. Going back to the issue of respect for people, I recall a manager with whom I worked who delivered excellent financial results. He was an able person and in fact his leadership was in many ways charismatic. Many people in his team worked for him with enthusiasm. However, he was also a bully; he could and did reduce people to tears of humiliation and terror. I personally do not believe that this is compatible with values that call for respect for people. After several discussions that did not lead to any change, we agreed that it was best for all concerned if he left the company. Had he stayed, not only would his career have been limited but, more importantly, flouting the values of the company would have been seen by all to have been tolerated. I thought of this when listening to a talk by the biographer of the late Steve Jobs. Jobs was clearly a brilliant man, and also one who commanded a loyal and devoted following who under his leadership have produced remarkable products. But I also got the impression that he had a darker side and could be very tough on individuals, to say the least. I fell to wondering if I would have found his behaviour towards individuals acceptable within Shell. Not having known him or worked with him I have no idea whether this would have been the case or not. But just supposing it was, would it have been right to fire a genius for behaviour? That is a difficult question to answer. Corporate life is not the place for those who cannot take a certain amount of stress and display some backbone and resistance, because there will be tough decisions that have to be taken. The counter-argument is that a bullying genius may well destroy others who are not only human, but who given the opportunity and encouragement may be an equally valuable source of ideas. Who knows? I would rather err on the side of humanity and create the sort of environment where both types can flourish.

In my experience, if a manager is failing in some way and making life difficult for those in his or her team, those in the organisation expect higher management to do something about it. They expect firm action, but they also want the action taken in a way that still shows respect for the individual. Likewise if cutting costs is essential to the health of an organisation and involves reducing staff numbers, this too must be done with respect. And that does not just mean not sending out redundancy notices by text message; it means careful evaluation and individual consideration, as well as supporting those leaving in the search for new positions. It is salutary, as well as sometimes quite encouraging, to review the current status of those who left a year or two after the event.

Corporations and the people in them are a part of society, so it is not surprising that the same issue arises elsewhere. I recall what for me was a seminal experience in the fuel crisis in the UK in 2000. In that year transport fuel prices had risen to heights that were causing great public unrest. Road-transport fuel prices in the UK are made up of both actual fuel cost and various forms of excise duty and taxation such that taxes make up three-quarters or more of the price. For some time there had been an escalator that increased the tax on fuel automatically well above the rate of inflation. By September, as a result of both high oil prices and the increases in tax, many farmers and hauliers were demanding that the government cut the taxation on fuel to prevent rises in pump prices. In an apparently spontaneous movement, truck drivers and farmers blockaded major refineries and fuel depots around the country to prevent the delivery of fuel by road to retail outlets. The supply of fuel to the general public as well as hospitals and other public services was beginning to be restricted or cut off.

The tanker drivers leaving the refineries were understandably reluctant to cross picket lines and there was also a question of the safety of fuel tankers passing through blockades outside refineries. We knew from our own contacts with the press that the government was using its press machine led by the then Director of Communications and Strategy Alistair Campbell to get the blame shifted onto the oil companies, suggesting that the companies were supporting the blockade because of industry opposition to the taxes. In fact fuel taxation at the pump is not a big issue for the oil companies; fuel demand in the short term is not very much influenced by fuel prices. We were actually just concerned to get fuel to our increasingly angry customers while also keeping our heads down.

As the fuel shortage bit and the crisis escalated, the Prime Minister Tony Blair called a meeting of all the major oil companies. On the government side, apart from Tony Blair, was John Prescott, who was not only Deputy Prime Minister but also Minister for Environment, Transport and the Regions. Lord Macdonald of Tradeston, who was the actual Minister for Transport, was also present, as were Jack Straw, as Home Secretary, and Sir Richard Wilson, Cabinet Secretary. Alistair Campbell sat on the far end of the government side.

Tony Blair opened the meeting by saying that a few days before the press had been suggesting that the oil companies were encouraging the blockade, but of course the government knew that to be quite untrue. This was an extraordinary statement as I, and I imagine everyone else on the oil company side, knew perfectly well that Alistair Campbell had been feeding the press that line. It was inconceivable that Blair did not know that. Had Blair started the meeting by saying that a few days earlier we had all been trying to protect our own patches, but the time had now come to stop these games and work together to solve the crisis I would have had some respect for him. As it was, he was being at very least disingenuous, which was not a good start. While Blair was saying this I stared at Campbell, who managed to look completely innocent and unconcerned.

What followed was almost equally disturbing. We were discussing practicalities of maintaining supplies in various eventualities when John Prescott's mobile phone went off in his pocket. Somewhat embarrassed he took it out, fumbled with it to turn it off and put it back in his pocket. Almost immediately it rang again. Tony Blair remarked that John was somewhat technologically challenged and the whole government side, including civil servants, giggled. I think if Prescott had had a knife he would have stuck it in Blair. On the business side of the table there was embarrassment. In most responsible companies if a member of the team does something inappropriate, you deal with it afterwards. You do not humiliate them in from of the rest of the team and visitors. That is just bad management. Some people may regard these two instances as minor, but they made an impression on me as indicative of the values of the Prime Minister.

One of the most difficult things in a corporation is to ensure that the values are absorbed by all and applied by all. This is of course an almost unachievable ambition. I recall once being at a meeting discussing the governance of NGOs. One chief executive of a major global NGO worried as to how it was possible to ensure that all of the thousands of their employees in all of the tens of countries in which they delivered services lived up to their high standards. Somewhat to his surprise, it was with great pleasure that I was able to welcome him the ranks of the 'multinationals'.

Many corporations lay great emphasis on training to instil values. Conventional training has limited effect. What is needed is training that involves a lot of free-flowing discussion and relating of personal experiences—what are sometimes referred to as 'war stories'. I recall listening to the chief executive of a major financial institution that had suffered from scandals relating to trading in Europe and to other events in Japan. He had put in place an impressive structured training programme delivered around the world through thousands of hours, with care to ensure maximum coverage (and documentation of the coverage). I was impressed by the effort and the systematic approach. Then, in my eyes, he blew it all by remarking somewhat wistfully of his errant traders that if they had done it to Goldman Sachs or Lehman Brothers it would have been all right. He plainly did not get it. Distorting the market, which is what the traders had done, is an abuse whether the victims are Goldman or Lehman or simple investors. The value is not dependent on the victim, although the severity of the crime may. Given this attitude of the chief executive, I suspect that the entire structured and rather legalistic training was wasted.

It is not enough simply to send out a message from the top and hope that people through the organisation absorb it and really take it on board. In the case of the BP Macondo (or Deepwater Horizon) disaster in the Gulf of Mexico in 2010, I am quite sure that both the then Chief Executive Tony Hayward and his predecessor, my industry colleague John Browne, believed that safety was more important than profit and would have emphasised this. Yet analysing the accident it is difficult to escape the conclusion that those involved in the region and the front line took a series of five or six decisions that were aimed at saving time and money at the expense of decreasing safety of the operation. Why?

In Shell in the 1990s our safety performance in exploration and production had plateaued after a period of improvement. An analysis of accidents showed that fatal accidents were more likely to occur when operations were started up before all was completely ready. It was also apparent that in the case of many accidents, someone had had some degree of prior concern or uneasiness about the situation but had not felt empowered to take action. So we sent out a strong message to all operations over my signature saying that anyone had a right to stop an operation if they felt that it was unsafe and that it was more important to ensure that all was ready—training and testing complete—than to meet a promised deadline.

For two or more years after that when I attended town hall type meetings with people on operations around the world, I found that at some point there would be a question along the lines of 'Mark, are we not sending out mixed messages on the importance of production versus safety?' Initially I was a bit irritated by the question, pointing to the letter I had signed and which I thought was absolutely clear. Could people not read? Very soberingly, I soon realised that it was not that people had not read my letter, but that they still had some doubts about what it really meant. Not to put too fine a point on it, they did not really believe the words or that I really meant what I said. The answer was not to make the message more strident, but to find operations that had been shut down for safety reasons or where start-up had been delayed and draw attention to them, publicly commending those concerned. If people see an action clearly costing the company money and yet which attracts commendation, they believe the message.

Establishing the principle that anyone involved has the right to shut down an operation if they feel that it is unsafe is important. It takes time to establish and can easily be destroyed. At the time of the UK fuel crisis in 2000 discussed above, I had a phone discussion with Tony Blair who was concerned that Shell tanker drivers might be supportive of the blockading truck drivers and refuse to deliver fuel through the pickets of the refineries and depots. I explained to him that I thought that this was unlikely; the reason that fuel delivery trucks were not driving through the blockade was a concern for safety. It was understandable if tanker drivers did not want to drive 40 tons of highly inflammable fuel through an angry mob even if they had the protection of the police. He asked whether it was possible to order them to do so. I explained that this would immediately destroy a principle that it had taken us years to embed.

A short time ago someone who on behalf of shareholders had been interrogating my successors in Shell on their approach to safety and what the checks were told me that the Shell representative had related a story of a cook on an offshore platform who had shut the operation down on a safety concern. I know no details, but was encouraged to hear it.

Cynthia Carroll adopted a similar approach when she became CEO of Anglo American. She had not been in the job for very long when there was a horrific string of fatal accidents in the majority-owned subsidiary Anglo Platinum. She announced that she was simply not prepared to be CEO of a company that killed people in that way. So she shut down the mines involved and had all the miners attend training on surface. This had a big impact. She was fully supported by the board—indeed I realised that we should have done it earlier. We announced what production would be lost and had not a single complaint from a shareholder although they could easily calculate the cost. There were some grumbles in the diehard South African mining community saying 'Does she not realise that mining is a dangerous business?', but I also had compliments from someone in the South African utility Eskom who remarked that it was a big help to him. He said they would love to do the same, but unfortunately if they did lights would go out in parts of South Africa. All is still not perfect, but Cynthia can take credit for saving many lives and preventing many disabling injuries.

Although the costs of a delay or a shut-down may appear great, they are in fact offset by the great improvement in efficiency that results from proper planning and also from the increase in trust and communication within an organisation. That trust and confidence extends to communications from senior management. Having said that, there will still be difficult decisions to be taken on risk. When failures are prevented, the initial costs are rapidly repaid by returns in efficiency. Collective behavioural change can be achieved at relatively low costs and deliver great benefits. There does, however, come a point of diminishing returns. In all aspects of daily life there are things which would increase safety, but which we rightly decide not to do because of trade-offs. A much lower universal speed limit on the roads would undoubtedly save lives, but the cost in terms of frustration, avoidance and delays is generally considered too high.

The impact of individuals

While it is certainly true that the character of people at the top of a company or heading a major division has a great impact on the ethos of an organisation as a whole, I find it very encouraging that many individuals lower down within a company can influence its course.

There is no doubt that Geoffrey Chandler had such an influence on Shell when he drafted the first set of Business Principles in the 1970s, principles that have been adapted and augmented since but largely incorporate the original. Shell had been shaken by a corruption scandal that affected all oil companies in Italy and in the 1970s there were severe criticisms of the activities of multinational companies. Geoffrey was what was then called 'Trade Relations Coordinator', which later morphed into the more conventionally named Head of Public Affairs. The Principles were originally in the form of a letter from Geoffrey to the operating units of the Group around the world. Clearly they had the support of the senior leadership of the time, the Committee of Managing Directors, but I am sure that they emerged as a result of Geoffrey's commitment and persistence. An individual can have a great influence in a corporation even if they are not at the very top.

In fact, influence is often at much lower levels in major corporations. I recall an occasion when some extremely aggressive speed bumps had been installed at the entrance to the car park of the Shell exploration and production offices in The Hague, so that any moderately low-slung vehicle tended to scrape on them. I had suggested several times that these be lowered to a more reasonable height, to no effect. Then one day I was being driven in from the airport by my regular driver when I noticed that the bumps had at last been lowered. 'Oh, Piet', I said, 'they have lowered the bumps.' He replied, 'Yes, I had a word with them a couple of days ago.' I then knew where real power lay. Not so long after that I was visiting the Président Directeur Général of Elf, Loïk Le Floch-Prigent[3] in his office in La Défense, Paris. When we left his office to go to the airport he kindly suggested that his driver could take us. The car was a standard black French government-type Peugeot and the driver clearly doubled as a bodyguard. All was fairly normal until we hit a traffic jam and the driver reached into a glove pocket, produced a magnetic stick of blue light for the roof that plugged into the cigarette lighter and turned on the siren. My colleague and I discussed whether we should try and look sick, important or like police officers. When I got back to Holland I told Piet that I now knew what to get him for Christmas. He was horrified and pointed out that even the Queen could not do that in Holland.

Another example of the power of individuals within large organisations was my last assistant in Shell, Barbara Baylis. Barbara is more or less the same age as I am (although she looks a good 15 years younger than I do), but she joined the company straight out of school. Shell (and indeed the country) was very different then. We retired at the same time with a joint farewell party. Barbara remembers being in the typing pool and having to ask to be excused if she needed to go to the toilet—and not more than twice in the morning. In those days when alcohol was drunk at lunch time she also remembers whose offices were off limits on a Friday afternoon if she had to deliver typed letters to those who had dictated them. Barbara had been the assistant of the Chairman of Shell in London for many years, alternating with a colleague. Each would serve until their Chairman retired and then revert to being the

3 See references to Le Floch-Prigent in relation to corruption in Chapters 2 and 8.

assistant of the number two until the succession changed. So Barbara and I worked together for many years, and her contribution and support were invaluable.

To celebrate her 40 years in the company, we organised a small reception. To be strictly accurate, Barbara organised it. She also decided on the guest list of our colleagues. When making a speech, I looked around the faces. They were a complete cross-section of those working in London, from managing directors, through division heads, to maintenance people, security people and receptionists. The list was very selective and I could see immediately the common characteristic. I was able to say to them that they had all clearly passed Barbara's tough test of competence and commitment. They were people who delivered what they said they were going to do and who could be relied on completely. That did not mean that they always achieved perfect results. If they failed for a good reason, Barbara would arrange things so that they were covered. They were part of a team, and I and my colleagues at the top of Shell were subject to the same evaluation. She might not say anything, but you could see from a flicker of an expression if she had her doubts. Any large organisation only works if people at all levels can be relied on to play their particular part, whatever level they are at. That is one reason why increasing remuneration and other differentiations to excessive levels are as damaging within an organisation as outside. As an assistant and colleague Barbara was exceptional, but I have been fortunate to have many exceptional people among the ten personal assistants in different countries and jobs that I have had in my career in Shell and later as Chairman of Anglo American.

How to check on the penetration of values within a company

Ensuring that the penetration and widespread absorption of the values and principles of a company is critical, but how can one check that it has been achieved? I believe that there are three ways; to sleep easily one needs to have all three in place.

The first is simply personal contact. With a global company this involves travelling a lot and spending time talking to groups of people and listening to their questions and comments. Clearly this depends on style and also on there being a feeling of openness. It does not have to be done by one person, even if this were possible, as almost all of us feel more at ease with some people than with others. With an open team and a network of people who can reflect the opinions and concerns of their colleagues, the coverage becomes very wide. Without people feeling free to ask me in meetings about what they saw as a mixed message on production versus safety I might not have realised that people had doubts on what the message was. I might have assumed, until something went wrong, that everyone had read and was acting on what I had thought was a clear message.

The second check is through very well-designed global surveys conducted independently with a guarantee of anonymity. Many people are sceptical about the usefulness of such surveys, saying that people do not bother to participate or else they do not put down what they really think. This is not my experience.

It is important that the results of the survey be independently analysed and fed back to people in organisational groupings that are large enough to protect the anonymity of any individual respondent. In that way people can compare the responses for their unit in relation to those of other units in the same business or region, as well as trends for the corporation as a whole at various levels of aggregation. It is equally important that there be open discussions on what changes in approach are needed to address issues that emerge from the survey and commitments be made at different levels in the organisation as to how this is to be addressed. People will only take part in a survey if they think that their views will be listened to and that action will be taken. An important signal from a global survey is whether participation is rising or falling. In a healthy company with an open environment for communication and where results are discussed and actions taken in response, participation rates can be above 90%.

Such a survey needs to be professionally designed and analysed. People experienced in this type of work will ensure that several questions asked in different ways seek to examine the same point. In that way there are internal cross-checks. Furthermore, professional organisations often have comparative results from other companies in the industry or of similar size and scope. I am not an expert in these matters but I have been impressed by the insights of those who are.

The third check is external and is obtained by engaging with those outside the company, both critics and others who are more supportive. Surveys can also be useful in this, but a lot of the feedback comes from merely listening carefully to those outside the company. People form an opinion of the behaviour and policies of a company based on their experience and their perceptions. It does not matter if those inside the company think that the perceptions are erroneous; they still need to be analysed carefully. Often reality lies somewhere between the perceptions of those inside and those outside the company. Closing the gap is important.

Shifting and distorting value frameworks

There is no doubt that the changing approach to risk is having a significant impact on business. There is also no doubt that many of the changes in, for example, the UK Corporate Governance Code[4] are useful codifications of what has been found by experience to be sound practice. However, we cannot regulate ourselves out of trouble. There was a rash of regulatory measures introduced in response to the Enron affair. Yet the failure in Enron was for the most part not a failure of regulation—regulations were in place—but a failure of values. I doubt that the bulk of those involved in Enron were inherently more wicked than the rest of us. The problem was that they were working in a system whose values had imperceptibly shifted over time without them realising it, so that essentially criminal misuse of accounting appeared normal to

4 The UK Corporate Governance Code, formerly the Combined Code, www.frc.org.uk/Our-Work/Codes-Standards/Corporate-governance/ UK-Corporate-Governance-Code.aspx. The latest edition is 2012.

them because they had convinced themselves that their behaviour was within accounting rules. There is a remarkable section of Enron's Risk Management Manual, apparently approved by their audit committee. This said:

> Reported earnings follow the rules and principles of accounting. The results do not always create measures that are consistent with underlying economics. However corporate management's performance is normally measured by accounting income, not by underlying economics. Risk management strategies are therefore directed at accounting rather than economic performance.

Accounting rules were devised to present a true and fair picture of the state of the business, yet here was a value system that had come to accept that the rules, even when out of line with reality, were more important than the real economic state of the business. With such values, it is unlikely that further regulation will provide a solution.

Changing value systems

How does a value system shift over time? Consider the case of cosmetic surgery. This is a technique developed to repair faces and bodies damaged in warfare. It was then usefully extended to making cosmetic improvements where the pre-existing condition was causing distress. These are all useful and commendable activities. But there is no doubt that it can go too far—in some parts of California it is acceptable and routine for people to make continuous adjustments in their appearance. This practice is encouraged by peer pressure. If I lived in that society I might well consider having the extra fold in my chin removed. The values of that society have changed—people who if they lived elsewhere would never think of cosmetic surgery suddenly find it normal or even desirable. I view this as a distortion of values, or put another way, a shift in the frame of reference of what is normal or acceptable. I suspect that serious damage is done—yet legislation is plainly not the answer. Closer to home, my wife and daughter both have pierced ears; Judy one hole in each ear, Elizabeth two in one and three in the other. For their respective ages this seems quite normal to me, although Liz will one day reach an age where different norms may apply. Travelling in the uplands of Borneo we saw Kelabit women with very heavy brass earrings that had stretched their earlobes into long loops reaching to the level of their chins. Carrying these weights, they move their heads in an elegant and stately way that I find attractive. I have no holes or rings, but if it were the norm I doubtless would not hesitate. In some parts of our society it is fashionable to have rings and studs in every appendage. I see this when travelling on the underground in London. To me it is quite bizarre. If multiple body piercing is bizarre, why do I not find the holes in my wife's or daughter's ears a little bit bizarre, or indeed the ears of the women of Borneo. It is just a question of frames of reference.

The only check on shifting frames of reference is to be open to input from outside the corporate or industry frame of reference. This involves being open to communication and having a capacity to listen to those with whom you do not necessarily agree—after all, they are by definition probably at least partly outside the corporate or industry frame of reference. Family members play a very important role in this checking on outside reality. As one discusses events or problems family members give you their own analysis and report on the perceptions of their friends and acquaintances. As Judy often points out, they are more closely connected to the 'real world' than a senior corporate executive working intensively in a corporate environment.

The dangers of 'groupthink' and the need for informed independent input

Even when referring to what appears to be someone outside your own frame of reference, one can be misled by widespread 'groupthink' or by a tacit agreement by large sections of society to simply assume that something that is in fact a well-known possibility will not happen. The Euro crisis is an example of this. It was well known and discussed at the time of formation of the Euro that there was an inherent problem in a monetary union without a fiscal union. I personally was well aware of this, but in spite of it I confess I was supportive of the Euro (and indeed at that time of the UK joining the Euro, something which few people nowadays confess to). Along with many others I thought that the trade advantages outweighed the risks. This was not an unknown risk, but just one that a large number of people chose to ignore. Likewise the fact that an Icelandic volcano could throw enormous clouds of ash into the sky across large areas of Europe was not unknown to geologists; it had happened before in historical times. We all chose to ignore the risk and therefore not do tests on what level of dust was acceptable for modern jet engines. As a result European airspace was shut down for days—some at least unnecessarily.

People were aware of these threats, but somehow the right questions had not been asked, or not asked in the right context. It is essential not just to ask the right questions but also to make plain your reasons for asking the question. We lived in Melbourne in the early 1970s. Before we arrived, a major bridge over the Yarra River had tragically collapsed due to a design error in its box-girder construction. The redesigned West Gate Bridge was being built, an elegant bridge high above the river. I asked a neighbour who was involved in the construction why it was so high. He told me the possibly apocryphal story that when the bridge was being designed the engineers contacted the Royal Australian Navy who had a dockyard just upstream of the bridge and asked them what was the largest ship that might need to enter. The answer was the aircraft carrier *Melbourne*. The questioner then asked how tall the mast on the *Melbourne* was and added a small safety factor to the answer. When the bridge was being built, the navy enquired why it was so high. They were told that it was because of the height of the mast of the *Melbourne*; to which the navy replied that the mast on the *Melbourne* could be folded down. This story may well be apocryphal, but it is a useful anecdote to illustrate why one should not only seek information but also give people a good briefing on the background to the questions.

In the banking crisis the fact that banks were overleveraged with large amounts of wholesale borrowings was not unknown. Yet I know that many shareholders of HSBC urged the bank to gear up its balance sheet, which they criticised as being hopelessly conservative. This was resisted. Although the executives of the bank and the board knew that some competitors were overleveraged, none of us foresaw wholesale meltdown. I think we imagined that perhaps one bank might have a difficult time. The regulators such as the Financial Services Authority, who were initially quite frank in confessing that they had been concentrating largely on protection of consumers from mis-selling and their own folly, have subsequently escaped quite lightly as popular fury focused collectively on 'the bankers', a view encouraged by politicians seeking to divert attention from their own short-sightedness. Although the banking industry understandably and rightly attracted opprobrium for excessive remuneration and dubious practices, in fact most sections of our over-leveraged Western societies share some of the blame.

Such almost wilful collective blindness is difficult to avoid. I believe that competent regulators have an important role to play, but regulators are potentially subject to the same 'groupthink' as the rest of us. For example, if the oil industry regulator in the US Gulf of Mexico had been active in enquiring as to the possibility of an uncontrolled blow-out from deep-water wells in the area such as BP's Macondo, I suspect that the initial answer they would have got from me and many colleagues in the industry would have been that while, of course, there was always some possibility of failure as the operators were human and the equipment made by fallible humans, the chances of such an event, given the multiple barriers and the existing checks and balances, was vanishingly small. If, however, they had persisted with the questioning, perhaps on an individual basis with key figures in the industry, and if they had focused the question on what the worst event could be and what precautions should be taken in the event of a failure, the answer would I suspect have been different. Deep-water wells have by definition to be highly productive; otherwise they would not be economic. So we knew that the uncontrolled flow rates would probably be unusually high. We also knew that the well-heads were in depths beyond the reach of divers, so that remote access would be necessary. The requirement foreseen would have been collective industry capacity to recover very large volumes of oil and oily water from the sea in all weathers[5] and various additional steps for remote operation or capping at the well-head. This indeed is what after the event the major companies got together to design and acquire, something that a combination of 'groupthink' and by contrast a lack of collective action, coupled with poor regulation, had prevented before the event. In fact, industry collective action to assemble from all over the world at great speed the traditional responses of dispersant and booms to trap the oil, as well as the fleet of boats and facilities necessary to deploy them, worked very smoothly. It was just inadequate to meet the new challenge. In their efforts to drill in arctic waters both Shell and the regulators will be asking themselves similar questions on what the worst case scenario might be and hopefully building in sufficient redundancy to cover the risk. This process is usefully stimulated by outside critics.

Probably the most important lesson for Shell from the crises of 1995 described in the previous chapter was to be more open to outside inputs and opinions. It is necessary for all organisations to make sure that the values of the organisation are thoroughly embedded and absorbed throughout the organisation, but perhaps equally important that the value framework has not shifted undetected by those within the organisation and is no longer consonant with those of society at large. Organisation, structure and corporate governance may play a part in this.

---

5 I believe that a design for such a vessel had actually been proposed to Exxon, who understandably said it was too expensive for a single company; clearly an industry solution mandated by a regulator was needed.

Chapter 13

Changes in structure and governance: Do they matter?

Although the principal factor determining the behaviour of a company is the approach taken by individuals within the framework of values that pervades it, organisational structure does play a role. With good-will and flexibility most organisational structures can be made to work, but some structures are more robust and provide a greater range of the checks and balances that may be needed from time to time.

While the review of principles and values in Shell was in train as described in Chapter 12, we were also looking at the organisational structure of the overall group. The Royal Dutch/Shell Group had consisted since its formation in 1907 of a joint venture between two public companies, Royal Dutch Petroleum and the quaintly named UK company The 'Shell' Transport and Trading Company,[1] with 60% and 40% of the joint venture respectively. The fact that this dual parentage made essentially no difference to those working in the Group, apart from ensuring an essentially international element in the DNA of the

---

1 The name was chosen by the founders of the UK company, Marcus Samuel and his brother Sam as a reflection of the original family business of trading seashells for the decorative boxes and trinkets common in Victorian times.

organisation, was due to the work of John Loudon in the 1950s and 1960s. John Loudon was the father of the post-war Shell Group. He retired as an executive in the same year that I joined Shell, but many years later I had the pleasure of meeting him on several occasions. I had a great admiration for him and benefited from the structure he had set up.

Underneath the two quoted parent companies of Shell were two holding companies, one Dutch and one British, each owned 60:40 by the parents. All the companies of the Group were owned by these two holding companies; which one was a matter of history and convenience, but it did not matter as all dividends flowed in the ratio 60:40 to the parents. Central functions were housed in two service companies likewise one Dutch and one British, located in The Hague and London. The entire focus of the Group was on the operating companies; this was emphasised by the fact that the central offices were just that; the phrase 'head office' was an anathema and never used. The basic unit of the Group was the national operating company, and the results of these companies were aggregated into regions. The bottom line was thus national and regional. The central organisational functions of Exploration and Production or Manufacturing[2] (located in The Hague) or Oil Products Marketing and Chemicals (located in London) delivered their expertise to the operating companies as advice, effectively through the regional organisations who had bottom-line responsibility and who actually appointed the management of the operating companies. That is not to say that the technical functions were powerless. Their 'advice' carried weight. An iconic global head of exploration, Erdi Fraenkel, was known to say to operating company exploration managers in his delightful Swiss German accent, 'I cannot tell you what to do, but I can tell you what your next job will be.'

A core creation of the Loudon structure, which was inaugurated in 1961 and which continued until the full merger of the two parent

---

2 Another Shell peculiarity: 'Manufacturing' would in most oil companies have been called Refining, although it was in fact wider than that.

companies in 2005,[3] was the 'Conference'. This was a meeting of the boards of the two parent companies—the supervisory board and management board of Royal Dutch in the split board of the Dutch system and the unitary board of Shell Transport: in other words, the executive and non-executive directors of both parent companies. This was a meeting with no corporate legal status, but all the board discussion and business was done in 'Conference'. Appropriate corporate action was later taken by the separate parent company and holding company boards in separate meetings without further discussion.

'Conference' was chaired by the Chairman of the Committee of Managing Directors (CMD), the most senior executive in the Group. As that individual also chaired the meeting of the Group's most senior executives (CMD) he was thus the closest thing Shell had to a Chief Executive leading an executive committee. In that way the Chairman of CMD (a very long and difficult title for outsiders) was not only effectively Chief Executive, but was also effectively the Executive Chairman of the Group.[4] The genius of this remarkably long-lasting construction was that the Dutch and British parents merged imperceptibly in 'Conference'. There was no feeling of which parent a member came from and no mention of 60:40 shares.[5] The meeting meant that all other board meetings necessary for legal corporate actions could be extremely brief and without

3 This merger was in fact precipitated largely by the reserves reporting scandal discussed below.
4 When I was Chairman of the Committee of Managing Directors I would sometimes introduce myself at gatherings of business leaders as 'the nearest thing Shell has to a Chief Executive' rather than as the Chairman of the Committee of Managing Directors of the Royal Dutch/Shell Group, which would have meant little to most people. The alternative was to say 'Chairman of Shell' but that was also inaccurate. In the official history of the Group (Jan Luiten van Zanden, Joost Jonker, Stephen Howarth and Keetie Sluyterman, *A History of Royal Dutch Shell* [4 vols.; New York: Oxford University Press, 2007]: vol. 2, 110), John Loudon is quoted as saying that the Chairman of CMD 'comes down to the same thing' as a recognised chief executive, with the extent of collegiality being largely dependent on its chairman's character. That of course is as true today as then of any executive committee of any company.
5 The only time that some differences of opinion between different parent company boards arose was on the level of dividend to be paid. Shareholders in

further discussion. However, this structure did have consequences for the Group as the world and business environment changed.

The process of change in the Shell Group

In the mid-1990s, Cor Herkströter, who was Chairman CMD from 1992 to 1997, initiated a review of the structure, something for which he deserves great credit for he certainly would not have received support for considering changes from many of the former executives who remained on the boards of the parents.[6] The period coincided partly with the traumas of 1995 that were described in Chapter 11, but had in fact commenced well before. The review process started with a large meeting of the most senior executives of the Group from around the world. All agreed that change was needed, but there were many different views on what form that change should take.

Almost all complex global companies operate either explicitly or implicitly a matrix structure that balances the requirements of geographies and the business lines. Shell was probably slightly unusual by the 1990s in that the geographical side of the matrix—national operating companies and the regions—was dominant and carried the bottom-line responsibility, while the business lines were in the advisory role. Of course nothing is ever quite as straightforward as that in most companies, and major businesses such as Exploration and Production in Shell did indeed wield a great deal of influence, particularly so as senior management in the group as a whole was predominantly technical in background rather than financial.

The Shell structure had been manifestly successful, at least up until perhaps the mid-1980s. The devolution of management to powerful national operating companies and the way in which those companies and their people had become part of the national fabric in each country

different markets might have differing expectations, and these had to be reconciled by discussion in Conference.

6 Although influential, these former executives did not make up the whole board.

287

operation was a contribution to that success. Shell became essentially part of the furniture in many countries. Perhaps the most notable independent operating company was that in the United States, always known as 'Shell Oil', which did indeed have a minority public shareholding until this was bought out by the parent companies. Many Americans simply assumed that Shell was a US company.[7]

In a world of high tariff barriers and slow communications, these independent national operating companies well embedded in their national environments were very successful. In the late 1990s, before Exxon's acquisition of Mobil, Shell generally beat Exxon on most measures—actual net income, revenues, volumes and so one. The one measure on which we never came near to Exxon was profitability. We produced approximately the same after-tax net income, but on a basis of $50 billion more capital employed. The reason for this was easy to see. Exxon's assets were optimised on a regional basis with relatively few large integrated facilities centrally managed. In Shell the optimisation was on a national basis, with each country often having its own facilities—refineries, petrochemical plants, lubricants plants and depots. Marketing benefited from this localisation in an era when movement of goods was more constrained by tariffs. Slow communications also gave the advantage to nationally devolved management. However, with the advent of globalisation and regional trade blocks reducing the importance of national boundaries, the Shell structure was at a major cost disadvantage. In terms of numbers of operational sites and facilities, in most regions Shell had an order of magnitude more than Exxon.

Of course the need, for example, to reduce refineries in Europe had often been discussed. A task force of technical people would agree the logical steps; but when they returned to their own countries, their conclusions would be greeted with shock and horror. The regional organisations, as 'shareholders', would be appraised of the political impossibility of closing a refinery in France, for example (actually this is in fact probably very true!), and as a consequence nothing would happen. Once the

---

7 Of course, in the 1960s and 1970s many people in Britain would have assumed that Vauxhall and Ford in Dagenham were British companies and not the local subsidiaries of General Motors or the Ford Motor Company.

European refineries were put in a single business organisation and made responsible for the European refining bottom line, the same decisions were not only rapidly arrived at but could be implemented. Everyone in the refining organisation owed their allegiance to their refining colleagues and not to their national chief executives. Like most things in business management, the answer is normally quite simple and straightforward; it is getting it done by building motivation and a feeling of ownership in organisations that is the difficult piece.

The process of change was slow. I would explain to financial analysts why this was so. The 'localness' of Shell operating companies was an enormous asset. I would describe it as the 'pearl beyond price'. What was needed was to change the structure without destroying the pearl. People who were worried about the change were in fact worried about protecting this pearl. We had consultants and business gurus to advise us. I recall the advice of one such guru that for progress one needed to identify in meetings those 'blockers' and fire them. This of course is foolish advice; if one takes every objector in a meeting outside and metaphorically shoots them, you pretty soon have no 'blockers' but also no thoughtful voices pointing out where things are going wrong or are likely to go wrong. So it is probably preferable to fire the guru. Of course, there will be those who cannot finally bring themselves to agree with the common direction. Those individuals will in the end have to leave and will probably want to do so. However, this is generally a question of honest disagreement after much discussion.

When I came to the top job in the late 1990s, we still had four very large European operating companies in France, Germany, the Netherlands and the UK. Each had a major office with a finance function, a treasury function, an oil-trading function and so on. There had to be major deconstruction and this involved a big battle. The then boss of Shell UK, Chris Fay, an engineer with a distinguished career in major operating companies and projects around the world, could see what was needed. He worked hard at the necessary deconstruction and essentially did himself out of a job. I will always be grateful to him for his commitment to getting the sensible and necessary things done and demonstrating how they could be achieved in practice. It is through that process

289

that the iconic Art Deco 1930s office building of Shell Mex House, 80 The Strand in London, once, I believe, the largest office building in Europe at 12 floors, ceased to be the headquarters of Shell UK and was in due course sold. Much of it is now occupied by Pearson plc.

The pendulum of organisational change swings and often swings too far. In spite of the desire to preserve the 'localness' of Shell operating companies and the importance of having a single individual in a country who leads Shell overall, a Country Chairman, we probably did go too far in some instances. It is certain that in some of the large meetings we went too far in our enthusiasm to promote change and encourage people to challenge ways of thinking. I seem to recall in 1997 a Buddhist monk attending a large gathering of managers in Maastricht in the Netherlands. There was also much prancing around on stage in supposedly liberated ways to restore circulation. Some of this consultant-driven activity was excessive, but some was necessary to change well-established ways of thinking and to break moulds. I think that nowadays the *Financial Times* columnist Lucy Kellaway would have had a field day. Fortunately, this was all before the age of Twitter and YouTube.

Although at the time, and perhaps subsequently, we may have gone too far and in some cases damaged the 'localness' of the company, from independent surveys of the views of Shell people from all around the world I know that we did manage to preserve the Shell ethos that permits people to make mistakes and learn from them and to express contrary opinions and be listened to thoughtfully. It is very important in any company to make sure that such channels of different thinking are open and contrary ideas can be discussed. I recall in the late stages of the Soviet Union travelling to visit a Gazprom operation in western Siberia with a senior Gazprom executive. Gazprom, the state gas monopoly (see also Chapter 8), was the closest thing in the Soviet Union to a Western corporation, with a clear corporate ethos, a record of remarkable achievement in developing the large Siberian gasfields and bringing the gas through a gigantic pipeline system to Western Europe in the face of US sanctions on equipment. Gazprom showed great interest in the structure and practices of Shell and as we travelled together on the plane, Mr Resunenko, whom I knew quite well, asked me how we handled dissent in Shell. That is actually a very good question and I had to think of examples of how I would welcome comments and disagreements from a young engineer when a project was in gestation, but that, when all the discussion had been finished and a common position adopted, continued dissent was unacceptable.

In my own career in Shell I benefited from the view that mistakes can be a form of learning. In the 1960s in Sarawak, the exploration team that I led made an interesting oil discovery in a thick and highly productive sandstone. We duly reported the discovery and the fact that on the upside it could be very large. We thought carefully about the wells necessary to confirm and appraise the discovery quickly. The discovery was quite shallow and the wells could be drilled quite rapidly. In the first of two fairly ambitious appraisal wells we drilled, the thick sand had pinched out and disappeared entirely. In the second, the reservoir was intersected below the water contact. So both wells were 'dry holes'. By that time (communication was slow) the head of Shell's production geology department was on his way out to see what we were up to. He analysed our decisions and pointed out that although they were quite rational in terms of giving a lot of (unfortunately negative) information rapidly, they were high-risk. Our advisers (and masters) in The Hague had rashly ignored the qualifications and assumed that our reported upside was a relatively realistic projection; now with two dry appraisal wells the discovery had very negative connotations. As my appraiser said, 'Mark, you have just ruined a perfectly good oilfield and slowed its development by over-enthusiasm. You should have drilled a couple of short outsteps[8] and confirmed a developable size of field.' Over dinner and a drink he later consoled me by saying, 'Never mind, if all you cost Shell in your career is a couple of million dollars, your education will have been quite cheap.' It was a good lesson for an enthusiastic 30-year-old, particularly in relation to external markets. The field was later developed.

8 Outstep: a well drilled outside the proven oil or gas area.

The barriers to diversity

By the time I arrived in the top position in Shell in the late 1990s, we had been recruiting able men and women of all nationalities, cultures and backgrounds for much of my career. Shell is a very international company and from the beginning of my career I never worked in an office or team that had less than seven nationalities in it. People of all nationalities and both sexes moved to work in other countries where they could test themselves and be tested against international competition. Yet the top of Shell remained uniformly male, white and either British or Dutch (with an occasional American).

There was clearly something wrong; the result was statistically simply implausible. Given all the talented men and women we had employed, it was improbable that the most able were men of those particular origins. I knew from my own experience over more than 25 years that this was not a matter of conscious discrimination; we had a very well-developed staff appraisal and planning system and for many years had worked hard at giving able people of any background the experience that they would need to reach senior positions. The old excuse that there were not many female engineers for a technology-based company to hire had long since ceased to be plausible in many countries, and in any case we had in fact been hiring able women for many years; they simply were not making it to the top. There had to be hidden barriers. Quite clearly carrying on with our current appraisal and promotion systems was not going to deliver the change we expected.

We did two things. We set up a Diversity Council consisting of men and women from all around the world from different levels in the organisation; some already quite senior but some graduates with five or ten years' experience. The challenge to the council was to identify the hidden barriers and to help eliminate them. At the same time, being a highly analytical sort of company, we decided to hire in some expertise. Perhaps inevitably, this came from the United States, a country that had only a few decades before suffered from serious racial and other forms of discrimination but by legal and practical means had managed to make tremendous progress. At the suggestion of John Hofmeister,[9] who was running the Human Resources function, we appointed a Head of Diversity, an able African American woman called Leslie Mays.

Leslie suggested that we organise a series of diversity awareness workshops right across the company and that I should attend one of the early ones. Any business manager will tell you that if you want to do something with effect across an organisation, you had better set an example. So I immediately agreed to attend a workshop, although frankly, privately, I could not see that I needed any coaching on the subject of diversity. I had lived in many countries, including a dozen or more years in countries where Islam was the dominant or a major religion. I could get by reasonably well in a number of languages and had friends in the company of many backgrounds. In spite of this, I readily agreed to go along to set a good example, and it was a good thing that I did as I learned a great deal.

We started with a discussion of our own backgrounds. We were asked what class of society did we consider our origins to be. I argued with this, saying that I had been brought up from my mother's knee to believe that things such as race and class are unimportant. Gradually the realisation dawned on me that these are indeed things that are not important if they do not affect your way of life or prospects. A little like money.

Having got over this discussion, we then considered which groups of people in Shell might be thought to be dominant or to have advantages over other groups. Again, we had considerable discussion on whether the concept of 'dominant groups' had any relevance in Shell, but in the end we were able to decide on characteristics likely to give an individual an advantage. We started with men and women, with the clear answer being men. When considering native English speakers versus non-native, we agreed that perfect fluency was an advantage. It also became fairly clear that being Dutch or British did confer some advantage. And so we went on: expatriates versus nationals in a country; graduates of Oxford,

9 John Hofmeister, after retiring from Shell as President of Shell in the US, wrote an interesting book on US energy policy with the somewhat racy title *Why We Hate the Oil Companies: Straight Talk from an Energy Insider* (New York: Palgrave Macmillan, 2011).

Cambridge or Delft versus those from other universities; highly mobile people versus those who stayed in one country; technical people versus non-technical; exploration and production versus marketing; people with dependent supportive spouses versus dual careers; and so on. When we had agreed on ten or a dozen categories without too much difficulty or disagreement, we all lined up; someone called out the advantaged categories and we took a step forward if we were in that category. I am in every single advantaged category and landed well ahead of everyone else. This was of course quite disturbing. I have always been aware that an element of luck plays a part in promotion; being in the right place at the right time, for example. This experiment illustrated that there were other factors, each of which might only confer a small advantage but which none the less cumulatively make a significant difference. Some of these factors, such as a good education, are quite logical, but some of the others bear no relation to ability to do an excellent job.

Shell had always put a premium on a high degree of mobility. Working in different countries and in different parts of the business does indeed give an individual wide experience and an overall knowledge of the company's operations. However, it militates against couples with dual careers, women and those who had particular requirements or wishes for the education of their children. We had already begun to address the requirements for dual careers, but clearly changes were necessary. It was noticeable that many able people from outside Europe and North America would leave the company at a certain level when progress to very senior positions would make it likely that they would have to live more or less permanently in London or The Hague. I was aware of the fact that although I was highly mobile, had I worked for a US company that required me for the last 10 or 15 years of my career to relocate semi-permanently to the United States I would have left that company. This was not because of any difficulty with living in the United States for a few years, but a semi-permanent move would have meant for me unacceptable sacrifices in terms of proximity to ageing parents and grown-up children. I had a dream that we could address this by distributing the senior positions to regional centres, locating the top positions in different continents. In the late 1990s technology promised this but was in fact barely able to deliver it. Now it is very much more possible. Accenture for example has no real corporate centre; the chief executive, legal counsel and finance director all live in different continents or cities. The price paid is a lot of travel, but even that can now be avoided by much use of teleconferencing suites for meetings. These are not cheap, but by using technology to configure a meeting room so that the other attendees appear on a screen on the other side of the table as if they were in the room, they are effective. The technology allows multiple equipped sites to interact, and all the nuances of expression and body language are visible. The ability to transmit large amounts of technical data in real time nowadays also means that technical experts in any company can work remotely and share ideas.

Many major companies in the latter half of the 20th century assumed that if they had sound evaluation and development systems in place, talent would be identified and rise to the top. Experience shows that this is not the case; unless one looks for and consciously identifies the small hidden barriers, real change will not happen. When I spoke to town hall type meetings in Shell on the statistical implausibility of only white Dutch or British males at the top and the need for change I would often get the reaction that we had always run a meritocracy, and surely what I was talking about was departing from a meritocracy. To be fair, another part of the audience would also express satisfaction that I had at last grasped something that they felt to be true. I would have to explain that we were still aiming for a meritocracy, but we had to look very carefully at the definition of merit. Where we did this, and looked seriously at what the requirements for a particular job really were, we often came up with a choice that might have appeared unconventional using previous criteria. When I joined the board of HSBC in 2000 it was surprising that there were few if any really senior Chinese executives. Yet here was a company born in Hong Kong, which recruited many able Chinese and, like Shell, considered itself a meritocracy. Again the outcome was statistically implausible and HSBC has been working hard to correct this.

After the end of apartheid in South Africa, many South African business people, including those in Anglo American, considered that given a proper appraisal and development system the racial imbalances would sort themselves out over time. Given the educational disadvantages of the black population this was clearly unlikely, but it was also true that there were similar hidden barriers in Anglo. Lazarus Zim, a senior black South African (a recipient of an Anglo American bursary and now a wealthy and independent businessman) was asked to make recommendations to accelerate the change. Two of his recommendations were to abolish the executive dining room, to which he had access, and get everyone to eat in the very good main cafeteria, and secondly to put names and job titles on the doors on the executive floors. To some both seemed trivial, and in a sense they were, although most European and North American companies had abolished executive dining rooms decades before. I knew exactly what Lazarus meant. On my visits to South Africa I would go into the executive dining room. All were very welcoming, but everyone else there had known each other for years, knew each other's families and probably spent spare time together. One felt that one was sitting in someone else's seat. If that was true of the Chairman, how much more so would it be true for a young black executive? The collegiality and business discussions over lunch had a value, but this was offset by the reinforcement of an exclusive group. Likewise, when I was faced with the long and daunting corridors of the executive floors, as Chairman I could stick my head round an unlabelled door and ask who was behind it and what they did, but it would be very intimidating for someone more junior.

Did this work on diversity have an impact on the composition of Shell at senior levels? I think it did. The percentage of senior women for example has increased and there have been women on the most senior executive committee. However, it remains a challenge. Probably in no country is the situation yet ideal, although the Scandinavian countries come closest to it.

Changes at board level

When a company is seeking to make changes it is essential that the composition of the board of directors also reflects the change. We appointed

Eileen Buttle, a distinguished scientist and Nina Henderson, a US business woman, to the board. Luis Giusti, head of the Venezuelan State oil
company PDVSA in the pre-Chavez period, and Teymour Alireza, head
of a major international Saudi company that also had some operations
in the oilfield supply industry, also joined the board. These appointments sent a signal that women and important areas of the world outside Europe and North America were represented at the highest level.
Perhaps more importantly, people with deep understanding of different
cultural backgrounds can help a board not to misinterpret signals from
governments and partners in negotiations. A purely European board
might interpret an action as indicative of a rejection or lack of interest,
when in fact it might simply indicate that some changes were needed.

The presence of a significant percentage of women at board level is
equally important, again not just to send a signal but also to change
the way of thinking and dynamics on a board. A decade ago Peninah
Thomson, of the consultancy Praesta Partners, launched an innovative
initiative to identify women in senior executive positions in FTSE 100
companies who were not yet on another company board as a non-executive director. The 'FTSE 100 Cross Company Mentoring Programme'
has morphed into the Mentoring Foundation, with Peninah as its Chief
Executive. The concept was that company chairmen identified women
in their own companies who could contribute as non-executive directors of another company. In the process, chairmen committed to mentor
women from another organisation and help them to prepare for a non-
executive role. In practice the programme gave a woman an independent
interlocutor with whom she could discuss in confidence not only what
non-executive positions she might be most suited to, but also someone
with whom she could discuss issues and opportunities in her present
executive role. This helps to address the issue that the biggest shortfall
in female representation is in fact at executive director level rather than
just as non-executive directors.

Simplifying the complex board structure at Shell

As the changes to the Shell structure initiated by Cor Herkströter evolved over the following years, with a simplification and removal of organisational layers and a switch from regional to business responsibility for the bottom line, it was apparent that we needed to look at the complex double-headed structure of the Group, which had served extremely well for many years but might now no longer be the most appropriate.

In January 1999, when I was Chairman of the Committee of Managing Directors, we decided to have a discussion of Conference, the unofficial meeting of the Shell parent company boards (Royal Dutch Petroleum and The 'Shell' Transport and Trading Company), in workshop mode, with small groups discussing issues of organisation and recording their conclusions on flipcharts to be combined later. This in itself was a departure. Conference normally met around a very large table with presentations and lively, although relatively formal, discussions chaired by the Chairman of the CMD. There were a number of reasonably common conclusions from the smaller groups in the workshop, with strong input from the non-executive directors. It was agreed that simplification was needed. The general feeling, including certainly that of the outside directors of both companies, was that the combined boards in Conference made for too big a meeting for easy discussion. The current number was 20. There was also agreement that there needed to be fewer former executives on the boards—there were then five, which together with the five current executive directors meant that only half of the combined boards were independent directors. The practice had been that former executive directors remained as non-executives on one of the parent boards for a maximum of ten years or until they were 70 (there was a mandatory executive retirement of 60). This practice had perhaps served well in ensuring a long corporate memory and was probably well adapted to a relatively slow-moving and conservative business world, but it was out of tune with the business environment as the 20th century came to an end. Cor Herkströter had already broken the mould by stepping down on principle from the board on his retirement as an executive director. In spite of the agreement on the need for simplification, there was disagreement on which of a range of possibilities for combining the two companies was better.

I was very encouraged by the willingness of the independent non-executive directors to change. In fact, with a small group of executives including Steve Hodge, Group Treasurer, and Tim Morrison, responsible for Group taxation, we had already worked on various possible ways of partially or fully combining the parent companies. Without further consultation I therefore presented at the next Conference a paper showing what board members had wanted and what could be the way forward. This proved to be a big mistake; one of the suggestions I made was that as Chairman of CMD I should cease to chair Conference and that this should be instead done by an independent chairman. I had always felt that being both to some extent chief executive and also chairman was uncomfortable. As the senior executive, one wanted to be able to argue with great energy for a proposal, while as chairman one had to be impartial and take into account all views. It is just possible that had I suggested that Conference be chaired by a senior former executive, the proposal might have been more palatable. As it was there was a violent counter-reaction. I came closer than I ever had done in my entire Shell career to being sacked.[10] Willie Purves, the former Chairman of HSBC, and a senior outside director of Shell Transport, was delegated to tell me, I think with some sympathy for my position, that the situation was such that I had better forget the whole idea for the time being and concentrate on fixing the business. This debacle was entirely my own fault in not preparing the ground more carefully and evaluating the strength of the opposition, much of which came from former executives on the board. Some of them were deeply concerned that we were tampering with a structure which had, as has been described, been successful for many years, albeit in a different business climate. As it was, no action was taken at the time; the structure and procedures of Conference remained the same and the boards remained the same size although the executive directors of Shell Transport agreed among themselves that

10 See J.L van Zanden, J. Jonker, S. Howarth and K. Sluyterman, *A History of Royal Dutch Shell* (4 vols.; New York: Oxford University Press, 2007): vol. 3, 296.

no more than one would remain on the board after retirement. Sir Peter Holmes and Sir John Jennings, my predecessors on the Shell Transport board, followed this pattern.[11]

The change came eventually six years later in 2005, when under strong pressure from shareholders and in the light of the reserves scandal (see following pages in this chapter), Shell was forced to modify and modernise its structure and make a full merger of the two parents. It would have been better to have done it at a time and in a manner entirely of our own choosing, probably pleasing the market, rather than being pushed into it.

The consequences of structure

Did the complexity of structure, which after all had worked well for a long time, really make a difference? At a time of a wave of industry mergers triggered by John Browne and BP's masterly acquisition of Amoco, I think it did.[12] With its double-headed complex structure it would have been extremely difficult for Shell to merge or acquire for shares another major company. At the time of the rumoured acquisition of Mobil by Exxon I had had a meeting with Lou Noto, the Chairman of Mobil. I pointed out to him that if Exxon and Mobil joined forces, Mobil would simply be absorbed into Exxon with Exxon dominating. Would not a merger with Shell, whose culture was closer to that of Mobil, make more sense? To which Lou replied that the corporate structure of Shell

11 This resistance to change by former executives on the board is the very good reason why this practice is discouraged by the UK Combined Code, and also why the separation of chief executive and chairman is best practice, with the chairman being independent. The strongest opponent in the former executive, even when no longer on the board, continued to regard the merger and change of structure as a disaster and a betrayal of history.

12 The acquisition by BP of Amoco allowed BP to build its gas business, an area in which it had been weak. It also significantly increased its size and began the process of amalgamation, which created the current 'super major' oil companies. The market timing was also very opportune.

was so complicated that it was just not worth considering. In response he asked me to tell him why Shell had merged its US operations in 1997 with Texaco instead of Mobil. I was able to give him the answer immediately. The choice had been driven by the very independently run Shell operating company in the United States, which had held a unique place in the Shell corporate structure even long after the buyout by the Shell parent of the minority US independent shareholding. Had the decision been driven by global considerations the decision would certainly have been to go with Mobil, with whom there were far more global synergies and whose culture was closer to that of Shell. Had the decision been otherwise the history of the major oil companies might have been very different.

Did the complex structure of Shell also play a part in the reserves scandal of 2004 in which both Phil Watts, by then Sir Philip Watts and Chairman of CMD, and Walter van der Vijver, head of exploration and production, lost their jobs and in the aftermath of which the two parent companies merged under shareholder pressure to reform their governance? In one sense the answer is no, as the dual-parent structure would have made it easier for a member of the board of management of Royal Dutch such as Walter van der Vijver to raise the issue with members of the Royal Dutch Supervisory board. In another sense it did. Had Phil Watts been a conventional chief executive of a UK plc, with an independent chairman playing the sort of role that a UK plc chairman plays, the stress and antagonism between him and his executive colleague Walter van der Vijver would have been apparent to the chairman, who could have addressed it earlier. It was well known that Phil and Walter were not the best of friends, but it would have needed the more intimate and day-to-day knowledge of a chairman to detect the dysfunctional level of antagonism. In Anglo American, as an independent chairman, I had an office between that of the chief executive and the finance director. Although not full-time in the office, without interfering in day-to-day operations I could talk to people in the office and in the staff restaurant. As a result, any stresses and strains in relationships as well as general morale became transparent.

Much has been written about the large restatement of Shell's reserves in 2004 and the background to it. I was still a non-executive director of Shell at the time. The mis-statement of reserves according to US Securities and Exchange (SEC) guidelines had built up over years and, as I had been directly responsible for Shell's exploration and production operations (and reserves reporting) in the first half of the 1990s, I recused myself from all board and audit discussions on the matter.

Some background on the way that various reserves figures are produced may help. Consider a major gas field in the North Sea such as Ormen Lange. This field was discovered by a joint venture of Norsk Hydro, Shell, Exxon, BP and Statoil and also with a direct state shareholding from the Norwegian government (apart from the Statoil share). As the development of the field was planned by the operator, all the partners would review the technical data and arrive at a joint figure for how much gas and oil could be recovered from the field. This figure would be debated using all the available well and seismic data and would be based on statistical probability estimates. This technically determined a best estimate of the reserves that would be accepted by all partners as the basis for development and planning—a development that would involve a commitment to billions of dollars of expenditure. Given the financial implications of the figure, the number would be examined carefully by every member of the consortium, based on their own review of the same seismic and well data.

Each company then reported publicly on proven reserves, generally based on the guidelines of the SEC. These guidelines were notably more restrictive than the techniques used by the companies themselves for their internal purposes. They had also been tightened progressively in the years leading up to 2004. For example, they did not allow for extrapolation using 3D seismic, and also had restrictions based on whether or not hydrocarbons had actually been produced to surface and whether or not a decision to develop the field had actually been taken by the company concerned. In deep water, the number of production tests made was generally limited due to expense.

It is understandable that the SEC guidelines were more restrictive than the commercial techniques used by the companies in their decision-making. After all, the rules had to apply to all companies in all circumstances. However, it is also understandable, although not acceptable, that reservoir engineers tended to concentrate more on the technical figure on which corporate investment decisions were taken than on the figures based on the SEC guidelines, which to many engineers appeared to place arbitrary restrictions on what could or could not be included in proven reserves. In addition, the SEC requirements had been progressively changed, which may have allowed for different interpretations.

In the case of Ormen Lange, the result was that the five commercial partners all came up with a different number for their SEC reported reserves. Expressed as a percentage of the mutually agreed reserve figure on which the investment decision was taken, Norsk Hydro and BP were at the high end with a figure around 80% of the technical figure. Shell was somewhat lower (initially around 50% as I recall) with Exxon and Statoil reporting a far lower figure at around 30%. In the process of correcting the Shell SEC reserve figure, Shell reduced the quoted SEC reserves in two steps, taking a very conservative approach, to somewhere around 20% of the technical figure. So far as I know the other companies did not change their figures at that time.[13] BP soon after this sold their interest in the field to the Danish natural gas company DONG.[14]

The restatement of Shell's reserves, not just in Norway, but in Nigeria, Australia and the Middle East, caused a great scandal.[15] There is

---

13 Norsk Hydro did apparently discuss the discrepancy with the SEC (see www.gasstrategies.com/publications/gas-matters/92511). For comments on the differences see also A.C. Inkpen and M.H. Moffett, *The Global Oil & Gas Industry: Management, Strategy & Finance* (Tulsa, OK: PennWell Books, 2011).

14 In extensive research using the Freedom of Information Act to access SEC correspondence Phil Watts demonstrated that the SEC had been inconsistent in their treatment of different companies. In 2006 Cambridge Energy Research Associates (CERA) recommended that the SEC use a consistent approach such as that of the Society of Petroleum Engineers (SPE). www.spe.org/press/docs/pr/7Feb2006.pdf.

15 The Shell Audit Committee commissioned an independent report into the matter by Davis Polk & Waldwell (see www.shellnews.net/classactiondocs/Binder1_405-6_OCR.PDF, 31 March 2004).

no doubt that as soon as the problem emerged Phil Watts should have alerted the board. He also should have immediately queried Walter van der Vijver on what he meant by an email saying that he was sick of lying.[16] Both of these were serious mistakes. Having known him for many years, I have the highest respect for Phil Watts's integrity[17] and I do not believe that in the case of either individual personal gain entered into their minds. In Phil's case he committed the grave error of not telling the board immediately of the problems and of trying to sort it out himself. Both men left the company.

Conclusions and lessons

What are the lessons of all of this? Corporate governance and corporate structure are not ultimate determinants of the performance and behaviour of companies, but when robust they help to build trust and confidence of shareholders. When something goes wrong, the flaws in structure and governance tend to become plain.

I am a strong supporter of the separation of the roles of chairman and chief executive. Shell in its Committee of Managing Directors structure had an excellent collegiate executive committee. Tradition had it that any member had a 'red card' or veto over something that they felt they could not support, but in practice that was never exercised. When a member felt uncomfortable, the reason for doubts or discomfort was explored and the resulting modifications nearly always resulted

---

16 *Ibid.*

17 Phil Watts was and is a practising Christian and has since entered the priesthood. He did an enormous amount of forensic work in the two or three years after his dismissal and demonstrated that there were significant shortcomings in conclusions in regard to his position in the independent report by the law firm Davis Polk into the affair that Shell had commissioned and published. His work also convinced the UK Financial Services Authority and subsequently the US Department of Justice to drop any attempt at prosecution and indeed any threat of extradition to the US under the draconian extradition laws. He also challenged the SEC based on their own records as to whether the Commission had treated all companies equally.

in a stronger proposal. A little bit of speed was sacrificed in order to achieve decisions that had indeed considered all angles, including the improbable downsides. The Chairman of the CMD would sum up the discussion in a way not unlike that in which Quakers at their business meetings seek the 'sense of the meeting'. This system also had its flaws in that the same Chairman chaired the joint boards in Conference, and for this reason I had in 1999 proposed splitting the jobs. The system was therefore in practice almost, although not quite, as vulnerable to a dominant and entrenched individual as is the archetypal and now partly historical US corporation headed by a combined chairman, president and chief executive with a board of old and compliant buddies. Such responsibility embodied in a single individual makes for clear and exec-utive decisions, but when things go wrong they go badly wrong. There are no checks or balances in such systems. I recall that when Shell was once seeking an investment from Warren Buffett's Berkshire Hathaway group, Buffett's long-term associate Charlie Munger explained that they were not going to invest in Shell because the business was altogether too complex. He said that they liked to invest in businesses whose model was so simple that they could be run by an idiot 'because sooner or later they will be'. For that same eventuality, corporations, just like nations, need constraints in their constitutions and structures. Having said that, I have served happily on boards that for one reason or another have had a former chief executive as chairman or where the roles of CEO and chairman were combined. In such a case, the independent directors have not only to be truly independent but also to make absolutely sure that the broader body of executives in the company are comfortable making independent contributions to discussions in the board and that presenta-tions are not simply carefully rehearsed and orchestrated before coming to the board.

Apart from the strong preference for the roles of chairman and chief executive to be split, the most valuable innovations of modern corpo-rate governance codes such as the UK's Combined Code is the insistence on proper board evaluations, preferably conducted through one-to-one discussions between board members and a knowledgeable and experi-enced outsider. These appraisals do much to improve the workings of the board, and they have also included specific appraisal of the chairman, with a discussion of what the chairman needs to do more of, less of or differently. That is something that I myself as a chairman have found very useful.

The original double-headed structure of Shell effectively prevented the company making a major acquisition for shares. Did this matter? Is sheer size important? I think that there are two points arising from this. The first is that, although mergers often fail to create value due to conflicts of corporate culture and a failure to integrate the two companies effectively, the major mergers in the oil industry have on the whole worked well, presumably because of sound preparation, alignment of cultures and careful integration. Shell might well have benefited from such a major merger. On the other hand, once a certain minimum size has been reached, size per se ceases to be critical, other than perhaps to egos. In the oil and mining industries that minimum size is the size at which a company has the capacity and the cashflow to carry an overwhelming majority share of the kind of large project that is so necessary. The funding requirements and scale of such projects have increased steadily over the last 20 years, as has the minimum size needed to convince markets and host governments that a company is large enough, and has the technology and knowhow, to be a really credible lead partner. Beyond that, simple increases in size are not essential and may in some cases even be counterproductive.

One of the criticisms levelled at Shell in the aftermath of the reserves scandal was that among the many criteria of profitability that were used to determine variable bonuses for management—safety, progress with projects and reputation—was a measure of reserves added. For a resource company, the finding and development of new commercial reserves is a critical success factor so it seems to me logical that it should be a factor in determining the rewards of individuals who contribute to finding new reserves. There was an argument put forward that this was inappropriate, as it would encourage people to try and overstate book reserves inappropriately, although the impact of the reserves on the bonuses of senior executives at the time of the reserves scandal would have been relatively small. This seems to me to be a strange argument coming from people who are in general in favour of incentivisation of individuals through financial rewards. It would suggest that any form of incentivisation might encourage improper behaviour. I am not a golfer, but I have always remembered the story of the golfer Bobby Jones. Apparently, in the US Open in 1925 Jones went to play his ball in the rough. Unnoticed by anyone else, as he went to play the ball, the ball moved and he immediately gave himself a one-stroke penalty. That penalty cost him the Open. He was widely praised for his sportsmanship in reporting something no one else had seen and thus losing the title. Jones was reported to have said, 'You may as well praise a man for not robbing a bank.'

This leads on to the challenges of incentivising performance through variable pay and the related issue of remuneration differences between those at the top and bottom of a company and wealth differences in society at large.

Chapter 14

Differences in remuneration and wealth in companies and societies

Whether your experience is in business, government or charitable organisations and whether your viewpoint is that of a recipient or of a person who decides on the pay of others (or, indeed, both), you will be very aware of all the challenges of determining the right pay for a job. Competitive market considerations, scarcity or surplus of people able to do the job, the amount of training required, and the value added by the individual all play a part in determining how much an individual is paid. One might think that the overall value to society at large of an individual's work might also play a role, but in real life this is not the case, or only remotely so. To further complicate matters, many people, including myself, believe that people doing the same job should not automatically receive the same reward; there should be some variation with the quality of performance. For the great majority of my career in business I received no bonus, but that did not mean that my remuneration was not performance-related. There was generally an annual salary increment that varied with performance; although in percentage terms this variation was small, it was cumulative (and pensionable) so the long-term impact was significant. In addition to this was the incentive of promotion as a reward for performance in terms of contribution or skills and experience gained.

In any corporate survey, the one answer certain to be negative is the answer to the question as to whether pay is sufficient. Whatever the rate or whatever the actual relativity, the answer is likely to be no. On the other hand, while no employee might like to admit that the pay is entirely reasonable, the simplest measure of its adequacy is whether or not people spend a lot of time talking about it over the coffee machine. When remuneration becomes a continuous subject of discussion, it is a sure signal that pay is out of line with the market. It is also a sign that the company is losing productivity as a result of not paying competitively and therefore having staff spend all their time discussing the fact. Unless action is taken rapidly, the next step is an exodus of skills that it will be difficult to stop.

An organisation with no variability in reward for performance, far from being a happy band of co-workers, can be a bunch of dispirited and demotivated people. People see their best efforts frustrated by those who are not doing a good job or who do not care about the result of their work; they become disillusioned and frustrated. I watched the transformation of one such organisation in Egypt in the 1990s. Exploration for oil and gas was carried out by a 100% Shell-owned company with normal Shell terms and conditions. This exploration company discovered oil and gas in the Western Desert of Egypt—in many cases the seismic parties had to be preceded by mine-clearing parties to remove the mines left over from the battles of the Second World War. In Egypt, as in Syria, the other half of the short-lived United Arab Republic, the actual field development was carried out by a joint venture company formed by Shell and the state oil company, the Egyptian General Petroleum Company (EGPC). Although the joint venture company (the Badr El Din Petroleum Company—BAPETCo) had a general manager and many technical staff seconded from Shell, the bulk of its employees came from EGPC or other parts of government service. We were permitted to pay the Egyptian engineers, able as they were, only at the low government rates. There was very little differentiation of remuneration between the most routine and relatively unskilled job and a highly trained engineer or earth scientist.[1] The Egyptian government service ethos was one of punishing any error severely on the one hand, while on the other hand not rewarding enterprise and success in any way. As a result, the engineers tended to be risk-averse and the operators in general were more interested in a quiet life than in maintaining production.

It was difficult for the Shell manager and Shell-seconded members of the management team to operate in this environment. To make progress, it was necessary to know how to operate within the accepted Egyptian framework. Although the manager of the company was from Shell, the chairman was from EGPC or the government. The chairman could aid or frustrate progress greatly. At a time when the BAPETCo chairman was to be changed, I discussed this problem with the then Egyptian Minister of Petroleum, Hamdi Al Banbi, himself very able and experienced in the oil industry. Dr Banbi, who was Minister when the agreement to export Egyptian gas to Israel was signed, explained to me that it would take time to find the right chairman for BAPETCo. Not all the foreign joint ventures were the same. He pointed out that the different companies had different characteristics and someone who might be good for the Gulf of Suez Petroleum Company with Amoco might not work with Shell. The requirement for a French or Italian joint venture would also be different. This was perceptive and very true. The ethos, culture and operating methods in US, French, British or Italian companies all vary.

The BAPETCo Chairman that the Minister appointed introduced a remarkable change to the remuneration system of the company, which in a short period of time transformed the atmosphere within the company and its performance. It was a unique system and one with particularly Egyptian characteristics.

First, 30 or 40 performance indicators were defined. These ranged from those with a major immediate impact on production, such as whether a production station or certain wells had shut down in an unplanned way, to longer-term items such as the availability of materials on site. The

---

1 See Chapter 5 for the somewhat similar experience in Syria and for the resulting expedient of transferring Egyptian engineers to Syria and vice versa so that each could be treated as an expatriate in the other country.

indicators also covered safety issues such as whether anyone had been reported for not wearing a seat belt or proper protective equipment or whether there had been a recordable safety incident. Indicators relating to transport and shift schedules were also covered. The indicators were such that everyone, from the top to the bottom of the company, had a direct impact on at least one and probably several of them. Each of these items was measured and reported every day. If all were positive it would be declared that this had been a 'perfect day'. If there were 20 perfect days in the month, it was declared a 'perfect month' and everyone in the company was paid a bonus for that month. In a Western company such a bonus would probably be a percentage of salary, but in Egypt it was a fixed sum of money, the same for the general manager as for a security guard or truck driver. Everyone had a contribution to make to ensure that the day was perfect. Everyone suffered if someone slipped up. Over two years the result was remarkable. One could sense the difference as one ate in a canteen in one of the fields in the Western Desert. The modest fixed-sum bonus was of greater importance to those in lower pay scales; those at higher levels had the satisfaction of seeing overall performance improve through a more aligned and cooperative workforce who had begun to understand the overall picture and their contribution to it. The added cost of the bonus was far outweighed by the efficiency improvement. To me this was a solution of near genius in its adaptation of a reward system to a particular circumstance and culture. I have stood on a platform on the London Underground on a Monday morning, when the trains on some lines were not running because of signal failures or staff shortages probably not unrelated to the weekend and the weather, and thought that the Egyptian system would have application closer to home. One's fingers sometimes itch to try it.

Variable remuneration and its pitfalls

Bonuses

In the UK the introduction of additional variations in pay in the form of a non-pensionable bonus seemed logical and a good idea. It could be varied with the ability of the company or unit within the company to pay, depending on market conditions. It was non-pensionable so did not create a long-term liability for the company. It could be based on various performance measures that could be varied with circumstances. I can still remember receiving my first bonus in Shell. It was quite unexpected but seemed a very nice gesture of appreciation from the company for a job well done.

I have chaired the remuneration or compensation committees of HSBC and Accenture and had a lot of input into those of Anglo American, Shell and Saudi Aramco. I have thus watched and participated in a system that in the United States and Europe has gone wrong in a number of ways.

The first mistake was a collective one, a herd or collective-thinking approach from which it was difficult for any individual company to opt out. From about the late 1990s onwards, in a departure from the previous norm, it became common in many companies, certainly in the UK, for management to receive base salary increments in the 5–8% range while the bulk of the company received increments of 2–5%. The previous norm, certainly in Shell, had been that effectively all employees, regardless of position, received the same average increment, naturally with variations for performance and for economic conditions in different geographies. With the new approach, the difference does not seem large in any one year but the cumulative effect is manifestly unsustainable. The multiple of the top salaries to the median or the lowest salary continually increased. This was not just in the banking sector but across the board.

That change in the approach to base salaries would already have caused a problem, but it was compounded by the addition of other elements of variable pay, bonuses and so-called Long-Term Incentive Plans (or Programmes) (LTIPs) which, while seemingly having a rational purpose, further increased the gap in income between the senior executives of the company and the rank and file.

The logic of bonus awards is quite clear; the object is to give a reward with significant variation in line with the performance in the year concerned. The factors on which bonuses are determined can be varied from year to year in line with the particular objectives of the corporation or the business unit within the corporation that year. The objectives can be quite specific, but ideally they have hard measures not just related to financial outcomes but also to factors that will affect financial outcomes in the medium term. For example, in some businesses an element can be related to customer satisfaction, something to which all can contribute. Or there can be an element relating to industrial safety, environmental performance, project completion, securing certain contracts or achieving other targets. Such measures are often combined into scorecards that balance various elements of performance—financial, customer-related, environmental, safety and so on. The total pool from which the bonuses are to be paid can be varied with the financial performance of the company as a whole, varying it business unit by business unit according to performance, in line with the achievement of the objectives. Even small teams can be differentiated. The pool for that unit can then be divided according to individual performance and contribution.

To work effectively, such a system has to be completely transparent and understood by everyone in the company. The variation in the size of pools has to be defensible and there should be participation from the top to the bottom of a company. I believe such a system has a role to play in any well-run organisation. In practice this is not difficult to devise, and in my experience already exists in many companies.

Not everything can or should be rewarded by bonus payments or rewards. As Chairman of the remuneration committee of HSBC I was sometimes asked by shareholders how we rewarded ethical behaviour. My reply was always that we did not; unethical behaviour led to dismissal. You cannot reward people financially for being 'more ethical'; ethics are not in general subject to gradation, although there might be a questionable case where a discussion of the background and intention and a warning might be appropriate.

So what are the problems that have arisen? Some, such as a misalignment of bonus payment with objectives, are easily remedied. As bonuses are paid on an annual basis there is less chance of misalignment between the performance of the company and the size of bonuses. However, the size of bonuses in relation to base salaries has become a problem, particularly in parts of investment banking. The theory was that the bonus pool was flexible and that therefore in more straitened times it could be radically reduced. Unfortunately, at least part of the bonus, and in some cases a very large part, had become to be seen as effectively part of base pay. In the first or second year of my board membership of HSBC, before I became involved in the board remuneration committee, I recall being approached at the end of an Annual General Meeting of the bank by an indignant young man (and shareholder) from a part of the Bank's investment banking side. He grumbled that he and his unit had had no bonuses at all that year. I asked him whether the unit had been profitable and he replied that it had not been. That seemed to me to answer his question, but he clearly regarded at least some bonus as part of his basic remuneration. That was a general view in much of the industry and in that year HSBC paid the price for what seemed a completely rational action by losing many of its staff in that area to other banks. The memory of that event also made it more difficult to recruit new staff. This was clearly a collective industry issue.

The second problem is the feeling that in some areas, particularly in banking, bonuses are or have been paid out for performances that turn out to be illusory. This can be addressed by attaching claw-back provisions to bonuses or ensuring that large parts of any bonus are paid in shares that cannot be sold for a number of years. Both approaches are becoming more common since the financial crisis.

The third argument against bonuses is that they reward short-term performance, while shareholders are potentially more interested in long-term performance. For this reason Long-Term Incentive Plans were developed; unfortunately, they have just compounded the expansion of overall senior executive rewards relative to those in the engine rooms of corporations.

Long-Term Incentive Plans

The aim of a Long-Term Incentive Plan is to provide a longer-term incentive that would align the motivation of a senior executive with those of longer-term shareholders. An award of shares is made, but the actual transfer of these shares to the individual (so-called vesting) is dependent on performance conditions. Objectives are set that depend on performance over three or five years. In the UK, such plans, including the measures and targets, have to be approved by shareholders in a specific vote at the Annual General Meeting.

Although the objective of introducing a longer-term element into performance compensation to complement the shorter-term element of an annual bonus appears sound, for a number of reasons I think that they have proved to be a very bad idea in practice.

First, on top of an increasing base salary and an annual bonus, LTIPs are just another element that has contributed to the overall unsustainable inflation of senior executive reward relative to others. Some of this is cosmetic, and some real. There is often an assumption in the press that such awards will undoubtedly pay out, and probably at the maximum, so the quoted figures for executive salaries are inflated. However, it is equally true that when the targets are hit and the plans pay out, the sums involved can indeed be very large.

Second, as an LTIP takes into account the performance over a number of years, it is not unusual for the measures to be met by performance over the three- or five-year period, but just at a moment when conditions are changing and the share price or some other performance measure has declined. This leads to apparently perverse rewards, a large payout just at a moment when shareholders and analysts are registering concern. This is obviously not good for public relations and image, however fair it may be in relation to the agreed longer-term performance measures in the LTIP.

The third problem relates to the actual performance measures in the LTIP. As these have to be agreed with shareholders there is often quite some discussion among them as to the most important measures. Should it be total shareholder return over the period (share price increase or decrease plus accumulated dividends)? Many agree that this measure

315

is often strongly affected by external general market factors and is not well linked to executive performance, unless the measure is performance relative to other companies in the same sector. Others argue that return on capital or earnings per share are more appropriate measures. To prevent spurious outcomes, often a number of additional indicators are included, making the calculation complex and opaque. In discussion with shareholders I noted a danger that people began to think that by adding mathematical complexity one could improve the correlation with performance. That is so, but this also brings the danger that people come to view performance in mathematical terms, an equation that can be tweaked financially. In fact, any individual's performance is as much linked to their working environment, satisfaction in the job and the morale and ethos within the company as to any reward system; any business or shareholder that seeks to develop complex reward schemes that obscure the more important non-financial elements does so at its peril.

A fourth problem with LTIPs is that, in my experience, however carefully one designs them, at the end of the three or five years of the performance period conditions will have changed and the measures originally chosen may be less relevant.

The final objection to LTIPs is that, in spite of the large potential rewards that draw negative comment in the press, executives do not attach value to the potential rewards. The indicators are complex and people regard the direct link to their own performance as weak. Even where the current state of the indicators is calculated and reported regularly to executives, they tend to think of them largely as a sort of Christmas present that you might or might not get and do not value it until it actually arrives. So, as a performance incentive, LTIPs are in my opinion seriously flawed. Worse, the incentives could actually be perverse. HSBC before the financial crisis was a bank with a conservative balance sheet and, in spite of problems with a mortgage provider acquired in the United States, a generally conservative approach to lending. Partly because of this conservatism, the share price underperformed some of the more adventurous UK banks and as a result for some time the HSBC LTIP did not pay out, while those of competitors did. When the crash came and those competitors had to be bailed out, their share prices crashed much more than that of HSBC, making it again theoretically easier for them to meet new LTIP targets. Thus the system appeared to reward those in banks with riskier business models that had had to be bailed out. In theory, in future this will be addressed by claw-back provisions allowing past payouts to be recovered, but such claw-backs of awards already paid over can be difficult to implement in practice.

The way forward for variable remuneration schemes

For some time now, I have personally recommended that LTIPs be scrapped. I believe that there is a growing movement now towards a reformed system that would have a number of elements. The position of Hermes Equity Ownership Services, where I am currently the Chairman, is broadly supportive of changes to the generally accepted remuneration models. Hermes, which represents a group of large shareholders, has also worked with the National Association of Pension Funds (NAPF) to develop new guidelines for remuneration.

In my view there are a number of steps that need to be taken. First, to prevent continued widening between the remuneration of those at the top of an organisation compared to the median remuneration, companies should report annually on how their remuneration policies have affected this multiple.[2] This would hopefully eliminate proposals that exacerbate the difference, and at least hold it constant or reduce it. This is not a simple matter given the variability of rewards with performance, both at the top and often through an organisation, but it should be possible to average figures over a number of years or at least provide in commentary indications of the direction of movement. Alternatively,

---

2 The US Securities and Exchange Commission is currently introducing a requirement for companies to report on the ratio of the chief executive's compensation to the median compensation of all employees. How this will work is as yet
unclear. To me the most important measure is not the ratio, which will vary with
the nature of the company and industry, but whether the differential is increasing
or not.

there could be a target range reported with the actual outcome for the current year.

Second, all variable pay should be concentrated on the annual bonus, with performance criteria linked to measures that reflect the strategy of the company. These measures would change annually with the business plan, but it does not mean that they need to be short-term. For example, a company could report annually on progress towards achieving an objective in three or five years. These annual bonus targets can be linked at all levels in the organisation to things that can be influenced by an individual, a team or a business line. Unlike LTIPs, which may pay out at a time when the shareholders are suffering, annual bonuses would be closely related in timing to events and share price movements affecting the company.

Third, to ensure long-term alignment with the shareholder, the bulk of these bonuses should be paid in the form of shares in the company, which should be held for a very long time. Some at least should be held until retirement. In my experience people value shares that are vested in their names that have to be held, in contrast to LTIP shares that may or may not vest at all. I believe that as long-term shareholders executives are relatively sanguine about the ups and downs in the share price. What they are interested in is the long-term performance of the stock, including dividends paid. Their position is thus fully aligned with that of any other shareholder who is a long-term holder of the stock. At the time of the financial crisis, some senior executives in HSBC and some other banks had large shareholdings in their own companies as a result of either past LTIP awards, executive board member shareholding requirements or simply personal decisions. In some cases the loss on these shareholdings probably outweighed any cash remuneration they earned in that year. In other words, their net wealth in terms of shares and annual remuneration probably decreased. I did not hear any complaint from the individuals. They realised, however painful they might find it personally, all other shareholders were suffering the same pain and it was their job to fix it.

I believe that these three relatively simple steps would do much to address the current concerns about measures for variable remuneration, claw-backs, rewards for failure and so on. What such a system only partly addresses is the challenge of the inflated quantum of remuneration and the wealth gaps in society.

Wealth differentials in companies and in societies

The attitude of society to inequality arising from wealth of different forms is interesting. If one leaves aside the stagnation of wages at the lower end of the spectrum, there are three forms of inequality arising from well-above-average income or wealth.[3]

The first is caused by inherited wealth, which has been with us always and always will be. Old wealth of this kind generally keeps its head down, with the exception of certain individuals such as Paris Hilton, whose anatomical exposure is not limited to heads. In general, however, inherited wealth is not particularly visible.

The second kind of wealth is generated by entrepreneurs, owner/operators such as Bill Gates or the founders of Google. This form of wealth differential, in general, does not cause strains. Most people recognise that these are people who invested their own money, took risks and built a successful business. Their wealth fundamentally comes from a significant shareholding in something they created, and few begrudge them. Society's perceptions are to some extent coloured by how the wealth was generated, whether in a reputable or disreputable way. If the money was made by creating something useful that society wanted, by innovating or inventing, people are not concerned that the founder may be very wealthy in comparison to other people in the organisation who work for normal wages, provided working conditions are good. In fact, the founder is generally regarded by society as a hero and role model, and

3 Some of the ideas I express here were published in the form of an interview in R. Berger, D. Grusky, T. Raffel, G. Samuels and C. Wimer, *The Inequality Puzzle: European and US Leaders Discuss Rising Income Inequality* (Berlin: Springer). A video posted on YouTube www.youtube.com/watch?v=QPKKQnijnsM, 20 November 2012, created from a variety of sources, gives an interesting graphic presentation on wealth distribution in the US.

wealth is largely irrelevant. Depending on what such people do with their wealth, and many such as Bill Gates or Warren Buffett are great philanthropists, such wealth will eventually elide into old wealth as it did with Rockefeller or Carnegie.

Where the issue of inequality comes to the fore is with regards to a third group of people who are essentially managing public companies. These are people who run and administer companies owned by other investors. Such people may also be very creative. They may grow the company and create new businesses, but they do it with other people's capital. My entire career has been in public companies, with a responsibility for managing other people's capital. The current issue has risen because of the very large growth in the differential between people at the top of major public companies and those within the company or in society at large. That is where the strains begin to grow. If on top of that organisations fail as a result of a fundamental failure of executives to steward the capital entrusted to them, the problem is further exacerbated. Everyone in the Western world has a stake in such companies in the form of investments through pension funds or through employment, direct or indirect. Society's feeling of betrayal in the case of failure is then greater.

There is no doubt that large and growing gaps in income and wealth cause strains in society. Those working within a company generally accept that the people at the top of the company are doing jobs that require special skills and should therefore be paid more, but those special skills are often less evident to those outside the company, particularly those who are not familiar with business at all. In the case of star footballers who earn similar or greater amounts of money than high-level corporate executives, almost everyone acknowledges that they possess skills that most of the rest of us do not, and that they compete in a field that is open to all.

Whether or not there are strains within a company depends on the atmosphere and ethos and whether there is a feeling of inclusion or exclusion. People want competitive pay. If those at the top are remunerated less than in peer companies, people lower in the organisation may worry that this applies to them too. However, they also do not want to see those at the top excessively remunerated. When Accenture was still a partnership, and for a couple of years after it became a public company in 2001, the remuneration of the 2,500 partners was put to a vote every year by all the partners. This transparent system kept the relativities in line at different levels. While I would not recommend this for a public company, and Accenture no longer does it, the principle of openness and of justifying the relativities is a valuable one.

How can excessively large differentials be reduced?

Clearly the first step that needs to be taken is to prevent the differential widening further. As a result of adverse publicity and the challenging economic climate, further widening of the differential has largely halted. This is not to say that there is no danger of expansion recommencing if and when good times return. Hopefully the lessons will have been learnt by both remuneration committees and shareholders, but that is by no means certain.

Actually shrinking the differentials is much more challenging. Shareholders do have power and are beginning to use it. In the past this has sometimes been slow as those in investment management and pension funds, who are the holders of the shares on behalf of their many clients, are part of the same financial industry. Their own remuneration is subject to the same norms and practices within a similar framework, so they do not see it as abnormal and, further, have little incentive to attack it. Shareholders are now beginning to address the fact that, in parts of the financial services industry, the division of income between shareholders and employees has been badly skewed in favour of some employees. In the HSBC remuneration committee we gave much thought to this issue, often, it should be said, with equally thoughtful and genuinely constructive input from executives. The practice had grown up in a few, fortunately very restricted, areas where the structure was almost that of a 50–50 joint venture between employees and shareholders. If a business used the bank's capital, clearly the shareholders should get by far the larger share. In some businesses where little or no use was made of the bank's capital, such as certain parts of private banking, and where the employees had a close and individual relationship with the customers, and who may indeed have brought the client to the bank, there is a stronger reason to allow the proportion of the profit taken by the employee to rise somewhat. However, even in those cases, the bank's brand and reputation was clearly being used, so the split should still be firmly limited. It is going to take a long time, with concerted pressure from shareholders, to correct this across the banking industry as a whole. There is something of a parallel with the hedge fund market where the eye-watering fees consist of a fixed 2% management fee plus a further 20% of the profit above a certain relatively low level also going to the management. This structure has long been the subject of criticism but is only now in more straitened times actually beginning to change.

While shareholder pressure is important, the most powerful weapon is often public outrage, nowadays magnified and accelerated by social media campaigns and petitions. This outrage, whether in fact or merely in prospect, has led many executives to waive bonuses or payments to which they are entitled. It has also led Starbucks to make a voluntary contribution of taxes when faced with an outcry over the fact that they had not paid corporation tax in the UK for some years. This occurred in spite of the fact that their tax returns had apparently been perfectly in line with the regulations. Similarly, Goldman Sachs dropped an idea of delaying bonuses in the UK so that their employees would pay tax at a lower rate in the UK, again in spite of the fact that the move was perfectly within the law and that a similar move had already been made in the United States without any public or congressional outcry at all.

Public outrage is a very powerful weapon. Unfortunately it is somewhat capricious and does not necessarily hit the most egregious offenders but rather those who happen to be visible or prominent. In this it has many of the characteristics of a lynch mob, being opportunistic and generally not subject to reason once outrage has been unleashed. It is encouraging that corporations are held to a standard of perceived good behaviour or fairness and not simply to what is legal; but there are slight concerns on the impact this might have on consistency and the rule of law. In some cases, in particular corporation tax, the existing approach to division of taxation of international business between countries may need to be modified in the light of the changed structure of modern business. This will require international discussion and is therefore unlikely to happen swiftly.

Chapter 15

The business of not-for-profit enterprises

Much of this book has been about commercial for-profit enterprises. There is another very large and important sector: the not-for-profit sector. This sector is not only important in delivering services and support to different sectors of society, but as discussed in Chapter 2 on Coalitions, the benefits of cooperation between the for-profit and the not-for-profit sector working together can be significant, so understanding between the two sectors is important.

The difference is not as great as is sometimes assumed. Many not-for-profit organisations are multinational enterprises delivering goods and services on behalf of their members, charitable foundations and governments. The term 'not-for-profit organisation' is clumsy. Civil society organisation (CSO) is better and like the alternative non-governmental organisation can be conveniently abbreviated. Paul Alofs suggested in an article in 2011 that it was more positive to look on such organisations in the light of what they actually do rather than what they do not do.[1] He sensibly suggested that the sector be called the 'social profit sector', but the term has so far not been widely adopted.

1 P. Alofs, 'It's Time to Say "Not" to Not-For-Profit', *Globe and Mail*, 31 October 2011.

Until relatively recently, statistics on the numbers and activities of such organisations were difficult to find. This has been to a great extent remedied by the work done by the Johns Hopkins Center for Civil Society. The United Nations has issued guidelines to national statistical organisations on the preparation of economic statistics relating to not-for-profit enterprises. Working with the United Nations on these statistics, a study by the Center led by Lester M. Salamon compiled economic data on not-for-profit enterprises for eight countries (Australia, Belgium, Canada, the Czech Republic, France, Japan, New Zealand and the United States), with the intention of working on a further 20 countries as data in the required statistical format becomes available. The findings of the study demonstrate the remarkable scale of not-for-profit activity.[2]

In an update of the same study[3] extending the work to 15 countries, the sector contributed on average 4.5% of GDP, with a range from 1.5% in Thailand to more than 8% in Canada. By comparison in the same 15 countries the construction sector averages a 5.5% contribution to GDP and agriculture 6.4%. Paid employees in the not-for-profit sector make up on average 5.2% of the total workforce. In the United States alone there are between a million and a million and a half such not-for-profit organisations, depending on the definition used. Research by the Urban Institute estimates that in the United States in 2010

> nonprofits contributed products and services that added $779 billion to the nation's gross domestic product; 5.4 percent of GDP. Nonprofits are also a major employer, accounting for 9 percent of the economy's wages, and over 10 percent of jobs in 2009.[4]

2 L.M. Salamon, M.A. Haddock, S.W. Sokolowski and H.S. Tice, *Measuring Civil Society and Volunteering: Initial Findings from Implementation of the UN Handbook on Nonprofit Institutions* (Working Paper No. 23; Baltimore, MD: Johns Hopkins Center for Civil Society Studies, 2007).
3 L.M. Salamon *et al.*, *The State of Global Civil Society and Volunteering: Latest Findings from the Implementation of the UN Nonprofit Handbook* (Baltimore, MD: Johns Hopkins University, Center for Civil Society Studies, 2013).
4 Urban Institute, www.urban.org/nonprofits/more.cfm.

In Canada, Statistics Canada divides the sector into health and education (hospitals, universities and colleges), which make up two-thirds of the sector and 'core not-for-profits', which make up the remaining third. In 2008 the core sector alone made up 2.4% of GDP, or CND$35.4 billion, and grew at 6%.[5]

Civil society organisations as enterprises

On any measure, even if the hospitals and universities are excluded, the not-for-profit, NGO or CSO sector is an important economic sector. Broadly speaking, as businesses they provide goods and services in exchange for income. For example, a biodiversity conservation organisation delivers conservation of species as a service to members or donors who wish to support such conservation, or as a consultancy service to companies seeking to protect biodiversity around their operations. An organisation dedicated to delivering emergency relief and development will derive its income to support these activities not only from individual donors, but also in a significant way from governments, which are thus essentially outsourcing the delivery of development aid.

Like any business, these organisations have diverse sources of income and business models. The original Johns Hopkins study showed that 38% of the income of not-for-profits in 2007 came from fees and charges, 35% from philanthropy, including gifts of time and 27% from governments.[6] They note that the government share is understated because the fees category also includes services to governments. They also note that voluntary support is significant, being on average some 60% of the philanthropy category, including gifts of time. In Canada, for the core category of not-for-profits (i.e. excluding health and educa-

5 Statistics Canada, www.statcan.gc.ca/daily-quotidien/101217/dq101217b-eng.htm.
6 L.M. Salamon, M.A. Haddock, S.W. Sokolowski and H.S. Tice, *Measuring Civil Society and Volunteering: Initial Findings from Implementation of the UN Handbook on Nonprofit Institutions* (Working Paper No. 23; Baltimore, MD: Johns Hopkins University, Center for Civil Society Studies, 2007).

tion where the government contribution to income is very high), sales of goods and services made up 45% of income, membership fees and donations 28% and government transfers 21%, the balance being transfers from businesses and investment income.

Clearly the sources of income of not-for-profits depend very much on the field in which they work. Human rights organisations such as Amnesty International or Human Rights Watch derive most of their income from individuals and foundations. A development and relief organisation such as Oxfam, on the other hand, currently derives only about a quarter of its income from donations, while 21% of its income comes from sales of donated goods and over 40% from governments. If an organisation provides effective development and relief services it is entirely natural that governments should be prepared to channel a portion of their development aid through them. This is the market in operation in what might appear to be an unlikely field.

In the environmental field there is a steady movement towards greater cooperation with companies. WWF still derives the bulk of its income (57%) from individuals, but 17% comes from governments and 11% from corporations. An organisation such as the Rainforest Alliance, which works very effectively with companies to improve the sustainability of products such as coffee and tea, now gets only 12% of its income from its members but 35% in fees for services and 27% from governments.

There is thus a wide and varied universe of business models aimed at delivering a social good in exchange for an income from one or other section of society. The sector is lively, competitive and creative. Just as in the private sector, organisations seek the most effective business model to earn the income necessary to enable the delivery of their particular product, while seeking to develop the most effective product.

One difference is that not-for-profit organisations rarely merge with each other. They compete strongly for funds, but unlike businesses seldom join forces to reduce overheads and costs. When I was chairman of the Global Business Coalition for HIV/AIDS, TB and Malaria, working with the late Richard Holbrooke, who was the critical driving force behind the GBC, we did manage to merge with a similar organisation,

Transatlantic Partners Against AIDS (TPAA). This may have been facilitated by the fact that TPAA's activities were mainly in an area, the former Soviet Union, not covered by the GBC and by the fact that due to
a vacancy we could put the joint organisation in the highly competent
hands of John Tedstrom, the CEO of the smaller TPAA. The merger was
very beneficial. The fact that the GBC's funding came entirely from business undoubtedly also facilitated the move.

Much to the frustration of the business community, which receives
many approaches from civil society organisations with similar objectives, such a merger is extremely rare. In business, shareholders are often
in favour of consolidation, while in general funders of not-for-profits
take relatively little interest in encouraging such matters. The result is
that with every new idea or variant on an idea, the number of not-for-
profit organisations inexorably increases, except when complete financial starvation and collapse overtakes one. Judy and I have closed down
two not-for-profit organisations that we founded, which operated in the
area of prevention of violence and restorative justice. We did so in an
orderly fashion because, although both did excellent and effective work,
the funding was simply not developing in a sustainable way.

In spite of the lack of growth by consolidation and merger, many not-
for-profit organisations are very large, with annual revenues in the order
of half a billion dollars. They face all the challenges of major international organisations in terms of developing people, with structured pay
scales and pensions. At the World Economic Forum in Davos in 2004 I
was once invited to speak at a side meeting with the subject of the meeting being whether or not NGOs should be regulated. I was concerned
lest this turn out to be a meeting with a bunch of business people suggesting controls for NGOs. I need not have worried. The bulk of the
attendees were from major not-for-profit organisations discussing how
to ensure that standards are maintained in the sector. There was concern
that bad behaviour by some organisations might damage the reputation
of the sector as a whole. That reputation is high and certainly very much
higher in terms of trust than commercial businesses.

It appeared from that meeting that there were already problems
emerging in India with what were described as 'briefcase NGOs', which

consisted of someone, often apparently a politician, raising funds for some worthy project and then misusing the funds. The response had been to form a group in the industry to develop standards. The Credibility Alliance is a consortium of voluntary organisations committed towards enhancing accountability and transparency in the voluntary sector through good governance. The Alliance has developed an Accreditation System and Peer Group Review Model to strengthen and enhance the legitimacy and the credibility of individual organisations within the NGO sector.[7]

This parallels the steps taken in the commercial world. In an unregulated market the first step is to establish a brand, with the reputation of the brand being the assurance to the consumer on the quality of the product. This approach goes back hundreds of years to when names and symbols on establishments would, as a reputation for quality was developed, become a form of assurance against adulterated or substandard products. The second step is for a group of companies to form a membership organisation with companies having to agree to meet certain standards in order to join. The International Council on Mining and Metals is such a membership organisation—not every mining company is admitted. In the travel industry this goes further, with members guaranteeing customers in the case of a member defaulting. The third step is the establishment by government of regulatory frameworks, with enforcement, in order to ensure that the laggards or ill-intentioned members of an industry are brought into line.

Many not-for-profit organisations have strong brands established over many years. These often reflect or represent the original aims of the organisation and its supporters. For example, the WWF logo of a panda is very well known. This represented the original aim of preventing the extinction of pandas, tigers and other large mammals. The work of WWF has since broadened greatly, taking into account biodiversity of the widest sort. The organisation works on the preservation of habitats and fisheries and makes careful studies of the livelihoods of fishermen and villagers who depend on or interact with the fauna. There

7 See www.credibilityalliance.org/home/index.php.

is a realisation that communities need to see the livelihood benefits of preserving the fauna and its habitats. WWF has moved far beyond the preservation of a few large woolly mammals, or what I think are known more properly in the business as 'charismatic mega-fauna', but you can be sure that at least a couple of times a year there will be publicity on programmes for preserving tigers in the Sundarbans or Sumatra or some such, because although this is only a small, admittedly important, part of the organisation's work, it is what the multitude of individual WWF donors around the world expect.

Similarly, Greenpeace is now a very thoughtful organisation with well-developed policy positions on many aspects of sustainability. Many of these policies, with the exception of their implacable and unconditional opposition to nuclear power and genetic modification of organisms, res-onate with business people. Their supporters expect activism, so if they are not seen to be zooming around in inflatables under the bows of some ship or abseiling down a corporate asset festooned with slogans, their supporters think that they have gone to sleep and take their support to a competing organisation. Within bounds such forms of protest are useful in drawing attention to issues, but they are also essential to Greenpeace as a way of connecting with their supporters who expect visible activ-ism such as recently abseiling down the tallest building in London, the Shard, in protest at Shell plans to drill in the Arctic, or their frequent presence dressed as polar bears at public meetings. Occasionally, in my opinion, they cross the limit and engage in criminal damage, but in gen-eral activism based on thoughtful analysis is a useful contribution the public debate. Greenpeace have recently discovered that this form of activism can provoke a very intolerant response in countries such as Russia and possibly lead to draconian penalties.

Not-for-profits thus sometimes get trapped by their brands or their origins, just as commercial companies do. Most large oil and gas com-panies have worked hard at transforming their image to that of 'energy companies'. The most notable example is BP's rebranding as Beyond Petroleum. Yet in the minds of the population such companies remain firmly labelled as 'oil companies', the role of natural gas, hydrogen and biofuels being largely forgotten.

Brands are not the only area of similarity between the two sectors. At the meeting in Davos previously mentioned, the chief executive of a large NGO admitted that he was concerned at how he could be sure that all of his organisation's 60,000 employees around the world were behaving in line with his organisation's principles. His problem was exactly the one I have tried to address earlier in Chapter 12 on the challenge of embedding values, whether the organisation is for profit or not for profit. The challenge is the same. In a public panel discussion on accountability, my fellow panellist Barbara Stocking, the chief executive of Oxfam, pointed out that many of their employees delivering food aid to undernourished people were in a position of power that could, unless checked, lead to arrogance. She pointed out that, unlike a commercial organisation's customers, the recipients of food aid did not have the option of walking away if they thought that the service was bad. Oxfam has done excellent work on developing and applying methods of appraising the results and performance of their work, but Barbara said that she sometimes envied the feedback that a commercial organisation gets from its customers exercising their choice. She said that Oxfam had had to develop performance appraisal systems in spite of the fact that many of their supporters thought that, as their objective was laudable, they could do no wrong. I confessed that that was one particular challenge that I had never faced in my career in Shell.

So are there essential differences that result from the not-for-profit or for-profit structure of enterprises? I think that there are two.

The capital challenge for not-for-profits

The first is in the ability to raise capital. I have already referred in Chapter 6 to being on the board of Nuffield Hospitals, a not-for-profit healthcare provider that owned and ran over 30 hospitals across the UK, providing private healthcare services. The origins of the group had been charitable, and indeed many of the hospitals had been originally built by charitable donations and collections in their local areas. The organisation had ceased to raise funds charitably—the growth of the

UK's National Health Service (NHS) had rendered this unnecessary—but many people still required an option with a degree of comfort and service (and it might be said efficiency), which the NHS found difficult to provide. Nuffield was commercially run, but had no shareholders. All profits from a revenue of around $750 million were ploughed back into the enterprise. New hospitals could be built from cash surpluses and from loans serviced from these surpluses, but expansion was limited by the loan-to-capital ratios that lenders would demand. There was no method of raising additional equity capital.[8] For that you need capitalists who are prepared to invest equity in return for a share of the profits. I once discussed this dilemma with Muhammad Yunus, the founder of Grameen Bank (see Chapter 6). Grameen has developed spinoffs such as Grameenphone, which operates a hybrid mode of a not-for-profit in partnership with a commercial organisation, the Norwegian company Telenor. Muhammad said that he had no difficulty raising patient capital from supporters. It was, however, clear that those willing to lend money on patient or uncommercial terms had in fact generated their capital from the capitalist system.

The bulk of not-for-profits are in fact capital-light. They do not have large manufacturing facilities or major capital investments. The exception is the healthcare sector and there the capital comes either from philanthropy or from government transfers.

Differences in remuneration

The second difference is in remuneration. It would appear that similar levels of responsibility are remunerated at a higher level in the private for-profit sector than in the not-for-profit sector. There would seem to be two reasons for this. First, shareholders who have invested their capital have historically been less concerned about the proportion of the revenue of a corporation that is taken by the employees and managers in

---

8 Nuffield Hospitals has recently raised finance by means of a corporate bond, which is a partial answer to this dilemma.

the form of remuneration than the donors to not-for-profits have been. This is beginning to change now, but the change has been slow. Shareholders have not focused on this aspect of the division of profit as long as profits were adequate. By contrast, those who contributed to not-for-profits have generally been concerned to ensure that the employees and managers of the organisation they were paying to deliver on their behalf some social good did not capture an excessive amount of their donation or subscriptions. As in the private sector there have been major outcries when remuneration has reached a certain level (for example, a controversy over the pay of the chief executive of Amnesty International[9]) but the threshold seems to be much lower. Commercially run not-for-profit organisations such as Nuffield Health or the Consumer Association, neither of which solicit donations, do in fact pay salaries that are closer to the commercial sector.

The fact that those working in the not-for-profit sector accept relatively lower remuneration is perhaps due to a sense of vocation in that sector, but also I believe partly linked to the greater social acceptability of working in the not-for-profit sector.

If this is so, I find it an interesting outcome. As a geologist who considered a career in academia, I actually joined a commercial organisation because in my particular field the commercial imperative meant that it was possible to fund greater amounts of data collection in order to use science to solve geological problems that would lead to the location of hydrocarbons. This meant secure funding of intellectually challenging scientific work. At the time, when I discussed this with an academic for whom I had a great admiration, he remarked that he could never work for a commercial organisation as he derived much of his satisfaction from publishing papers and from their appreciation by scientific

---

9 See N.M. Young, 'Paying off Khan was "least-worst option" according to Amnesty's IEC chair', *Civil Society*, www.civilsociety.co.uk/governance/news/content/8481/paying_off_khan_was_least-worst_option_according_to_amnestys_iec_chair, 1 March 2011. And see also complaints in October 2013 about the remuneration of heads of charities at www.telegraph.co.uk/news/politics/10236183/Nine-British-charities-paid-staff-over-300k-each-last-year.html.

colleagues. This would not be possible in general in a commercial organisation. It would appear that a particular sort of social standing compensates for lower remuneration. Or is it just vocation?

In my own case, I have always regarded the finding and provision to the world of reliable and low-cost energy to allow economic development as an entirely worthwhile occupation. Although more latterly the impact of fossil fuels on the global climate has meant that we now know this cheap and reliable energy comes with clear downsides, this is a matter to be addressed, not regretted, given the role of energy in development for the past century. Although one can never be sure of one's own motivations, I believe that, had my chosen path led to a generally lower level of remuneration, I would have continued in it. Had society at large regarded my efforts as a contribution to society, as opposed to in many cases regarding it as a detriment (in spite of the universal use of the products), my decision might have been further reinforced.

The interplay of for-profit and not-for-profit sectors is complex, as is society's judgement on the merits of the two. Although many would deny it, the interplay is in a way just an example of the almost ubiquitous operation of market forces.

Building trust to work together

In addressing many of the issues that face the world, particularly in areas where governments are failing in their duties to the societies they govern, it is essential that business and civil society organisations work together for the common good (see Chapter 2). If this is to happen, businesses need to work to develop the trust of civil society organisations, without which cooperation will be impossible.

Trust in business is low. The best way of restoring it is by exceptional transparency and by reporting on exactly what business is doing and where. This transparency should cover both the positive things and the negative things.

This reporting is a central theme of both the Global Reporting Initiative and of the UN Global Compact signatories' commitment to deliver

Communications on Progress. These reports are public and open to scrutiny by all. In many cases they are verified by independent organisations. Where there are negative impacts, there should be an honest discussion of what needs to be done to alleviate this impact and how the steps towards that elimination can be reported on and tracked.

Once NGOs and businesses begin to realise that there is a common goal, it becomes easier to discuss a preferred solution and to work towards it together, with each side contributing. There are two things that militate against such cooperation.

Businesses sometimes think that, if they work with an NGO, the NGO should cease its criticism of business, or at least their particular business. For reasons of brand and business model discussed above, this is not possible. Even when cooperating with Shell, Greenpeace has to retain the right to make attacks elsewhere. This is part of Greenpeace's credibility with its donors and it cannot give this up. I think that businesses just have to recognise this as a part of the Greenpeace business model and accept that there will be some difficult times.

There are, however, limits. Friends of the Earth (FoE) tends to position itself as the last barrier against global domination by large businesses. This is an essential part of its brand value and its position is almost entirely anti-business. This makes cooperation very difficult if not impossible and there are few businesses that successfully work with Friends of the Earth. The exception is Eurostar, which cooperates with FoE in a carbon reduction programme and some renewable energy businesses. To be fair, what I describe as a result of a generally anti-business approach putting off potential business partners FoE ascribes to its own selective approach to partnership.

Organisations in each sector have to look at the gains that can come from cooperation. As enterprises, each has to understand the drivers of the other's model. The potential for positive change that can be achieved by improving the workings of business and its contribution to improvement of society are, I believe, much greater than that of a civil society organisation working on its own. In addition to this, there are the unique advantages that can be gained when both sectors work together in development and in areas where government is failing and where both would gain from government fulfilling its essential role.

Afterword

Family beginnings

I was born in Antigua on 15 September 1940, the youngest of six children, on the day on which the Battle of Britain reached its climax more than 3,000 miles away. My father wanted to christen me Spitfire, but fortunately my mother's good sense prevailed. I was delivered by Dr (later Sir) Wesley Winter, the first black doctor on the island. It was my father who proposed Dr Winter as the first black member of the New Club, the planters' gathering place at the head of town.

My mother's family had lived in Antigua from the 17th century, mainly as doctors or sugar planters. My father, Alexander, came to Antigua after the First World War where he had been wounded in action and been awarded the Military Cross at the same ceremony with the same award as his elder brother Mark. My paternal grandfather, George Moody-Stuart,[1] was a partner in a city firm Henckell DuBuisson, which pioneered the concept of a central sugar factory. The central Antigua

---

1 My great-great-great-grandfather served for 40 years in the army of the East India Company, retiring as a general. He did much genealogical research and entailed some property in Perthshire so that it could only be owned by a Stuart. Alexander Moody, my great-grandfather and a minister in the church, married the General's granddaughter, Jessie Stuart, the eldest of four girls and the heiress. To preserve the land, no longer in the family, they put his name before hers.

Sugar Factory, or simply 'the Factory', was built by my mother's father, Leonard Henzell, together with the railway system to bring the cane from the outlying estates. The steam engines were all called after members of the family.[2] Meanwhile, most of the sugar estates on the island joined together in the Antigua Syndicate of Sugar Estates, which was managed by my father.

When I was a teenager, my father asked me what I planned to do with my life. I replied that I thought I would like to be a sugar planter just like him. He told me that our forefathers had brought most of the people to the island many years ago and that he thought that the time had come to hand things over to them; I should find something else useful to do.

The sugar industry was taken over by the government after a difficult period of drought and closed in the early 1970s. The first Prime Minister of an independent Antigua, 'Papa' Vere Bird, the boss of the labour union in my father's time and founder of the Antigua Labour Party, lived after his retirement in the simple stone-built three-bedroom house that my father had built for us in the late 1940s. Papa Bird is now buried in the front lawn. He is surrounded by the little blue flowers of the plumbago hedge that had been planted and lovingly tended by my mother. This is strange, but somehow appropriate. I hope that the two old sparring partners are enjoying posthumous discussions and reminiscences, perhaps enlightened and enabled by the blaze of absolute truth and clarity of intentions that is never really available to us during our lives. Much mythology has been developed about the labour movement in Antigua and I have even seen my father described as the last slave owner.[3]

---

2 One engine, called after my Aunt Joan, was preserved and restored by enthusiasts and is still working on the Welshpool and Llanfair Light Railway in Wales (www.wllr.org.uk).

3 There is a foundation myth on the island, commemorated by a memorial, of a confrontation in 1951 between Papa Bird, the union leader, and my father on a white horse. The legend has it that in there was no sugar cane cut that year. Records in the Antigua Museum show that in fact production in 1951 was fairly normal. My father also never rode a white horse.

Although my childhood was an extremely happy and relatively care-free one, we were a family that had been divided by the war. My eldest brother George and my sister Lena had had polio before the war. George was only 18 months old at the time and it was feared that he might never walk again. Long before I was born my mother took him to England and spent more than two years there living with my grandfather and my father's unmarried sister Marion. Eventually George was left with my Aunt Marion, or Minna as she was known. So when the war came, George was in England and so was my eldest sister Marion. My second eldest sister Lena was at school in Jamaica, so throughout my early years I was used to being with just two of my five siblings, Margo and Len. Lena left for England when I was five; I saw her again when I was ten. My eldest sister Marion I first met when she came out to Antigua in 1948 after service in the WRNS in the war. I first met George when I went to England at the age of ten in 1950. In spite of what was initially considered to be an almost incapacitating handicap, George led an active life at school and subsequently in business. I never once heard him complain about his condition; he was an inspiration to me and to many others, doing pioneering work in the fight against corruption and working very successfully in agro-industrial development in many developing countries. In spite of these early prolonged separations we remain a close family.

Education

My first school was the Antigua Girls High School, which took boys up to the age of seven. After that I attended the Convent High School in St John's. In 1950, the year I was ten, Margo and I were sent to boarding school in England. I went to prep school at The Old Hall in Shropshire. I was very happy, but Margo, being very independent and in any case not keen on school, was not happy at her girls' school in Berkshire. In the holidays we stayed with our spinster aunts Minna and Margaret. We saw our parents once a year for the summer holidays, either going back home to the island or my mother would spend the summer with us staying with relatives.

At 13 I went on to school at Shrewsbury School. I did not have a particularly distinguished career at Shrewsbury. I was moderately academic, but I am quite uncoordinated when it comes to sports involving balls, so I did my best to avoid such sports by taking up rowing and cross-country running.

My A-Level results enabled me to scrape a place at St John's College Cambridge. Because of the end of national service, my place was deferred for a year as the universities needed to provide for those completing national service as well as those relieved from that obligation. I spent much of the year learning German and working in Germany. This period in Germany not so long after the war, talking to Germans in their own language about their experiences in the war from the Eastern Front to Italy, opened my eyes. As a boy of 19 I had only so far been aware of the Second World War from a British point of view and seeing the still very visible bomb destruction of buildings in London. I remain enormously grateful to these Germans for spending time with an inexperienced British boy and telling me of their experiences in the war, remarkably without rancour.

University

I went up to Cambridge in October 1960 to read Natural Sciences, specialising in Geology. To engage the attention of a sensible young woman at Cambridge in 1960 when the ratio of male students to possible females was 18:1 was a terrifying challenge. Judy was also reading Natural Sciences, but with an emphasis on Chemistry. She did also do some geology. Judy remembers my footsteps coming up behind her outside the Sedgwick Museum of Geology and asking her somewhat shyly if she would like to come with me to the birthday party of a friend of mine the following day. She assumed from the last-minute invitation that I had been stood up by another girl and said yes out of sympathy. She now knows that I had been working up courage for at least a week to ask her, and had thus left it until the unavoidable last minute. That began what has been over 50 years of a most active and happy partnership.

At the end of my first year I joined the Cambridge Spitsbergen Expedition as an assistant to Peter Friend who was a lecturer in the Geology Department, so it was natural that as I approached the end of my final year I planned to do postgraduate studies for a doctorate on fluviatile sediments in Spitsbergen. Together with Peter Friend, who would supervise my thesis, I had worked out an area of study and an interesting topic. As it involved something of interest to the oil industry in defining the extent of the sandstone reservoirs that sometimes contain oil, Shell was prepared to award me one of its postgraduate studentships.

I reckoned that while I would probably not get a first-class degree, I should get an upper second, which was the requirement for doctoral studies to be funded by the Natural Environment Research Council. However, I made a significant hash of one paper and only managed a lower second.[4]

This was a potentially fatal setback. I asked Professor Oliver Bulman whether I could still carry out my project. He said that as long as I could find the funding I could keep my place. Thus armed, I approached Shell. Their reply was that as long as Cambridge would have me to study for a PhD they would not withdraw their offer of funding. The circle was thus squared.

Meanwhile, Judy and I became engaged and she got a job as a research assistant to the late Norman Hughes. He was a botanist working on statistical approaches to defining species of fossil plants from their spores. Judy developed standardised methods of extraction to eliminate bias and then measured and counted different species. Norman and she published several papers demonstrating the statistical variation within and between species.

---

4 I believe that even at Cambridge there has been grade inflation in degree classes. First-class degrees are much more common, as are upper seconds. Lower seconds are rarer and third-class degrees, which in the 1960s were not unusual, are now also very rare.

In 1964 Judy and I married, with Dan McKenzie as best man, and we all moved in together. Dan's research[5] was funded by a Natural Environment Research Council research grant, I was on a Shell studentship of £500 a year and Judy was earning £600 a year as a research assistant, so the three of us were reasonably solvent most of the time. I also made a small amount of money as a demonstrator to students in the Geology Department and Judy translated some French and Norwegian geological books.

On completing my doctorate, I applied to Shell and was given a job as an exploration geologist.

Field geology in Shell: Spain and Oman

In September 1966 Judy and I moved to Holland. We lived in a rented flat where our first son Alexander was born. I joined the extensive Shell training programme, which indoctrinated me into the mysteries of drilling wells and seismic and aerial photographic interpretation.

In early 1967 I was posted as a field geologist to Spain. I was told that there would be no accommodation for my family in Spain, so Judy packed up our few belongings and the baby and returned to England. Returning to Holland after Spain, I was shocked and very annoyed to be told that I should go to Oman as a field geologist, again on a bachelor basis, to join a team on a research project in the Oman mountains.

At that time, to refuse a posting was tantamount to resigning. I counted up my non-existent savings and prepared to leave Shell. In fact, the person responsible for my assignment confessed that they had not taken my family situation into account. If I did not want the job, I did not have to take it. I asked what the alternatives were and he explained that I would go on a further period of training and await another posting, probably to Aberdeen. I said that I would have to consult Judy

---

5 Dan McKenzie's research in theoretical physics and geophysics led to groundbreaking papers in the emerging theory of plate tectonics. He is now a very eminent scientist and is considered one of the pioneers of plate tectonic theory.

before taking a decision, but I would let him know as soon as I had done so. He said he guessed that would mean that the answer would be no; I pointed out to him that that was not inevitable; he did not know my wife.

There followed a long night's discussion in my parent's flat in Shropshire, with Judy and I alternating in what was best to do. In the end Judy said that I should not pass up the opportunity of such a great job for a geologist as mapping the Oman mountains; she would take Alexander and return to her research job in Cambridge, renting a house. This she did, taking Alexander to work with her and putting him under the desk while she worked on her microscope, or when he began to walk letting him play football in a long laboratory with one of the lab assistants. This was all quite unprecedented and irregular. There had never been a baby in the Sedgwick Museum. Judy was simply operating on her life-long principle that you should not ask a question to which the answer can be no; better simply to assume it is OK and deal with any objections as they occur. There were no objections and the ritual academic breaks for communal coffee and tea became somewhat livelier and the average age dropped considerably.

Field geology, whether in the Arctic, Spain or Oman, is fascinating but sometimes stressful work. In a largely unmapped area one is confronted initially with a jumble of rocks and one is never sure whether one is going to be able to crack the code and sort their history and present state into some kind of coherent story. When one begins to have some success, the sense of excitement and achievement is stimulating. It is very good training for starting any job anywhere, with new and as yet unconquered challenges, and gradually through application beginning to get on top of it. After doing this a few times, one develops some confidence, in some cases rashly, that the complex challenges are resolvable.

Exploration geology: Brunei, Australia and the North Sea

In 1968 we were posted to the Sultanate of Brunei in Borneo, where I worked initially as an operations and well site geologist, liaising with or working on the offshore drilling rigs drilling exploration wells in Brunei and the neighbouring waters of the South China Sea off the East Malaysian states of Sabah and Sarawak. We were there for four years and after a while I joined one of the three exploration teams, and ultimately became the leader of one of the teams. Exploration activity was at a high level. The wells were quite shallow so the three teams were drilling over 30 wells a year.

Our next two sons, Douglas and Thomas, were born during that time in Brunei. Judy would get a kind of wanderlust and set off for several days with Alexander and later with Douglas up the major rivers by long boat into the hinterland, visiting some of longhouses and Chinese trading posts. Small children provide an immediate bond whatever the language, although Judy could speak reasonable Malay, which was the lingua franca in the jungle, as we had both spent time trying to learn it. I always tease Judy that her Malay has a French accent as she sat next door to a Frenchman during lessons. She sometimes crossed into Indonesian Kalimantan but said you could only tell which side of the border you were by whether the official photograph on the wall was of President Suharto or of the Yang di-Pertuan Agong, the king of Malaysia.

After in many ways idyllic years in Brunei, we were transferred to Shell Australia, where I became chief geologist. We lived in Melbourne, where our last child, Elizabeth, was born. Exploration consisted of some onshore exploration in Victoria and offshore in South Australia, both unfortunately unsuccessful, and participation in the very active exploration and production joint ventures of the North West Shelf in Western Australia.

In Melbourne, we lived a consciously ordinary suburban life in South Caulfield, with the children in the primary school just up the road. Family life with the children was blissfully normal for the last time before, due to our travels, the children in turn went to boarding school. Aged eight, and well endowed with the vocabulary of Australian state school playground (words that Judy suggested should be kept for 'garden use' only), Alexander calmly agreed to go to UK boarding school if it meant fewer changes of school. The others followed him at two-year intervals, making a valuable connection with Judy's mother in Sussex. It was that same boy who, a couple of years later, told Judy, 'You know Mum, you've only got to learn "how to live away from home" once.' Our philosophy was to take a risky joint decision on a new posting, schools, family, health. etc., then simply make that decision work. Hugely to the children's credit, as a family we agreed that Shell's work always came first—unless there was a crisis.

People often ask for our 'favourite posting'—it does not exist. We learned from all the places where we've lived, learned from our children and from one another. Our parents, siblings and the children have generously accepted life on our terms, a huge support as we shifted between 11 different homes, and tents, camper vans and boats, in our 35 years on the move. We do have northern European roots, an expatriate still belongs somewhere; but Judy has enthusiastically adapted to the international nuances of being what she calls a 'wife-of'. I remember initially in Brunei explaining that even if she would prefer to do all her own washing, housework and baby care, there were people locally who wanted work, could help and the payment would enrich their lives.

In 1976 we were transferred to London where I became responsible for leading the Shell exploration teams in the North Sea. It was a very exciting period in the UK oil industry, but Britain was not in a happy state. There were frequent strikes of transport and even teachers. There was relatively high inflation and a wage freeze. We even had the formation of a national oil company, the British National Oil Corporation (BNOC). Shell had been successful in exploration under the leadership of the late Myles Bowen, the UK exploration manager.

Oilfield operational experience: Brunei and Nigeria

After only two years in London, I was asked if I would return to Brunei to take up a new position as Services Manager. The idea was to combine in one large department engineering maintenance, procurement (then called Materials in Shell) and transport logistics. This would be a purely operational job, very different from the exploration in which I had spent my first 12 years in Shell.

Exploration team leadership was in part based on the knowledge that I could do almost all the jobs in the team and had developed experience from involvement in many exploration programmes. In Brunei I now dealt with aspects of the industry—maintenance, procurement and logistics—where I certainly could not do the job myself and where I had no direct experience of managing such disciplines. The three departments were headed by very experienced people with between them over a hundred years of service in the company; the youngest of them had joined the company when I was six. Fortunately, they were patient in explaining the darker arts of their professions and more importantly were willing to explain the factors that were causing them difficulty in getting their part of the job done. In the part of a business where the overall objective is extremely clear—keeping equipment running and delivering supplies and people to the job efficiently—a big role of management is finding out what is stopping people doing their part of the job efficiently and removing that blockage. It also consists of making sure that the different parts interface efficiently and do not get in each other's way.

I found that there was another big difference. In an exploration department, people derive their satisfaction from applying science and pitting their strengths to develop a clear picture of what is going on beneath the earth. The challenges facing an instrument maintenance engineer, a helicopter pilot or someone responsible for the supply of materials are different but no less challenging. Each appeals to different people, just as different people want to be farmers, doctors or blacksmiths. Satisfaction comes from doing their particular job successfully, seeing how it fits into the whole operation and being recognised as delivering an essential contribution. Management thus becomes a matter of understanding the interrelationships, working to remove the barriers and frictions that are preventing different people delivering their contribution, and making sure that everyone recognises and appreciates the essential nature of others' contributions as well as that of their own. This is not a matter of remuneration; it is a question of the great feeling of satisfaction for a job well done, both your part of it and that of the whole.

In 1979 we went to Nigeria, my job being Divisional Manager in the Western Division based in Warri. This was essentially a pure operations job; the planning for exploration and field design was done in Lagos and the two divisions drilled the wells, built the facilities, and produced and exported the oil. My opposite number as Divisional Manager in the East was Nigerian, initially Babs Komolu and later Emeka Achebe. We would talk to each other frequently on the phone and exchange views and experiences and, once a month, travel up to Lagos for a management meeting.

A manager's job with responsibility for an oilfield producing four or five hundred thousand barrels a day is all-consuming. You are responsible for making sure that everything works. This includes not just the wells and production facilities, but support facilities as well. Shell in Nigeria was staffed at that time to a level of over 95% by Nigerians. To attract able Nigerians as well as people from overseas to areas away from the big cities such as Lagos it is necessary to provide not just housing, but schools, hospitals and clinics, and sporting and recreational facilities. These all have to be at high international standards and supported by reliable utilities—electricity and water. None of this is easy in an environment where facilities in the country as a whole struggle to operate. In addition, there is responsibility for relations with communities around operations, for acquiring land on which wells and facilities can be established and for relations with local government. I imagine that it must be like being captain of an enormous aircraft carrier, but one that has spouses and children on board and is not sailing independently on the high seas but is permanently moored in a lively and busy port with its own preoccupations. If you noticed a truck in the field engaged in an unusual activity, a hole in a fence somewhere, or a crack at the bottom of a swimming pool on a Sunday afternoon, you made a mental note to speak to someone about it. If you wanted to communicate remotely you used a radio, as mobile phones were not yet available.

One holiday we drove back across the Sahara with a Malaysian colleague Ibrahim Ahmad, our seven-year-old daughter and a Welsh woman called Carole whose husband was working for an Italian contracting firm. Ibrahim wanted to be the first Malaysian to drive across the Sahara; I suspect he probably was. Alas it is not so easy or safe nowadays to camp in northern Nigeria and Niger.

Judy established and ran a youth club for Nigerian children in the housing area. She promised to go back and see them after we left and did so after the military coup that brought the period of civilian government that we had enjoyed to an end. We still know the children of Nigerian colleagues and see Nigerians when they come to London, as well as those living there.

Management beyond exploration and production:
Turkey and Malaysia

Shell's operations in Turkey consisted of relatively small oil production in eastern Turkey in the area around Diyarbakir, with its mainly Kurdish population, a joint venture refinery in Mersin, a large retail marketing business and a chemical products business. The job to which I went in 1982 was one of 'country manager' or Country Chairman in Shell parlance. This meant having bottom-line responsibility for all the business lines. For me this was my first job in wider management outside exploration and production and the first time that I had overall responsibility for a large marketing organisation and for the Shell brand as a whole. For the rest of my time in Shell I would worry not just about the operational matters that filled one's day in Nigeria, but about the state of every Shell station we drove past, every Shell advertisement seen and every mention of Shell in the press or interaction with the public. One had become, at least in that country but partly globally, part of the public face of Shell. That is of course true to some extent of anyone in the organisation, but much more so at country manager level. If someone had a problem or wanted a relationship with the company, they turned to you.

In my opinion, one cannot really begin to understand a culture unless one speaks at least some of the language. Judy and I took lessons separately. For the four years we spent in Turkey, three times a week on the way to the office I would spend two hours with Gönül Çapan, wife of the Turkish author and poet Cevat Çapan. Over the years, this was not just a matter of learning the language, but of discussing cultural and social backgrounds and trends from an academic left-of-centre rather than business view. Judy meanwhile lectured in the English Literature faculty of Istanbul University in Beyazit Square.

After four years in Istanbul, we moved in 1986 to Kuala Lumpur where I took up a similar position as country manager for Shell in Malaysia. Shell in Malaysia had a much larger exploration and production operation, with significant oil production as well as a natural gas liquefaction joint venture in Bintulu in Sarawak. The marketing organisation was sophisticated and Shell had a large share of the market; there was also a refinery in Port Dickson and another smaller one in Lutong in Sarawak.

I was familiar with the East Malaysian oil and gas operation from my earlier involvement of its exploration when based in Brunei. In fact, in our second spell in Brunei I had spent much time splitting the operation so that the Malaysian part could be operated from within Malaysia. By 1986 the Malaysian national oil company Petronas wanted to establish its own operating arm, Petronas Carigali, for exploration and production. This process is described in Chapter 1. Its smooth implementation involved my building close relationships and trust with Petronas, in particular with its Chairman, the late Tan Sri Azizan Zainul Abidin, a person of great wisdom and integrity.

At the same time there were ongoing negotiations on increasing the size of the Liquefied Natural Gas Plant in Bintulu, a joint venture with Petronas, on how and by whom such extensions would be operated and where the gas supply would come from. We also negotiated and prepared for the world's first commercial gas-to-liquids project in Bintulu, a small plant but a pioneering one.

For me another first in Malaysia was being Chairman of a public company. The Shell refining company in Port Dickson had outside shareholders and the shares were quoted on the Kuala Lumpur Stock Exchange. This was my first interaction with individual shareholders at lively Annual General Meetings. It is through such meetings that one becomes truly aware of the responsibility to the thousands, and in some cases indirectly millions, of individuals who have put some of their savings into the company for which you are responsible. And a very salutary experience it is too. Unlike an individual entrepreneur who can sometimes put at risk their entire venture and personal possessions, the manager of a public company is steward of other people's savings and has different constraints and responsibilities to both shareholders and fellow employees.

The Hague and London

In 1990 I returned to The Hague to become responsible for Shell's global exploration and production business. This was the first time I had ever worked in Shell's Central Offices, having for the past almost 25 years successfully evaded such a period in favour of working in operating companies. In 1994 we returned to London and a flat in Wapping. Much of the content of this book is based on the years at the top of Shell and Anglo American since 1990. They are also built on the background described above.

Index

Abacha, Sani 26, 122, 179, 181–2, 248, 250–51, 253
Abubakar, Abdulsalemi 26–7, 32
Abuja 16–17
Accenture 171, 264, 295, 312, 320–21
accountability 65, 194, 215, 329, 331
Achebe, Emeka 20, 346
activism 26, 244–5, 330
  see also public campaigns; public protests
Adams, Gerry 109
Ademiluyi, Adegoke 20
Afghanistan 73, 88, 90, 92
African National Congress (ANC) 79, 80–81
Agazadeh, Gholamreza 85, 87, 90, 92
Agip 175–6, 203
agriculture 11, 23, 24–5, 84, 217–21, 226, 237
Ahmad, Ibrahim 172, 346–7
Alien Tort Claims Act (US) 73–4, 251–2
Alireza, Teymour 297
Alofs, Paul 324
American Petroleum Institute (API) 142
Amnesty International 39, 89, 105, 327, 333
Amoco 246, 300, 310
Anderson, Brian 122, 251
Anderson, David 145

Anglo American
  anti-bribery policy 171, 192–3
  and apartheid 80–82
  in Australia 144
  in China 234–5
  and climate change 144, 163
  in Colombia 41
  company values 264, 273
  and corruption 171, 192–3
  corporate governance 301
  in the Democratic Republic of Congo 192–3
  donates to ICF 222
  educational projects 212–13
  and entrepreneurship 213–15
  and equality of opportunity 295–6
  and HIV/AIDS 209–12
  job creation projects 213–15
  remuneration committees 312
  and safety 234–5, 273
  in South Africa 80–82, 209–15, 273, 295–6
  training of security forces 41
  and the UN Global Compact 56
Anglo Platinum 46–7, 137, 273
Anglo Zimele 213–14
Annan, Kofi 53–5, 205, 206
Antigua 146, 336–8
Antigua Syndicate of Sugar Estates 337
antiretroviral therapy (ART) 209–10, 211
apartheid 78–81, 212, 295–6

Arab Spring   118
Arakis Energy   103
Aram, Robin   55, 258
arms industry   175, 176, 177
arrests   26, 42, 100, 116–17, 119,
   122–5
artisanal refining   27, 28–9
Aspen Institute   75
al-Assad, Bashar   97–8, 113, 118
al-Assad, Hafez   96–7, 111–18
Association of Southeast Asian Nations
   (ASEAN)   100–101, 103
Australia   16, 143, 144, 281, 303,
   343–4
automotive industry   135–7, 157, 162,
   167
Awolowo, Obafemi   24

Babangida, Ibrahim   26, 249
Badr El Din Petroleum Company
   (BAPETCo)   309–11
BAE Systems   176
Baha'i   92
Ban Ki-Moon   56–7, 76
Al Banbi, Hamdi   310
Bangladesh   62–3, 176
Bank of America   219
banks   43–4, 72, 180, 203, 281–2,
   312–14, 316–17, 318, 321–2
al-Bashir, Omar   68–9
Bavinton, Owen   192–3
Baylis, Barbara   275–6
Beckett, Margaret   37
Berkshire Hathaway Group   305
Berlusconi, Silvio   198
Biafra, Republic of   17, 249, 252
bidding processes   176–7, 178, 185,
   193–4
Biko, Steve   82
biogas   238
biofuels   134–5, 156, 220, 238, 330
biomass   140, 148
Bird, Vere   337
Black Economic Empowerment
   (BEE)   13

Blair, Tony   88, 152–3, 161, 205, 206,
   270–71, 272–3
boards of directors   285–6, 297–300,
   304–6
Body Shop, The   37, 253–4
bonuses   21, 306–8, 311–18, 322
Botswana   203
Bouteflika, Abdelaziz   206
Bowen, Myles   344
boycotts   78–9, 244
BP   19–21, 39, 103, 141–2, 246, 271–2,
   282–3, 300, 302–3, 330
branding   246, 322, 329–30, 335
Brasilia   16
Brazil   16, 147, 183, 200, 228, 236
Brent Spar   242–8, 253–4
bribery   30, 33, 56, 170–73, 176, 183,
   184–8, 192–3, 197–8
Bribery Act (UK)   176
Brink, Brian   209, 210–11
Britain   see United Kingdom
British Museum   107–8
British National Oil Corporation
   (BNOC)   344
Browne, John   141–2, 246, 271–2, 300
Brunei   13, 120, 178, 179, 342–3,
   344–5, 348
Buffett, Warren   305, 320
Buhari, Muhammadu   25–6
building regulations   62–3, 165, 230–31
Bulman, Oliver   340
Burkina Faso   171, 222
Burma   74, 100–103, 119
Bush, George W.   89, 93, 150, 152
Business and Society Programme   75
business education   75
Business for Peace initiative   67, 108
business registration   222
Buttle, Eileen   297

Cambridge University   339–41, 342
Cameroon   49, 50
Campbell, Alistair   269, 270
Canada   46, 66, 103–4, 125, 145,
   326–7

Canberra 16
Çapan, Cevat 43, 348
Çapan, Gönül 43, 347–8
capitalism 127–8, 332
carbon capture and storage
(CCS) 154–5
carbon credits 145–7
Carbon Price Floor 145
carbon prices 141, 154, 166
carbon trading schemes 142–7, 166
Carey, George 89
Carroll, Cynthia 273
cars 135–7, 157, 158, 159–64, 167
cassava 24, 217, 220
catalytic converters 135–7, 165
Catholicism 18, 112
Cambridge Energy Resource Associates
(CERA) 303
Chad 48–51
Chad–Cameroon export pipeline 48–51
Chamber of Mines 209
Chambers of Commerce 54, 222, 265
Chandler, Geoffrey 105, 106, 107, 254,
274
charcoal 219–20
charitable donations see philanthropy
Chartered Bank 203
Chavez, Hugo 197
chemical weapons 97
Cheney, Dick 150
Chevron 48–9, 74
child labour 54
child mortality 9
China 3, 57–8, 63, 66, 144, 147, 158,
166–7, 200, 202, 218, 226–41
China Council for International
Cooperation on Environment and
Development (CCICED) 227
China Development Forum 144, 227,
228, 229, 237
China Development Research
Foundation 236–7, 239–40
China National Offshore Oil
Corporation (CNOOC) 226–8

China National Petroleum Corporation
(CNPC) 66, 67, 103
Chirac, Jacques 205–6
Chrétien, Jean 206
Christianity 18, 32, 112, 123, 124–5
civil partnerships 110–11
civil society organisations
branding 329–30
coalitions with business 2–3, 34–9,
44, 47–8, 104, 204, 206–7,
334–5
criticism of business 142, 335
embedding values 271, 331
as enterprises 326–31
and the Extractive Industries
Transparency Initiative 194
and the G8 Task Force on Renewable
Energy 149
and the Global Reporting
Initiative 261–2
governance of 271, 326–31
and legislation 70
legitimacy of 46
and markets 127–8
opposition to Chad–Cameroon
pipeline 49
and overseas development aid 200,
201, 217
and poverty eradication 201, 217
raising of capital 326–7, 331–2
regulation of 328–9
remuneration of staff 332–4
and Shell's refuelling of planes in
Sudan 106–7
size and nature of sector 324–6
and the UN Global Compact 55, 56,
57, 202–3, 208
withdrawal from Democratic Republic
of Congo 120
civil war
Chad 49
and conflict diamonds 45
Democratic Republic of Congo 120,
129
Nigeria 17, 19, 27, 180, 249
Sudan 66, 103–4
Syria 97, 121
claw-back provisions (bonuses) 314,
317

Clean Air Act (UK)   165
Clean Development Mechanism (CDM)   143, 145–7, 166
CleanStar Mozambique venture   219–20
climate change   37, 138–69
Clini, Corrado   147–8, 150–51
Clinton, Bill   85, 95, 150
Club of Rome   139
coal   135, 139–40, 164–5
coalitions   2–3, 34–9, 44–8, 201, 205–7, 334–5
Collège de Contrôle et de Surveillance des Ressources Pétrolières   50
collusion   178
Colombia   39–40, 41, 58, 66–7
colonialism   31, 46, 73, 123, 249
Commission for Africa   222
commissions, payment of   83, 193
Commonwealth   250
compensation   27, 28, 101, 233–4, 249
competition   131–2, 136–7, 160, 162–3, 193, 208, 222, 261
compliance   72, 230–31, 240–41
concession agreements   13–14
conflict diamonds   45
conflicts of interest   47, 116
Congo   see Congo Brazzaville; Democratic Republic of Congo
Congo Brazzaville   187
Conoco   85
Corporate Average Fuel Economy (CAFE) standards   161
corporate governance   278–9, 284–307
corporate values   75, 110, 263–83, 331
Corporation, The (Abbott and Achbar)   31
corruption
   author's instances of   170–73
   in China   230–31, 233, 234
   company policies on   171, 186, 187–8, 266, 274
   complexities of   188–92
   and costs of refusal   192–5
   in Egypt   98
   in Elf   48–9, 175
   exposing of   195–8

and the Extractive Industries Transparency Initiative   44–6, 194–5, 252
   government involvement   174–7
   grand corruption   174–7
   and the Investment Climate Facility for Africa   222
   in Italy   198
   judicial   72
   in Kazakhstan   188
   legislation on   72, 176–7
   in Malaysia   125
   measures against   177–88
   in Nigeria   23, 25–7, 33–4, 171–3, 178–83, 252
   public acceptance of   198–9
   reporting of   185–6
   and the 'resource curse'   5
   in South Africa   198
   and taxation   144
   and Transparency International   174, 183–4, 193–4
   in Turkey   188–9
   in Ukraine   189–92
   and the UN Global Compact   55–7, 63, 202
   in Venezuela   197
   see also bribery; collusion; extortion; kickbacks
Credibility Alliance   329
cultural diversity   264–7, 293, 297

Dalan, Bedrettin   188
Damascus   96, 111–12
de Klerk, F.W.   78
de Segundo, Karen   255
Déby, Idriss   49
Deepwater Horizon disaster   271–2, 282–3
Democratic Republic of Congo   120, 129–31, 192–3
Deng Xiaoping   226
detention without trial   123–5
development aid   99, 200, 201–2, 215, 326–7
Dhaka   62–3
disability   62, 238

discrimination   12, 54, 79, 266–7,
    292–3
diversity   264–7, 292–7
Dodd–Frank legislation (US)   195
domestic fuel   164–5, 216, 219–20, 238
drinks industry   203, 219

economic growth   11, 87, 115, 226,
    232, 234
economic liberalisation   83–4, 96–9,
    115–16, 118
Economist, The   50, 208–9
education
    author's   338–41
    business education   75
    in China   230, 231, 233, 236–7,
        239–40
    corporate investment in   212–13, 346
    development aid for   200, 202
    higher   81, 239–40
    in Nigeria   18, 31, 346
    in Oman   6
    in South Africa   81, 212–13, 296
    in Syria   113
    tax revenue used for   215
    for women   90
Eggar, Tim   244, 246
Egypt   9, 68, 74, 98–9, 113, 118, 309–11
Egyptian General Petroleum Company
    (EGPC)   309–11
Eigen, Peter   56, 174
elections   18, 23, 25, 26–7, 32, 78, 101,
    102, 125–6
Elf   48–9, 175, 275
Elkington, John   261
Elshafie, Mohamed   105–6
employment   10, 14, 29, 62, 67, 201,
    212, 226, 232, 266–7
energy efficiency   61, 156–7, 160–67
Engen   79
Enron   278–9
entrepreneurship   201, 203, 213–17,
    226, 319–20
    see also small businesses
environmental damage   27–9, 188–9,
    249, 252
    see also climate change

environmental regulation   230–31
    see also Kyoto Protocol
environmental standards   53–4, 71,
    72–3, 202, 260
environmental targets   230–31, 232
Equator Principles   72
Ericsson   203, 205
ethanol   134–5, 220
Ethiopia   205
European Union (EU)   91, 93, 100, 103,
    120, 121, 142–3, 166
European Union Emissions Trading
    Scheme (EU ETS)   143, 145
Eurostar   335
Evren, Kenan   42
executions   26, 29, 32, 42, 181–2,
    232–3, 250–51
extortion   56, 191
Extractive Industries Transparency
    Initiative (EITI)   44–6, 52, 84,
    194–5, 252
extraterritorial legislation   52, 70–74,
    195
Exxon   13–14, 48–9, 190, 246, 288,
    300, 302–3

fair trials   267
family values   31, 263–4, 280
Fay, Chris   244, 289
financial crisis   144, 155, 161, 230,
    280–82, 314, 316–18
Financial Services Authority   282
fire safety   62–3
fish farming   24, 217
Fitzgerald, Niall   222
five-year plans   229–32
forced labour   54
Ford, Bill   156–7
Ford, Henry   70
Foreign Corrupt Practices Act (FCPA)
    (US)   176, 188
foreign exchange   25, 116, 131
Forest Stewardship Council   38–9
Fox, George   122, 126
fracking   133–4, 155
Fraenkel, Erdi   285

France   19, 43, 48–9, 57, 175, 275, 289
fraud   143, 183, 187, 191
   see also corruption
Friend, Peter   340
Friends of the Earth   149, 207, 335
Fu Chengyu   63
fuel crisis (UK)   161, 269–70, 272–3
fuel oil   94–5, 140
fuel prices   161–2, 166, 269–70
   see also oil prices

G8 Task Force on Renewable
   Energy   147–54
Gaddafi, Muammar   68, 98, 110, 122
gas   *see* natural gas; shale gas extraction
Gasunie   190
Gates, Bill   224, 319, 320
Gates Foundation   224
gay marriage   110–11
Gazprom   190–92, 290–91
GBC Health   209, 327–8
Gegan, Scott   148
genetic modification   330
Germany   57, 244, 247, 254, 289, 339
Giffen, James   188
Giusti, Luis   297
Global Business Coalition for HIV/AIDS
   (GBC)   209, 327–8
Global Climate Coalition   141–2
Global Compact Foundation   59
Global Compact Leadership
   Summit   59, 75
Global Compact Local Networks   59,
   60–64, 65–7, 72, 74, 76, 107, 208
Global Compact Office   58–9
Global Peace Index   67
Global Reporting Initiative   65, 248,
   261–2, 334–5
Global Witness   44
globalisation   288
Goldemberg, José   148
Goldman Sachs   322
Good Friday Agreement   109
Gowon, Yakubu   18, 20, 22, 249
Grameen   128, 332

Grayson, David   38
grand corruption   174–7
Greater Nile Petroleum Operating
   Company (GNPOC)   103
Greenpeace   37, 149, 243–8, 330, 335
groupthink   280–83
Growing Sustainable Business (GSB)
   initiative   203, 205–7
Gueneau, Jacques   187
Gulf Cooperation Council   61

H&M   63
Hague, The   275, 285, 349
Hama   113
Harrabin, Roger   163
Hart, Stuart   205
Hayward, Tony   271
health and safety   15, 62–3, 119, 154,
   260, 311
health insurance   230, 232, 233, 237,
   238
healthcare
   in China   230, 231, 233, 236–7, 238
   and civil society organisations   331–2
   corporate investment in   67, 81, 82,
      104, 209–12, 346
   development aid for   200, 202
   in Nigeria   346
   in Oman   6, 7, 9
   and public–private
      partnerships   223–5
   in South Africa   81, 82, 209–12
   in Sudan   66, 67, 104
   tax revenue used for   215
Hemingway, Janet   224
Henckell DuBuisson   336–7
Henderson, Ian   255
Henderson, Nina   297
Henzell, Leonard   337
Herkströter, Cor   250, 287, 298
Hermes Equity Ownership Services   65,
   171, 317
higher education   81, 239–40
Hilmy Mohd Nor   122–3, 124
HIV/AIDS   209–12, 327–8
Hodge, Steve   299

Hoffman, Kurt 215
Hofmeister, John 293
Holbrooke, Richard 327–8
Holmes, Peter 20, 79, 300
homosexuality 110–11
house arrests 42, 100, 116–17, 119
housing 6, 9, 23, 47, 189, 214, 238, 346
HSBC 171, 227, 264, 281–2, 295, 312–14, 316–18, 321–2
Hughes, Norman 340
hukou system 228
human rights 39–41, 53–4, 63, 71, 101–4, 138, 196, 202, 228, 248, 257, 266
    abuses of 3, 26, 40, 97, 98, 100, 103–6, 109–26
Human Rights Watch 39, 327
Hussein, Saddam 83, 88–9
hybrid vehicles 157, 163, 164, 167
hydro power 148, 153–4
hydrogen 156, 330

ICM 219
Igbo people 17–19
incentives
    for companies 146, 149, 231
    for individuals 306–7, 308–9, 311–19
Inclusive Market Development (IMD) programme 207
India 2, 16, 57, 66, 112, 147, 158, 166, 216, 328–9
Indonesia 25, 123
IndustriALL Global Union 63
infrastructure 17, 22–3, 27, 118, 200, 202, 215–16, 226, 228, 236–7
Inkatha Freedom Party (South Africa) 79
Innovative Vector Control Consortium (IVCC) 224–5
insecticides 223–5
Institute for Economics and Peace 66–7
Integrity Pacts 193
Intergovernmental Panel on Climate Change (IPCC) 138–9, 147, 156

internal migration 218, 227–8
Internal Security Act (ISA) (Malaysia) 122–4
international aid 99, 200, 201–2, 215, 326–7
International Alert 108
International Chamber of Commerce 54
International Council on Mining and Metals 72, 206, 329
International Criminal Court (ICC) 52, 68–9, 73, 97–8
International Energy Agency 149
International Finance Corporation (IFC) 151
International Institute for Environment and Development (IIED) 206
International Institute for Sustainable Development (IISD) 73, 145
International Institute for Tropical Agriculture 24
international legislation 52, 70–74, 195
International Monetary Fund (IMF) 45
international trade agreements 72–3
investment 64–9, 83–4, 96–9, 101–4, 107, 145, 202–5, 213–22, 265–6
Investment Climate Facility for Africa (ICF) 222–3
investment trusts 12–13
Iran 84–8, 89, 90, 92–6, 108, 121, 136
Iran and Libya Sanctions Act (ILSA) (US) 84–5
Iran–Iraq War 86, 87, 161
Iranian Revolution 85, 86, 160
Iraq 73, 82–3, 88–96
Ireland 91, 157
Ironsi, General 18
Isdell, Neville 222
Islam 17, 18, 32, 90, 92, 124, 293
Islamic bonds 12
Israel 84, 89, 90–91, 92–3, 99–100, 115, 310
Istanbul 188–9, 348
Italy 176, 198, 274

Jamaica 338

Japan 57
Jennings, John 300
Jennings, Philip 63
job creation 29, 201, 213–17, 226, 232
Jobs, Steve 268
Johns Hopkins Center for Civil
    Society 325, 326
joint ventures 14, 20–22, 48–9, 111,
    113–18, 121, 180–83, 190–92, 220–
    21, 302–3, 309–11
Jonathan, Goodluck 27
Jones, Bobby 307

Kazakhstan 188
Keeton, Margie 82
Kell, Georg 58, 59, 203
Kengo Wa Dondo, Léon 129–30
Kerry, John 100
Khartoum 105–6
kickbacks 170
Killelea, Steve 66
Kimberley Process (KP) 45
Kinshasa 120, 129–30
Klein, Diana 108
Korea see North Korea; South Korea
Kuala Lumpur 16, 123, 348
Kuchma, Leonid 191
Kumolu, Babs 20, 346
Kuti, Fela 32
Kyoto Protocol 141, 142–3, 145–7,
    156

labour standards 21, 53–4, 61–3,
    70–73, 202, 266–7
labour unions 36, 55, 56, 62–3, 70, 80,
    202–4, 208, 262, 337
Lagos 20, 32, 172, 346
land ownership 222–3, 233–4
Lazarenko, Pavlo 191
Le Floch-Prigent, Loïk 48, 175, 275
lead-free petrol 136, 165
Least Developed Countries (LDCs) 203,
    205
Lebanon 88, 115
legislation 52, 70–72, 136, 176, 184,
    194, 195

see also regulation
Li Shi 236–7
Libya 68, 84–5, 98, 110
Lion Mountains project 220–21
Liquefied Natural Gas (LNG) schemes
    Brunei 179–80
    Malaysia 179, 348
    Nigeria 27, 179–83, 253
Litvin, Daniel 2
Liverpool School of Tropical
    Medicine 224
Lockheed 176
London 160, 164–5, 189, 197, 285,
    289, 344, 349
Long-Term Incentive Plans
    (LTIPs) 312–13, 315–17, 318
Loudon, John 285
Louis Dreyfus Commodities 221
Lu Mai 237–40

Macalister, Terry 88–9
Macdonald, Lord 270
MacGregor, Neil 107
McGuinness, Martin 109–10
McKenzie, Dan 341
Madagascar 205
Mahathir bin Mohamad 15–17, 122–3,
    125
Major, John 244, 246
Make Poverty History campaign 201
malaria 209, 223–5, 327
Malaysia 10–17, 25, 30–32, 112, 122–
    6, 179, 343, 348–9
Malaysian Industrial Development
    Authority (MIDA) 14–15
Mali 171
Malloch-Brown, Mark 205, 206
Mandela, Nelson 78
Mandelson, Peter 109
Maputo 219–20
Marine Stewardship Council 38
markets 114–16, 127–37, 140–47, 149,
    151–2, 154, 160–63, 165–9, 222,
    334
Marks & Spencer 157
massacres 113

Mays, Leslie 293
Mbeki, Thabo 210
medical care *see* healthcare
medical insurance 230, 232, 233, 237, 238
Mehta, Vikram 16
Melbourne 281, 343–4
Mentoring Foundation 297
mergers 300–301, 306, 327
Mexico 135
migrant labour 61–2, 80, 228, 267
migration, internal 218, 227–8
military aid 99
military coups
  Nigeria 18, 20, 22, 25–6, 32
  Turkey 41–3
military intervention 42–3, 84, 88, 97
mining industry 44–7, 194–5, 197, 206, 209–12, 234–5, 273, 306, 329
Mining, Metals and Sustainable Development Initiative 206
Mitterrand, François 175
Mitterand, Jean-Christophe 175
Mkapa, Benjamin 222
Mobil 79, 288, 300–301
Mobutu Sese Seko 120, 129–30
Mondi 38–9
Montreal Protocol 71, 166
Moody-Stuart, Alexander 341–2, 343–4
Moody-Stuart, George 174–5, 178, 338
Moody-Stuart, Judy 1, 43, 89, 112, 129, 172–3, 279–80, 328, 339–44, 346–8
Morrison, Tim 299
motor industry 135–7, 157, 162, 167
Mouana, Bakamana 129
Movement for the Survival of the Ogoni People (MOSOP) 249, 252–3
Mowlam, Mo 109–10
Mozambique 219–20
Mubarak, Hosni 98–9, 113
Mugabe, Robert 82
Muhammed, Murtala 18, 20
Munger, Charlie 305

Munsiff, Jyoti 92
Muslim Brotherhood 113
Myanmar 74, 100–103, 119

Nabulsi, Nader 116–18
Najib Tun Razak 123
Nasser, Gamal Abdel 9
National Association of Pension Funds (NAPF) 317
National Health Service (NHS) 332
National Iranian Oil Company 86, 87, 88
National Land Center (Rwanda) 222–3
National League for Democracy (NLD) (Myanmar) 100, 101
National Party of Nigeria 23
national pride 15–17, 52, 182
national sovereignty 33, 41, 45, 48, 51, 194
national values 6, 7, 89, 92
Natural Environment Research Council 340, 341
natural gas 85–6, 125, 133, 140, 189–92, 330
  see also liquefied natural gas (LNG) schemes; shale gas extraction
Nelson, Jane 38
Nestlé 203, 218–19
Netanyahu, Binyamin 99
Netherlands 105, 114, 129, 140, 190, 255–6, 267, 275, 284–5, 289, 341, 349
New Delhi 16, 166
New Economic Policy (NEP) (Malaysia) 12, 15
newspapers 79, 80, 124, 198
Nigeria 2, 16–33, 39–40, 122, 171–2, 176–83, 217, 221, 247–53, 257, 303, 346–7
Nigerian National Petroleum Corporation (NNPC) 20–22, 25, 27, 180–81
non-governmental organisations (NGOs) *see* civil society organisations
non-interference policies 2, 30, 32–3, 119

Norsk Hydro 302
Norske Veritas 245
North Korea 84, 89
Northern Ireland 68, 90–91, 109–10, 267
Norway 46, 190, 194, 245, 302
not-for-profit enterprises *see* civil society organisations
Noto, Lou 300–301
Novozymes 219–20
nuclear power 98, 153–4, 330
nuclear weapons 84, 88
Nuffield Health 127, 331–2
nutrition 239

Obama, Barack 87, 99–100, 161
Obasanjo, Olesegun 20, 22, 26–7, 32, 206, 250
OECD Convention on Combating Bribery 176
offsetting (carbon emissions) 145–7, 157
Ogoni people 26, 182, 248–54
Ohunyon, Chief 24
Oil and Natural Gas Corporation (ONGC) 66, 104
Oil-for-Food policy 82–3
oil leaks 27–8
oil prices 23, 50–51, 83, 117, 132, 160–61, 269
Ojukwu, Colonel 18–19
Oman 6–10, 30–32, 341–2
Omene, Godwin 20, 24–5
Oppenheimer, Harry 80, 81, 212–13
oppression 97, 100, 113, 188
Organisation of African Unity 20
organisational structure 284–307
Organization of the Petroleum Exporting Countries (OPEC) 9, 132–3
Ormen Lange gas field 302–3
overseas development assistance (ODA) 99, 200, 201–2, 215, 326–7
Oxfam 218, 327, 331

Pakistan 66
Palestine 89, 90–91, 92–3, 99–100, 115

palm oil 25
Pax Christi 105
pension funds 64–6, 320, 321
pension provision 230, 232
People's Democratic Party (PDP) (Nigeria) 27
People's Liberation Army (China) 233
performance measures 231, 309–12, 313, 315–16, 318, 331
Permodalan Nasional Berhad (PNB) 12
personal savings 230
personal transportation 135–7, 157, 158, 159–64, 167
PetroChina 66
Petronas 13–14, 50, 103, 125, 348
Petronas Towers 16
pharmaceutical industry 203
philanthropy 207, 208–9, 320, 326–7, 331–2
Phoenix Africa Development 220–21
planning permission 189
pollution 27–9, 188–9
  indoor 216, 219
positive discrimination 12
poverty 3, 49, 200–202, 216–18, 226–41
Powell, Colin 89–93, 150
Prahalad, C.K. 204–5
precautionary savings 230
Prescott, John 270
press 79, 80, 124, 198
Principles for Responsible Management Education (PRME) 75
Principles for Responsible Investment (PRI) 64–6, 72, 107
production-sharing contracts 13–14, 117
property registration 222–3
Protect, Respect, Remedy framework 71, 107
protectionism 73
public campaigns 36–8, 322
  see also activism
public outrage 182, 242, 244, 247–8, 253, 322–3
public–private partnerships 222–5

public protests   97, 98, 100, 118, 330
  see also activism
public scrutiny   69–70, 198
public services   127, 232, 233, 269
  see also education; healthcare; social
    security
public transport   160, 166
Publish What You Pay campaign   44,
  194–5
Purves, Willie   299
Putrajaya   16–17

Qaboos bin Said, Sultan of Oman   9
Qaddafi, Muammar   68, 98, 110, 122
Quakers   70, 89, 122, 129, 255, 305

racial violence   11, 18, 123–4
Raina, Jyrki   63
Rainforest Alliance   327
Ramphele, Mamphela   81–2
Rana Plaza building collapse   62–3
rebellions   8, 113
recycling   232, 243, 247
regulation
  automotive industry   136–7
  building regulations   62–3, 165,
    230–31
  of civil society organisations   328–9
  and climate change   154, 157, 159,
    162–7
  and corporate governance   278–9
  and energy efficiency   157, 162–3,
    165–7
  environmental   230–31
  financial   278–9, 282
  and groupthink   282–3
  and markets   128–31, 160
  oil industry   282–3
  and renewable energy   154
  safety regulations   62–3
  of shale gas extraction   133–4
  see also legislation
religion   see Christianity; Islam;
  Quakers
Relly, Gavin   80, 81
relocation   46–7, 104, 227–8, 236, 238
remuneration   21, 113–15, 215, 232,
  276, 282, 308–23, 332–4

renewable energy   147–54, 156, 157,
  159, 335
reporting   65, 248, 261–2, 334–5
reputation   204, 253–4, 322, 328–9
reserves scandal (Shell)   301–4, 306
resource curse theory   5, 7
respect   265, 268–9
retail industry   114, 157
Rhodesia   see Zimbabwe
Rich, Marc   95
Rifkind, Malcolm   113
Rio Convention on Environment and
  Development   53
Rio+20 World Summit   76
Rio Tinto   206, 215
riots   11, 123
risk   40, 64, 74, 102, 133, 154, 180,
  192, 204, 274, 278–9, 280–83
Roddick, Anita   253–4
Rouhani, Hassan   87
Royal Dutch/Shell Group   284–91,
  298–300
  see also Shell
Ruggie, John   71, 104, 107
Runnalls, David   145
Russia   39, 93, 94–5, 97, 115, 190–92,
  328, 330
  see also Soviet Union
Rwanda   222–3

SABMiller   219
Sachs, Jeffrey   5
safety   15, 62–3, 119, 154, 260, 271–3,
  311
Said bin Taimur, Sultan of Oman   6–7,
  8, 9
Saigon   120
Salamon, Lester M.   325
Salim, Emil   47
Samuelson, Judith   75
sanctions   3, 20, 77–9, 82–8, 96–101,
  103, 116, 120–21
Sandbrook, Richard   206–7
Saro-Wiwa, Ken   26, 29, 181–2, 247,
  248–54
Saudi Arabia   92, 176, 186, 265

Saudi Aramco   171, 186, 264, 265, 312
Schwab, Klaus   89
secularism   43
Securities and Exchange Commission
    (SEC)   302–3
security   39–41, 43–4, 66, 67, 68, 101,
    202
security forces   39–41, 43–4, 101, 104
Sellers, Rick   149
Senegal   206
service industries   229, 232
Shagari, Shehu   23
shale gas extraction   133–4, 155
share-based incentives   314, 315, 318
Shell
    affiliate businesses   203–4
    anti-bribery policy   33, 171–3, 185,
        187–92
    in Australia   343–4
    author awarded studentship
        by   340–41
    author's career with   340–49
    and the Brent Spar   242–8, 253–4
    in Brunei   342–3, 344–5
    in Chad   48–51
    in China   226–8
    and climate change   140–45, 147–8,
        163
    community development   29, 33
    company values   30–31, 129–31, 264,
        265, 272–3, 274–6
    corporate governance   284–307
    and corruption   33, 171–3, 177,
        178–83, 185, 187–92
    in Democratic Republic of
        Congo   129–31
    in Egypt   309–11
    and entrepreneurship   201, 203–4,
        205
    General Business Principles   105, 107,
        242, 254, 256–61, 274
    and Greenpeace   37, 243–8, 330, 335
    and human rights   105–7, 118–26
    and investment trusts   12–13
    in Iran   85–7, 92–6
    job creation   29, 201, 203–4
    and Ken Saro-Wiwa   29–30, 181–2,
        248–53

in Malaysia   12–14, 122–6, 291,
        348–9
    in Myanmar   102
    in Nigeria   2, 19–30, 122, 171–3,
        178–83, 221, 248–53, 346–7
    non-interference policies   2, 30, 32–3
    in Oman   341–2
    organisational structure   284–307
    remuneration of staff   113–15, 309–
        11, 312
    and renewable energy   147–8
    reserves scandal   301–4, 306
    and safety   272–3
    and security   43–4
    Shell Foundation   215–17
    Society's Changing Expectations
        programme   255–62
    in South Africa   78–9
    in Spain   341
    staff development   33
    in Sudan   105–7
    and sustainable development   215–17
    in Syria   111–18, 121
    tanker intercepted by US Navy   92–6
    in Turkey   41–4, 188–9, 347–8
    in Ukraine   190–92
    and the UN Global Compact   55, 56
    in Vietnam   120
    withdrawals from ventures   50–51,
        106–7, 121, 249–50
Shell Foundation   215–17
Shell General Business Principles   105,
    107, 242, 254, 256–61, 274
Shell Mex House   290
Shell Oil   96, 288, 301
Shengman Zhang   230
Shonekan, Ernest   26
Short, Clare   88
Siemens   184–5
Sierra Leone   220–21
Singapore   11, 94, 241
Sinn Féin   109–10
small businesses   206–7, 208, 213, 223
    see also entrepreneurship
Smith, Adam   129
Smith, James   248
Snowden, Edward   87
social media   36, 241, 322

social security   230, 231, 232
Society's Changing Expectations
    programme   255–62
solar power   148, 216
Soros Open Society Foundation   44
South Africa   13, 20, 46–7, 78–82, 121,
    198, 209–13, 273, 295–6
South Korea   57
sovereignty   33, 41, 45, 48, 51, 194
Soviet Union   19, 39, 96, 115, 116,
    189–90, 229, 290–91, 328
    see also Russia
Spain   57, 99, 341
Sri Lanka   66–7
Standard Chartered   203
Starbucks   322
State Oil Marketing Organisation
    (SOMO) (Iraq)   83
state violence   97, 100, 103–4, 113
Statoil   302–3
steel industry   23, 230
Stiglitz, Joseph   144–5
Stocking, Barbara   331
Straw, Jack   270
subsistence farming   11, 217, 218
Sudan   39–40, 65–9, 103–7
sugar industry   336–7
Sullivan, Leon   79–80
supply chains   56, 67, 76, 201, 207,
    213, 214, 266
surveillance   87, 111–12
SustainAbility   261
sustainable development   37–9, 73,
    201–25, 227, 248, 257, 261
sustainable energy   134–5, 147–54, 156,
    157, 159, 335
Suu Kyi, Aung San   100, 101, 102–3,
    119
Syria   67, 74, 96–8, 111–18, 119, 121,
    309
Syrian Petroleum Company (SPC)   96,
    113, 116

Tabung Haji   12
Taib Mahmud   125–6
Taliban   90, 92

Talisman   66, 103–4
Tan Sri Azizan   125, 348
Tanzania   205
Tarallo, André   48
Tarmac   234–5
taxation   23, 33–4, 144–5, 159, 161–2,
    179, 214–15, 222, 237–8, 269,
    322–3
Tedstrom, John   328
Tehran   136
telecoms industry   131–2, 203
teleconferencing   295
Telenor   332
terrorism   88, 109, 123–4
Texaco   301
Thailand   101
theft   27, 28, 34
Thomson, Peninah   297
tobacco industry   203
Total   85, 101–2, 119, 121, 203, 205
tourism   10, 16–17, 329
trade agreements   72–3
Trahar, Tony   209–10
training
    anti-bribery   184
    for employees   33, 67, 114, 184, 271,
        272, 273
    and safety   272, 273
    for security forces   40, 41, 44
    and values   271
Trans Niger pipeline   27
Transatlantic Partners Against AIDS
    (TPAA)   328
transparency   116, 129, 160, 163, 176–
    7, 193–4, 198–9, 329, 334–5
Transparency International   26, 56, 174,
    183–4, 193–4
travel industry   329
trust   89, 107, 126, 129, 131, 231, 256,
    273–4, 334–5
tuberculosis   209, 210, 327
Tukaki, Matthew   60
Tunisia   118
Turkey   41–4, 67, 91, 112, 188–9,
    347–8
Tymoshenko, Yulia   192

UK Corporate Governance Code   278, 305
Ukraine   190–92
UNI Global Union   63
Unilever   38, 203, 219
Union Solidarity and Development Party (USDP) (Myanmar)   101
United Africa Company   26
United Arab Emirates   61, 85
United Energy Systems (UES)   191–2
United Fruit Company   2, 32
United Kingdom
   author's education in   338–41
   author's family remain in   342
   bonuses   312, 315
   and the Brent Spar   243–4, 246
   Carbon Price Floor   145
   Clean Air Act   164–5
   and climate change   145, 152–3, 157
   colonialism   20, 31
   and corruption   176, 177
   and the Extractive Industries
      Transparency Initiative   46, 194
   fair trials   267
   fuel crisis   161, 269–70, 272–3
   fuel prices   161, 166, 269
   government surveillance   87
   healthcare   331–2
   and Iraq   88–9
   labour standards   70
   national values   110–11
   and Northern Ireland   68, 90–91, 267
   planning permission   189
   public transport   160
   remuneration   312, 315
   and renewable energy   152–3, 157
   sanctions   20
   security policy   123–4
   Shell in   284–5, 289–90, 344, 349
   signatories to the UN Global
      Compact   57
   supports government in Nigerian civil
      war   19
   taxation   161, 166, 322
   and the Voluntary Principles
      on Security and Human
      Rights   39

United Malays National Organisation (UMNO)   123, 124
United Nations   83, 91, 93, 120–21, 325
United Nations Convention on Corruption   56
United Nations Development Programme (UNDP)   9, 205, 206, 207
United Nations Economic and Social Council (ECOSOC)   203
United Nations Environmental Programme (UNEP)   29, 64
United Nations Framework Convention on Climate Change (UNFCCC)   143, 166
United Nations Global Compact (UNGC)   53–76, 103–4, 107, 119, 201–8, 227, 257, 261–2, 334–5
United Nations Human Rights Commission   104
United States
   Alien Tort Claims Act   73–4, 251–2
   automotive industry   160–61
   biofuels   134–5
   bonuses   312
   and carbon trading   166
   and the Clean Development
      Mechanism   145
   and climate change   133–5, 142–3, 150–52, 158, 160–61, 166
   convicts Pavlo Lazarenko   191
   and corruption   176–7, 178, 188, 191
   does not accept ICC   52
   extraterritorial legislation   52, 73–4, 251–2
   and G8 Task Force on Renewable
      Energy   150–52
   intercepts Shell tanker   92–6
   and Iran   84–5, 86–7, 92–6
   and Iraq   83, 89–92
   and Israel   99–100
   and Kyoto negotiations   142–3
   and Myanmar   103
   natural gas   133–4, 140
   not-for-profit sector   325
   oil industry in   132
   and Palestine   99–100
   refuses to export compressors to Soviet
      Union   190

remuneration 312
sanctions 84–5, 94–7, 103
shale gas extraction 133–4
Shell Oil 288
signatories of the UN Global
    Compact 57
sustainable energy 133–5
and Syria 96–7
taxation 322
in Vietnam war 120
and the Voluntary Principles
    on Security and Human
    Rights 39
Universal Declaration on Human
    Rights 53, 71
US Climate Action Partnership 142

values
    corporate 75, 110, 263–83, 331
    family 31, 263–4, 280
    national 6, 7, 89, 92
van der Vijver, Walter 301, 302–3
variable remuneration 308–19
Venezuela 197
Vietnam 120
violence see civil war; massacres;
    military coups; racial violence;
    rebellions; state violence
Voluntary Principles on Security and
    Human Rights 39–41, 72, 101–2,
    104
Vyakerev, Rem 190

Wade, Abdoulaye 206
Wakoson, Elias Nyamlell 68–9
Wang Meng Kui 236
Wang Sangui 236–7
Wang Xiaolu 236–7
Warri 20, 23, 25, 171, 172, 178–9, 346
water usage 66, 230, 232
Watts, Phil 179, 181, 255, 301, 302–3
wealth differentials 276, 312, 317,
    319–23
Wen Jiabao 231, 234
West, Chris 215
whistle-blowing 185–6, 187–8
Williams, John 255
Wilson, Brian 177

Wilson, Richard 270
Wilson, Robert 206
wind power 148, 152
Winter, Wesley 336
withdrawal (companies from
    countries) 78, 79–80, 104–5, 106–
    7, 120, 121
Wiwa, Ken 252
women
    education 90
    employment 14, 90, 105–6, 129
    as entrepreneurs 213
    political participation 9
    and promotion prospects 292–4,
        296–7
    respect for 265
working conditions 21, 53, 61–3, 70,
    71, 202
World Bank 47, 50–51, 72, 82, 151,
    174, 182, 213, 228
World Bank Group Extractive Industry
    Review 47
World Bank International Finance
    Corporation 50, 213
World Economic Forum 53, 89, 328–9,
    331
World Food Programme 105
World Health Organisation 225
World Resources Institute 75
World Summit on Sustainable
    Development 37, 44, 201, 205
World Wildlife Fund (WWF) 38, 327,
    329–30

Yang Quarry 234–5
Yar'Adua, Umaru 27
Yemen 10, 68, 187
Yergin, Daniel 169
Yoruba people 18, 27
Yunus, Muhammad 128, 332

Zain 203
Zaire see Democratic Republic of
    Congo
Zambia 80
Zhou Shengxian 227
Zim, Lazarus 296
Zimbabwe 20, 45, 82